Unsaying God

ACADEMY SERIES

SERIES EDITOR
Aaron W. Hughes, University at Buffalo

A Publication Series of
The American Academy of Religion
and
Oxford University Press

THE CREATIVE SUFFERING OF THE TRIUNE GOD
An Evolutionary Theology
Gloria L. Schaab

A THEOLOGY OF CRITICISM
Balthasar, Postmodernism, and the Catholic Imagination
Michael P. Murphy

INCARNATION ANYWAY
Arguments for Supralapsarian Christology
Edwin Chr. Van Driel

DISABILITY AND CHRISTIAN THEOLOGY
Embodied Limits and Constructive Possibilities
Deborah Beth Creamer

MEETING GOD ON THE CROSS
Christ, the Cross, and the Feminist Critique
Arnfríður Guðmundsdóttir

MUSLIMS, SCHOLARS, SOLDIERS
The Origin and Elaboration of the Ibādī Imāmate Traditions
Adam R. Gaiser

RACE AND RELIGION IN AMERICAN BUDDHISM
White Supremacy and Immigrant Adaptation
Joseph Cheah

JOURNEY BACK TO GOD
Origen on the Problem of Evil
Mark S. M. Scott

BEYOND THE WALLS
Abraham Joshua Heschel and Edith Stein on the Significance of Empathy for Jewish-Christian Dialogue
Joseph Redfield Palmisano, SJ

TYPES OF PENTECOSTAL THEOLOGY
Method, System, Spirit
Christopher A. Stephenson

OTHER DREAMS OF FREEDOM
Religion, Sex, and Human Trafficking
Yvonne C. Zimmerman

LIBERALISM VERSUS POSTLIBERALISM
The Great Divide in Twentieth-Century Theology
John Allan Knight

IMAGE, IDENTITY, AND THE FORMING OF THE AUGUSTINIAN SOUL
Matthew Drever

RIGHTEOUS RHETORIC
Sex, Speech, and the Politics of Concerned Women for America
Leslie Durrough Smith

ENFOLDING SILENCE
The Transformation of Japanese American Religion and Art under Oppression
Brett J. Esaki

LONGING AND LETTING GO
Christian and Hindu Practices of Passionate Non-Attachment
Holly Hillgardner

MEANING IN OUR BODIES
Sensory Experience as Constructive Theological Imagination
Heike Peckruhn

THE GOODNESS OF HOME
Human and Divine Love and the Making of the Self
Natalia Marandiuc

Unsaying God

Negative Theology in Medieval Islam

AYDOGAN KARS

OXFORD
UNIVERSITY PRESS

OXFORD
UNIVERSITY PRESS

Oxford University Press is a department of the University of Oxford. It furthers the University's objective of excellence in research, scholarship, and education by publishing worldwide. Oxford is a registered trade mark of Oxford University Press in the UK and certain other countries.

Published in the United States of America by Oxford University Press
198 Madison Avenue, New York, NY 10016, United States of America.

Library of Congress Cataloging-in-Publication Data
Names: Kars, Aydogan, author.
Title: Unsaying God : negative theology in medieval Islam / Aydogan Kars.
Description: New York, NY : Oxford University Press, [2019] |
Includes bibliographical references.
Identifiers: LCCN 2018048099 |
ISBN 9780190942458 (hardcover) | ISBN 9780190942472 (epub)
Subjects: LCSH: God (Islam)—Proof—History of doctrines. |
Negative theology—Islam. | Islamic countries—Intellectual life.
Classification: LCC BP166.2 .K28 2019 | DDC 297.2/11—dc23
LC record available at https://lccn.loc.gov/2018048099

1 3 5 7 9 8 6 4 2

Printed by Sheridan Books, Inc., United States of America

To Aslı:
We have grown a flower that
No longer fits the pot.

Contents

Acknowledgments

REFLECTING ON SUFISM and companionship, Henry Corbin said decades ago that "the Absolute has no face; only the person has a face permitting the 'face to face' encounter." This book owes a lot to my recent encounters, some face to face, some virtual, and some, yes, imaginal. First, it is the relentless support and guidance of Richard McGregor that made this study possible. He has been continuously, gently, and naturally embodying the meaning of scholarship. Next, it is my two companions at Vanderbilt University, Ashkan Bahrani and Mohammad Meerzaei, who have been providing me with scholarly dialogue and enduring support that was indispensable in the ripening of this work. I am also thankful to my other teachers and colleagues from the beautiful city of Nashville: David Wasserstein, Lenn Goodman, Ellen Armour, and last but not least, Allen Hibbard, whose friendship I am very much missing.

I am also indebted to various scholars who reviewed chapters of this book and generously shared their insightful comments with me: Peter Adamson, Livnat Holtzman, Khalil Andani, Samer Akkach, and Ken Avery. Especially Mohammed Rustom illuminated my dark Ramadan nights with his candid emails and insightful, meticulous responses to my puzzled ideas.

My sincere thanks to my colleagues here at Monash University, who joined me in reflecting on my project as it gradually evolved. Constant Mews, Al Thomson, Peter Howard, Raphael Dascalu, Nathan Wolski, Julian Millie, Bain Attwood, Susannah Radstone, Georgie Arnott, Ruth Morgan, Tim Verhoeven, Daniella Doron, and Tamara Prosic: it has been a privilege of mine to be working with these distinguished researchers.

This book was written in a world where it is difficult to concentrate on research. I acknowledge the energy that I received from solidarity with the Academics for Peace (Barış İçin Akademisyenler) in Turkey that kept me intellectually alive in the last few troubled years. They made me better realize that I am part of multiple stories, many of which are just slightly different narrations of ʿAṭṭār's *Conference of the Birds*.

This humble book is my way of thanking my family. Rūmī said that "the mirror of the soul is the face of the beloved," to which his beloved responded: "words are for the other, my dear."

Unsaying God

Introduction

ON A BEAUTIFUL FRIDAY, according to an Anatolian anecdote, two villagers eventually decided to begin performing the daily prayers that they had neglected. They went to the mosque of their village and began listening to the Friday sermon. Yet the sermon turned out to be infuriating. The preacher was uttering only negative statements, occasionally decorating his sermon with quotations from the Qurʾan: "God is not similar to what you imagine; God cannot be compared to anything; God is elevated from anything you say; God is not this, and God is not that." One of them could not stand it anymore, and whispered in the ear of his fellow: "This despicable man is trying to say that there is no God, but he just cannot daresay it."

This book is about what medieval Muslim scholars did actually say about God, though in order to negate it. It examines the intellectual formations and historical developments of negative speech performances—specifically, negative theological movements concerning the divine essence that developed in medieval Islam. It presents a broad analysis of various Islamic disciplines and schools to unearth diverse theological positions as well as figuring out the intellectual contexts where negative discourses were performed.

Negative theology is difficult to pin down in Islamic intellectual history, as our sources provide a rich variety of possibilities. When introducing the Ismāʿīlīs, for example, the theologian ʿAbd al-Malik Imām al-Ḥaramayn al-Juwaynī (d.1085) employs a term that is a literal Arabic counterpart for the Latin *via negativa*—the path of negation: "The path of Ismāʿīlīs is via negativa [*sulūkihim maslak al-nafy*] instead of the affirmation of divine attributes. If they are asked whether the creator exists, they negate it, and say: '*He is not not-existent.*'"[1] Al-Juwaynī was rather hostile to Ismāʿīlīs, but

1. Al-Juwaynī, *Kitāb al-Irshād*, 37.

the position he described was emphatically confirmed by famous Ismāʿīlī scholars of his time, as we will explore in due course. Yet Abū Tammām (fl.l.10th CE), himself an Ismāʿīlī doxographer of the time, ascribes a comparable double negation of speech to another group, a Zaydī branch of Shīʿism in Yemen. Accordingly, the group—called Khalafiyya—resisted any positive, and indeed, negative speech when it comes to God:

> These people will not describe God with any description that is suitable for created things nor will they say of Him that He is either knowing [*ʿālim*] or not not knowing [*lā lā ʿālim*], not powerful [*lā qādir*] or not not powerful [*lā lā qādir*], not a thing [*lā shayʾ*] or not not a thing [*lā lā shayʾ*], not confined [*lā maḥdūd*] or not not confined [*lā lā maḥdūd*]. They speak about the creator neither on the basis of reality nor through metaphor. They rather talk by approximation [*taqrīb*]. Thus if they were asked about God, "do you recognize Him?" They would remain silent. They will not say that we recognize Him [*naʿrifuhu*] or that we do not not recognize Him [*lā lā naʿrifuhu*]. For them, if they were to recognize Him, their recognition of Him would encompass Him. Whoever is recognized and becomes recognizable to his recognizer cannot be a god.[2]

Theological negativity, however, was by no means perceived to be exclusive to Ismāʿīlī or Zaydī groups. Among the foremost "negators," according to the jurist Ibn Ḥazm (d.1064), were the Peripatetic philosophers. Ibn Ḥazm accused al-Kindī (d.873) of contradicting his own negativist [*salbī*] theology when al-Kindī tried to demonstrate that God is the cause of all creation, after claiming that nothing can be applied to, thought of, or said about Her. Ibn Ḥazm's concerns were not unfounded. When it comes to negating discourse on God's essence, on the other hand, it was such scripturalists and jurists who strictly applied the "without asking how" [*bilā kayfa*] principle to cut off any discursive access to God's nature. In a similar spirit of prudence, legal scholars and traditionists would often refuse to answer various theological questions, recommend another expert to respond, or simply say "I don't know." As his favorite pupil famously

2. Abū Tammām, *Kitāb al-Shajara*, 96 (Arabic text). The English translation provided by Madelung and Walker as "knowing or not knowing, powerful or not powerful, a thing or not a thing, confined or not confined" omits the double negations in the original Arabic text. Cf. ibid., 92 (English translation).

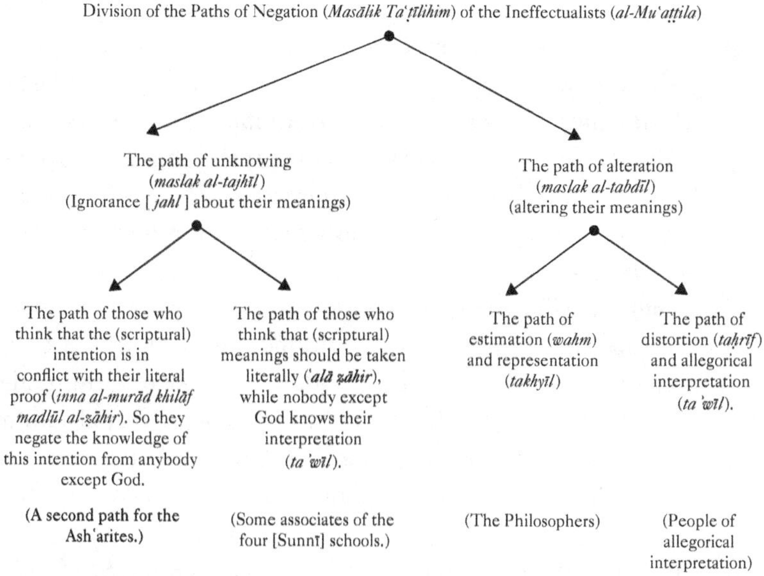
Division of the Paths of Negation (*Masālik Taʿṭīlihim*) of the Ineffectualists (*al-Muʿaṭṭila*)
The path of unknowing (*maslak al-tajhīl*) (Ignorance [*jahl*] about their meanings)
The path of alteration (*maslak al-tabdīl*) (altering their meanings)
The path of those who think that the (scriptural) intention is in conflict with their literal proof (*inna al-murād khilāf madlūl al-ẓāhir*). So they negate the knowledge of this intention from anybody except God.
The path of those who think that (scriptural) meanings should be taken literally (*ʿalā ẓāhir*), while nobody except God knows their interpretation (*taʾwīl*).
The path of estimation (*wahm*) and representation (*takhyīl*)
The path of distortion (*taḥrīf*) and allegorical interpretation (*taʾwīl*).
(A second path for the Ashʿarites.)
(Some associates of the four [Sunnī] schools.)
(The Philosophers)
(People of allegorical interpretation)

FIGURE I.1 Division of the Paths of Negation (*Masālik Taʿṭīlihim*) of the Ineffectualists (*al-Muʿaṭṭila*)

Al-Tamīmī in al-Dhahabī, Kitāb al-ʿArsh, 1:36; cf. al-Tamīmī, Muʿtaqad Ahl al-Sunna wa-l-Jamāʿa fī Asmāʾ Allāh al-Ḥusnā, 13.

reports: "More times than I can count, I asked Aḥmad Ibn Ḥanbal (d.855) about something and he just said, 'I don't know.'" Another pupil remarks that Ibn Ḥanbal used to say "I don't know" as a proper response, before citing various opinions.[3] If we listen to the scripturalist theologian of Saudi Arabia, Ibn Khalīfa al-Tamīmī (b.1959), the entire world of Sunnī Islam that he otherwise fervently promotes has long been associated with a "path of unknowing" [*maslak al-tajhīl*] and learned ignorance about the divine message and ipseity (or identity). For his readers he provides a prefatory schema of Muslim negativist approaches toward the meaning of the holy scripture, as illustrated in Figure I.1.

While al-Tamīmī's admittedly biased categorization and examples provide an exciting starting point to delve into negative theology in Islam, it curiously omits probably the most celebrated school of thought. In terms of notoriety, the prize for championing all "negators" in the tradition will arguably go to the Muʿtazilites. The negative statements of Muʿtazilite

3. See Ibn al-Jawzī, *The Life of Ibn Ḥanbal*, 147.

theologians inundated many pages in the works of later doxographers. However, when we look at the academic literature, it is yet another group, the Sufis, who are more intensively cited since the 1970s as the best exponents of Muslim *apophasis*—a Greek term commonly translated as "negative speech," or "unsaying." Ibn al-ʿArabī (d.1240) and Rūmī (d.1273), two great Sufi masters and both among the most influential Muslims who ever lived, are widely depicted as the most prominent representatives of Muslim negative speech on God.

Which group embodied the negative theological tradition of Islam? The sheer variety of possibilities sketched in Figure I.1 indicates that the search for a singular "Islamic negative theological tradition" or school is misguided at the outset. Yet another hostile yet fascinating schema that al-Tamīmī introduces to us illustrates that even the so-called radical ineffectualists that he rather dislikes are perceived as a rich and heterogeneous category, as indicated in Figure I.2.

These fascinating groups and their labels in al-Tamīmī's Salafī mind point to a rich variety among those "radicals" who defend an apophatic approach to God's nature and also in their performative strategies of negating the theological discourse. Al-Tamīmī is far from being impartial on the topic, yet he can still identify important differences in the apophatic strategies that each group adopted: paradoxicality, silence, double negation, and perpetual negation. In the light of this plurality, we are better off abandoning the rather commonplace talk about *negative*

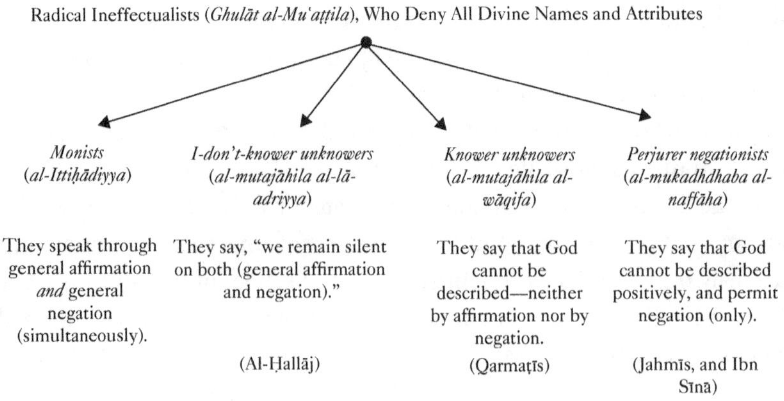

FIGURE I.2 Radical Ineffectualists (*Ghulāt al-Muʿaṭṭila*), Who Deny All Divine Names and Attributes

Al-Tamīmī in al-Dhahabī, *Kitāb al-ʿArsh*, 1:37.

theology in favor of *negative theologies*, as we acknowledge the possibility of producing multiple and heterogeneous self-negating theological discursive formations.[4]

We shall rephrase, then, our initial question. *Which groups embodied the negative theological traditions of Islam?* This study begins with asking this simple question, and then proceeds to sharpen it.

Why Sufism, and Why the Thirteenth Century?

Traveling across negators, denialists, ineffectualists, paradoxographers, naysayers, ignorance-pretenders, unknowers, I-don't-knowers, and taciturns, this book aims to introduce the apophatic theological positions that developed in the medieval Islamicate world. It is particularly interested in tracing their circulation among Sufis, and specifically in the thirteenth century. I should add a note, however brief, in justification of my choice to concentrate on thirteenth-century Sufism in this book. I will mention only three main reasons, which respectively correspond to the current literature on apophasis in Islam, comparative mysticism, and theories of mysticism.

First, Sufis of the thirteenth century compose the most unexpected yet prominent group cited in the current scholarship of apophaticism in Islam. The 1970s witnessed the rise of the concept "apophasis" in the study of religion, as a term that indicates not just a speech-act but also a new, ethicalized divine transcendence associated with mysticism. Within this broader turn in reinterpreting negative speech in religion and philosophy, a large body of works on Islam has cited primarily thirteenth-century Sufi masters, especially Ibn al-ʿArabī and Rūmī, as the foremost representatives of Islamic apophasis or negative theology.[5] In this

---

4. See Kars, "Two Modes of Unsaying in the Early Thirteenth Century Islamic Lands."

5. Corbin, "De la Théologie Apophatique comme Antidote du Nihilisme"; Corbin "The Paradox of the Monotheism"; Schimmel, *Mystical Dimensions of Islam*, 49; Schimmel, *Pain and Grace*, 63; Schimmel, *As Through a Veil*, 79; Schimmel, *The Triumphal Sun*, 10; Katz, *Mysticism and Language*, 3–32; Sells, *Mystical Languages of Unsaying*; Franke, *On What Cannot Be Said*, vol.1; Harmless, *Mystics*, 237; Almond, *Sufism and Deconstruction*; Huntington, "A Way of Reading," 283. For apophasis in other mystics, al-Ḥallāj (d.922), and al-Niffarī (d.af.965), see Mayer, "Theology and Sufism," 259. Here Mayer argues that "in common with other mystical theologies, it [i.e., Sufism] strongly inclined to an apophatic rather than a kataphatic approach to the divine mystery, expressing God through denial, not affirmation, through 'unsaying' rather than saying."

background of scholarship, it is paradox and mysticism that widely come to mind when we talk about apophaticism. Ibn al-ʿArabī and Rūmī are by far the most cited names for apophasis in Islam, while Henry Corbin's (d.1978) list added Persian Sufi masters who lived in the same century, such as Najm al-Dīn Kubrā (d.1221), ʿAlāʾ al-Dawla Simnānī (d.1336), and ʿAzīz Nasafī (fl.l.13th CE). A closer focus on this period and its figures not only reveals how forms of apophaticism adopted by these Sufis fit into the larger Islamicate world but also elucidates what was apophatic in theological context—in which sense, under which specific historical conditions and discursive regulations, and with which peculiar performative dimensions. Through a focus on Sufism, I will test whether the common equivalence of mysticism and negative theology is tenable. This study suggests that it is not.

Second, the description of thirteenth-century Sufism as the pinnacle of Muslim apophaticism reflects the broader description of the period in a comparative scholarly perspective. These were the most exciting times for the study of apophaticism—the golden age of Abrahamic apophatic theologies—as Michael Sells remarked:

> The 150-year period from the mid-twelfth to the beginning of the fourteenth century constitutes the flowering of apophatic mysticism. Almost simultaneously, the apophatic masterpieces of the Islamic, Jewish, and Christian traditions appeared, which would include, among others, the writings of Ibn ʿArabi (d. 1240), Rumi (d. 1273), Abraham Abulafia (d. ca. 1291), Moses de Léon (d. 1305), the twelfth- and thirteenth-century Beguine mystics culminating with Hadewijch (fl. 1240) and Marguerite Porete (d. 1310), and Meister Eckhart (d. ca. 1327).
>
> Apophasis lived on after this period in the post-exilic Kabbalah of Isaac Luria [d.1572], in the Spanish mystics, in Jacob Boehme [d.1624], and widely throughout the Islamic tradition. Yet it never again held as central a place in mystical language.[6]

---

6. Sells, *Mystical Languages of Unsaying*, 5. Sells adds that a convenient end-date for these heydays of apophatic mysticism would be 1492, "the year Jews and Arabs were expelled from Spain, the colonial age began, and the civilization held in common by Jewish, Christian, and Muslim cultures began to break apart into increasingly separate spheres" (Ibid., 221 n15.)

This argument is extremely enticing for any student of comparative mysticism. What might be the reasons for such a synchronic and widespread blooming—if indeed this was the case—of apophaticism across kin religions? Why did such apophaticism never resurface?

While the depictions of the thirteenth century as the pinnacle of Sufism are widespread, the extent to which these representations inherit the earlier orientalist or Muslim modernist baggages is not always clear. The preeminent British scholar of Sufism, Arthur Arberry (d.1969), for example, adopted an essentializing yet popular decline paradigm of Sufism, wherein the thirteenth century became the period when Islamic mysticism reached its climax and then gradually decayed (for nearly eight centuries!), never to recover.[7] An in-depth study of apophaticism in Islam up to the end of the thirteenth century provides a better understanding for such larger comparative perspectives on mysticism. The present study does not find substantial evidence in support of a conspicuous flowering of apophaticism on the divine essence among Muslims during this period. Paradoxical forms of negative theologies did intensify, but we also witness the decay of other forms that were more powerful in the previous centuries. Hence this study refuses to uphold the thesis of the thirteenth-century flowering of apophatic theologies among "the daughters of Abraham." We will unearth strong trans-religious interactions of apophaticism, particularly among the Muslim and Jewish mystical and philosophical traditions. On the other hand, these cross-pollinations developed much earlier than the thirteenth century, and mostly beyond the mystical currents of these religions.

The final reason is related to an even broader theoretical challenge on the relationship between mysticism and its institutionalization. The

---

7. "The age of Ibn al-Fāriḍ [d.1235], Ibn al-ʿArabī and Rūmī represents the climax of Sufi achievement, both theoretically and artistically," writes Arberry. "Thereafter, although through the numerous and ever multiplying Religious Orders the influence of Sufi thought and practice became constantly more widespread, and though sultans and princes did not disdain to lend the movement their patronage and personal adherence . . . the signs of decay appear more and more clearly, and abuse and scandal assail and threaten to destroy its fair reputation. . . . The history of the decline varies from country to country according to circumstance, but the general pattern, though admitting differences of detail, is fairly consistent throughout." (*Sufism*, 119.)

As Weismann observes in Arberry's approach, "apart from the salient essentialism of the text, it also hides the underlying modernist-orientalist presupposition that Sufi shaykhs lack agency and merely succumb to the external action of the forces of modernity. As in other cases of subaltern studies, this presupposition proved utterly false." ("Sufism in the Age of Globalization," 265.)

supposed opposition between mysticism and institutional religion has long overshadowed the study of religion as well as Sufism. Like Arberry, Spencer Trimingham (d.1987) in his *Sufi Orders in Islam* (1971), among other influential studies, depicted a progressively institutionalized history of Sufism, which meant for both men the gradual regression of authentic mysticism in Islam. This commonly presumed opposition between institutional religion and mysticism has been challenged since the late 1970s. Most remarkably, a group of comparative religionists developed what is called the constructivist approach, which has literally reversed the perennialist claims on mysticism and highlighted the importance of religious institutions, doctrines, scriptures, and established norms and practices in grounding, catalyzing, and even constructing mystical experiences.[8] Accordingly, mysticism is not the experiential, authentic seed of religious institutions and doctrines but rather their fruit. Within this theoretical context, how apophaticism relates to the institutionalization of mysticism emerges as a pivotal question that awaits a historically grounded answer. Depending on the theoretical position a religionist adopts, the expectations will be diametrically opposed to each other. Does the organization of mysticism in the form of orders [*ṭawāʿif*] and idiosyncratic methods [*ṭarīqāt*] associated with specific eponymous Sufi masters inhibit, or rather intensify apophaticism among Sufis?

The assumed flowering of apophatic mysticism curiously follows the beginning of the long process of the formation of Sufi orders. Yet an unresolved theoretical dilemma appears here: many scholars, including those who assume a golden age in the thirteenth century, also hold that apophaticism is inherently resistant to institutionalization, systematization, formality, and organization. Hence the relation of apophaticism with institutionalization is yet to be addressed on historical grounds. With its focus up to the beginning of the organization of Sufism in the form of orders, the current study traces whether the emerging institutionalization catalyzed or hindered Sufi variations of apophaticism in the thirteenth century. The present analysis does not find any tangible intensification or waning in apophatic theologies as a direct result of the institutionalization of mysticism in the form of nascent Sufi groups beginning to construct and gather around the lineages, methods, and practices associated with charismatic eponymous figures. The absence of such correlation further

8. For example, Katz, *Mysticism and Philosophical Analysis*; Proudfoot, *Religious Experience*; Katz, *Mysticism and Language*.

suggests that the ubiquitous association of mysticism with apophaticism is a problematic one.

A Guide to Negative Theology: Are the Muʿtazilites Negative Theologians?

So who were the negative theologians among medieval Muslims?[9] Until recently scholars of religion associated negative theology or negativist forms of theology in Islam particularly with a group of speculative theologians who emerged in eighth-century Iraq: the Muʿtazilites. Doxographers of other theological schools usually called them "the negators," or "deniers," of God's attributes. When Abū al-Ḥasan al-Ashʿarī (d.936) introduced the Muʿtazilite view on divine unity in a few sentences, he employed the Arabic negations some seventy times in a dizzying one-page "description," if it can be called that, as shown in Figure I.3.

The image of Muʿtazilites as the most famous standard-bearers of Islamic negative theology has persisted right up into modern scholarship, though what is meant by "negative theology" is rarely explained. The Muʿtazilite doctrine indeed indicates a fundamental weakness of "negative theology"—the standard term via which modern scholars of religion conceptualize apophatic performances in theology. While the Muʿtazilites firmly negated the reality and applicability of divine attributes to God, they did not follow the unknowability principle widely associated with negative theology. They maintained that God's essence, or the truth of Her ipseity [*ḥaqīqat dhāt Allāh*], was rather *knowable*. Fakhr al-Dīn al-Rāzī's (d.1209) observation is perceptive:

> Ḍirār [d.815] among the theologians, and [Abū Ḥāmid] al-Ghazālī [d.1111] among the later ones, argued that we do not know the truth of the ipseity of God—which is the claim of the philosophers. *The majority of the theologians among us* [i.e., the Ashʿarites] *and among the Muʿtazilites have argued that She is, indeed, knowable* [*annahā maʿlūma*].[10]

9. The discussion that follows relies on my longer analysis of the concept of "negative theology." See Kars, "What Is 'Negative Theology'? Lessons from the Encounter of Two Sufis." Also see Kars, "Sufis and Muʿtazilites: Theological Engagements of Ibn ʿArabī."

10. Al-Rāzī and Ṭūsī, *Muḥaṣṣal Afkār al-Mutaqaddimīn*, 188. Also see Jaffer, "Muʿtazilite Aspects of Faḫr al-Dīn al-Rāzī's Thought," 520 (emphasis mine).

وهذا شرح قول المعتزلة فى التوحيد وغيره

أجمعت المعتزلة على أن الله واحد ليس كمثله شىء وهو السميع البصير ، وليس
بجسم ، ولا شبح ، ولا جثة ، ولا صورة ، ولا لحم ، ولا دم ، ولا شخص ، ولا جوهر ولا
عرض ، ولا بذى لون ولا طعم ولا رائحة ولا مجسة ، ولا بذى حرارة ولا برودة ولا رطوبة
ولا يبوسة ، ولا طول ولا عرض ولا عمق ، ولا اجتماع ولا افتراق ، ولا يتحرك
ولا يسكن ، ولا يتبعض ، وليس بذى أبعاض وأجزاء ، وجوارح وأعضاء ، وليس
بذى جهات ، ولا بذى يمين وشمال وأمام وخلف وفوق وتحت ، ولا يحيط به
مكان ، ولا يجرى عليه زمان ، ولا تجوز عليه المماسة ولا العزلة ولا الحلول فى
الأماكن ، ولا يوصف بشىء من صفات الخلق الدالة على حدوثهم ، ولا يوصف بأنه
مُتَنَاه ، ولا يوصف بمساحة ولا ذهاب فى الجهات ، وليس بمحدود ، ولا والد ولا مولود ،
ولا تحيط به الأقدار ، ولا تحجبه الأستار ، ولا تدركه الحواس ، ولا يقاس بالناس ،
ولا يشبه الخلق بوجه من الوجوه ، ولا تجرى عليه الآفات ، ولا تحل به العاهات ،
وكل ما خطر بالبال وتُصُوِّر بالوهم فغير مشبه له ، لم يزل أولاً سابقاً متقدما
للمحدَثات ، موجوداً قبل المخلوقات ، ولم يزل عالما قادرا حيا ، ولا يزال كذلك ،
لا تراه العيون ، ولا تدركه الأبصار ، ولا تحيط به الأوهام ، ولا يُسمع بالأسماع ، شىء
لا كالأشياء ، عالم قادر حىّ لا كالعلماء القادرين الأحياء ، وأنه القديم وحده ،
ولا قديم غيره ، ولا إله سواه ، ولا شريك له فى ملكه ، ولا وزير له فى سلطانه ،
ولا معين على إنشاء ما أنشأ وخَلْق ما خلق ، لم يخلق الخلق على مثال سبق ،
وليس خلق شىء بأهون عليه من خلق شىء آخَر ولا بأصعب عليه منه ، لا يجوز
عليه اجترار المنافع ولا تلحقه المضار ، ولا يناله السرور واللذات ، ولا يصل إليه
الأذى والآلام ، وليس بذى غاية فيتناهى ، ولا يجوز عليه الفناء ، ولا يلحقه العجز

FIGURE 1.3 Key Muʿtazilite teachings on the divine nature according to al-Ashʿarī. Each of the boxes on the page is an Arabic negative particle. This passage has been called the "*credo* of Muʿtazilism . . . and a declaration of negative theology."[a]

[a]Al-Ashʿarī, *Maqālāt al-Islāmiyyin*, 1:216; Alami in Bennett, "The Muʿtazilite Movement (II)," 152.

Al-Rāzī's point about the essential accessibility of God to human intellect is widely supported by a variety of prominent sources. Hence there is an unjustified leap from the *negation of attributes* to the *divine unknowability and inaccessibility* in calling a Muʿtazilite scholar a negative theologian. Medieval scholars were keenly aware of the difference between the two theological questions, and the Muʿtazilites embodied a reference point for scholars to clarify their own positions. In his correspondence with the eminent philosopher Naṣīr al-Dīn Ṭūsī (d.1274), the Sufi master Ṣadr al-Dīn Qūnavī (d.1274) argued that "everybody who ponders seriously agrees that the divine reality is unknowable [*majhūla*]."[11] In his response, Ṭūsī felt obliged to correct Qūnavī's generic statement, clarifying the philosophical stance that he followed:

> it was necessary for Qūnavī rather to say: "the philosophers have agreed upon this (unknowability)." For, the Muʿtazilite masters among the theologians assert that the *divine reality is rather knowable to human beings as She is* [*ḥaqīqatihi taʿāla maʿlūma lil-bashar kamā hiya*].[12]

In turn, Qūnavī indeed agrees with the refinement that Ṭūsī brings to divine unknowability. In his response to Ṭūsī's correction, Qūnavī indicates that he actually meant the Aristotelian philosophers and the verifier Sufis, and not theologians, by the phrase "everybody who ponders seriously."[13] While Sufis and philosophers agree on divine unknowability, the Muʿtazilites state the opposite, both for Ṭūsī and Qūnavī. Observers like Ibn Taymiyya (d.1328) and al-Dhahabī (d.1348), however dissident they were toward these traditions, confirmed their schema.

The claim that "God is known" (in the sense of both *maʿlūm* and *maʿrūf*) is repeated and underscored in Muʿtazilite texts from early on. In the *Epistle of Whoever Seeks Guidance* [*Kitāb al-Mustarshid*] al-Qāsim ibn Ibrāhīm (d.860) employs both Arabic verbs to emphasize that God is knowable: "people know that things can be perceived as they really are and certainly known even if they are absent from us, for God is *cognized* and

11. Ṭūsī and Qūnavī, *al-Murāsalāt*, 50; also see Madelung, *Studies in Medieval Muslim Thought*, XI, 7.

12. Ṭūsī and Qūnavī, *al-Murāsalāt*, 100.

13. Ibid., 165–166.

known" [*fa-Allāhu yuʿlam wa yuʿraf*]. The head of the Basran Muʿtazilites, Abū Rashīd al-Nīsābūrī (d.ca.1068), also criticizes the defenders of divine unknowability, such as Ḍirār. His *Topics of Controversy* [*Masāʾil al-Khilāf*] follows the more celebrated summa *The Sufficient* [*al-Mughnī*] of his master al-Qāḍī ʿAbd al-Jabbār (d.1025), defending God's essential knowability by human reason, and goes so far as to discuss whether children can attain it. The later Muʿtazilite Taqī al-Dīn al-Najrānī (l.12th-ea.13th CE) also penned a long chapter devoted to the refutation of various possible arguments for divine unknowability.[14] Accordingly, creation is full of immediate proofs that can logically demonstrate to *every* rational person that they are created by an essentially omnipotent, self-sufficient, all-knowing, and just creator. Once this fundamental epistemological principle is logically proven, and the divine essence is known, one can be sure that the scriptures, as well as the ethico-legal systems explained through them, are revealed in order to sustain justice and help creation flourish. Otherwise, even miracles will prove nothing. Similarly, only after knowing the divine essence with its necessary positive and negative attributes can we derive other, non-essential attributes of God. If the Muʿtazilites tended to negate some the attributes of God, it is because they have certain knowledge about the divine nature.

Can We Still Speak of Negative Theology Tout Court?

It can be justifiably argued that the Muʿtazilites adopted a negative theological approach to the applicability of *divine attributes*; yet most of them were far from being negative theologians on the question of the knowability of the *divine essence*.[15] These two questions were held by Muslim theologians to be closely related, yet distinct and different. Many present-day studies, failing to recognize the distinction that was made in precolonial intellectual landscapes, run the risk of confusing different positions on the divine attributes and divine essence. Indeed, the widespread contemporary

---

14. Al-Najrānī, *al-Kāmil fī al-Istiqṣāʾ fīmā Balaghnā min Kalām al-Qudamāʾ*, 325–334; Abū Rashīd al-Nīsabūrī quoted in Ansari and Schmidtke, "Muʿtazilism after ʿAbd al-Jabbār," 248–249; al-Qāsim ibn Ibrāhīm, *Anthropomorphism and Interpretation of the Qurʾan*, 66–67; Abrahamov, *Islamic Theology*, 64.

15. The discussion that follows relies on my longer analysis of the concept of "negative theology." See Kars, "What Is 'Negative Theology'?' Lessons from the Encounter of Two Sufis."

appeal to the designations "negative theologian" or "apophatic thinker"—in addressing Ibn al-ʿArabī, Muʿtazilites, Ismāʿīlīs, Rūmī, al-Ghazālī, or the Jewish scholar Moses Maimonides (d.1204)—hides more than it reveals. First, negating all attributes from God, as many Muʿtazilites and Aristotelian philosophers did, does not support the overly hasty leap to an unknowable, ineffable divine essence. Also, an emphasis on an apophatic divine essence does not necessarily mean that all attributes are to be negated from God. The singular, generic term "negative theology" ignores not only the plurality of negative paths concerning a specific theological question but also the more elusive yet fundamental distinction between diverse theological questions, such as the nature of divine attributes and the divine essence.

Second, in a broader sense, "negative theology" inevitably assumes that one is adopting a negativist position in the entire field of theology. Yet it inescapably fails to define what a negativist position is in terms of a broad variety of questions that are widely considered "theological": issues including religious leadership, anthropomorphism, predestination and free will, theodicy, eschatology, the status of prophecy, the nature of the divine word, and divine love. "Negative theology" not only fails to identify the specific question and its terms, but it also reduces the rich field of theology down to a single issue—that is, God's nature—into *theomania*, and its supposedly triumphant negation. What would a negative theology of theodicy, or of religious leadership look like? We are yet to conceptualize and analyze these themes, exactly because the blanket term "negative theology" monopolizes the broad field of theology with its narrow lens on the divine essence and inhibits the analysis of other theological questions. The very fact that precolonial Muslim scholars applied the terms for negation to diverse theological questions indicates that their conception of theological negativity was much broader, and probably less theomaniac, than ours.

Who, then, were the negative theologians among medieval Muslims? The question does not have a proper answer, mainly because "negative theology" is too broad and vague a term if we survey the theological questions that they asked, and recall the vast dimensions of theology. "Negative theology," when a specific theological problem is not defined, is a generic concept with limited, if any, explanatory power. Do we mean a negative theology of the divine essence, divine attributes, theodicy, divine will, religious leadership, free will, or divine love? One can adopt a negative theology on any one of these questions, but this does not make one negativist in all these other fields of theology. The Muʿtazilites might have a negative theology of *divine attributes*, but the majority of them were far from adopting a negative theology of *divine essence*. If the question for negative theology is about the discursive or visionary accessibility of the divine nature, Muʿtazilites do not qualify as negative theologians even though their long series of negations inundate many pages. "Negative theology" is contextual, at least in the sense that an apophatic approach to a specific theological question does not automatically entail apophaticism on another theological question even if they are closely related. In other words, the unqualified employment of the term "negative theology" in the study of religion indicates that its content is already presumed, generally betraying our contemporary interests and anxieties, at the expense of a better understanding of what is really negative or positive in different theological positions in historical context.

Moving Forward

We now have some justification for the five conceptual and contextual moves that the following chapters make. These theoretical arguments emerged through an analysis of medieval Islamic texts, contexts, and pretexts. Yet I venture that the conceptual conclusions are general enough to apply to the study of Christian and Jewish negative theologies.

First, "negative theology" *unqualified* is also *disqualified*. The so-called negative theologians will change depending on the specific theological questions we are dealing with. Therefore, we will not encounter the unqualified term "negative theology" anymore, lest it causes confusion between different questions that we will examine. The following chapters of this study differentiate "negative theologies of the divine essence" from "negative theologies of divine attributes" and discourage the unqualified application of the term "negative theology."

Second, in the following chapters we will analyze one specific question within theology as a gateway to think about various (religious or nonreligious) forms of apophaticism in Islamic heritage. It revolves around the nature and accessibility of the divine ipseity [*dhāt*]—the motherland of "theo-logy" that relates to a wide range of problems but is still *a* question of theology. However pivotal in approaching other questions, the divine nature is only one problem within the broad field of inquiry called "theology" that I define in this book as "talking about God," or "God-talk in all its forms."[16] Hence the apophatic dimensions of vast fields under the rubric of theology, including religious leadership, anthropomorphism, predestination and free will, eschatology, the status of prophecy, the nature of the Qurʾan, theodicy, the origin and return, divine love, and divine attributes will be beyond our scope unless they directly relate to the human access to, or speculation on, God's essence. Similarly, if Islamic schools of thought have peculiar apophatic contributions in fields beyond theology or in subfields of theology other than the divine nature—and they obviously do—they will remain unexplored in this study.

Third, the case of Muʿtazilites shows us that hunting for negative particles and statements and labeling them "negative theology" or "apophaticism" would be misguided from a historical perspective. Such a strategy would mislead us also from a theoretical perspective. Equating negative statements with "apophaticism" would mark the inability to differentiate a twitch from a wink—a failure of the thick description of a communicative act with multiple layers of meaning. Denys Turner's *Darkness of God* made a similar point arguing that negation is performed in accordance with the rules of a given theological discourse that cannot be reduced to grammar. If the Qurʾanic statement "God is closer to you than your jugular vein" is understood as "God is physically proximate," which is a grammatical possibility, it could be negated by adding a negative particle: "God is not physically proximate." This statement can indeed properly negate an anthropomorphist theology, but for many schools of Islamic thought it actually misses the very point of a foundational Qurʾanic metaphor. In this particular theological setting, "God is closer to you than your jugular vein" is understood as a metaphor for divine immanence. Thus the person who appears and says, "No, God is not physically near to this vein in human body," actually does not participate in the particular language of that theological discourse. "What negates a metaphor is only another metaphor."[17] In that discourse, the statement "God is closer to you than your jugular vein" could be meaningfully negated in a few, yet not infinite, ways. One popular option could be another Qurʾanic statement, "Nothing is like unto God," which indicates divine transcendence in its terminology. Or, a ritual performance, a supplication, or silence could serve as a negation depending on the context. In these cases, theological discourse is

16. Walker, *Early Philosophical Shiism*, 84; Chittick, "Worship," 221.

17. Turner, *Darkness of God*, 37; Geertz, *The Interpretation of Cultures*, 5–10. See Qurʾan (hereafter abbreviated as Q.) 50:16; Q.42:11.

properly negated without explicitly appealing to a negative particle, while the negative statement fails to relate to the discursive space in the first place. Immediately when we reduce apophaticism to negative statements, we actually deprive ourselves of apprehending the historically changing, context-specific rules that govern the discourse and define how it can be meaningfully negated via its own repertoire.

Fourth, once we concentrate on the divine ipseity as a springboard to analyze the related negative theological currents in the Islamicate context, we now have justification for skipping the famous negators—that is, the Muʿtazilites—and approaching Sufis, Aristotelian philosophers, and others. Now we have a more refined sense of what we are looking for in order to understand the apophatic theologies of the divine essence. It is not pages-long negative statements that we will be hunting, even though we will catch them abundantly in what follows. Rather, we are undertaking thick descriptions of discursive formations that cancel themselves to perform the unsayability and unknowability of their saturated theme through negating their own acts of saying about knowing.

Fifth, al-Tamīmī's generous use of the labels such as "negators," "unknowers," and "negativists" to attack his rivals and to promote his own exclusivist scripturalism helps us question whether "negative theology" has an objective historical reality. The ascription of these labels was, as it still is, politicized and generally did not correspond to these self-negating performances.[18] Therefore, we will not be tracing an objectively defined or fixed (say, "Neoplatonic") group or school of "negative theology." Rather, we will examine self-negating strategies, the historical significance and performers of which were unstable and debated.

Coming to Terms: "Apophasis," "Performance," and God's Gender

As already implied, this study approaches apophaticism as a self-negating speech-act performed within a specific discursive field. In this lens, I define negative (or apophatic) theologies of the divine essence as all forms of self-negating performative speech formations on the divine ipseity. In other words, this book is studying particular theological speech performances that negate themselves by employing the very tools, repertoire, and

18. Cf. Asad, *Genealogies of Religion*, 29.

discursive methods of theology itself. Beyond this linguistic, performative definition, no inherent connection of apophaticism with critical thinking, mysticism, theology, paradoxicality, anti-institutionalism, or morality is made in this book. Each one of such problematic yet popular associations will be rather challenged in what follows.

Throughout the book, the reader will often encounter the terms "performance" and "performativity." I am using these terms in line with the speech-act theory of John Langshaw Austin and John Searle rather than the social theories of Michel Foucault or Judith Butler. My aim is to examine how the utterance of a negative statement *does* various things in different levels of meaning, and how the same utterance can *do* diverse things depending on the ritual or institutional context.[19] I will focus on this dimension particularly in the chapter on paradoxical apophaticism. There I will argue that the particular ritual context organized by specific Sufi institutions defines the performative success of a paradoxical utterance.

Last but not least, the language of this book carries a deliberate tension. In terms of gendered pronouns, I make a clear distinction in the book between my own voice and that of the sources I translate. My Arabic sources generally use the singular third-person male pronoun "He" [*huwa*] when addressing God. This *huwa* in medieval theological context was in most cases a pronoun that not only indicates masculinity but also transcends it when addressing God. This is a "He beyond he and she" for most of the scholars that we will encounter. Accordingly, God is "He" in a way that transcends gender binaries as God has both feminine and masculine names and attributes.[20] In what follows, we will encounter scholars arguing that

19. See, e.g., Austin, *How to Do Things with Words*, 4–11.

20. While defining divine attributes in terms of masculinity and femininity was common, the school of Ibn al-ʿArabī has also defended the superiority of the feminine over the masculine in the divine nature. ʿAbd al-Razzāq Kāshānī (d.1330) wrote:

> The origin of anything is called the "mother" [*umm*], since the branches branch off from the mother. Do you not see how God says, "[Fear your Lord, who created you from a single soul,] and from her he created her spouse, and from the two of them scattered forth many men and women" [Q.4:1]"? "Women" are feminine, while the "soul" from which creation took place is also feminine. In the same way, the root of the roots, beyond which there is no beyond, is called the "Reality" [which is feminine]. . . . The same is true of "Entity" and "Essence"—all these words are feminine.
>
> [Women] embrace the meaning of being the root from which things branch off. The same is true of Nature, or rather, of the Reality. Although the Reality is the father of all things because She is the Absolute Agent, She is also a mother. She brings together activity and the reception of activity. Hence She is identical with the locus of receiving activity in the form of that locus, and She is identical with the agent in the form of the agent. Her own reality demands that She bring together entification and

"He is beyond 'h' and 'e,'" as God transcends, or unites, gender binaries. In other words, God as *huwa* in medieval Islamic contexts can be male or trans-male, and the ambiguity is real, especially in the more anthropomorphic approaches we will analyze in the last chapter. In standard Arabic grammar, it is again the male pronoun that describes mixed genders. On the other hand, Persian pronouns for God are epicene (i.e., gender-indefinite), but semantically they still operate largely under the shadow of Arabic grammar in the medieval theological context. Therefore, I will mostly use androcentric (i.e., male-biased) pronouns when addressing God, aiming to be a faithful translator. In some cases—for example, if the referent is divine quiddity [*māhiya*], reality [*ḥaqīqa*], ipseity [*dhāt*], or God as the first cause [*ʿilla*]—the pronouns in my sources will become female, insofar as "quiddity," "reality," "ipseity," and "cause" are feminine terms in Arabic. It is indeed impossible to talk about God without using feminine names and pronouns, as emphasized eloquently by Ibn al-ʿArabī and his students.[21] In any case, I will remain as faithful as possible to my sources when introducing gendered terms or pronouns.

On the other hand, I hope that I will not upset my reader if I do not feel myself bound by the grammatical boundaries or theological inclinations of my sources. This book must rather address readers of English, which has its own boundaries and conventions. In Islamic studies and beyond, scholars today commonly use singular third-person male pronouns assuming that the gender ambiguity and the trans-male use of *huwa* can be transferred into English only via "He." But why should I impose a gender-biased and probably theologically loaded language on my English readers by assuming that only "He" (rather than "She" or "It") can be read as a term that transcends gender? The employment of these English pronouns in the study of religion is driven by language ideologies and the particular grammatical, lexical, or referential roles they attribute to gender. This book

---

> nonentification. Hence She becomes entified through every male or female entification, just as She is incomparable with every entification. (ʿAbd al-Razzāq Kāshānī in Murata, *The Tao of Islam*, 197.)

21. From Ibn al-ʿArabī:

> *If you want to say* [that he does not come into being from the Essence, but] *from a divine attribute, "attribute"* [ṣifa] *is also feminine. If you want to say* [that he comes into being] *from the divine power, "power"* [qudra] *is also feminine. Take whatever position you like. You will not find anything but the feminine having priority, even in the case of those who claim that God is the "cause" of the cosmos, for "cause"* [ʿilla] *is feminine*" (in Ibn al-ʿArabī in Murata, *The Tao of Islam*, 197; italics in original).

wants to resist the common temptation to unjustifiably promote a specific linguistic gender ideology and theology over others.

As a native speaker of Turkish, my natural choice would be "it" as a pronoun to address God, for three reasons. First, Turkish pronouns are referentially epicene, hence "it" sounds to me more natural, plain, and accurate. Many Turkish-, Kurdish-, or Persian-speaking Muslims could not even consider the possibility to talk about God as "He," until they learn languages with gendered pronouns, such as English, German, or Arabic. God would be a personified "It" for them, and they would be surprised to learn that English-speaking Muslims prefer "He" rather than "It," even though the latter is a viable grammatical possibility in English. This book analyzes mainly Arabic and Persian sources, while its author, no matter his ethnic or religious background, must himself avoid tacitly endorsing the gender ideology of any of these languages as the sole or normative voice of Muslim theological reflection. Second, "it" would better fit my own ecocentric perspective that entails gender-justice as an organic ingredient of environmentalism. In brief, I do not feel the pressure to employ feminine pronouns in order to undermine the hegemony of androcentricism and to promote gender-justice. Finally, such a choice would free me from capitalizing the first letter of the pronoun, which imposes a binary of God versus creation, or divine versus profane, on me and the scholars we are exploring. The perspective shifts in the Qur'an, and the ambiguities in the intimate conversations of al-Niffarī (d.af.965) or the ecstatic writings of al-Ḥallāj (d.922) remind us again and again that in Islamic mystical writings the referents of pronouns were often unfixed, sometimes on purpose. Anybody who has tried to translate Rūmī's devotional poems addressing his divinized, beloved companion, Shams Tabrīzī, will know that it is not only difficult but sometimes just wrong to introduce capitalization, even when the term is "qur'ān" or "divine" rather than a mere pronoun. I understand, however, that "it" lacks the conventional sense of the personified, living, active, or intimate dimension of the divine for many English readers. I also know that forsaking capitalization will render this book more tiresome to read. Moreover, such a gender-indefinite choice will erase the original gender play that inheres in many male and female pronouns in my Arabic sources.

Still, digressing from the common Anglophone scholarly tradition of employing male pronouns, as the author I will choose the singular female pronoun in addressing God. In other words, while the quotations address God mostly via singular male pronoun, the very sentence before or after the quotations will consistently use singular female pronoun. In both cases, the pronouns addressing God will be capitalized. I find four benefits in distinguishing my voice from the voice of my sources in terms of gender, creating a tangible tension. First, it faithfully transmits my original sources. Subtle examples of gender play in my sources will become visible, and possible anthropomorphic inclinations will make better sense, as we will see particularly in the final chapter. Second, the gender difference between the voices of author and of the sources and scholars explored in the book will better highlight the gender tension inherent in Islamic theological writings. It will constantly remind the English reader that the Arabic "He" of my sources is predominantly a term that transcends gender when referring to God. The popular Muslim conception of "He beyond 'h' and 'e' " will be better transmitted to the English reader. Third, differentiating my voice will distance me from the conventional linguistic practice in Anglophone scholarship. Through this distance, I will be able to challenge the implicit normativity of an English and Arabic (rather than, say, Persian or Turkish) theology and gender ideology in academic writing. "He" is a valid pronoun to address God only in some of the languages that Muslims speak, and this author aims to avoid the common practice of endorsing theologies that are meaningful only in these languages. Finally, my use of feminine pronouns will not only remind us of the trans-male nature of the referent, but also the unjustifiable use of male pronouns today as a transgender term in Anglophone scholarship. I hope to resist the hegemony of androcentrism in academic and theological discourse without compromising historical rigor in rendering my sources.

Compass

The current chapter has introduced the framework, content, and the basic conceptual problems in discussing "negative theology" as such. Accordingly, the move from "negative theology" to "negative theologies" is not sufficient to solve our conceptual problem in approaching Islamicate theological landscapes. Any question about "negative theology," in singular or plural, does not have a precise answer, mainly because "negative theology" is too broad and vague a term if we survey the theological questions that were asked or if we recall the breadth and depth of theological discourses. The current chapter has provided a conceptual introduction and narrowed down the scope of the next chapters to the negative theologies of the divine essence.

The following four chapters of the book thus focus on the wellspring of the field of theology: the divine ipseity. Within this narrower theological and clearer conceptual topography, they trace four distinct yet interconnected paths of negative speech on the nature of God that widely circulated in the medieval Islamicate world. These families of negative speech formations are loosely defined as "double negative," "philosophical," "paradoxical," and "amodal" apophatic paths. The formation and career of each of these paths are analyzed in a separate chapter of this book. These studies suggest that Islamicate scholars could apply more than one of these methods of negating the discourse on God's essence in different works or contexts. Moreover, the same methods of negation could be adopted by rival groups. For example, the set of strategies that define philosophical apophaticism were also adopted by the critics of philosophy in the twelfth and thirteenth centuries. In the transmission of philosophical apophaticism in Andalusia from al-Kindī to Moses Maimonides, not only polymaths like al-Baṭalyawsī (d.1127), but also surprising names such as the ascetic mystic Ibn Masarra (d.931) played significant roles. On the other hand, the Jewish theologian Nethanel al-Fayyūmī (d.1165) and the Shāfiʿī judge of Fāṭimid Cairo, al-Quḍāʿī (d.1062) followed Ismāʿīlī apophaticism by adopting not only their famous "double negation" but also their complex cosmology. In the same vein, the apophatic strategies that Sufis applied were often shared with non-Sufis, and even anti-Sufis. The cases the book introduces illustrate not only the plurality of negative theologies of the divine essence but also the porousness of intellectual boundaries between schools, sects, and religions, Judaism and Islam in particular. Conversations on "Islamic," and for that matter "Jewish" or "Christian," negative theologies, should bear in mind the theological osmosis that took place across religious traditions. If we tend to define religions as separate belief systems—and we still widely do—such definition attributes theology a decisive yet undeserved role in determining religious differences and boundaries. This study encourages finding another definition of religion that goes beyond beliefs and ideas, insofar as it demonstrates that theologies were shared intellectual projects that had little respect for religious boundaries.

The presence of multiple ways of negating discourses on divine essence indicates that there is no single "negative theological tradition" even with reference to one problem within the Islamic intellectual heritage. While there is no unified theology or creed among Muslims in the absence of an authoritative "church," clergy, or consistent state regulation, the questions asked and the answers provided were not only diverse and contextual but also considerably overlapping among scholars and intellectuals from different backgrounds and religious affiliations. From a wider methodological perspective, the study adopts a historicist, contextualist approach to the study of negative theologies and apophasis. Accordingly, every discourse is composed of a finite set of connected propositions and performatives, and there is neither one method nor infinite methods of negating a given discourse. Apophatic possibilities are discourse-dependent insofar as the rules, methods, performative dimensions, and wider implications of negating a discourse are partially defined by the discourse itself. The book hopes to convince the reader that there is no unbounded, absolute, or infinite negation; negative speech is a historically embedded performance that should be contextualized within the multilayered discursive spaces that it affirms in order to operate.

This study displays the inherent affirmativity in any given speech performance, and its findings are in stark contrast with the popular associations of "negative theology" with broad themes like "infinite critique," antidogmatism, mysticism, or morality. Yet, the book avoids extended theoretical discussions, comparisons, or reflections on the contemporary significance of, or appeal to, apophasis and negative theology in philosophy, comparative religion, or constructive theology. The primary purpose of the current book is to inform readers about negative theologies of divine essence in Islam, introducing a historical perspective, vast fields of scholarship, and diverse intellectual schools and figures. It has a clear theoretical framework, while theoretical discussions are either completely removed or minimized in favor of deeper analysis of Islamic intellectual history. Such valuable and unavoidable philosophical discussions and comparisons should wait until we have a better grasp of Muslim negators, denialists, ineffectualists, paradoxographers, naysayers, ignorance-pretenders, unknowers, I-don't-knowers, and taciturns. Their diverse self-negating speech formations not only stated but also performed the unsayability of the excessive, saturated theme of theological discourse through their own failure of saying.[22]

---

22. All quotations from Arabic, Persian, and Turkish throughout the book are my own translations into English, unless solely a published English translation is cited. When I provide my own translation, I will also cite, if available, an existing English translation of the source for my readers. When I directly quote from an existing translation, I will often make some minor modifications to preserve terminological or formal consistency as I will denote in each case.

The majority of the works consulted in this study have not been translated into English. I will provide a courtesy translation of the titles of all of these works, and often use these English titles rather than the original names in order to make the book more accessible to my readers.

PATH ONE

Double Negation

ISMĀʿĪLĪ APOPHATICISM

THIS CHAPTER INTRODUCES the contours of the classical Ismāʿīlī negative theology of the divine essence that is often called the path of double negation. The apophatic path developed by Ismāʿīlī scholars had distinct cosmological markers and a logical structure that enabled the performative self-cancellation of discourse about the inaccessible divine essence. Respecting their diversity, and without essentializing or dehistoricizing them, we can highlight three general features that widely circulated among Ismāʿīlī thinkers until the Mongol invasion: (1) They put the divine essence beyond the divine word (or command), which lies beyond the first creation, the universal intellect. Creation emerges from the divine word's conjunction with the universal intellect, which compromises the former's oneness and makes it knowable to intellect only as the one-many, yet still unknowable in its relative oneness. (2) The relative oneness of the divine word can be transcended only by two negations. The first one negates the positive ground and relationality, and the second cancels all (positive and negative) discursivity in order to indicate the beyond of the relative oneness beyond creation. This "via negativa duplex" of the classical Ismāʿīlī theological tradition indicates the inapplicability and failure of any statement on God through its own performative self-cancellation. "Negating the divine attributes" means their *inapplicability*, rather than their *negative applicability*, which they criticized. (3) The absolute oneness of God is unknowable, beyond the impenetrable oneness of the divine word.

Texts written by or about Sufis began to employ the double negation in the thirteenth century when Sufism and Ismāʿīlīsm developed creative interactions, particularly in Iran and Central Asia. The post-Alamūt coalescence of Ismāʿīlism and Sufism in these territories strongly corroborates this premise.

The Background: "Radicals of All Radicals"

Muʿtazilites were depicted as the foremost champions of an extreme negative theology by their adversaries and the later tradition. This depiction, as we have seen, needs to be qualified: it could be appropriate to call the Muʿtazilites "negative theologians" in terms of the nature of the divine attributes, not that of God's essence that this study explores. Thus we should visit the runner-up. In the accounts of medieval doxographers, the names of Muʿtazilites were generally accompanied by another group of "negators": "the Esoterics" [al-Bāṭiniyya]. When introducing the Esoterics, Imām al-Ḥaramayn al-Juwaynī writes:

> Some sects of Esoterics say, "*Nothing can be attributed to God.*" . . . They believed that if one describes beginningless as the "necessary being," this will entail likening Him to creation, as they are existent [too]. Hence their path is via negativa when asked to affirm the attributes. If they are asked whether the Creator exists, they negate it, and say "*He is not not-existent.*"[1]

Al-Juwaynī's plural term "some sects of the Esoterics" [*ṭawāʾif min al-Bāṭiniyya*] describes a heterogeneous group of theological currents that were associated with the official Islam of the Fāṭimids (r.909–1171), Ismāʿīlism. Among the Esoterics, the Qarmaṭīs were particularly well-known for adopting such double negations. Another hostile observer, Ibn Taymiyya reports:

> They say, "He is named neither affirmatively nor negatively. He is called *neither existent nor not not existent* [*lā lā mawjūd*], *neither living nor not not living* [*lā lā ḥayy*], insofar as there is comparability to

1. Al-Juwaynī, *Kitāb al-Irshād*, 37.

existents in affirmation, and comparability to non-existents in negation. All of it [i.e., speech] contains comparability."[2]

Echoing this double negation, Ibn Taymiyya calls the Esoterics in a way that doubles the tone of radicalism he ascribes them. "They are *the most radicals of all radicals* [*ghulāt al-ghulāt*]." They negate from Him all binaries [*al-naqīḍayn*], and say, "[He is] *neither existent nor non-existent, neither living nor dead, neither knowing nor ignorant.*"[3]

Mention of the "Bāṭiniyya" does not even appear in al-Ashʿarī's earlier doxography, and the "Ismāʿīlīs" are briefly mentioned as a rather insignificant Shīʿite sect among many others. However, in less than a century—thanks to the rise of the Fāṭimids in Egypt, the expansion of the originally Zaydī then Imāmī Būyids (r.933–1056) from northern Iran to Iraq, and the intensive, organized proselytization of Ismāʿīlism around the world—"Bāṭiniyya" becomes a major theme of the Sunnī doxographers with increasing intolerance toward what they perceive as their foremost religious and political threat. More harshly than al-Ashʿarī, Abū al-Muẓaffar al-Isfarāʾīnī (d.1079) removes Ismāʿīlism, now called the "Bāṭiniyya," from the category of "Shīʿites," and puts it under "the Resemblers" [al-Mushabbiha], who claim to be Muslims, but do not constitute one of the seventy Muslim sects. Here al-Isfarāʾīnī was following the hostile categorization of the influential doxographer, ʿAbd al-Qāhir al-Baghdādī (d.1038). In a debate on Ismāʿīlism and its critics, Fakhr al-Dīn al-Rāzī sniffed at ʿAbd al-Qāhir's doxographical work as it was bigoted and hostile toward other schools. Yet al-Rāzī's own succinct doxography, the *Beliefs of Sects* [*Iʿtiqād al-Firaq*], its innovative dimensions notwithstanding, does not deviate from their categorization that wants to exclude Ismāʿīlīsm from the abode of Islam. In 1257, when the Īlkhānid pagan warlord Hūlāgū (r.1256–1265) destroyed the Ismāʿīlī stronghold in Iran, his official court historian ʿAṭāʾ Malik Juvaynī (d.1285) would compare the conquest dramatically to that of Khaybar, and to the struggle of the Prophet with the disbelievers. By the time of the Imām al-Ḥaramayn's student Abū Ḥāmid al-Ghazālī, "Bāṭiniyya" already meant the Ismāʿīlī umbrella first and foremost, but it could be employed to accuse anybody of diversion from their

---

2. Ibn Taymiyya in al-Dhahabī, *Kitāb al-ʿArsh*, 1:69–70.

3. Ibn Taymiyya and al-Tamīmī in ibid., 1:76.

own standards of normative Islam and succumbing into esotericism. For example, Ibn Taymiyya, whose polemical attacks had a wider scope than most, applied the term "Bāṭiniyya" not only to Shīʿites wholesale but also to specific Sufi groups and to elitist philosophers such as the famous Ibn Rushd (d.1198).[4] Ibn Taymiyya's doubled hostility toward Ismāʿīlis was not merely about their double negation.

Medieval Ismāʿīlīs are well known—or better said, stereotypically known—for a peculiar appropriation of a notoriously broad and fuzzy term, "Neoplatonism," into their theological system. For early Ismāʿīlīs, in line with Plotinus (d.270), God was the unknowable absolute One who can be neither comprehended by reason nor accurately described. Their doctrine removed all the attributes, including "being," from God, and unlike the majority of the Muʿtazilites, they kept Her essence utterly unknowable and ineffable. They even avoided the name "God," and rather preferred "the Originator" [al-Mubdiʿ]—a vague, directional designation—as noted early on by non-Ismāʿīlī scholars like Abū Manṣūr al-Māturīdī (d.944) far away in Samarqand.[5] As early as the beginning of the tenth century, they developed a radically apophatic theology via a method of "two negations" [*salibatān*], which employed a self-cancelling theological "discourse" that removed God from the realm of discursivity. The "description" of divine identity [*huwiyya*; literally, "He-ness"] in Abū Yaʿqūb al-Sijistānī's (d.972) *Wellsprings of Wisdom* [*Kitāb al-Yanābīʿ*] is extremely difficult to translate due to the originality of its language, which stretches the limits of Arabic as much as it can:

> The pure He-ness [*al-huwiyya al-maḥḍiyya*] associated with the glorified Originator transcends "He" and "not-He." It is not that He-ness is existent and not-He-ness [*lā-huwiyya*] is not-existent. . . . The Originator is not "He" unlike the He-ness of the existents, and not "not-He" unlike the not-He-ness of the non-existents. His He-ness

4. "Copy of the *fatḥnāmā* of Alamūt: '*Praise be to God, Who keepeth His promise, and aideth His servant and strengtheneth His host, and routeth the sects, He alone'!*" (ʿAṭāʾ Malik Juvaynī, *Jehān Gūshā*, 622, 618; Hodgson, "Bāṭiniyya"). See Abū al-Muẓaffar al-Isfarāʾīnī, *al-Tabṣīr fī al-Dīn*, 140–142; ʿAbd al-Qāhir al-Baghdādī, *Kitāb al-Farq bayn al-Firaq*, 247–255; Fakhr al-Dīn al-Rāzī, *Munāẓarāt*, 39; Fakhr al-Dīn al-Rāzī, *Iʿtiqād al-Firaq al-Muslimīn wa-l-Mushrikīn*, 263–264.

5. Walker, *Ḥamīd al-Dīn al-Kirmānī*, 87; al-Māturīdī, *Kitāb al-Tawḥīd*, 162. As an early critical and perceptive reader of Ismāʿīlism, al-Māturīdī challenged the Ismāʿīlī negation of naming, arguing that naming does not cause any similarity or comparability [*tashbīh*] among the named. (See al-Māturīdī, *Kitāb al-Tawḥīd*, 162–163.)

> is the manifestation of the negation of the He-nesses and not-He-nesses from the transcendent Originator.[6]

Here al-Sijistānī's experimental, twisted language is negating all possible descriptions of God and all discursive identities attributable to Her. *God's identity is a negation of all discursive possibilities, including this very negation itself.* Hence the negativity in this line differs from the Muʿtazilite negation of the divine attributes, which kept the divine essence knowable. Most evidently, Ismāʿīlī scholars not only negated attributes but also their negations. One of the most controversial of these negations concerned, commonsensical though it may seem, divine "thingness" [*shayʾiyya*] where Ismāʿīlīs diverged from virtually all prominent Muslim schools of thought.

Thingness of God?

Al-Sijistānī refuses to apply not only "identity," or "he-ness," but also their negations, even if one supplies these attributes with an emphasis on divine incomparability. This double negation was a radical critique of widespread theological approaches to the divine transcendence circulating among different schools. The Zaydī and Muʿtazilī polymath of Yemen, Nashwān al-Ḥimyarī (d.ca.1194) illuminates this major point of divergence, focusing on the applicability of *thingness*:

> Ismāʿīlīs among the Jaʿfarīs say: "God is not a thing [*lā shayʾ*], and not not a thing [*lā lā shayʾ*]. For, if one says 'He is a thing,' they will compare Him; and if one says 'He is not a thing,' they will deny Him." So they say this both in terms of negation and affirmation altogether [*fa-qālu fīhi bi-l-nafy wa-l-ithbāt jamīʿan*]."[7]

The term *shayʾ* that the Ismāʿīlīs negated meant grammatically much more than what "thing" signifies in modern English. The Arabic term indicated the entire field of *logos* in its widest sense possible. The influential Basran grammarian Abū al-ʿAbbās al-Mubarrad (d.898), for example, declared that *shayʾ* was the most universal noun. The doyen of Arabic

6. Abū Yaʿqūb al-Sijistānī, *Kitāb al-Yanābīʿ*, 71. For Walker's English translation, see Abū Yaʿqūb al-Sijistānī, *Wellsprings of Wisdom*, 49–50. Also see Alibhai, *Abū Yaʿqūb al-Sijistānī and Kitāb Sullam al-Najāt*, 44–47.

7. Al-Ḥimyarī in Ansari, *al-Mutabaqqī min Kutub Mafqūda*, 119.

grammar, Sībawayh (d.796), is reported to have said that it is "the most universal of universals" [*aʿamm al-ʿāmm*]. The negation of thingness, from a grammatical perspective, was radical enough to cancel *any* mental and linguistic, hence discursive, possibility. Muʿtazilites at large would follow the position that *shayʾ* was the most broadly applicable category in reality, and they argued that *shayʾ* encompassed the two subcategories "existent" [*mawjūd*] and "non-existent" [*maʿdūm*]. As al-Māturīdī explains, *shayʾ* is only "a name of establishment, and a negation of ineffectuality [*ism al-ithbāt wa nafy al-taʿṭīl*]." Its negation [*lā shayʾ*] meant either the negation of the reality of that thing or diminution of something established [*nafy al-ḥaqīqa aw taṣghīr al-thābit*]. Later al-Bāqillānī (d.1013) would echo this commonplace position that saw thingness as grounding *logos* rather than a superadded attribute or a construct.[8]

Shayʾ was, in other words, a term that based the very discourses on divine incomparability and transcendence. Prominent Sunnī as well as Shīʿī scholars at least from the eighth century onward—such as Muḥammad al-Bāqir (d.733), Hishām ibn al-Ḥakam (d.ca.815), al-Kulaynī (d.940), al-Māturīdī, and Ibn Bābawayh (d.991)—developed popular discourses of transcendence for God, often employing catchphrases such as "God is a thing not like anything [*Allāhu shayʾun lā ka-l-ashyāʾ*]."[9] Those who appealed the phrase were called by the Ismāʿīlī doxographer Abū Tammām "the Weeds" [Nābita]—a derogatory term for intellectually poor scripturalism. But admittedly it was used ubiquitously and applied almost by every other school of theology. Shīʿī imāms Jaʿfar al-Ṣādiq (d.765) and

---

8. Al-Māturīdī, *Kitāb al-Tawḥīd*, 105–106; al-Bāqillānī, *Tamhīd al-Awāʾil*, 34–35, 265–266; Frank, "'Lam Yazal' as a Formal Term in Muslim Theological Discourse," 268n44; Wisnovsky, "Avicenna and the Avicennian Tradition," 105.

Algebraists also conceptualized *shayʾ* as a kind of universal variable (Wisnovsky, "Notes on Avicenna's Concept of Thingness," 183).

From an alternative grammatical perspective, we can see the negation of thingness as an even more direct gesture toward divine unknowability. The grammarian al-Zajjāj (d.923) describes *shayʾ* as anything that is knowable [*kulli maʿlūmun huwa shayʾ*]. (See Frank, "'Lam Yazal' as a Formal Term in Muslim Theological Discourse," 257.) Insofar as the claim that God is knowable [*maʿlūm*] was popular among the Muʿtazilites, the refutation of divine knowability could have ultimately led the Ismāʿīlī scholars to the more radical negation of *shayʾ*, pertinent to their defense of divine unknowability.

9. Ibn Bābawayh, *al-Iʿtiqādāt fī Dīn al-Imāmiyya*, 22; al-Māturīdī, *Kitāb al-Tawḥīd*, 104–107. Also see Cerić, *Roots of Synthetic Theology in Islam*, 150–151. For the *Fiqh al-Akbar II*, which was attributed to Abū Ḥanīfa (d.767), but was written much later, see Abū Ḥanīfa in Wensinck, *The Muslim Creed*, 190.

Muḥammad al-Jawād (d.835) argued that thingness had to be applied to God in order to remove Her beyond the two limits of ineffectualism [*taʿṭīl*] and comparability [*tashbīh*]. Like his forerunner ʿAbd al-ʿAzīz al-Makkī (d.854), al-Ashʿarī applied the term and approvingly reported that the vast majority of Muslims [*ahl al-ṣalāt*] attribute "thingness" to God, while it was only Jahm ibn Ṣafwān (d.745) and a group among the Zaydīs who avoided employing the name.[10] Ibn Ḥanbal, who wrote a refutation to Jahm, was among those who found the phrase self-contradictory. Yet, some Jahmites and the followers of Ibn Ḥanbal, like Abū Muḥammad Rizq Allāh al-Tamīmī (d.1095) used the phrase. Works attributed to Abū Ḥanīfa (d.767) including the *Greatest Insight* [*Fiqh al-Akbar*], Abū Muṭīʿ Makḥūl al-Nasafī's (d.930) refutation to Jahm, and later Ḥanafī creeds such as Maymūn ibn Muḥammad al-Nasafī's (d.1114) *Ocean of Discourse* [*Baḥr al-Kalām*] and the famous *Fiqh al-Akbar II* invariably employ "thing" for God. Most of the Zaydites, the Ashʿarites, Māturīdites, and Karrāmites as well as Muʿtazilites like al-Ṣāliḥī (fl.ca.913) and al-Qāsim ibn Ibrāhīm shared this view. The prominent Ibāḍite theologian al-Fazārī (8th CE) also applied the attribute "thing" to God, even though its meaning is a negation—that is, God's being not non-existent [*laysa bi-maʿdūm*]. The application of *shayʾ* to God makes the very discussion of the beatific vision in the afterlife possible, as the recorded discourses of the Sufi master ʿAbd al-Qādir al-Jīlānī (d.1166) indicate. Other Sufis like Ibn Khafīf (d.982), in the line of his teacher al-Ashʿarī, claimed that God is a thing unlike things. In Andalusia, the physician Jamāl al-Dīn Ibn Tūmart (d.1001) employed the term *shayʾ* in an emphasis on divine otherness with a set of negations. Philosophers also did not hesitate to call God a "thing" in order to enable speech about Her, even if it is employed metaphorically in order to preserve divine dissimilarity and transcendence. Abū Naṣr al-Fārābī (d.950), for example, agreed with the Muʿtazilites in holding that "thing" is the supreme genus, which can be distinguished into the species "existent" and the species "non-existent." Due to Her transcendence of these species, God cannot be called "existent," but She can be called "thing." Ibn Miskawayh (d.1030) follows al-Fārābī, and the Sufi intellectual Ibn Sabʿīn

10. Williams, "A Body Unlike Bodies," 35; Amir-Moezzi, *The Divine Guide*, 44; al-Ashʿarī, *Maqālāt al-Islāmiyyin*, 2:180; al-Qāsim ibn Ibrāhīm, *Anthropomorphism and Interpretation of the Qurʾan*, 12, 73–84; Ibn Taymiyya, *Darʾ Taʿāruḍ al-ʿAql wa-l-Naql*, 187. As the Ismāʿīlī doxographer Abū Tammām informs us, at least the Khalafiyya branch of Zaydiyya in Yemen refused to apply the term; see Abū Tammām, *An Ismaili Heresiography: The Bāb al-Shayṭān*, 96 (Arabic text), 92 (English translation).

(d.1269) argues that God is *the* Thing—the term applies to Her eminently [*via eminentiae*]. These discourses of divine transcendence based on God's dissimilarity to other "things" were ubiquitous. Indeed, they were so popular that it was seen as problematic enough to stir a heated debate among philosophers when Abū Zakariyyā al-Ṣaymarī (fl.11th CE) in Abū Ḥayyān al-Tawḥīdī's (d.1023) circle refused to call God "thing."[11]

It is in this grammatical and theological context and widespread agreement that Ismāʿīlīs of the tenth and eleventh centuries negated the applicability of *shayʾ* to God. The report from the Yemenī scholar al-Ḥimyarī is corroborated by other observers like al-Māturīdī in Samarqand. Al-Ḥimyarī's contemporary Ismāʿīlī fellow countryman Ibn al-Ḥusayn al-Ḥāmidī (d.1162) vocally criticized all of those who claimed that "God is a thing unlike anything." Al-Sijistānī had already seen in these supposedly negative statements blatant anthropomorphism as they still indicate a shared basis, in this case thingness, for comparability. The *Treasures of Proof* [*Khazīnat al-Adilla*], composed during the reign of al-Ḥakīm (r.996–1021), probably by a disciple of Ḥamīd al-Dīn al-Kirmānī (d.1021), devoted a chapter explaining that God is not a "thing."[12] Ismāʿīlīs stood against the tide by refusing the applicability of a key term that made theological

11. For more about this debate, see, al-Tawḥīdī, *al-Muqābasāt*, 186–188. For examples of calling God "thing," see Frank, "'Lam Yazal' as a Formal Term in Muslim Theological Discourse," 268n44; Abū Ḥanīfa in Wensinck, *The Muslim Creed*, 190; also Abū Ḥanīfa in Watt, *Islamic Creeds*, 63; cf. Q:67:3; Rudolph, *Al-Māturīdī and the Development of Sunnī Theology in Samarqand*, 90; Maymūn ibn Muḥammad al-Nasafī, *Baḥr al-Kalām*, 99; Abrahamov in al-Qāsim ibn Ibrāhīm, *Kitāb al-Dalīl al-Kabīr*, 31–33; al-Qāsim ibn Ibrāhīm, *Anthropomorphism and Interpretation of the Qurʾan*, 12–13, 73–84; al-Fazārī, *Early Ibāḍī Theology*, 176; al-Fārābī, *Kitāb al-Wāḥid wa-l-Waḥda*, ch.1–2; Wisnovsky, "Avicenna and the Avicennian Tradition," 105–107; Ibn Miskawayh, *Miskawayh: De l'âme et de l'Intellect*, 141; Ibn Sabʿīn, *al-Kalām ʿalā al-Masāʾil al-Ṣiqilliyya*, 40; al-Jīlānī, *al-Fatḥ al-Rabbānī*, ch.33, 134. For an English translation, see al-Jīlānī, *The Sublime Revelation (al-Fatḥ al-Rabbānī)*, ch.33, 209; al-Daylamī, *A Treatise on Mystical Love*, xxxiii; Jamāl al-Dīn Ibn Tūmart al-Andalusī, *Kanz al-ʿUlūm*, 37; Wisnovsky, "Notes on Avicenna's Concept of Thingness."

Ibn al-Sīd al-Baṭalyawsī represents another exceptional case demonstrating that not all philosophers in Andalusia agreed with this popular position regarding the thingness of God. See al-Baṭalyawsī, *al-Ḥadāʾiq fī al-Maṭālib al-ʿāliya al-Falsafiyya al-ʿAwīṣa*, 95.

12. Ivanow, *A Creed of the Fāṭimids*, 10–11; Abū Yaʿqūb al-Sijistānī, *Kitāb al-Maqālīd al-Malkūtiyya*, ch.11; Walker, *Early Philosophical Shiism*, 77; Ibrāhīm ibn al-Ḥusayn al-Hāmidī, *Die Ismailitische Theologie*, 14–15; al-Māturīdī, *Kitāb al-Tawḥīd*, 163.

A similar critique comes from the Andalusian grammarian and philosopher al-Baṭalyawsī, as discussed below. The parallels between al-Sijistānī and al-Baṭalyawsī are eye-catching. See al-Baṭalyawsī, *al-Ḥadāʾiq fī al-Maṭālib al-ʿāliya al-Falsafiyya al-ʿAwīṣa*, section 3.2.2.1.

discourse possible. They could stand firm against the thingness of God, as we will see below, only until the twelfth century.

But what remains sayable on God once the very grammatical ground of theological discourse is removed? And then this very removal is removed?

Double Negation: The Repetitive Form

Al-Sijistānī asks the same question, though, admittedly, in a more sophisticated style: "If the Originator, transcendent as He is, had a comparable He-ness within creation other than negating He-nesses and Not-He-nesses, then with what would creation compare Him?"[13] Accordingly, what can only be said of the divine ipseity is its abstraction as a negation from creation and all discursive spaces. Any discourse that claims to address God's absent ipseity should be negated, and then re-negated in order to indicate the limits of all discursivity. Al-Sijistānī calls for an unprecedented, repetitive form of double negation, saying,

> There does not exist a glorification [*tanzīh*] more brilliant and more splendid than that by which we establish the absolute transcendence of our Originator through the use of these phrases in which a *negative*, and a *negative of a negative* apply to the thing denied.[14]

Al-Sijistānī's first negation cancels any positive discourse on God by removing all attributes. The second negation cancels the negative discourse of the first step itself, by canceling all, including negative, discursive possibilities. Al-Sijistānī carefully emphasizes that the second move is directed toward the entire act of the discursive negation of the first step, not just toward its content.[15] Trivial as it might appear, the difference is enormous

13. Abū Yaʿqūb al-Sijistānī, *Kitāb al-Yanābīʿ*, 71. For an alternative English translation, see Abū Yaʿqūb al-Sijistānī, *Wellsprings of Wisdom*, 50.

14. Abū Yaʿqūb al-Sijistānī in Madelung, *Religious Trends in Early Islamic Iran*, 78 (my emphasis). Also see Walker, "An Ismaili Answer to the Problem of Worshipping the Unknowable, Neoplatonic God," 18; De Smet, "Ismāʿīlī Theology."

15. Walker, *Early Philosophical Shiism*, 78. Morrow assumes that the first step negates a positive statement—such as "God is Merciful"—and the second negates this affirmation—such as "God is not Merciful." (*Islamic Images and Ideas*, 13.) This is evidently different from what is happening in al-Sijistānī's and al-Kirmānī's works. Alibhai rightly points out that the

for the classical Ismāʿīlī theology. Accordingly, the form of negative theology that focuses on removing attributes from God falls into anthropomorphism by tacitly affirming the objecthood (or thingness) itself. The first directly targeted group in his *Book of Keys* [*Kitāb al-Maqālīd*] are "*those who worship God by denying his attributes and limitations.*" According to al-Sijistānī, these negativists, who would embody "the perjurer negationists" [*al-mukadhdhaba al-naffāh*] in the table of al-Tamīmī, "do not worship God in a beneficial manner since such is applied to some created beings." Thus the via negativa of the Muʿtazilites, philosophers, and Jahmites is theologically defective. Indeed, in al-Sijistānī's *Book of Keys*, such negationism is listed under the heading "hidden anthropomorphism" [*tashbīh khafiyy*]! "Whoever worships God by denying the attributes falls into a *hidden anthropomorphism*, just as someone who worships Him by affirming them falls into *obvious anthropomorphism*." These hidden anthropomorphists, argues al-Sijistānī, "*maintain that God is indescribable, indefinable, uncharacterizable, unseeable, and not in a place.*"[16] A major difficulty of this method of constant negation of attributes is that it can also be applied to heavenly sublime entities, not just God. But even more importantly, such perpetual negation indirectly affirms the presence, thingness, or existence of its object. The statements "G is not X," "G is not Y," or "G is not Z" all assume cognitive access to G. If the double negations were in the form of "G is not not X," "G is not not Y," "G is not not Z," then they would be still operating on the same discursive ground. They would still presume the comparability between G and the attributes X, Y, Z that are negated. Instead, the second step of the double negation should negate the entire negative discourse, such as "not (G is not X)," "not (G is not Y)," or "not (G is not Z)." Only in this way God will be removed from the space of both

---

two negations refer to two different domains, but these domains are for him merely the bodily [*jismānī*] and spiritual [*rūḥānī*] domains. Al-Sijistānī's apophaticism goes beyond that. (Alibhai, *Abū Yaʿqūb al-Sijistānī and Kitāb Sullam al-Najāt*, 52.)

For other summaries of the double negation, see Walker, "An Ismaili Answer to the Problem of Worshipping the Unknowable, Neoplatonic God"; Daftary, "The Iranian School of Philosophical Ismailism"; Poonawala, "Al-Sijistānī and His Kitāb al-Maqālid al-Malakūtiyya," 173–183.

16. Abū Yaʿqūb al-Sijistānī, *Kitāb al-Maqālīd al-Malkūtiyya*, 61, 77–82. Also see Abū Yaʿqūb al-Sijistānī in Walker, *Early Philosophical Shiism*, 75; Walker, *Abū Yaʿqūb al-Sijistānī*, 88–92. For examples of the criticized approach, see Ibn Bābawayh, *al-Iʿtiqādāt fī Dīn al-Imāmiyya*, 27; al-Fazārī, *Early Ibāḍī Theology*, 172–176. For al-Māturīdī's parallel critique of the Muʿtazilite master al-Kaʿbī (d.931), see Rudolph, *Al-Māturīdī and the Development of Sunnī Theology in Samarqand*, 293.

positive and negative discourse. Al-Sijistānī's fellow Ismāʿīlī intellectual Ḥamīd al-Dīn al-Kirmānī aims to clarify this process, by giving propositional examples to his bewildered readers indicating their subtle difference from the path of the perpetual negators. "God cannot be named" is the first step and "not 'God cannot be named'" is the second step that removes God—*not (not transcendent She is)*—beyond the discursive field in its own failure.[17]

The double negation of al-Sijistānī and al-Kirmānī presents a unique form of apophatic theology that is even more radical than it appears when we put it in context. Earlier Neoplatonic representatives of negative theology on divine nature are known to situate the ineffable One beyond the first emanation, the universal intellect. Ismāʿīlīs go beyond this classical Neoplatonic system, which was widely accepted by the Peripatetic philosophers. In their cosmology Ismāʿīlī thinkers creatively put the divine word [*kalima*], or the divine command [*amr*], above the universal intellect, which is itself unknowable in its oneness. Such an addition of the word between the One and the universal intellect did not emerge in the common Neoplatonic scheme of cosmic emanations, although Iamblichus (3rd-4th CE) and Proclus (5th CE) added, for various reasons, other entities or hypostases between the One and the intellect. The shorter version of *Theology of Aristotle*—the Arabic translation and adaptation of Plotinus' *Enneads*—follows the common Neoplatonic system, yet it was the Arabic original of the longer version that adds the divine word between the One and the universal intellect. Discovered in 1929, it is this longer version, which antecedes the Latin translation, that uniquely combines the scriptural language with an emanation system where God's command functions as the immediate cause of the process. When we talk about the beyond of the intellect, it relates to the creative divine word before actually coming to God. As the *Epistles* [*Rasāʾil*] of the Brethren of Purity [Ikhwān al-Ṣafāʾ] (fl.l.10th CE) put it succinctly, "The realm of intellects is devised by the divine word, which cannot be comprehended by human thought."[18] Thus the Ismāʿīlī

---

17. Ḥamīd al-Dīn al-Kirmānī, *Rāḥat al-ʿAql*, 148–149. For an interesting comparison of the Ismāʿīlī double negation with that of Pseudo-Dionysius the Areopagite (fl.5th-6th CE) and Theodor Adorno (d.1969), see Finlayson, "On Not Being Silent in the Darkness," 17–19.

18. Ikhwān al-Ṣafāʾ, *Rasāʾil*, 4:199; Ebstein, *Mysticism and Philosophy in al-Andalus*, ch.1; Baffioni, "The Role of the Divine Imperative (*Amr*) in the Ikhwān al-Ṣafāʾ and Related Works," 69; Walker, "An Ismaili Answer to the Problem of Worshipping the Unknowable, Neoplatonic God," 20–21; Plotinus, *Enneads*, 7.6.6: 322–327; Rudolph, *Al-Māturīdī and the Development of Sunnī Theology in Samarqand*, 276–277; Landolt, "Khwājah Naṣīr al-Dīn Ṭūsī

cosmology deepens the divine transcendence and prepares the metaphysical ground for the second negation. As a typical Ismāʿīlī gesture of his times, al-Sijistānī depicts the divine command, instead of God Herself, as the effective cause of the celestial intellects:

> We negate all He-nesses from the real Originator because every He-ness requires a cause. We found that the most noble of those things possessing a He-ness is the intellect, and the He-ness of the intellect necessitates a cause, which is the divine command, may His glory be exalted. It is thus "He" who is the true Originator without a cause—exalted is "He" above that—and accordingly "He" does not require a He-ness. "He" does not require a He-ness, nor the negation of it—"He" is not the negation of He-ness either. Thus, *beyond the non-He-nesses there is no affirmation of a thing that is "He."*[19]

The apophatic cause of the first creation is not God, but Her command, which doubles the divine transcendence. The conjoining of the divine word as the one-many with the universal intellect marks the emergence of plurality, coloring, and creation. "Origination" via which God relates to the divine word beyond intellect is a negation beyond negation. Accordingly, origination was "not" [*lays*], which is neither being nor not-ness [*nafy al-aysiyya wa-l-laysiyya*]—a second, hyper negation. Let alone the absolute One (God), even the divine word (i.e., the numerical one, or the one-many below it) cannot be known in its self-contained oneness. This Ismāʿīlī deepening of negativity through cosmology is overlooked if it is reduced to a decontextualized, generic "Neoplatonism." The Ismāʿīlī via negativa duplex in this repetitive form was unprecedented.

(597/1201–672/1274), Ismāʿīlism, and Ishrāqī Philosophy," 365–374; Daftary, "The Iranian School of Philosophical Ismailism," 18.

19. Abū Yaʿqūb al-Sijistānī, *Kitāb al-Yanābīʿ*, 72; Abū Yaʿqūb al-Sijistānī, *Wellsprings of Wisdom*, 50.

For the explanation of the role of the divine command, see Abū Yaʿqūb al-Sijistānī, *Kitāb al-Yanābīʿ*, 73–75; Abū Yaʿqūb al-Sijistānī, *Wellsprings of Wisdom*, 51–52. For the non-numeric oneness of the designation "*al-wāḥid*," see Abū Ḥātim al-Rāzī, "On al-Wāḥid/al-Aḥad," 509–511.

Permutations and Performances

With the trans-transcendence of the unknowable God beyond the divine word, which is beyond the universal intellect, the Ismāʿīlī apophaticism was philosophical and refined. It differentiated God as the apophatic one from the divine word, or the universal intellect, which was "one" in terms of its negative relation with God, but ready to be multiplied as the source of creation via emanation. In a dense passage, Jaʿfar ibn Manṣūr al-Yaman's (d.957) *Secrets of the Speaker-Prophets* [*Sarāʾir al-Nuṭaqāʾ*] explains the apophatic origination of the one-many, the first intellect, and then, the latter's creation of the universe. Per al-Sijistānī, Jaʿfar experiments with language to indicate the negativity of God beyond the negativity of the divine word:

> He forged a continuous link [*sabab*] between Himself and His creation, and prevented them from knowledge of Him except through His link. He veiled Himself from His creation with the veil of His eminence. He signified Himself with Himself. The eminence of His lordship was so concentrated that it could not be realized by sense or known by touch, and His essence could not be known by *jinn* or human. In His kingship, He partners with no one.
>
> Origination [*ibdāʿ*] preceded creation [*khalq*], so He transcends comparability [*tashbīh*] with what He originated. Rather He made His strength and majesty, the brilliance of His light and the splendor of His power emanate upon *His origination, which negated divinity from his he-ness [nafy ʿan huwiyyatihi al-ulūhiyya], and confessed the unicity [waḥdāniyya] of his Originator.* If he had not applied the negation to himself from the beginning [*ibtidāʾ*] of his *logos* [*nuṭqihi*], then none would have a path to the knowledge of their object of worship [*maʿbūd*]. Yet, no confession was affirmed: *the negation was affirmative* [*fa-kāna al-nafy tathbītan*] as his saying "*but God*"—this indicated the Originator Divinity to the origination. Hence *the origination's negation of divinity from his ipseity was an affirmation of his Originator.* And *this affirmation of divinity after the negation was a link [sabab] for the appearance of creation.* So the originated one was the creator [*khāliq*], elevating [*tanzīhan*] the Originator and exalting [*taʿẓīman*] His power. Thus, origination was from "not" [*lays*], and creation was from "not/all" [*ays*].[20]

---

20. Jaʿfar ibn Manṣūr al-Yaman in Hollenberg, *Interpretation after the End of Days*, 246 (Arabic text). For Hollenberg's own English translation, see ibid., 221–222.

In this fascinating section, like other Ismāʿīlī scholars, Jaʿfar is naming the first origination, that is, the first (or universal) intellect "the creator," which was otherwise an inalienable name of God for other prominent Muslim schools of thought. This first intellect, as it relates to God via origination, was but pure negation: it affirmed nothing but the negation of his own godhead. From the perspective of the lower intellects, the excess of negativity in the saturated gift of the first intellect serves as the only affirmation of its apophatic beyond. The "link" with beyond intellect is, thus, a joint negation and "affirmation," which is geared to an excess of negation. Accordingly, the declaration of faith [*tahlīl*] "There is no god but God" summarizes this apophatic position; an excessive, impenetrable negation, and an affirmation which is actually based on negation, are united. Divine negativity is manifested through the affirmative gift of the intellect, which in fact is a deeper negation. As an explanation of this point difficult to digest, the Egyptian *dāʿī* Abū ʿĪsā al-Murshid (d.ca.980) speaks on behalf of the first intellect. When realizing how it is self-negatively connected to the Originator, which it cannot know, the first intellect can only declare, "*There is no god but God—that is, 'I am not god'!*"[21]

A fundamental yet subtle peculiarity in terms of the divine attributes resides in the insistent critique of philosophers and Muʿtazilites by many Ismāʿīlī masters. One might tend to lump the Ismāʿīlī negation of divine attributes together with that of the philosophers. Yet their negations in terms of divine attributes are different, and even antithetical to each other. In the Ismāʿīlī apophaticism of the divine essence, negating the divine attributes indicates their *inapplicability* instead of *their negative application* that we find among early Ibāḍīs, Jahmīs, some Muʿtazilīs, and philosophers. Al-Ḥāmidī repeats what earlier Ismāʿīlī scholars had underlined—attributes or names simply do not apply to God:

> [He is] the negator of the created idols from His divine ipseity; that which reflections do not dare upon; minds do not enclose; eyes do not perceive; *transcends* [*al-munazzah*] *the names and attributes*; unsullied by the resemblance to any states; beyond the occupations of

21. Abū ʿĪsā al-Murshid in Hollenberg, *Interpretation after the End of Days*, 244 (my emphasis).

the dwellers of the two worlds and the heavens; so there is no opposite nor par unto Him.[22]

One should negate the attribute, and then negate the very negative discourse, in order to cancel the binary and to testify the inapplicability of divine attributes to the apophatic ipseity. This perpetual self-cancellation of theology through double negation is in stark contrast to the via negativa of the philosophers. As we saw in al-Tamīmī's exclusivist yet perceptive chart, "negating the divine attributes" for most of the philosophers means to read them as negations, per the Arabic Aristotle, Ibn Sīnā (d.1037), Maimonides, or Thomas Aquinas (d.1274). While the philosophical negation (i.e., negative indication) of divine attributes follows that of some Muʿtazilīs, Jahmīs, and perhaps the earlier Ibāḍīs, the Ismāʿīlī negation (i.e., inapplicability) of divine attributes accuses the former of not properly defending divine incomparability. Philosophers negate only divine immanence [*tashbīh*] in underscoring their indispensable principle of divine dissimilarity and incomparability [*tanzīh*]. The only way of "expressing" God's non-discursive trans-transcendence for the Ismāʿīlīs is rather the self-canceling double negation of both God's immanence and incomparability. Classical Ismāʿīlī theologians diverged from philosophers (and converged with the paradoxographer Sufi strands) in disqualifying divine incomparability, the glorious maxim owned by virtually all other major Islamicate intellectual traditions.

Observers did not have a uniform way of expressing the double negation of the classical Ismāʿīlī theologians. They sometimes quoted the repetitive negation "not not," but more frequently they would go with another logical format: "neither nor." This bivocality mirrors two common tropes among Ismāʿīlī theologians. Most Ismāʿīlīs preserved the double transcendence of God beyond the beyond-intellect without employing the repetitive "not not" of al-Sijistānī and al-Kirmānī. Instead, they indicated this beyond discursivity by the more straightforward way of negating all binary attributes through radicalizing the negation in favor of God's trans-transcendence, associating it with the apophatic declaration of faith "There is no god but God."[23] In other words, both steps of the double negation remained the same, yet they were expressed in the form of negative

22. Ibn al-Ḥusayn al-Ḥāmidī, *Die Ismailitische Theologie*, 1.

23. For the Egyptian *dāʿī* Abū ʿĪsā al-Murshid on the *tahlīl*, see Hollenberg, *Interpretation after the End of Days*, 243–244.

conjunction, "neither (G is X) nor (G is not X)," which is actually the logical equivalent of the conjunction of the two steps of the repetitive negation, "G is not X" and "not (G is not X)." Negative conjunction was already prominently applied by many Ismāʿīlī scholars, including al-Sijistānī and al-Kirmānī themselves. Indeed, one of the earliest Ismāʿīlī scholars whose writings survive, Abū Ḥātim al-Rāzī (d.934) rather preferred this structure of double negation over the repetitive negation. He already claimed that all positive and negative attributes had to be constantly negated if one wanted to address God:

> No attribute can ever belong to the Originator [al-Mubdiʿ], glorious and exalted. And we do not describe Him [even] as the "perfectness" or the "perfect" One. . . . We do not say either that He (i.e., God) is perfect, that He is perfectness [itself], that He is not perfectness [itself], nor that He is not perfect.[24]

Such a method of perpetual double negation and inapplicability of all binaries removed not only all relationality and discursivity, thus the ground for anthropomorphism, but at the same time the misplaced negation associated with the Muʿtazilites. Arguably Abū Ḥātim al-Rāzī's "neither nor" form was pedagogically, rhetorically, liturgically, and defensively a more viable option than its rigorous equivalent "not not." The repetitive negation appeared mainly in the works written for advanced Ismāʿīlī scholars. Per Abū Ḥātim, al-Sijistānī and al-Kirmānī themselves had employed the negative conjunction in their writings even more intensively than the explicit, repetitive negation as the former was extensively shared with other Ismāʿīlī thinkers. In the same vein, Muḥammad al-Nasafī (d.943), the politically controversial *dāʿī* active in Transoxania, disqualified all possible ascriptions, including being and its negation, from the apophatic divine ipseity. "Non-being and nothingness, like being, follow being; they are negations of an existent."[25] Compared to the "not not" strategy, perpetual double negation of binaries through negative conjunction could be employed more widely, in the texts addressing the novice. It was suitable even for the public sermons of the Ismāʿīlī imāms! At the Major Festival during

---

24. Abū Ḥātim al-Rāzī in Nomoto, *Early Ismāʿīlī Thought on Prophecy*, 176. For the divine unknowability and human incapacity, see Abū Ḥātim al-Rāzī, *The Proofs of Prophecy*, 29–30.

25. Walker, "The Ismāʿīlīs," 79.

the siege of the Khārijite leader Abū Yazīd at Kiyāna in 947, the Fāṭimid caliph al-Manṣūr (r.913–953) opened his oration [*khuṭba*] as follows:

> Praise be to God, unified through His lordship, solitary in His oneness, praised with power and permanence, glorified by majesty and grandeur, the first without limit, the last without end, exalted from the anthropomorphism of the ignorant, definitions of the describers, the conditions of the attributers, and the comprehension in visions of those who speculate.[26]

The caliph's public performance of this apophatic theology was symptomatic of its larger proliferation and influence. The psychological and practical impacts of such an apophatic sermon on soldiers on the eve of a physical confrontation is difficult to estimate. But it probably worked, not just because the army triumphed. Other Ismāʿīlī leaders, such as the most celebrated Fāṭimid theologian of his time, al-Muʾayyad fī al-Dīn al-Shīrāzī (d.1078) followed the caliph al-Manṣūr in preaching apophatically. Having attained the highest ranks of "the Gate of Gates" [*bāb al-abwāb*] and "chief missionary" [*dāʿī al-duʿāt*], al-Muʾayyad fī al-Dīn was probably the most influential and popular preacher of the time. According to the Yemenī Ismāʿīlī theologian al-Ḥāmidī, in his public orations al-Muʾayyad strongly negated the applicability of all attributes, names, and discourses to God. In one of these sermons probably delivered to a large crowd, al-Muʾayyad fī al-Dīn preached as follows:

> One cannot speak of the unseen, transcendent and glorified is His majesty, with a name among names; He cannot be described with what His origination is associated; but there is no way around appealing the beautiful names as metaphors [*istiʿāra*]. . . . So professing His unity [*tawḥīd*] is coming to know one's limits. Negation [*salb*] of

---

26. Caliph al-Manṣūr in Walker, *Orations of the Fāṭimid Caliphs*, 18 (Arabic text); my emphasis. Walker's translation missed the key movements indicating God's transcendence. He translates *mutawaḥḥid* as "unites," but this should be "unified," because it is the human action that the text emphasizes. More importantly, the unusual choices of *mutaʿazzīz, mutajabbīr*, and *mutaʿalī* instead of *ʿazīz, jabbār*, and *taʿāla* in the original text indicate that *God gets these attributes artificially from human discourses*: translating them as "almighty" and "all-powerful" ignores the key aspect of these attributes. God becomes "almighty" by human ascriptions of names, but God in Himself is beyond being almighty. Cf. Caliph al-Manṣūr in Walker, *Orations of the Fāṭimid Caliphs*, 107 (English text).

> divinity from them has His purification [*tajrīd*]; negation of names and attributes from Him has His incomparability [*tanzīh*]. He is the transcendent: not-negated, not ineffectualized [*lā yuʿṭal*], nothing said about His creation can be said on Him, and not annulled [*lā yubṭal*].[27]

These public performances illustrate the wide and sustained diffusion of apophaticism on the divine nature among Ismāʿīlīs. As we move to the eleventh and twelfth centuries, variations on apophaticism become more visible among Ismāʿīlī theologians. First, the negative conjunction "neither nor" becomes increasingly popular rather than its logical equivalent of repetitive negation— the "not not." This formal change will make it increasingly difficult to distinguish the Ismāʿīlī double negation from the paradoxical forms of apophaticism that circulated particularly among Sufis. Second, it will not be always easy to distinguish the double negation from the perpetual negation of philosophers that earlier Ismāʿīlī masters fiercely opposed. The Ismāʿīlī *dāʿī* Aḥmad ibn Ibrāhīm (fl.ea.11th CE) of Nishapur, for example, expressed divine transcendence by employing a curious apophatic strategy:

> All those who know the created beings realize their inability and deficiency, *negating divinity from them until negating divinity from all created beings*. Thus, unity is left unmingled, without anthropomorphism [*tashbīh*] or ineffectualism [*taʿṭīl*].[28]

The self-negation of deity from creation echoes a common Ismāʿīlī theme we encountered most clearly with Jaʿfar ibn Manṣūr al-Yaman, Abū ʿĪsā al-Murshid, al-Muʾayyad fī al-Dīn, and, later, Ibn al-Wālid (d.1215). On the other hand, it is not immediately clear whether al-Naysābūrī is following the defining aspect of Ismāʿīlī theology, the negation of all binaries, or a preference in favor of a negative language similar to what we find among philosophers. We have interesting evidence suggesting that his style of perpetual negation is still situated against the Aristotelian philosophical

27. Al-Muʾayyad fī al-Dīn in Ibn al-Ḥusayn al-Ḥāmidī, *Die Ismailitische Theologie*, 11–12.

28. Al-Naysābūrī, *Degrees of Excellence*, 7 (Arabic text). I did not follow the original translation, which did not preserve the reiterated employment of *nafy*. Cf. ibid., 36–37 (English text).

negative application of discourse. In his early Ismāʿīlī autobiography, the young philosopher Naṣīr al-Dīn Ṭūsī, who studied in Nishapur for a few years, passionately celebrates the Ismāʿīlī via negativa. His praise depicts the Ismāʿīlī path as an infinite self-negation, in the same way al-Naysābūrī did. The young Ismāʿīlī philosopher writes as follows in Persian:

> [God] is more glorious and exalted than to be the fount of two opposites, the origin of two contraries, the source of unity and plurality, the cause of the absolvement [*tanzīh*] and non-absolvement [*lā-tanzīh*] (of attributes). He is beyond any attribute by which something could be qualified, whether it be non-existent or existent, negative or positive, relative or absolute, verbal or in meaning [*lafẓī yā maʿnavī*]. *He is beyond, and also beyond the beyond, and so forth* . . . [N]o one maintains such pure unity [*tavḥīd-i ṣirf*], such unconditioned absoluteness [*tanzīh-i mahż*], except the *Taʿlīmiyyān* [the Ismāʿīlīs].[29]

Ṭūsī's comprehensive challenge to all binaries goes against divine absolvement, which was championed by philosophers (among others). While adding a perpetual negation of all discursivity from the divine essence, Ṭūsī still self-consciously adopts the Ismāʿīlī cosmology, negative conjunction, and the pertinent critique of philosophical emphasis on divine absolvement that has strong parallels with Abū Yaʿqūb al-Sijistānī's double negation.

These examples highlight the variations among the ways in which the double negation was performed by Ismāʿīlī scholars. A similar diversity can be observed in the way the primal source is defined and related to the universal intellect. Yet, all in all, both the double negation, and the cosmology doubling divine unknowability embodied common building blocks of the classical Ismāʿīlī self-negating theologies of the divine nature. Insistence on an apophaticism that depicted God as the unknowable beyond of the beyond of all negations (and their negations) spread from North Africa to greater Persia and Transoxania where Ismāʿīlī *dāʿīs* were active.

29. Ṭūsī, *Contemplation and Action*, 11 (Persian text), 37 (English translation). Cf. Abū Yaʿqūb al-Sijistānī in Madelung, *Religious Trends in Early Islamic Iran*, 78.

Disseminations: Ismāʿīlī Apophaticism beyond Ismāʿīlīs

The expansion of Ismāʿīlī ideas to Andalusia seems to have had sustained effects on the indigenous intellectual and mystical traditions. The continuities of Ismāʿīlism with the great Sufi master Ibn al-ʿArabī is probably one of the most intriguing of these intellectual connections. Ismāʿīlī impact on his thought, particularly the parallels in terms of the mediating role of the divine word and divine will, letter mysticism and occult sciences, hierarchy of saints, and the theory of the perfect man has been the subject of recent studies. On the other hand, I would argue that an elusive yet most characteristic Ismāʿīlī theological impact on Ibn al-ʿArabī, particularly significant in terms of apophaticism, has been neglected. This is exactly the point where Ismāʿīlī scholars, with their particular negative theology on the divine nature, resisted the grammatical and theological agreement of other schools of thought. As highlighted above, this is the applicability of "thingness" to God. Quite boldly, Ibn al-ʿArabī not only refuses to call God a "thing," but also reverses the authoritative grammatical claim of Sībawayh that "thingness" is "*the most universal of universals.*" Accordingly, the word "thing" is rather "*one of the most indefinite of indefinites*" [*min ankar al-nakirāt*], since it can be applied to anything at all, except only God Herself:

> As for ourselves, we do not affirm that the word "thingness" can be ascribed to the essence of the Real, since [such ascription] has not come down to us, nor have we been addressed by it, and courtesy [*adab*] is to be preferred. In the verse "Everything is annihilated" [Q.28:88], every *thing* is annihilated. That is why we negate from the Real the ascription of the word "thing" to Him.[30]

Furthermore, this rejection of divine thingness is directly related to Her unknowability for Ibn al-ʿArabī:

> The negation of thingness from Him is one of His essential attributes, just as is the negation of "withness" [*maʿiyya*] from things. He is with the things, but the things are not with Him, since "withness"

30. Ibn al-ʿArabī in Chittick, *Sufi Path of Knowledge*, 88 (with my minor modification).

follows from knowledge: He knows us, so He is with us. We do not know Him, so we are not with Him.[31]

Ibn al-ʿArabī's critique of popular conceptions of divine transcendence, his dissatisfaction with both negations and affirmations when it comes to God, and his paradoxical negative theology of the divine essence that we will examine below will all have significant parallels with Ismāʿīlism, although I will point to some key divergences as well.

Along with Ibn al-ʿArabī, the enigmatic, ascetic mystic and intellectual of Cordova, Ibn Masarra is generally pointed out as such an influence, even though he was active before the organization of the Fāṭimid state. From Ibn Saʿīd al-Andalusī (d.1070) onward, prominent historians like al-Qifṭī (d.1249) and al-Shahrazūrī (d.1288) called Ibn Masarra an "Esoteric," associating him with Ismāʿīlī theological ideas.[32] Ibn Ḥazm's discussion on Ibn Masarra and his self-styled successor Ismāʿīl al-Ruʿaynī (d.ca.1040) provides an important evaluation of the extent of Ismāʿīlī influences in his theology and cosmology. Accordingly, Ibn Masarra was known to defend the idea that God was too sublimely transcendent to have any direct contact with creation. Hence it was not God Herself, but Her throne [*ʿarsh*]—that is, the primal matter from which the universe is created—that was the governor of the world [*al-mudabbir li-l-ʿālam*]. This argument ascribes to Ibn Masarra no less than God's abdication of the governance of creation, transferring the task to Her first creation. Such a depiction strongly resonates with medieval Ismāʿīlī theology. Yet, Ibn Ḥazm notes that al-Ruʿaynī's own son denied that his father actually defended this removal of God from divine governance. Ibn Ḥazm's suspicion is justified: Ibn Masarra's extant writings, including his *Epistle on Contemplation* [*Risālat al-Iʿtibār*] abundantly address God as the creator, and governor, of the universe.[33] Ibn Masarra's very depiction of the divine throne as the

---

31. Ibn al-ʿArabī, ibid.

32. Al-Qifṭī, *Taʾrīkh al-Ḥukamāʾ*, 16; Shams al-Dīn al-Shahrazūrī, *Nuzhat al-Arwāḥ*, 83–84; Morris, *Ibn Masarra: A Reconsideration of Primary Sources*; Ebstein, *Mysticism and Philosophy in al-Andalus*. While Ebstein's analysis is fundamentally important in displaying doctrinal convergences between Ismāʿīlism and Ibn al-ʿArabī, his analysis does not entail the twelfth century—the key period when a new form of orthodoxy emerged in Andalusia. For an analysis of that period, see Casewit, *The Mystics of al-Andalus*, ch.1–2.

33. Ibn Hazm, *al-Fiṣal fī al-Milal*, 4:151; Ibn Masarra in Garrido Clemente, "Edición Crítica de la Risalat al-Iʿtibar de Ibn Masarra de Córdoba," 91, 95, 98, 100; Stroumsa and Sviri, "The Beginnings of Mystical Philosophy in al-Andalus"; Morris, *Ibn Masarra: A Reconsideration of*

first creation also manifests a subtle yet important cosmological difference that hints at Ibn Masarra's closer relationship with another intellectual tradition growing in Andalusia. As we will elaborate in the next chapter, Ibn Masarra did profess a powerful negative theology of the divine essence, yet it was more in line with that of the philosophers than that of the Ismāʿīlīs. Still, Ibn Masarra does embody profound parallels with the forming Ismāʿīlī doctrines. Convergences with Ismāʿīlism are particularly clear in Ibn Masarra's letter mysticism and the prominence of the divine command in his cosmology.[34] Already in the tenth century Ismāʿīlīsm had become a powerhouse of ideas no longer limited to Ismāʿīlīs, but circulated among scholars of diverse orientations under their intellectual and political sway, and beyond.

The adoption of Ismāʿīli teachings was evident, especially in areas under their direct rule. Ismāʿīlī apophaticism on the divine nature made a great impact in Yemen as well as in Upper Egypt, which would remain the realm of political upheavals and religious dissidence under the Ayyūbids after Saladin's (r.1174–1193) final blow to the Fāṭimid rule in 1171. For instance, the head of the Jewish community in Yemen, Nethanel ben al-Fayyūmī, surprising as it may sound, adopted the Ismāʿīlī negative theology of the divine essence. In the opening of his popular theological Judeo-Arabic compendium titled *Orchard of Intellects* [*Bustān al-ʿUqūl*], he lays all key markers of this peculiar apophaticism:

> In the name of God, the merciful and compassionate, do I begin. . . . Praised be God, yea the God of Israel, the first preceding every primeval thing; *the cause of the cause of causes. . . . Nothing is like unto Him*; He created all things out of nothing. *Unto Him we cannot apply definition, attribute, spatiality or quality*. He has no throne that would imply place nor footstool that would imply sitting. He cannot be described as rising up or sitting down, as moving or as motionless, as bearing or being born, as having characteristics or as in any way defined. . . . He does not enter or go out, descend or ascend. He is far beyond the reach of the human intellect, transcending apprehension, conception, and even conjecture. His essence is indescribable

---

Primary Sources, xxv; Abrahamov, *Ibn al-ʿArabī and the Sufis*, 101; Stroumsa, "The Muʿtazila in al-Andalus: The Footprints of a Phantom."

34. Ebstein, *Mysticism and Philosophy in al-Andalus*, 86; Stroumsa and Sviri, "The Beginnings of Mystical Philosophy in al-Andalus."

> and cannot be grasped by means of the attributes. *He is exalted even beyond the sublimity and the greatness ascribed to Him by the philosophers*, as the Prophet, peace be with Him, praised Him and said in his outburst of praise: "Let them bless Thy glorious Name—Thy name be exalted above all blessing and praise! [Nehemiah 9:5.]"[35]

What the scholarship on al-Fayyūmī does not realize in this passage is that al-Fayyūmī is not only citing the Torah but also the Qurʾan. "Nothing is like unto Him" [*laysa ka-mithlihi shayʾ*], biblical as it might appear, is unmistakably a Qurʾanic phrase, and arguably the most widely quoted verse among Muslims at large in reference to divine transcendence. The verse, Q.42:11, is cited on the divine oneness and attributes even in the oldest Muslim theological texts that have survived.[36] Al-Fayyūmī is clearly participating in the ongoing theological discussions on anthropomorphism, including major controversies revolving around the descent [*nuzūl*], throne, footstool, or physical descriptions, of God.

Manifested in the pervasion of negations in the opening, al-Fayyūmī's approach to the divine nature is in the Ismāʿīlī line. A second manifestation is the way he addresses God. Instead of calling God "the cause of

35. Al-Fayyūmī, *The Bustan al-Ukul*, 1 (Judeo-Arabic text), 1–3 (English translation; with my modifications).

36. Al-Fazārī, *Early Ibāḍī Theology*, 178, 185. The sophisticated treatment of the divine attributes in these Ibāḍī theological texts indicates that this subject developed considerably earlier in Islamic theology than previously accepted in modern scholarship.

For the employment of the verse in the service of divine transcendence by the early Persian Sufi exegete Rashīd al-Dīn Maybudī (fl.af.1126), the Ashʿarite polymath Fakhr al-Dīn al-Rāzī, and the compiler of Zaydī exegesis al-Sharafī (d.1651), see Hamza, Rizvi, and Mayer, *An Anthology of Qurʾanic Commentaries*, 386, 515, 555. For others, see Ibn al-Wālid, *Tāj al-ʿAqāʾid*, 30; Ibn Masarra in Stroumsa and Sviri, "The Beginnings of Mystical Philosophy in al-Andalus," 224 (for the Arabic text itself, see Ibn Masarra in Garrido Clemente, "Edición Crítica de la Risalat al-Iʿtibar de Ibn Masarra de Córdoba"; Ibn Masarra in Morris, *Ibn Masarra: A Reconsideration of Primary Sources*, 257–258); al-Junayd in Qushayrī, *Epistle on Sufism*, 6; Abū Bakr al-Wāsiṭī in Silvers, *Tawḥīd in Early Sufism*, 142–143 (also in al-Sīrjānī, *Sufism, Black and White*, 52); Abū Ḥāmid al-Ghazālī, *Iḥyāʾ ʿUlūm al-Dīn*, 1:89; al-Bayhaqī, *Kitāb al-Asmāʾ wa-l-Ṣifāt*, 27; al-Sarrāj, *Kitāb al-Lumaʿ*, 29 (Arabic text); Muḥammad Ibn Tūmart, *Sharḥ Murshida*, 21; Muḥammad Ibn Tūmart, *Aʿazz mā Yuṭlab*, 216; Abrahamov, *Islamic Theology*, 50; Ibn Barrajān, *A Qurʾan Commentary*, 167; Ibn Barrajān in Casewit, *The Mystics of al-Andalus*, 175, 262; Ibn al-ʿArabī in Elmore, *The Fabulous Gryphon (ʿAnqāʾ Mughrib)*, 144, 246; al-Māturīdī, *Kitāb al-Tawḥīd*, 121, 138; Aḥmad al-Rifāʿī, *Kitāb al-Burhān al-Muʿayyad*, 19; Ibn Bābawayh, *al-Iʿtiqādāt fī Dīn al-Imāmiyya*, 22; al-Ḥakīm al-Samarqandī in al-ʿOmar, *Doctrines of the Māturīdīte School with Special Reference to As-Sawād al-Aʿẓam*, 167; Abū Ṭālib al-Makkī, *Qūt al-Qulūb*, 3.33:1173; Aḥmad al-Ghazālī, *al-Tajrīd fī Kalimat al-Tawḥīd*, ch.43, 106–107; Jamāl al-Dīn Ibn Tūmart al-Andalusī, *Kanz al-ʿUlūm*, 30.

creation" as most if not all theologians and philosophers were doing, he rather chooses to describe Her as *"the cause of the cause of causes."* This doubling of causality is a clear reference to the Ismāʿīlī cosmology where "the cause of causes" characterized the divine word as the cause of the universal intellect. In his *Book of Enlightenment* [*Rūshanāʾīnāma*], for example, the Persian writer Nāṣir Khusrav (d.1088) wrote that "the first cause is the cause of all causes. God Himself, in His singleness [*fardāniyyat*], is free from being either a cause or the result of causation." Accordingly, this cause of causes is the word, while universal intellect is the first creation, or "the first caused" [*maʿlūl-i avval*], and in turn, "the source [*aṣl*] of everything that has existence."[37] For al-Fayyūmī too, it was not God, but Her word, who acts as the efficient cause of universal intellect, hence creation. He writes: "The first creation of God was the universal intellect—the origin of life, the fountain of blessings, the well-spring of happiness. . . . God made it by His word and His will, not from anything and not in anything, not with anything and not through anything."[38]

Al-Fayyūmī clearly shares the Ismāʿīlī placement of the one-many divine word between the apophatic One, and the first creation, the universal intellect. Hence the indescribable God is placed further beyond the divine word beyond the intellect. Finally, the critique of Aristotelian philosophers within such a negativist description of the divine nature is of particular importance in betraying the Ismāʿīlī tone of the work. Finding philosophical negativity unsatisfactory, he claims that attributes do not apply to Her. Disqualifying the philosophical negation as insufficient and divine attributes as inapplicable were two major markers of Ismāʿīlism both owned by al-Fayyūmī. The interpenetration of rabbinic Jewish and Ṭayyibī Ismāʿīlī cosmology, prophetology, numerology, and hermeneutics is so powerful in the case of al-Fayyūmī that "Jewish Ismāʿīlism" is probably the most accurate term to define al-Fayyūmī's apophatic theological hermeneutics.

Another significant example of the sway of Ismāʿīlī apophaticism is the Sunnī-Shāfiʿī judge of Fāṭimid Cairo, Abū ʿAbd Allāh al-Quḍāʿī. As a senior government official, al-Quḍāʿī worked as a judge over the Sunnī subjects under Fāṭimid rule, traveled to Constantinople as Fāṭimid emissary to the

---

37. Nāṣir Khusrav, *Six Chapters; or, Shish Faṣl: Also Called Rawshanāʾī-nāma*, ch.1–2 (with my minor modification).

38. Al-Fayyūmī, *The Bustan al-Ukul*, 2 (Judeo-Arabic text), 2 (English translation; with my minor modification). Also see Kiener, "Jewish Ismāʿīlism in Twelfth Century Yemen," 262; Ebstein, *Mysticism and Philosophy in al-Andalus*, 38–40.

Byzantine court, served in their chancery—being scribe for a time for the vizier ʿAlī ibn Aḥmad al-Jarjarāʾī (d.1045)—and had close contact with eminent Fāṭimid scholars. Even though he lived under Fāṭimid rule, al-Quḍāʿī's scholarship was highly respected among Sunnī scholars, especially as a reliable scholar of prophetic reports. His *Compendium for the Cornerstones of Wisdom* [*Dustūr Maʿālim al-Ḥikam*] is among the earliest and best-known extant compilations of ʿAlī's (d.661) sermons, sayings, and teachings. Even though al-Quḍāʿī is not a Shīʿī scholar himself, the sayings on the divine essence that his compilation attributes to ʿAlī mirror the powerful Ismāʿīlī apophaticism of his time and display the available Shīʿī resources for facilitating it:

> The first part of religion is knowledge of God. Knowledge of Him is perfected by the declaration of His oneness. The declaration of His oneness is perfected by sincere allegiance to Him. Sincere allegiance to Him is achieved by *negating all attributes* [*nafy al-ṣifāt*] *from Him, by the testimony of every attribute that it is other than the thing described, the testimony of every described thing that it is other than the attribute, and the testimony of both of these that they have newly come into being and thus cannot be eternal.*
>
> Whosoever describes God has circumscribed Him. Whosoever circumscribes Him has quantified Him. And whosoever quantifies Him has invalidated His eternity. Whosoever asks "How?" has sought a description of Him. Whosoever asks "In what?" has confined Him. Whosoever asks "On what?" has made another space empty of Him. Whosoever asks "Where?" has defined Him. Whosoever asks "Where to?" has made Him cross over a path.[39]

Al-Quḍāʿī's early collection ascribed ʿAlī an emphasis on the inapplicability of attributes, names, and discourse when it comes to God. The tenth to twelfth centuries witnessed a proliferation in the circulation of such ʿAlīd traditions under Fāṭimid rule, suggesting that the influence of Ismāʿīlī apophaticism was not confined to circles of theologians. The *Book of Unveiling* [*Kitāb al-Kashf*] compiled by Jaʿfar ibn Manṣūr al-Yaman

---

39. ʿAlī ibn Abī Ṭālib and ʿAlī al-Qāḍī al-Quḍāʿī in ʿAlī ibn Abī Ṭālib, ʿAlī al-Qāḍī al-Quḍāʿī and al-Jāḥiẓ, *A Treasury of Virtues*, 7.23:170–171. Also see ibid., 7.24:171–174.

The supplications attributed to the fourth Imām ʿAlī ibn al-Ḥusayn Zayn al-ʿĀbidīn (d.712) contain similar negations. (ʿAlī ibn al-Ḥusayn, *Psalms of Islam*, Supplications 1-2:15–21.)

contains such prophetic reports with strong negations. Similar ʿAlīd traditions are quoted by the Yemenī Ismāʿīlī scholar al-Ḥāmidī. The human incapacity as the ultimate limit of human attainment, or the *docta ignorantia* as Nicholas of Cusa (d.1464) would put it, is tellingly attributed to Abū Bakr (d.634) among Sunnī scholars including Sufis like Abū Naṣr al-Sarrāj (d.988) and Ibn al-ʿArabī. Al-Ḥāmidī rather attributes the tradition to ʿAlī, putting it into rhymed verses as well as a strongly apophatic context:

> [ʿAlī ibn Abī Ṭālib said:] Whatever your fantasy discerns as the most truthful meanings related to Him, indeed, *have nothing to do with Him, and return to you, as they are created and originated.*
>
> He said:
> Incapacity to attain is the attainment
> Seeking the secret of the core of the ipseity is polytheism
>
> Unveiling the depths of the unseen is blindness
> To the one whose horizon is but the darkness of incapacity.[40]

Ismāʿīlīs and Sufis could negotiate which companion of the Prophet uttered the principle of docta ignorantia. But there is more at stake between them in this brief report: the apophatic insight that "human discourse on God returns to itself" that al-Ḥāmidī ascribes to ʿAlī widely circulated among the most popular Sufi manuals and was connected to Sufis like al-Shiblī (d.946), who were active in Baghdad, rather than ʿAlī.[41] Sufis usually converged with Ismāʿīlīs in their balanced dissatisfaction with the applicability of any negative and affirmative discourse and their defense of the docta ignorantia and divine unknowability. Such parallel theological ideas could often point to shared discursive spaces of exchange, dialogue, adoption, adaptation, and transformation, as well as potential negotiation and competition.

---

40. Ibn al-Ḥusayn al-Ḥāmidī, *Die Ismailitische Theologie*, 10. Cf. Idrīs al-Qurashī, *Zahr al-Maʿānī*, 25; ʿAlī ibn al-Ḥusayn, *Psalms of Islam*, "Fifteen Whispered Prayers," 12:253; al-Sarrāj, *Kitāb al-Lumaʿ*, 36 (Arabic text); Ibn al-ʿArabī in Elmore, *The Fabulous Gryphon (ʿAnqāʾ Mughrib)*, 142; Gillon, "Aperçus sur les Origines de l'ismaélisme à Travers le Kitāb al-Kašf," 105. Cf. Nicholas of Cusa, "On Learned Ignorance," 360–366.

41. See, e.g., al-Qushayrī, *al-Risāla al-Qushayriyya fī ʿIlm al-Taṣawwuf*, 496. For an English translation, see al-Qushayrī, *Epistle on Sufism*, 310. See also al-Ṭabarī, *Salwat al-ʿĀrifīn*, 18 (Arabic text); al-Sīrjānī, *Sufism, Black and White*, 52 (Arabic text); al-Sarrāj, *Kitāb al-Lumaʿ*, 36 (Arabic text); Ibn al-ʿArabī in Elmore, *The Fabulous Gryphon (ʿAnqāʾ Mughrib)*, 142; Thiele, "Abū Hāshim al-Jubbāʾī's (d. 321/933) Theory of 'States,'" 367.

Later Developments

The Ismāʿīlī apophatic theology with its rationalist, perpetual double negation of attributes from an unknowable God spread widely with the Ismāʿīlī *invitation* [*daʿwa*]. Al-Muʾayyad fī al-Dīn al-Shīrāzī in Egypt; Ibrāhīm ibn al-Ḥusayn al-Ḥāmidī in Yemen and India; and Nāṣir Khusrav, Ḥasan Ṣabbāḥ (d.1124) and al-Shahrastānī (d.1153) in Persia provide us exquisite examples of this peculiar apophatic theology moving into the eleventh and twelfth centuries. The Ḥanafī theologian of Samarqand, Abū Manṣūr al-Māturīdī was already familiar with the popular Ismāʿīlī ideas, including their distinction between God and the creator to whom they ascribed the divine attributes. He narrates how Ismāʿīlīs argued that "*there is no name for Him*" [*laysa lahu ism*], and similar versions of this idea, such as "*He does not have any essential name or essential attribute*" or "*God—Who has no essential name.*"[42] Al-Māturīdī's reports on the unnamability are testified not only in earlier Ismāʿīlī sources but also in later ones, such as Nāṣir Khusrav.

In the *Book of Enlightenment*, Nāṣir Khusrav rejected the application of philosophical names of such as being, existence, and causality.[43] His *Twin Wisdoms Reconciled* [*Jāmīʿ al-Ḥikmatayn*] criticizes the employment of a wider array of theological names, showing that each of them assume the accessibility, relationality, or plurality of the divine essence. A major point of his divergence from theologians of other schools is about naming God at all in the first place:

> It is clear that to call God "knowing" is polytheism [*shirk*]. And if these theologians assert that God is "powerful" . . . this too is polytheism. And if these theologians say that God is "living" . . . this

42. See, e.g., al-Māturīdī, *Kitāb al-Tawḥīd*, 161–162.

43. See Nāṣir Khusrav, *Six Chapters; or, Shish Faṣl: Also Called Rawshanāʾī-nāma*, ch.1 (with my minor modification):

> He is beyond being or not-being. And thou must realize that everything to which thou mayest attribute existence, may also be predicated with non-existence as an opposite state. . . . Existence and non-existence are the opposite of each other. And nothing which has an opposite can be a god. . . . It is impossible to attribute to God being either a cause or the result of causation because both these categories have been produced by Him. . . . We are saying all this metaphorically, not discussing the reality, because discourse cannot deal with the matters concerned with divine unity, dealing with them directly. Speech and speaker are both dependent on what has been created by Him. Discourse is powerless, unable to penetrate the true realities and understanding of His ipseity. This is because, as we have already said, speech and the speaker are both below the intellect, and therefore they cannot perceive anything except what is under it.

> is polytheism. If these theologians establish that God—praise be to Him—is "hearing" . . . this is an innovation [*bidʿati*] which this group has created; *in their ignorance they have imposed these names on God.*[44]

The trans-transcendence of God in Khusrav's theology is also clear in his poems, where he warns not to confuse the universal intellect with the Originator, Who is rather beyond the divine word beyond the universal intellect. His commentary on the earlier Ismāʿīlī poet Abū al-Haytham al-Jurjānī's (fl.10th-ea.11th CE) apophatic couplets on "the One" proposed to address the problem of whether the absolute one can be called "One." Naming something "one" will add to it the attribute of oneness, which will, in turn, violate that absolute oneness. Addressing the problem of namability of the absolutely one, al-Jurjānī and his commentator Nāṣir Khusrav were inheriting an ancient problem tracing back to Plato's *Parmenides*, and even Pythagoras. In a classical Ismāʿīlī spirit, al-Jurjānī problematized calling the absolute, apophatic One anything, including "creator":

> What is the One in whom the many exist, absolute in uniqueness?
> *Why do you call Him "creator" and "compeller"?*
> One whom neither doubling nor halving affects;
> Who neither increases nor lessens in number?
> *One by necessity or by approximation, not by exactitude*
> How can such statements be understood?[45]

In his commentary on al-Jurjānī's exquisite lines, Khusrav distinguished the absolute One from the multiple one, "from which the order of numbers comes, and which is multiple, is composite, formed of oneness and of that substance which is receptive to oneness." The latter is the numeric one, which is the principle of all numbers and the source of the infinite multiplicity. Once the latter is united in its one-manyness with the universal intellect, it becomes the first existent and gives birth to creation. Let alone the absolute One, even the multiple one cannot be known in its unity. All relationalities belong to the realm under the universal intellect,

---

44. Nāṣir Khusrav, *Between Reason and Revelation*, 65, 41–71 (emphasis mine); Idrīs al-Qurashī, *Zahr al-Maʿānī*, 23–24. Also see Jackson, *On the Boundaries of Theological Tolerance in Islam*, Introduction.

45. Abū al-Haytham al-Jurjānī in Nāṣir Khusrav, *Between Reason and Revelation*, 135; Nāṣir Khusrav in Schimmel, *Make a Shield from Wisdom*, 50–51; Plato, *Plato's Parmenides*, 137b–144e.

and they are not applicable to what is beyond. Only by approximation can one imagine what the oneness of the multiple one would be. But neither it nor the absolute One beyond it can be known.[46] Only double negation of all possible imaginable names helps un-knowing the absolute One, because it is beyond the multiple one, which is itself approximated via negation.

In questioning the applicability of names, including "creator," al-Muʾayyad fī al-Dīn joined the chorus of al-Sijistānī, Jaʿfar ibn Manṣūr al-Yaman, al-Jurjānī, and Nāṣir Khusrav. He rejected the applicability of any term that indicates God's being the cause, source, or originator of creation in any sense: "He is beyond the attributes 'the creator,' 'the maker,' 'the originator.' " This rejection of causality was a challenge to all other schools but was particularly aimed at the philosophical stance that typically depicted God as the effective cause of creation. It seems that al-Muʾayyad performed these negations, again, during a public performance: an oration. In light of this public apophaticism, it is also unsurprising that per al-Jurjānī and Nāṣir Khusrav he negated the well-known Qurʾanic attributes that were popularly assumed, especially among Sunnīs, to be essential to God. Al-Ḥāmidī reports al-Muʾayyad fī al-Dīn's refusal to admit any of these otherwise well-established divine names:

> He is glorified: He does not enter under the sway of any name or attribute; He cannot be approached by indications with qualities. One cannot say that He is all-living, nor omnipotent, nor omniscient, nor intellecting, nor perfect, nor complete, nor agent, because He is the Originator of all-living, omnipotent, omniscient, intellecting, perfect, complete, and agent. One cannot claim "ipseity" about Him, insofar as every ipseity bears attributes, such as matter or nine accidents, and soul and its attributes.[47]

Al-Muʾayyad fī al-Dīn moves to terms like "substance," "accident," "cause," and then to adverbs, and discusses extensively and exclusively what *cannot* be said of God. The inapplicability of any name, including the more conventional and widespread names, reemphasizes the importance of Ismāʿīlī cosmology in further deepening Plotinus' apophaticism. The attributes that Ashʿarites ascribe to God actually belong to the universal

46. Nāṣir Khusrav, *Between Reason and Revelation*, 136–137.

47. Al-Muʾayyad fī al-Dīn in Ibn al-Ḥusayn al-Ḥāmidī, *Die Ismailitische Theologie*, 13–14.

intellect, which ranks below the divine word below the apophatic God. As al-Muʾayyad fī al-Dīn puts it clearly, " 'all-living,' 'omnipotent,' 'eternal,' 'omniscient' –this is the first existent," not God hidden far beyond.

Nizārī Ismāʿīlism in Iran of the twelfth and, indeed, thirteenth centuries, even though the records we have are scanty, continues this form of apophaticism. Al-Shahrastānī, whom Naṣīr al-Dīn Ṭūsī calls "the chief Ismāʿīlī master" [*dāʿī al-duʿāt*] in his autobiography, presents a highly vague Arabic summary of the originally Persian treatise of the great Nizārī master Ḥasan Ṣabbāḥ. Ḥasan denied the human ability to know God without the guidance of a living teacher; his paradoxical discourses on truth and error, and on the formula of *tahlīl* ["There is no god but God"] would boil down to this point:

> [Ḥasan] put truth and error and the similarity between them on the one hand, and the distinction between them on the other hand—opposition on both sides, and order on one of the two sides—as a balance to weigh all that he uttered on the matter. He said: "This balance is simply derived from the formula of *tahlīl*, which is compounded of negation and affirmation, or of negation and exception thereto." He said: "*It does not claim the negation is erroneous, nor does it claim the affirmation is true.*" He weighed therewith good and evil, truth and falsehood, and the other opposites. But his point was that he came back, in every doctrine and every discourse, to affirming the teacher. [48]

According to al-Shahrastānī's rather enigmatic report, Ḥasan Ṣabbāḥ was following the classical Ismāʿīlī double negation in its popular, negative conjunction form. Besides, like Abū ʿĪsā al-Murshid and Jaʿfar ibn Manṣūr al-Yaman, Ḥasan was depicting the declaration of faith as the best summary of their apophatic theology. The formula "There is no god but God" was glorifying God by negating all real or imaginable relations and binaries, as it indicates the limitations of both affirmative and negative statements in its balance. For Ḥasan, as al-Shahrastānī reports, the formula of divine unity was "balancing a feather against a feather." Al-Shahrastānī himself adopts a similarly balanced approach to the *tahlīl* and also criticizes the supposed negativism of the theologians as well as philosophers.

---

48. Al-Shahrastānī in Landolt, *An Anthology of Ismaili Literature*, 151 (with my minor modification); Ṭūsī, *Contemplation and Action*, 3 (Persian text), 26 (English text).

For al-Shahrastānī, their negative language on the divine nature not only violates the divine unknowability which philosophers otherwise profess—it also runs the risk of anthropomorphism. Here al-Shahrastānī is undertaking the same critique of "hidden anthropomorphism" with Abū Yaʿqūb al-Sijistānī:

> does he [Ibn Sīnā] not understand that *the negation of many deficiencies from the Real (exalted is His majesty) is a deficiency for Him*? As the weavers amongst the literalists and the lowest story-tellers say: "Neither body, nor substance, nor something shaped, nor measured, nor elongated, nor round, nor square, nor pentagonal, nor obligated, nor put together," and the rabble of humanity respond, "Glorified is God! Glorified is God!" So Ibn Sīnā set about protracting the chapters in his books with the negation of the like of these attributions from the necessary being in Himself, prior to proving Him. . . . This is nothing but haphazardness and shooting in utter blindness, and *a negation of deficiencies which is an affirmation of deficiencies*![49]

Proper apophaticism is not the *negative applicability* of divine attributes for al-Shahrastānī. It is rather admitting their *inapplicability*. Negative statements are to be re-negated in order to perform the incapacity of the theological discourse. "God" is marked by an excess of negation. Al-Shahrastānī's discussion of the phrase "God" [*Allāh*] as an apophatic designation that negates all identities and ipseities has evident parallels to earlier Ismāʿīlī theologians:

> Nothing is grasped of the majesty of God (exalted is He) except His He-ness [*huwiyya*] alone, for *He is He*; amongst the established supplications is: "O He who is He." . . . The name "God" bestows the idea of His divine status through the negation of quiddity; "the One" bestows the idea of pure monotheism through the negation of quantity; and "the Absolute" bestows the idea of exaltation through the negation of quality [*maʿnā al-ulūhiyya bi-nafy al-māhiyya; maʿnā al-tawḥīd bi-nafy al-kamiyya; maʿnā al-tamjīd bi-nafy al-kayfiyya*].[50]

---

49. Al-Shahrastānī, *Struggling with the Philosopher*, 36, 56 (with my minor modification).

50. Al-Shahrastānī, *Keys to the Arcana*, 82–83 (Arabic text), 144–145 (English translation).

The meaning of "divinity" as the inapplicability of quiddity was a theme suggested by prominent Ismāʿīlī intellectuals such as al-Sijistānī, Jaʿfar ibn Manṣūr, and al-Ḥāmidī. Moreover, also very characteristically, al-Shahrastānī defends the position that creation arose through the divine command [*amr*], which first wrote the *tahlīl*—as suggested by Jaʿfar ibn Manṣūr and Abū ʿĪsā al-Murshid.[51]

Although the available sources get more meager, we can still trace the Ismāʿīlī negative theology of the divine essence into the thirteenth century. The *Crown of Creeds* [*Tāj al-ʿAqāʾid*] penned by the fifth Yemenī *dāʿī*, Sayyidnā ʿAlī ibn Muḥammad Ibn al-Wālid (d.1215), demonstrates how the main components of Ismāʿīlī apophaticism were carried into his times. While we observe terminological, cosmological, and thematical differences, this Ismāʿīlī creed clearly continues the apophatic teachings of the earlier masters with its dizzying negations that take pages and pages. Accordingly, the creator [*mubdiʿ*] of the universe is not the Originator [*Ṣāniʿ*] Herself, Who is exalted from such relations in Her non-numerical oneness [*wāḥid lā min ʿadad*].[52] The primal source [*al-mabdāʿ al-awwal*] of the universe is the universal intellect [*al-ʿaql al-awwal*], which was symbolically hinted at in the Qurʾan as the "heavenly pen" [*qalam*]. It is eternal, complete, perfect, and subsistent. All perfect attributes that fellow Muslims ascribe to God, such as "all-living," "omnipotent," "omniscient," "intellecting," "perfect," "complete," and "agent," befit the first creation. Hence Ibn al-Wālid's exposition of the one-many is in perfect structural harmony with that of the earlier tradition of the Ismāʿīlī negative theology of the divine essence. With his work's dense apophaticism, Ibn al-Wālid does something fascinating yet elusive: he goes so far as to employ the declaration of faith with regard to the universal intellect, and not God! His closing of the relevant section is extraordinary:

> This first existent is that of which the prophetic law reports as "the pen." Its ipseity is the one-many [*al-wāḥida al-mutakaththira*] in its relations, attributions, and conjugations. He [rather] transcends His

---

51. See al-Shahrastānī, *Keys to the Arcana*, 84 (Arabic text), 146 (English translation); Steigerwald, "The Divine Word (Kalima) in Shahrastānī's Majlis."

52. One of the puzzles that surface in the *Crown of Creeds* is the employment of *al-Ṣāniʿ*, in addition to, and sometimes in opposition to, the classical Ismāʿīlī designation of God, *al-Mubdiʿ* (e.g., Ibn al-Wālid, *Tāj al-ʿAqāʾid*, ch.2, 20). How these two terms relate to each other is not fixed.

existents, and His agent is complete and perfect. *There is no God but He who acts, which is the complete and perfect existent.*[53]

Within this Ismāʿīlī cosmology, Ibn al-Wālid's God is utterly unknowable, far beyond comprehension, limitation, or definition. Discourse [*ʿibāra*] cannot reach anything about Her; anything that can be known or spoken of is created. The Originator is not a body, not a substance, not an accident, not a matter, not a form, not in space, not in time, not comparable to anything, not speakable, and so forth. Scattered among thousands of negations, we find separate sections, such as "on the Negation of Naming from Him" and "on the Negation of Attributes from Him," where negative statements attain an ecstatic, incantational nature. The approach to the relationship between the divine essence and divine attributes is a familiar one: all attributes should be negated in the sense of their utter *inapplicability*.[54] Neither an attribute nor its negation apply to Her. The double negation unfolds itself in the more common form of negative conjunction—"neither nor." This sophisticated apophatic theology can be traced further into the thirteenth century, in creative and surprising interactions with Sufism particularly in Persia and Central Asia.

Ṭūsī: Sufi Paths of Ismāʿīlī Apophaticism

Khvāja Naṣīr al-Dīn Ṭūsī was arguably one of the greatest thinkers in history, and his exposition of Sufism, *Attributes of the Illustrious* [*Avṣāf al-Ashrāf*] was penned toward the end of his life, after his public conversion from Ismāʿīlism to Imāmiyya.[55] The work describes the Sufi path in six chapters, which, in turn, are composed of six stations. The discussion here will focus on the last two chapters only, as outlined in Figure 1.1.

The fifth chapter concerns the stations of the most distinguished wayfarers who have attained union [*ahl-e vuṣūl*]. It contains the stages of *complete trust in God* [*tavakkul*], *resignation* [*rižā*], *submission* [*taslīm*], *unification* [*tavḥīd*], *conjunction* [*ittiḥād*], and *union* [*vaḥdat*]. The sixth and last chapter

53. Ibn al-Wālid, *Tāj al-ʿAqāʾid*, ch.21, 44. For a brief English summary of ch.20–22, see Ivanow, *A Creed of the Fāṭimids*, 31–32.

54. Ibn al-Wālid, *Tāj al-ʿAqāʾid*, 30. In these sections, Ibn al-Wālid employs the two popular terms for negation, *nafy* and *salb*, interchangeably.

55. This section is adapted from my broader analysis devoted to Ṭūsī's apophaticism. See Kars, "Ṭūsī Reloaded: Ismāʿīlī Paths of Sufi Wayfaring and Sufi Paths of Ismāʿīlī Apophaticism."

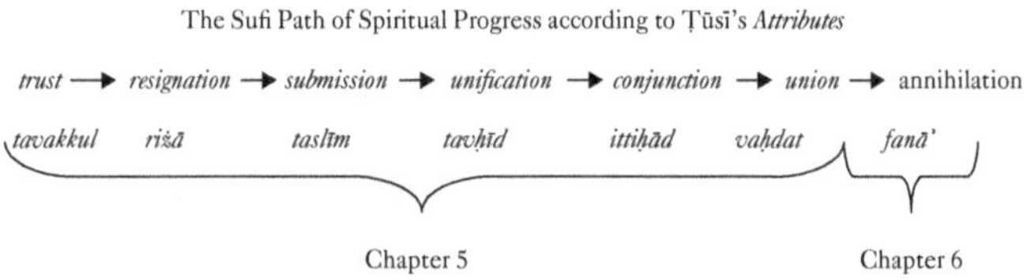

FIGURE 1.1 The Sufi Path of Spiritual Progress according to Ṭūsī's *Attributes of the Illustrious*

is an exception as it is devoted to one theme only: its title is "*annihilation*" [*fanā*ʾ], and its content is still *union* but of a different kind.

Since the ninth century onward Sufis have defined such systems of spiritual progress. Ṭūsī's list of stages, however, has (to my knowledge) no precedent in the Sufi literature. In particular, "submission" did not surface in thirteenth-century or earlier Sufi manuals. It was the presence of this term, which had evident significance in Ismāʿīlī theology, that made Ṭūsī's Sufi path unprecedented.[56] Indeed, an Ismāʿīlī path of Sufism—the same order of stations, with a minor yet curious difference—appears in Ṭūsī's earlier Ismāʿīlī eschatology, *Origin and Destination* [*Āghāz va Anjām*]. Here Ṭūsī explains that the return to divine oneness requires first the annihilation of the volition that lifts one to the rank of resignation. Then, with the annihilation of one's power, one attains the stage of complete trust. In the next step, one's knowledge must be annihilated in God's knowledge, which brings the stage of submission. Finally, "one's existence must be annihilated in God's existence, to the extent that one should become nothing on their own. This is the rank of the people of unity [*maqām-e ahl-e vaḥdat*]."[57] In other words, the places of the stages of resignation and complete trust are reversed in *Attributes of the Illustrious* and *Origin and Destination*, while other stages and themes are identical. Even the Qurʾanic

56. "Complete trust in God" and "resignation" are depicted as two consecutive Sufi stages in the descriptions of al-Sarrāj (*Kitāb al-Lumaʿ*, 51–54, Arabic text) and al-Kalābādhī (*Kitāb al-Taʿarruf*, 118–121). The Qurʾanic verses cited by al-Sarrāj and Ṭūsī in the sections on "complete trust in God" and "resignation" are identical. While we can surmise that Ṭūsī had access to al-Sarrāj's well-known work, both al-Sarrāj and al-Kalābādhī (d.990) have other stages and stations that are very different from those of Ṭūsī.

Nor does it look like Ibn Sīnā's "Stations of the Mystics." Cf. Ibn Sīnā and Ṭūsī, *al-Ishārāt wa-l-Tanbīhāt*, 4:76–95.

57. Ṭūsī, *Āghāz va Anjām*, 82.

verses that Ṭūsī cites for the stages of resignation, complete trust, and submission are the same.[58]

Why are the steps of resignation and complete trust reversed in the "Ismāʿīlī" eschatology and the "Sufi" manual? Ṭūsī's brief exposition of the Sufi path in his letter to Ṣadr al-Dīn Qūnavī unveils the mystery. Here, Ṭūsī has another, however brief, account of Sufi wayfaring. Accordingly, resignation and complete trust constitute a binary; they represent one single station, and Ṭūsī does not employ them separately.[59] When one transcends "the station of resignation and complete trust," one attains union, which is beyond unification as well as conjunction. This depiction in the letter is in perfect harmony with the accounts in *Attributes of the Illustrious* and *Origin and Destination*. Hence we have three texts written for very different readers in different periods of Ṭūsī's career that strongly cohere in their description of the spiritual path. Ṭūsī calls these most distinguished travelers both "those who have attained absolute union" [*ahl-e vaḥdat-e muṭlaq*] and "the people of communion" [*ahl-e vuṣūl*]—both of the designations appear in *Attributes of the Illustrious* and *Origin and Destination*. The "Sufi" path of Ṭūsī's *Attributes of the Illustrious* and the *Letters* he sent to Qūnavī is thus paved by a unique approach to spiritual progression with an Ismāʿīlī flavor. However, not only the path of spiritual progress is in line with his Ismāʿīlī writings in the *Attributes of the Illustrious*. Arguably, the work also adopts a distinctly classical Ismāʿīlī apophatic approach to the divine nature.

Major features of Ismāʿīlī negative theology are dressed in a Sufi garment in the *Attributes of the Illustrious*. Striking parallels can be found even in rhetorical gestures—such as the opening of the book, or the devotional expressions. Ismāʿīlī texts typically began in a powerfully apophatic manner; we find the strongest emphasis on divine unknowability and the inapplicability of language both positive and negative. *Attributes of the Illustrious* opens in an eye-catchingly apophatic manner, very similar to the works of earlier Ismāʿīlī scholars:

> Incomparable thanks to God, because no intellect has the power to access His truth, and no thought or knowledge can comprehend the fullness of His gnosis. Every expression that aims at His description

58. Q.9:72, Q.65:3, and Q.4:65 for "resignation," "complete trust," and "submission" respectively.

59. Ṭūsī and Qūnavī, *al-Murāsalāt*, 91.

> and every utterance that verbalizes his identity is perceived only via the blemish of comparability [*tashbīh*] if it is affirmative; its perception is not freed from the scourge of ineffectualism [*taʿṭīl*] if it is not affirmative.[60]

In the very opening of the work on Sufism, Ṭūsī cancels divine knowability as well as positive and negative discourse on God. The double threat of comparability and ineffectualism, common as the binary might appear, displays a much deeper skepticism concerning the limitations of language than it seems. Sufis and theologians employed the "two limits" of *tashbīh* and *taʿṭīl* predominantly to underscore the dangers in interpreting the divine attributes, the reported [*khabarī*] physical attributes in particular. Not only Imāmī and Sunnī scholars who penned influential theological works and creeds popular in Central Asia but also Sufi masters like ʿAbd al-Qādir al-Jīlānī, Aḥmad al-Rifāʿī (d.1182), Abū al-Najīb al-Suhrawardī (d.1168), ʿUmar al-Suhrawardī (d.1234), Ibn al-ʿArabī, and ʿIzz al-Dīn Kāshānī (d.1334) all used the binary of *tashbīh* and *taʿṭīl* when addressing divine attributes, specifically within the context of anthropomorphic depictions of God.[61] For Ṭūsī, however, the danger of falling into one of these fallacies was a generic philosophical problem inherent in any utterance on God. It was not such celebrated Sufi eponyms or theologians but other sources that nourished Ṭūsī's skeptical opening. Ismāʿīlī texts, with their powerful, apophatic openings and common depiction of the tension between *tashbīh* and *taʿṭīl* as general problems of descriptive language, provide the most likely possibility. For example, the Ismāʿīlī *dāʿī* of Nishapur Aḥmad ibn Ibrāhīm had also suggested a via negativa that would yield divine unity purified both from *tashbīh* and *taʿṭīl*.[62]

The more we proceed through Ṭūsī's stations, the more his apophatic theology with its double negation reveals itself in the Sufi terminology.

60. Ṭūsī, *Avṣāf al-Ashrāf*, 3. Cf., e.g., al-Sijistānī, *Kitāb al-Yanābīʿ*, 55; Ḥamīd al-Dīn al-Kirmānī, *al-Risāla al-Durriyya*, 89; Ibrāhīm al-Ḥāmidī, *Die Ismailitische Theologie*, 1.

61. Al-Ḥakīm al-Samarqandī in al-ʿOmar, *Doctrines of the Māturīdīte School*, 167–169; al-Ṭaḥāwī in Watt, *Islamic Creeds*, 49–50; Abū al-Muẓaffar al-Isfarāʾīni, *al-Tabṣīr fī al-Dīn*, 162; al-Jīlānī, *al-Fatḥ al-Rabbānī*, 21, 95; al-Rifāʿī, *al-Burhān al-Muʿayyad*, 19–20; Abū al-Najīb al-Suhrawardī, *Ādāb al-Murīdīn*, 1–3; ʿUmar al-Suhrawardī, *Aʿlām al-Hudā*, 69–71; Ibn al-ʿArabī, *Kitāb al-Masāʾil*, 310; Izz al-Dīn Kāshānī, *Miṣbāḥ al-Hidāya*, ch.1. sec.3, 25; Amir-Moezzi, *The Divine Guide*, 44–46.

62. Al-Naysābūrī, *Degrees of Excellence*, 7 (Arabic text). 36–37 (English translation). Cf. Chittick, *Faith and Practice*, 40–41; De Smet, "Ismāʿīlī Theology," 317.

Step four of the Sufi path, unification, brings the seeker to the realization that the attribute "being" should be negated from creation because only God deserves it:

> [Unification is] to cut off oneself from the vision of plurality and to consider everything One, and to see all One. Once the seeker unifies in the depth of his soul all in Oneness, he moves from the station of "He is One and there is none who shares with Him in divinity" to the station of "He is One and there is none who shares with Him in being.[63]

Unification thus separates God's being from creation, insofar as only God is the real Being—the term applies to Her *via eminentiae*. The limits of this act of negation, however, become clear once the seeker progresses on the Sufi path, and achieves the next step, *conjunction*. "'Unification' is to *make* one, while 'conjunction' is to *become* one. . . . In unification there is a blemish of limitedness that does not exist in conjunction."[64] More clearly, unification is the realization of the seeker that God is the only real being. This is very much like the necessary existent [*wājib al-wujūd*] of the Peripatetic philosophers, who is the only real being and the source from which all beings emanate and all attributes are to be negated. Conjunction is going beyond this philosophical negative theology with realizing that the divine otherness cannot be limited with existentiating causality. The station of conjunction is the realization of the still positive, causal ground of being, and negating it in favor of the non-discursive, ineffable, visionary testimony of oneness: "[Conjunction] is to see that all is He, without limiting Him by saying that 'everything other than Him exists through Him, so all are one.'"[65] Conjunction negates from God the attribute of being, along with ontic, causal relationality. This disqualification of the popular philosophical theologies of the divine nature through a further radicalization of negation was the hallmark of classical Ismāʿīlī theologians. With this first negation, the text self-consciously goes beyond the philosophical via negativa and leaves no positive language for God, including being.

---

63. Ṭūsī, *Avṣāf al-Ashrāf*, 93.

64. Ibid., 95.

65. Ibid., 95. Cf. Awḥad al-Dīn al-Balyānī (misattributed to Ibn al-ʿArabī), *Whoso Knoweth*, 24–25.

Still, says Ṭūsī, "conjunction means to become one, but it has the smell of plurality."[66] The very discursive act of negating God's being along with everything else needs to be negated with a second move in order to indicate pure oneness beyond all binaries. We move to a second negation, which, now, targets the entire discursive field, both positive and negative. This is the sixth and final station, divine union [*vaḥdat*], where discourse, with its endless binaries, cancels itself, as Ṭūsī moves to negative conjunctions:

> Rest and motion, contemplation and remembrance, journey and wayfaring, desire, desirer and desired, deficiency and perfection are all non-existent in oneness. "*When discourse arrives at God, rein back!*"[67]

This final step of union is the second performative negation that cuts all, positive and negative, discursive fields in order to indicate divine union. This was the end of their journeys, and the self-negation of language, for the most advanced Sufis. Indeed, the Ismāʿīlī path described in Ṭūsī's *Solidarity and Dissociation* [*Tavallā va Tabarrā*] ends exactly at this point, where it clearly overlaps with the *Attributes of the Illustrious*. The former treatise is written for the novice Ismāʿīlī seekers of union [*ṭālib-e vaḥdat*], and similarly it depicts the station of union as the stage where discourse cancels itself, after having removed its ground, both positive and negative:

> There is neither knowing nor known, neither lover nor beloved. All will be God and God alone. . . . [T]his is a rank that no creature can describe. That which can be described in words cannot be free from denial [*kufr*] and ascribing partners to God [*shirk*].[68]

The realm of union described in this Ismāʿīlī text as the self-cancellation of all binaries and discursive spaces overlaps fundamentally with the one we find in the *Attributes of the Illustrious*. The station of union in these works corresponds to the numeric oneness of the divine word in the Ismāʿīlī apophatic tradition that Ṭūsī inherits. It can be indicated only with the self-canceling double negation. Step five, conjunction, negates all positive

---

66. Ṭūsī, *Avṣāf al-Ashrāf*, 96.

67. Ibid.

68. Ṭūsī, *Tavallā va Tabarrā*, 32.

statements about God, while the final step, union, cancels both positive and negative language.

We have no way to experience, or know, and no language to indicate God's absolute oneness beyond the numerical oneness of the divine word. Hence *Solidarity and Dissociation*, Ṭūsī's earlier work for Ismāʿīlī novices, ends when we arrive at the end of discourse via double negation. The *Attributes of the Illustrious*, however, wants to elaborate what it means to talk about divine oneness beyond the one-many. Hence it adds a sixth chapter that has no sections or stations but is, rather, composed of a few sentences. It is telling that the content of this new chapter is not different from the sixth and last step of the fifth chapter: it is still elaborating union, but now Ṭūsī is addressing the divine oneness beyond the oneness of the divine word. The chapter "explains" this non-journey of unknowing the beyond of the beyond-intellect. Ṭūsī associates this "non-journey" with non-discursive negation, by calling the chapter "annihilation," the "beyond" of double negation:

> In union, there is no wayfarer and wayfaring, journey and aim, desire, desirer and desired: "everything perishes except His face" [Q.28:88]. Also *there is no affirmation of this discourse, and it cannot be uttered; and there is no negation of this discourse, and it cannot be uttered. Affirmation and negation are binaries, and duality is the source of multiplicity. There is no affirmation or negation there. Negation of the negation, or affirmation of the affirmation, also is not there. Negation of the affirmation, or affirmation of the negation, also is not there.* . . . Whatever comes to tongue, imagination, or reason is to be negated. "To Him all matters are returned" [Q.11:123].
>
> It was this that we aimed to address in this compendium, and here the discourse is terminated.[69]

This concluding chapter not only echoes the dizzying passages of the earlier Ismāʿīlī theologians on the divine nature, but such an ending is in stark opposition to the Sufi, and also philosophical, formats we know. Sufi texts neither depict annihilation as the final culmination of the path, nor employ the term without its typically superior counterpart of "subsistence" [*baqāʾ*], or "annihilation of annihilation" [*fanāʾ al-fanāʾ*]. For Ṭūsī, however,

69. Ṭūsī, *Avṣāf al-Ashrāf*, 101.

there is no subsistence, life, being, or any other positive (or indeed, negative) ground to talk about. This "station" is called "annihilation" not because there is something that has been, or can be, annihilated but only because it is a common, negative linguistic performative signal to absence. "[Sufis] call it annihilation, because the return [*maʿād*] of creation is by annihilation, as its origin [*mabdaʾ*] was from non-existence [*ʿadam*]."[70] There is no way from the numeric oneness to the absolute oneness; there is only annihilation if we want to address divine oneness—*neither a negation nor an affirmation, nor their negations.* Here at the end of a uniquely Ismāʿīlī path of Sufi wayfaring, we are nowhere else other than the double negation of classical Ismāʿīlī apophaticism on the divine nature.

Ṭūsī's apophaticism presents irreducible Sufi themes profoundly blended with the heritage of al-Sijistānī, al-Kirmānī, and other Ismāʿīlī masters. The negation of the applicability of all attributes and even of being is mixed with a rational, intellectualist self-negation of discourse that leads to the unknowability of the trans-transcendent God. Ṭūsī's apophatic Sufi-Ismāʿīlī theology in the *Attributes of the Illustrious* displays two key interrelated phenomena: the theological and thematic porosity of Sufism and Ismāʿīlism in thirteenth-century Persia and the continuity of the Ismāʿīlī apophatic tradition, in different forms, after the Mongol invasions. The porosity of negative theology on the divine essence should not be mistaken for harmonization in the case of Ṭūsī, because he neither considers himself a Sufi in any sense nor does he aim to integrate Sufism and Ismāʿīlism. The *Attributes of the Illustrious* is not a Sufi-Ismāʿīlī (or Ismāʿīlī-Sufi) treatise that wants to harmonize the two. Instead, it is Ṭūsī's empathetic but also naturally "Ismāʿīlized" depiction of pious Sufism to the powerful Īlkhānid vizier Shams al-Dīn Juvaynī's (d.1284) ill-fated son Bahāʾ al-Dīn (d.1279), who was already an admirer of Sufi saints [*muḥibb al-avliyāʾ*] according to Ṭūsī's own testimony. The theological disparity becomes clear at the very beginning of the treatise, when Ṭūsī is describing the prerequisites of wayfaring for the Sufi novice in the very first station of the first chapter. This is "faith" [*īmān*], and it requires the affirmation of the certain knowledge [*ʿilm qaṭʿī*] of God's eight essential attributes.[71] This Sunnī theological stance was not acceptable to Ṭūsī as we know from his other writings, but it was an accurate description of a widespread Sufi

70. Ibid., 101.

71. Ibid., 4, 9.

creed of the time. Even though Ṭūsī adds Ismāʿīlī apophatic themes to his treatise on Sufism, he appears as more of an outsider describing a form of Sufism that was already incorporating sustained Ismāʿīlī teachings. Reading his *Attributes of the Illustrious* in the light of his oeuvre—especially the *Letters* and *Origin and Destination*—indicates a very different trope than that of bringing Sufism and Ismāʿīlism together. Instead, in Ṭūsī's oeuvre they are already and imperfectly blended together, which provides important insights into later Ismāʿīlism as well as Sufism.

Dimension of Apophatic Theology in Later Sufi and Ismāʿīlī Connections

Looking at the relationship between Sufism and Ismāʿīlism after the thirteenth century from the angle of apophaticism on the divine nature highlights a coalescence of themes, practices, cosmologies, hermeneutical strategies, and institutions, instead of a one-way relationship of "influence." These overlaps are particularly visible among Ismāʿīlīs who stayed in Persia and began living outside of their traditional closed communities, instead of migrating to Badakhshan in Central Asia or to the Indian subcontinent after the Mongol invasions. Nizārī Qūhistānī's (d.1321) Persian poetry, for example, indicates not only his affiliation with Sufi institutions and his adoption of Sufi themes, but it also has Ismāʿīlī dimensions, some of which relate to apophaticism on the divine nature.[72] Such apophaticism was still prominent among later Ismāʿīlīs, affiliated with Sufism or not, as demonstrated in the writings of Pīr Ṣadr al-Dīn (fl.14th CE). Perhaps the most prolific of the Ismāʿīlī authors in the Subcontinent in his times, he employs negative conjunctions in describing the divine essence:

> Friend! The religious scriptures and books cannot fathom this, for there is
> Neither day there, nor night, neither sun, nor shade.
>
> Friend! My lord is not such that he can be spoken of. He is to be seen—for
> He is indescribable, and nameless.

---

72. Lewisohn, "Sufism and Ismāʿīlī Doctrine in the Persian Poetry of Nizārī Qūhistānī," 238. For more information on Qūhistānī and Sufism, see Virani, *Ismailis in the Middle Ages*, 66–70.

> Friend! How sweet is that lord, indescribable, nameless. Says Pīr Ṣadr Al-Dīn, truly, with my own eyes, I have seen him! [73]

Pīr Ṣadr al-Dīn is simultaneously defending the unknowability of the divine nature and defending its transcendence of names, descriptions, and binaries. Yet we also observe the mark of visionary experience as the highest form of knowledge, as we already saw in Ṭūsī's Ismāʿīlī's eschatology and Qūhistānī's poems. By the mid-fifteenth century, when Nizārī Ismāʿīlī imāms emerged in the guise of Sufi masters [*pīrs*], Ismāʿīlī and Sufi themes cannot be disentangled within Ismāʿīlism in Persia. Theology is included in this coalescence. An apophatic poem of the Ismāʿīlī master ʿAbd al-Salām (d.ca.1493), for example, explains the recognition of the imāmate through his own spiritual reality, which the Ismāʿīlīs of his period equated with the divine command. The poem has clear Sufi dimensions. Still it adopts some long-standing strategies of Ismāʿīlī apophaticism, such as the negative conjunction, a challenge to the most common, philosophical definition of God as the necessary being, and the disqualification of otherwise popular idea of divine dissimilarity:

> Whither can you behold me in this dusty realm, with these eyes? For I am in a place yet placeless, beyond place and habitation. . . . Count me not to be this, consider me not that; for in the world of ineffability, I am beyond body, even soul. *Neither am I existent, nor non-existent, neither perceptible, nor comprehensible to the mind; neither ineffable, nor effable, neither in a place, nor placeless.*[74]

Within a universalistic tendency of Persian poetry, a message of moral ecumenism coalesces with an apophaticism on God that is both Ismāʿīlī and Sufi at the same time. As Davlatshāh (d.af.1487) writes in his *Biographies of Poets* [*Taẕkirat al-Shuʿarāʾ*], some claimed that Nizārī Qūhistānī was a mystic [*muvaḥḥid va ʿārif*], and some associated him with Ismāʿīlism. Whatever he was, says Davlatshāh, "he was a man of gnosis and truths [*maʿārif va ḥaqāyiq*].[75] The turn from theological tracts

73. Pīr Ṣadr al-Dīn in Virani, *Ismailis in the Middle Ages*, 181.

74. Imām ʿAbd al-Salām in Virani, *Ismailis in the Middle Ages*, 176 (emphasis mine).

75. Davlatshāh, *Taẕkirat al-Shuʿarāʾ*, 233; Lewisohn, "Sufism and Ismāʿīlī Doctrine in the Persian Poetry of Nizārī Qūhistānī," 246–247.

into poetry with Nizārī Qūhistānī, Pīr Ṣadr al-Dīn, and ʿAbd al-Salām signifies that theological paradigms and their nuanced markers play an insignificant, or even corruptive, role in this emerging visionary and aesthetic framework. Unlike Ismāʿīlism, politically and discursively powerful Sufism could claim to name it. The pen name of Imām ʿAbd al-Salām symbolizes the Sufi label of this coalescence: "Dervish." On the backdrop of Ṭūsī's description of the dervishes in his Ismāʿīlī eschatology as the noblest yet hidden saints, who will skip the step of reckoning in the afterlife, it is hardly a surprising choice.[76] Divested from its deep cosmology and its initiatory preference for negation over affirmations and divine incomparability over divine immanence, the double negation of Ismāʿīlism appears to have transformed directly into self-contradictory statements—that is, paradoxes, which are expressed with an intensified experiential dimension in line with the dominant Sufi epistemology.

The dissolution of Ismāʿīlī theological and cosmological markers into a broad crucible of Persian Sufism was already underway in Ṭūsī. The early thirteenth century might have provided the Ismāʿīlī ground for such a deep interpenetration by not only defining Sufi-Ismāʿīlī apophatic theological paths but also by performing, disseminating, or even institutionalizing it. On the other hand, apart from Ṭūsī's works that complicate the picture, we do not have reliable earlier evidence of a conscious Ismāʿīlī Sufism that preserves this peculiar form of apophaticism. The theological ideas of Ṭūsī's early Ismāʿīlī gnostic master Kamāl al-Dīn Muḥammad Ḥāsib (d.1242) are yet to be uncovered. Kamāl al-Dīn's master, Bābā Afżāl al-Dīn Kāshānī (d.1213) is of special importance at this point. Bābā Afżāl, as his sobriquet might suggest, was apparently not just a philosopher and poet but also perhaps a practicing Sufi. His known works do not give us hints of his following the double negation in the Ismāʿīlī line. On the other hand, the only precedents for the work *Jāmiʿ al-Ḥikma*—attributed to Kāshānī—are distinctly Ismāʿīlī: Nāṣir Khusrav's *Vajh-e Dīn* and the Persian abridgment of the *Epistles* of the Brethren of Purity known as *Mujmal al-Ḥikmat*.[77] It is

---

76. Ṭūsī, "Āghāz va Anjām," 69–70. Cf. Ikhwān al-Ṣafāʾ, *Rasāʾil*, 1:97–99; Q.5:54; Kars, "Ṭūsī Reloaded: Ismāʿīlī Paths of Sufi Wayfaring and Sufi Paths of Ismāʿīlī Apophaticism."

77. Garakani and Negahban, "Bābā Afḍal"; Chittick, *The Heart of Islamic Philosophy*, 26–27; Nasr, "Afḍāl al-Dīn Kāshānī and the Philosophical World of Khwāja Naṣīr al-Dīn Ṭūsī," 251.

Al-Ḥāmidī cites the *Epistles* of Ikhwān al-Ṣafāʾ in the context of divine unity but attributes it to the eighth Ismāʿīlī imām, Wafī Aḥmad (d.ca.828). Such attributions may suggest that the *Epistles* were secretly disseminated during the reign of the ʿAbbāsid caliph al-Maʾmūn

this work attributed to Kāshānī that negates "being" from God, in order to indicate Her transcendence beyond causality. The issues discussed in the treatise are also key themes in the Ismāʿīlī repertoire. If authentic, *Jāmiʿ al-Ḥikma* would indicate Kāshānī as a pivotal source that culminates in Ṭūsī's organic Sufi-Ismāʿīlī philosophical amalgam. But the fact that other writings of Bābā Afżāl do not cohere with this treatise makes the ascription doubtful. For Ṭūsī himself, Bābā Afżal was a philosopher who excelled in logic, unlike Kamāl al-Dīn Muḥammad Ḥāsib, a master of esotericism. In the *Collection of Mysteries* [*Jāmiʿ al-Asrār*], Ḥaydar Āmulī (d.1385) mentions Bābā Afżāl as one of the greatest of those who, "having deepened philosophy and the official exoteric sciences, returns to the way of men of God." Along the lines of Ṭūsī and Āmulī, Quṭb al-Dīn Shīrāzī (d.1311) and Mullā Ṣadrā (d.1640) described him as a philosopher par excellence who mastered logic.[78] His known theological writings are distinctly philosophical, which fundamentally differ from the double negation of classical Ismāʿīlism.

Ṭūsī and his masters of "esotericism" in Persia are symptomatic of the intellectual exchanges among Ismāʿīlīs and Sufis without an explicit process of integration. The thirteenth century marks a period of intensive organic interpenetrations among Sufis and Ismāʿīlīs. The Ismāʿīlī tradition has indeed claimed many Sufi masters of the century. Nizārīs of Central Asia consider ʿAzīz Nasafī as their co-religionist.[79] On the other hand, the legendary accounts of Shams al-Dīn Muḥammad (d.ca.1310), the son and

---

(r.813–833). (See el-Bizri in Ikhwān al-Ṣafā', Epistle 22, *The Case of the Animals versus Man*, x.) In al-Ḥāmidī's narration, the *Epistles* said the following in terms of the divine attributes:

> One must glorify [*tanzīh*] the Originator from that which reason and soul describe, insofar as they are originated and created. . . . Demonstrably, reason and soul cannot comprehend His attributes. . . . His hiddenness is unlike veilings; His manifestation is unlike the manifestations of His creatures; He is veiled with His light, as His manifestations and splendor is with His light. . . . Eyes are blocked from His vision, and thoughts are perplexed seeking reality of His attributes. (Ibn al-Ḥusayn al-Ḥāmidī, *Die Ismailitische Theologie*, 12.)

78. Garakani and Negahban, "Bābā Afḍal"; Vasiltsov, "Afḍal al-Dīn Kāshānī and His Treaties 'The Book of Everlasting,'" 7.

79. "Nasafī never identifies himself directly as a Sufi but clearly sympathizes with those he usually calls *ahl-i vaḥdat*; and the expression *ahl-i vaḥdat* is found in the Ismāʿīlī works of Naṣīr-al-Dīn Ṭūsī in the first place." (Landolt, "Nasafī, ʿAzīz.") More significantly, in the *Book of Descent*, Nasafī differentiates the "Sufis" from the *ahl-i vaḥdat* and deliberately hides his own affiliation: "Now I do not reveal my own opinions, so they cannot accuse me of infidelity. I relate and I say, 'The *ahl-i vaḥdat* say this and the Sufis say that.'" (ʿAzīz Nasafī in Ridgeon, *Cambridge Companion to Sufism*, 141.)

designated successor of the last ruler of Alamūt, Rukn al-Dīn Khurshah (d.1257), has been identified with the famous Sufi master of Rūmī, Shams Tabrīzī (d.1248) within the Ismāʿīlī tradition. We find, for example, a narrative according to which Shams' father was an Ismāʿīlī master named Khāvand Jalāl al-Dīn. The report on Shams' supposedly Ismāʿīlī lineage might be widely circulating already in the fifteenth century: Davlatshāh transmits it in detail before claiming that Shams' father was actually a mercer [*bazzāz*] from Khurasan.[80] Among such claimed Sufi-*cum*-Ismāʿīlī identities of the time, two prominent Persian Sufis, Farīd al-Dīn ʿAṭṭār (d.1221) and Maḥmūd Shabistarī (d.1320), are worth mentioning. Shabistarī's famous *masnavī* titled the *Rose-Garden of Mystery* [*Gulshan-i Rāz*] shows familiarity with certain Ismāʿīlī doctrines and actually became one of the most popular texts among Persian Ismāʿīlīs. We know that Nizārī Qūhistānī's Sufi master, Amīn al-Dīn Balyānī of Tabriz, was also the master of Maḥmūd Shabistarī. Indeed, the Ismāʿīlīs of Persia and Central Asia generally consider the *Rose-Garden of Mystery* as belonging to their own literature. On the other hand, ʿAṭṭār's interpretation of the relationship between soul and body in the afterlife seems to be peculiar among Sufis, and Hermann Landolt has argued that it is closely connected with the eschatological position declared in the Ismāʿīlī sources of the time.[81] It is also very likely that ʿAṭṭār's *Book of Secrets* [*Asrār-nama*] employed the term "the cycle of Adam." The term appears in the Imāmī sources such as the *Mother of the Book* [*Umm al-Kitāb*] (wr.late 8th CE), which was preserved among the Nizārī Ismāʿīlīs in its Persian version, or directly in Ismāʿīlī theological texts such as Abū Yaʿqūb al-Sijistānī's *Unveiling of the Hidden* [*Kashf al-Maḥjūb*]. Based on these convergences, Landolt goes so far as to read ʿAṭṭār's *Conference of the Birds* [*Manṭiq al-Ṭayr*] as well as the *Book of Secrets* in the light of Ismāʿīlī eschatology. What Landolt neglects is the presence of this term in the writings of ʿAṭṭār's Sunnī Kubrawī master, Majd al-Dīn Baghdādī (d.1219).[82] In theological and hermeneutical terms,

80. Davlatshāh, *Tazkirat al-Shuʿarāʾ*, 195.

81. See Landolt, "ʿAttar, Sufism and Ismailism." On the other hand, in his letter to Quṭb al-Dīn Shīrāzī, a certain scholar named Aḥmad reports the eschatological position of "a group" [*qawm*], which is strikingly similar to that of ʿAṭṭār. Cf. Aḥmad in Walbridge, *The Science of Mystic Lights*, 203 (English text); 237 (Arabic text).

82. Abū Yaʿqūb al-Sijistānī, "Unveiling of the Hidden (from Kashf al-Maḥjūb)," 122; Anonymous, "The Mother of Books (from *Umm al-Kitāb*)," 29–30; Meier, *Essays on Islamic Piety and Mysticism*, 278; Daftary, *Ismailis in Medieval Muslim Societies*, 185–187; Landolt, "ʿAttar, Sufism and Ismailism."

ʿAṭṭār is strikingly consistent with the Kubrawī Sufis of the time, more than Ismāʿīlism.

None of the Sufis mentioned above clearly resonates with the classical forms of Ismāʿīlī apophaticism on the divine nature. Yet they all point to a major transformation in the thirteenth century: intensive overlaps in claims on Persian mysticism, and in Sufi and Ismāʿīlī identities and discourses. Not only increased institutionalization of Sufism but also fatal political losses for Ismāʿīlism define the context of these overlaps. However, major theological breaks with the earlier Ismāʿīlī apophaticism predate the thirteenth century and the Mongol invasions. The Ismāʿīlī double negation was already in decay in the twelfth century. Key dimensions of earlier Ismāʿīlī apophaticism gradually cede their place to more conventional theological positions, and particularly to negative conjunctions and paradoxes on the divine nature that were intensively employed by Sufis.

The *Crown of Creeds* compiled by the Yemenī *dāʿī* Ibn al-Wālid, the clear manifesto of Ismāʿīlī apophaticism, provides insights into this gradual move. The negation of the term "thing" [*shay*ʾ], which was a core apophatic theological topic for key Ismāʿīlī intellectuals, does not actually appear in the *Crown of Creeds*. The absence of such a fundamental topic is quite surprising considering the abundance of negations that inundate the text—thousands, not hundreds, of negations! Ismāʿīlī negation of *shay*ʾ was an insistent yet radical gesture toward divine unknowability and undermined the very possibility of God-talk. The *Crown of Creeds* is rather silent on such a strong Ismāʿīlī negative theological position on the divine essence. Rather, it adopts more popular, hence less radical positions on the term. Relevant discussions even imply that Ibn al-Wālid actually did call God a "thing" unlike things: "He is End-less, and *no thing was with Him* [*lam yazal wa lā shay*ʾ *maʿhu*]." Similarly, the universal (or primal) intellect is also described here as the "first thing" [*al-shay*ʾ *al-awwal*]. Ibn al-Wālid also penned a work titled the *Falsification of the Vain* [*Ḍamīgh al-Bāṭil*]—a rebuttal of Abū Ḥāmid al-Ghazālī's attack on Ismāʿīlism. Such polemics evidently had an impact on Ibn al-Wālid's Ismāʿīlī theology. The theological changes that we observe in the *Crown of Creeds* are visible also in the works of al-Shahrastānī, who managed to square his Ismāʿīlī commitments with Ashʿarism. His *Keys to the Arcana* [*Mafātīḥ al-Asrār*] also attributes thingness [*shay*ʾ*iyya*] to God. Three centuries later, the nineteenth *dāʿī* in Yemen, Idrīs ʿImād al-dīn al-Qurashī (d.1468), would return to the teachings of al-Ḥāmidī and prohibit calling God a "thing."[83] Yet the twelfth and early thirteenth centuries already witnessed important shifts within Ismāʿīlī apophaticism on God, even before the Mongol destruction of the Ismāʿīlī strongholds in Iran.

Intensive theological convergences between Ismāʿīlīs and Sufis on the negative theology of the divine nature also precede the Mongol invasions. We can trace apophatic theological thematical convergences among Sufis and Ismāʿīlīs farther back to their formative periods. An intriguing example comes from the early Sufi of Baghdad, al-Shiblī. Sufi historians Abū Naṣr al-Sarrāj, al-Sīrjānī (d.1077), al-Qushayrī (d.1072), Abū al-Khalaf al-Ṭabarī (d.1077), and later, ʿAyn al-Qużāt Hamadānī (d.1131) and ʿIzz al-Dīn Kāshānī—among many others—narrate al-Shiblī's famous "explication" of divine unity. In al-Sīrjānī's narration, al-Shiblī "described" divine unity as follows:

> Woe! The one who explains divine unity with words is a heretic; who indicates it is a dualist; who speaks about it is ignorant; who remains silent about it an ignoramus; who thinks that he has attained it has rather missed it; whatever your fantasy discerns as the most truthful meanings related to Him, indeed, have nothing to do with Him, and return to you, as they are created and originated.[84]

These Sufi reports on al-Shiblī are identical with Yemenī Ismāʿīlī theologians al-Ḥāmidī and Idrīs ʿImād al-dīn's later narrative on ʿAlī ibn Abī Ṭālib's response to Kumayl Ibn Ziyād's (d.707) inquiry on the divine unity.

---

83. Al-Shahrastānī, *Keys to the Arcana*, 144 (English translation), 82 (Arabic text).

It is "not from a thing, not through a thing, not in a thing, not for a thing, and not with a thing—He is the first thing" (Ibn al-Wālid, *Tāj al-ʿAqāʾid*, ch.22, 44–45). Also see ibid., 26, 38–39.

A major exponent of later Ismāʿīlism, Idrīs ʿImād al-dīn writes that "thing" can be said only of the origination, and not of God (Idrīs al-Qurashī, *Zahr al-Maʿānī*, 25).

According to Muḥammad Ibn Tūmart (d.1130), "God was, and no thing was with Him" was actually a prophetic tradition, hence the safest position one could adopt on the application of *shayʾ* to God (Ibn Tūmart, *Sharḥ Murshida*, 17). Cf. al-Bayhaqī, *Kitāb al-Asmāʾ wa-l-Ṣifāt*, 20–21, 112.

84. Al-Sīrjānī, *Sufism, Black and White*, 52 (Arabic text); al-Sarrāj, *Kitāb al-Lumaʿ*, 30 (Arabic text); Abū Khalaf al-Ṭabarī, *Salwat al-ʿĀrifīn*, 18 (Arabic text); ʿAyn al-Qużāt Hamadānī, *Tamhīdāt*, 332; ʿIzz al-Dīn Kāshānī, *Miṣbāḥ al-Hidāya*, ch.1, 2, 19; al-Qushayrī, *al-Risāla al-Qushayriyya fī ʿIlm al-Taṣawwuf*, 496. For an English translation, see al-Qushayrī, *Epistle on Sufism*, 310; cf. Idrīs al-Qurashī, *Zahr al-Maʿānī*, 22.

The influential *Paradise of Submission* [*Ravża-yi Taslīm*] commissioned by Naṣīr al-Dīn Ṭūsī also narrated the report, without citing any name. Long before Ṭūsī, the Brethren of Purity was citing another prophetic saying popular among Sufis, within strongly pro-Sufi discourses. Describing the "poles" [*quṭb*] among the "friends of God" [*awliyā*ʾ], the Brethren quote the prophetic saying "*if present, they are not recognized, and if absent they are not missed.*" Accordingly, the *awliyā*ʾ embody the noblest group on the day of resurrection, wear coarse wool clothes [*al-ʿabāʾ; al-khashin*], pray in seclusion [*khalwa*], "do not fear the blame of any blamer," and ultimately remain hidden from creation.[85] All of these concepts and principles embodied the major themes of the Path of Self-Blame [Malāmatiyya], which originated in Nishapur in the ninth century and became widespread after its quick incorporation within Sufism. A later example for such parallel traditions and anecdotes particularly in terms of divine unknowability can be found in the *Crown of Creeds* as well. The Ismāʿīlī creed gestures toward the maxim "only God knows God," which was defended by a plethora of prominent Sufis like al-Kharrāz (d.899), Yūsuf ibn al-Ḥusayn al-Rāzī (d.916), al-Junayd (d.910), Dhū al-Nūn (d.861), Abū Ḥāmid al-Ghazālī, Ibn al-ʿArabī, Najm al-Dīn Dāya Rāzī (d.1256), Sharaf al-Dīn Balkhī (fl.ea.13th CE), Majd al-Dīn Baghdādī, Farīd al-Dīn ʿAṭṭār, ʿAzīz Nasafī, and ʿIzz al-Dīn Kāshānī.[86] On the other hand, apophatic traditions compiled under Ismāʿīlī rule also proliferated among Sufis. In his Qurʾanic commentary, which was attributed to Ibn al-ʿArabī, the Imāmī Akbarī Sufi ʿAbd al-Razzāq Kāshānī (d.1330) cites the ʿAlīd tradition that "the perfection of sincerity to God lies in the negating of attributes from Him."[87]

---

85. Ikhwān al-Ṣafāʾ, *Rasāʾil*, 1:97–99; Q.5:54; Kars, "Ṭūsī Reloaded: Ismāʿīlī Paths of Sufi Wayfaring and Sufi Paths of Ismāʿīlī Apophaticism."

86. Abū Ḥāmid al-Ghazālī, *al-Maqṣad al-Asnā*, 33–34; ʿAzīz Nasafī in Ridgeon, *Cambridge Companion to Sufism*, 135–136; Abrahamov, *Ibn al-ʿArabī and the Sufis*, 63; Lāhījī in Corbin, *Man of Light in Iranian Sufism*, 118; ʿIzz al-Dīn Kāshānī, *Miṣbāḥ al-Hidāya*, ch.1.3, 24–25; Ibn al-Wālid, *Tāj al-ʿAqāʾid*, ch.18, 30; Kars, "What Is 'Negative Theology?' Lessons from the Encounter of Two Sufis," 17–19.

87. Later, the prominent Imāmī scholar Fayḍ Kāshānī (d.1681) ascribed this saying to the fifth Imām Muḥammad al-Bāqir.

ʿAbd al-Razzāq Kāshānī in Hamza, Rizvi, and Mayer, *An Anthology of Qurʾanic Commentaries*, 1:550; Ṭūsī, *Paradise of Submission*, 27 (Persian text), 28 (English translation); Ibn al-Ḥusayn al-Ḥāmidī, *Die Ismailitische Theologie*, 10; Badakhchani in Ṭūsī, *Paradise of Submission*, 250–251n19.

It can be surmised that at least since the tenth century onward the negative theological themes and traditions on the divine essence circulating among Sufis and Ismāʿīlīs had important overlaps. Not only an emphasis on divine unknowability but also an otherwise rarely found, simultaneous rejection of divine incomparability [*tanzīh*] and divine immanence [*tashbīh*], as well as an inclination toward paradoxes, can be found among the earliest Ismāʿīlī as well as Sufi sources. With the thirteenth century, the more Ismāʿīlī apophaticism was divested of its radical negativity, distinct cosmology, and the double negation that at least initially preferred divine incomparability to divine immanence, the more it approached the regular paradoxes that find divine immanence and divine incomparability equally insufficient.

Summary

The apophatic theology of God's nature developed by Ismāʿīlī scholars since the early tenth century has clear cosmological markers and a logical structure. It puts the divine essence beyond the divine word, which lies beyond the first creation. The divine word is essentially a negation, and its conjoining with the first creation marks the effective cause of creation. Addressing the divine word necessitates a negative language, and addressing its beyond demands the self-cancellation of this negative language through a second negation. These two steps could be performed via not only two repetitive negative particle, but also via their logical equivalent, a negative conjunction. Most of these defining features recall the insufficiency of generic concepts such as "Neoplatonism" and "negative theology" in understanding the classical Ismāʿīlī apophaticism in context and over time.

Classical Ismāʿīlī apophaticism has a unique combination of double negations, the unknowability of God, and an intellectual, nonmystical self-cancellation of theological discourse. This apophatic theology expanded widely from Andalusia to Central Asia in the tenth century and made its mark as witnessed by the long-standing, mostly hostile and reductive depictions of Ismāʿīlīs as "the negators." In the thirteenth century however, this powerful form of apophaticism did not play a major role outside the Ismāʿīlī context. Neither the Sufis nor scholars who had close relations with specific Ismāʿīlī networks such as ʿAzīz Nasafī and Bābā Afżāl seem to have adopted it. Still, Ibn al-ʿArabī's significant convergences suggest that the diffusion of Ismāʿīlī themes and ideas would have an elusive yet profound impact on Sufism. The case of Ṭūsī also indicates that it was in Iran and Central Asia where Ismāʿīlī double negation was preserved and put into creative interactions with Sufism in the thirteenth century. The post-Alamūt organic coalescence of Ismāʿīlism and Sufism in these territories strongly corroborates this premise.

PATH TWO

Necessarily Dissimilar

PHILOSOPHICAL APOPHATICISM

IN THE CENTURIES following al-Kindī, Muslim philosophers developed a coherent family of apophatic theological positions on the divine essence and its accessibility. The recurring aspects of this philosophical apophaticism were (1) a negative theology of divine attributes that reads them as negations, (2) the unknowability of the divine essence, closely connected with an Aristotelian version of the Neoplatonic distinction between discursive thought [*dianoia*] and non-discursive intellection [*noēsis*], (3) the necessary dissimilarity [*mukhālafa*] of God as the first cause of everything else, and (4) a philosophical hermeneutics that protects divine oneness and dissimilarity. Most of these aspects were established in conversation with the Muʿtazilites. As early as al-Kindī, Muslim philosophers adopted such a philosophical apophaticism of the divine nature, which later would take diverse forms, while preserving strategic resemblances.

With a few notable exceptions that we will explore, Sufis of the thirteenth century did not adopt this form of apophaticism mainly because a negativist reading of the divine attributes did not proliferate among them. Still, the philosophical apophaticism of al-Ghazālī, Qūnavī, Ibn Sabʿīn, and the early Kabbalist Azriel of Girona (d.1238) indicate the intellectual porosities not only between Sufism, mysticism, and philosophy but also between religious traditions in the thirteenth century. As philosophical ideas transcended disciplinary and religious borders, the philosophical apophaticism associated with it also found expressions across traditions. The employment of a negative language around the declaration of faith, "There is no god but God," by two Kubrawī Sufis of the thirteenth century, is of particular importance as it demonstrates two key aspects of Sufi variations on philosophical apophaticism. First, in order to sustain divine unknowability, Sufis had to negate not only discourse on the divine essence but also unveiling and vision—the superior epistemological sources in Sufism. Second, the negation of divine attributes in philosophical apophaticism transformed into a negation of human attributes in the hands of these Sufis.

Beginnings: The End-less

Along with the Ismāʿīlīs, the depiction of the Peripatetic philosophers as defenders of an unknowable God, to whom nothing can be ascribed, was a popular theme in theological discussions in the precolonial period. Indeed, many scholars believed that the famous negative theology of the Muʿtazilites on God's attributes was in fact borrowed from the philosophers. The Sufi philosopher Quṭb al-Dīn al-Aharī (d.1260) argued that the Muʿtazilites misunderstood the Greek philosophers' subtle distinction between non-existence and nothingness, and ended up negating [*nafy*] the existence of matter, which he finds despicable. The Muʿtazilites are just "poor philosophers," and ungrateful "thieves" [*sarrāq al-ḥukamāʾ*] who stole wisdom from the ancients that they did not appreciate or even understand at all according to al-Aharī.[1]

On the other hand, Muslim doxographers including al-Ashʿarī and Fakhr al-Dīn al-Rāzī thought that the Muʿtazilites were influenced not only by the ancient philosophers but also by the Arabic philosophers of the Islamic era. More importantly, more than being mere thieves distorting the legacy of the philosophers, the Muʿtazilites were in general faithful to their spirit in negating the divine attributes. In his section on the Muʿtazilites, al-Ashʿarī observes that negating all attributes, they reduced them into a single meaning:

> Those who negated the attributes of the lord said: "God, glorious is His praise and holiest are His names, has no attributes, no knowledge, no power, no life, no hearing, no vision, no glory, no majesty, no magnificence, no greatness"; and so on they said about the various attributes of God, the glorious, the majestic, with which He is described. This is a word that they [Muʿtazilites] have borrowed

1. Al-Aharī, *al-Aqṭāb al-Quṭbiyya, aw, al-Bulgha fī al-Ḥikma*, 105.

> from their brethren, the would-be-philosophers [*ikhwānihim min al-mutafalsafa*], who alleged "The all-knowing end-less creator is not all-knowing, not all-powerful, not all-living, not all-hearing, not all-seeing, not eternal." They explained this, and said, "We say: '[God is] but the End-less Itself [*ʿAynun Lam Yazal*],' " and they did not add anything else.[2]

Al-Ashʿarī further explains that the Muʿtazilites negating [*nafy*] the Qurʾanic attributes of God were only following the spirit [*maʿnā*] of what the philosophers did overtly. Scattered reports from al-Ashʿarī on the philosophers display a consistently apophatic theology of divine names that firmly negates all possible ascriptions, including eternity [*qidam*], from God. All of these negations serve to indicate God's utter transcendence as opposed to Her similarity to creation. As in the previous report, it is the non-Qurʾanic term "End-less" [Lam Yazal] that designates this negative essence:

> They differed in the expression "God is all-knowing, all-living, all-powerful, all-hearing, all-seeing." . . .It is narrated from one of the philosophers that there is no partnership [*shirk*] between the Producer [*al-Bāriʾ*] and others in these names. The Producer is not named "all-knowing," and not to be called "all-powerful," "all-living," "all-hearing," "all-seeing." They said: "*He is but the End-less.*"[3]

Only "End-less," a curious negative designation, is employed by the philosophers because no other name can apply to God, as all names in our language, even the most qualified ones, entail comparability and sharing, which violate God's incomparable, transcendent oneness. Al-Naẓẓām (d.835 or 845) and later Ibn Kullāb (d.855) and Abū ʿAlī al-Jubbāʾī (d.916) employed the phrase *lam yazal* as an adverb in discussing divine attributes, as in "God is *endlessly* all-knowing," "God is *endlessly* all-hearing," and "God is *endlessly* eternal." But some Muʿtazilites of the time followed the philosophical path, as they employed *lam yazal*, while, as al-Ashʿarī observed, "they did not add anything else." Such usage converted *lam yazal*, like its cognate *al-azalī*, into a proper noun, Lam Yazal—a negative

2. Al-Ashʿarī, *Maqālāt al-Islāmiyyin*, 2:156, emphasis mine. Ibn Taymiyya would cite this passage in various works he penned.

3. Ibid., 1:240; 2:156–157.

designation of God. ʿAbbād ibn Sulaymān (d.864) of Basra, as the most striking example, explicitly criticized the appeal to *lam yazal* in conventional, adverbial contexts. He insisted on employing the phrase as the only proper noun that designates the divine essence. *"He said: The all-hearing is End-less, and (His) hearing is End-less. He said: I don't say 'the all-hearing does not end,' or 'He is endlessly all-hearing.'"*[4] This self-conscious rejection of the adverbial use and insistent adherence to the proper noun version was a theological nuance that al-Ashʿarī was able to catch. Along with ʿAbbād, other Muʿtazilites Hishām al-Fuwaṭī (d.825) and Abū Zufar (fl.ea.9th CE) negated various attributes, interpreting all of them as reducible to God's End-lessness. The nominal appeal to Lam Yazal was creative, and indeed initially awkward from a grammatical perspective, but it spread in Muslim theological discourse, increasingly and widely appealed to in diverse contexts. The Sufi Bāyazīd al-Bisṭāmī (d.848 or 875), the traditionist ʿAbd Allāh al-Dārimī (d.865), and the jurist Ibn Khuzayma al-Nisābūrī (d.924) employed Lam Yazal in nominal form in their theological expositions, even if their approaches to the divine attributes and the divine essence differed. Al-Ashʿarī himself frequently appealed to Lam Yazal as a proper name to designate God [Allāhu Lam Yazal] throughout his works.[5]

A non-Qurʾanic description, the rise of the proper noun "End-less" in theological discourse seems to be germane to the negative theology of the divine attributes associated with the Muʿtazilites and philosophers of the ninth century. Both the proper noun and the negativist approach to the divine attributes ascribed by doxographers to "philosophers" find full expression in Yaʿqūb ibn Isḥāq al-Kindī's corpus, along with an apophaticism on the divine essence. In the categorization of different kinds of knowledge, al-Kindī puts "First Philosophy" on the top, which is the

---

4. ʿAbbād in al-Ashʿarī, *Maqālāt al-Islāmiyyin*, 1:233; Wisnovsky, *Avicenna's Metaphysics in Context*, 229–232.

Technically, *lam yazal* is operating as an "incomplete verb" [*fiʿl nāqiṣ*], or an "adverbial verb" [*fiʿl ʿibāra*] in the first grammatical structure—i.e., in "He is endlessly all-knowing" [*huwa lam yazal ʿalīmun*]. In the latter grammatical structure, *lam yazal* is operating as a "complete verb" [*fiʿl tām*]—a *Vollverb* as Josef Van Ess recognizes—i.e., "He is End-less" [*huwa lam yazal*]. (See Van Ess, *Theologie und Gesellschaft im 2. und 3. Jahrhundert Hidschra*, 4:20n.5.) Here I am simplifying the advanced discussions on Arabic grammar in Richard M. Frank's analysis of the emergence of *lam yazal* as a formal term in Muslim theology; see Frank, "'Lam Yazal' as a Formal Term in Muslim Theological Discourse."

5. Al-Sarrāj, *Kitāb al-Lumaʿ*, 29 (Arabic text); al-Ashʿarī, *Maqālāt al-Islāmiyyin*, 1:218; 1:240, 2:180.

"knowledge of the First Truth [*ʿilm al-Ḥaqq al-Awwal*] Who is the cause [*ʿilla*] of all truth."[6] On the other hand, the passages actually addressing the First Truth, or the First Cause, are extremely limited in his *On First Philosophy*, and they are in the form of a sequence of negations. *On First Philosophy* discusses extensively the general principles of causation and being. Through its *silence* the work is "telling us that all we can know about the First Truth, i.e., God, is that our knowledge of all else is not applicable to Him; or, more positively put, He is what the world is not."[7] This negativity is expressed in al-Kindī's work via the proper noun "End-less" ["Lam Yazal" or "al-Azalī"]—a complete semantic entity that designates God. Only God is Lam Yazal, because "that which is not Lam Yazal is created." Al-Kindī's argument for the alterations and created nature of heavenly spheres relies on a similar syllogism in which only God is by definition Lam Yazal. Somewhere else he describes God as "the true essence that never ceased to be nor will ever cease to be. *The End-less, and the Cease-less forever*" [*Huwa al-inniyya al-ḥaqq allatī lam takūn laysa wa lā takūn laysan abadan; lam yazal wa lā yazāl aysa mā abadan*].[8] On the other hand, al-Kindī's standard designation of God is the name "the Eternal" [al-Azalī], which is cognate and semantically identical with the ascription God "the End-less" [Lam Yazal] reported by al-Ashʿarī. The definition that he gives for "al-Azalī" is identical with the use of "Lam Yazal," and both indicate a rather negative semantic field:

> Al-Azalī: that which cannot become nothing [*laysa*]; is not in need of something else for its self-standing [*qiwāmihi*]; does not need something else for its self-standing; does not have a cause; that which does not have a cause is ceaseless forever [*dāʾim abadan*].[9]

Such substantive appeals to Lam Yazal and al-Azalī to define God, grammatically awkward and non-Qurʾanic as they were, spread from the ninth

6. Al-Kindī, *Al-Kindī's Metaphysics: On First Philosophy*, 56; al-Kindī, *Rasāʾil al-Kindī al-Falsafiyya*, 30.

7. Ivry in al-Kindī, *Al-Kindī's Metaphysics: On First Philosophy*, 17.

8. See Frank, "'Lam Yazal' as a Formal Term in Muslim Theological Discourse," 260–262; Yaman, *Prophetic Niche in the Virtuous City*, 232.

9. Al-Kindī, *al-Ḥudūd wa-l-Rusūm*, 194.

century onward in Muslim theological discourses.[10] Al-Kindī's one-page description of the "Eternal" [al-Azalī] contains around forty Arabic negative particles. Simply put, God's being the cause [ʿilla] of creation makes Her uncaused, ineffable, unknowable, and utterly transcendent. She is the source of all multiplicity; and She is beyond the multiplicity and unity that belongs to creation. As the true One, She cannot be spoken of in the way creation is spoken of. "God, 'the true One,' is completely transcendent, in the precise sense that nothing can be said of Him."[11] Al-Kindī writes:

> The true One is not one of the intelligible things, and is not matter, not genus, not species, not individual, not specific difference, not property, not common accident, not motion, not soul, not intellect, not whole, not part, not all, not some. It is also not one in relation to anything else, but is an absolute one, not augmentable, not composed, not multiple. Nor is it one of the sort which we mentioned in which kinds (of one) exist, (of) all the kinds of one which we mentioned, and that which is attached to their names is not attached to it. . . . The true One, therefore, has no matter, no form, no quantity, no quality, no relation, is not described by any of the remaining intelligible things, and has no genus, no specific difference, no individual, property, no common accident, no movement; and it is not described by any of the things which are denied to be one in truth. It is, accordingly, pure and simple unity, i.e., (having) nothing other than unity, while every other one is multiple.[12]

Al-Kindī's philosophical apophaticism is paradoxically a form of God's proof. The ultimate cause of creation should be beyond all multiplicity and unity that exists therein. Human categories cannot be applied to their apophatic source. As the unique source, God is the "true One" [*wāḥid bi-l-ḥaqīqa*], while unity exists in creation only metaphorically [*bi-l-majāz*]. The distinction is not quantitative but categorical, as the absolute One

10. Frank, "'Lam Yazal' as a Formal Term in Muslim Theological Discourse," 261; also see al-Bāqillānī, *Tamhīd al-Awāʾil*, 36.

11. Al-Kindī, *Al-Kindī's Metaphysics: On First Philosophy*, 67. See also al-Kindī, *Rasāʾil al-Kindī al-Falsafiyya*, 25–27; Adamson, "Al-Kindī and the Muʿtazila," 49.

12. Al-Kindī, *Al-Kindī's Metaphysics: On First Philosophy*, 112 (with my slight modification). See also al-Kindī, *Rasāʾil al-Kindī al-Falsafiyya*, 104. See Yaman, *Prophetic Niche in the Virtuous City*, 230–231.

cannot be comprehended by expanding or narrowing a genus in human thought. Divine oneness thus cannot be apprehended. Not only the unity we perceive in creation, but even the intellectual principle of it—that is, the numerical one—cannot be applied to God. The numerical one, al-Kindī explains, is not a number; it is the matter [*hyle*] of the world, and in this sense, it is the one-many, which cannot be used to designate the absolute One.[13]

Al-Kindī's apophaticism on God's nature displays a fundamental ambivalence. On the one hand, God is fully removed from the realm of creation and discourse, utterly unknowable, transcendent, and dissimilar. On the other hand, one can discursively prove that God is the ultimate, real agent of creation. In other words, while following a classical Platonic style of argumentation to explain the oneness in all other things, al-Kindī's proof of God is nevertheless a negative one based on dissimilarity [*mukhālafa*], insofar as nothing else is truly one, or "ceaseless forever." As various scholars have underlined, his account of the divine essence "pictures a *connection* that articulates a *distinction*."[14] God's being the unique source of creation simultaneously removes Her beyond all and culminates in al-Kindī's apophaticism. This is a relationship that refuses all relationality vis-à-vis God. Every attribute should be negated, because She is the source of our language, world, and all that exists and does not exist. All attributes of creation—that is, the caused world—should be negated from the cause, insofar as the cause precedes all and differs necessarily. Al-Kindī's *Epistle to Ibn al-Jahm on the Unity of God* confirms the apophatic causality that was found in his *On First Philosophy*:

13. Al-Kindī, *Al-Kindī's Metaphysics: On First Philosophy*, 95–98; al-Kindī, *Rasāʾil al-Kindī al-Falsafiyya*, 83–88; Netton, *Allah Transcendent*, 49.

"The cause of unity in unified things is accordingly the true One, the First, and everything which receives unity is caused, every one other than the One in truth being one metaphorically and not in truth." (Al-Kindī, *Al-Kindī's Metaphysics: On First Philosophy*, 13; al-Kindī, *Rasāʾil al-Kindī al-Falsafiyya*, 105 (with my minor modification.)

14. See Druart, "Metaphysics," 331; Yaman, *Prophetic Niche in the Virtuous City*, 231.

God's being the unique origin of everything else is a form of connecting Him to the world that disconnects Him from it. This simultaneous "distinction" and "connection," in David Burrell's terms, is a key aspect of philosophical apophaticism we identify in thinkers of different religious traditions, Ibn Sīnā, Maimonides and Thomas Aquinas being the most shining examples. See Burrell, *Knowing the Unknowable God*, 1–32.

> He is not many but One, without multiplicity. May He be praised and elevated high above the qualities which the heretics attribute to Him. He does not resemble His creation for multiplicity exists in all creation but absolutely not in Him. For He is the creator (*mubdiʿ*) and they are the created.[15]

Al-Kindī is clear about this difference: he repeats in various contexts that "*something is necessarily generated from its contrary*. . . . [E]verything that is generated is generated from 'not-it' [*lā-huwa*]."[16] His philosophical apophatic causality relies on this key approach to God as the negation of creation that will have wide and long term repercussions.

The convergences are clear between al-Kindī and the Muʿtazilites in terms of this negative theology of the divine attributes. The negative proof for God's necessary existence as the inherently dissimilar cause of creation, a major argument that philosophers and later theologians intensively applied, was developed by the Muʿtazilites. Moreover, the reflection of the necessary dissimilarity of God on the inapplicability of divine attributes, including oneness, circulated among Muʿtazilites as well. Hence it is not surprising to find that al-Qāsim ibn Ibrāhīm's exposition of the divine oneness is quite similar to al-Kindī's apophatic approach:

> He is One with whom there is not a second. He has no like in attribute, in essence, in saying, in action, or in any of the senses. He has no like in attribute or in the sense of eminence and superiority. This sense of eminence will never disappear from God in any way, for there is nothing like Him and He is unlike anything. If it were possible for God to have a like in any sense and this likeness were eminence, it would be possible for God to be like another in every sense and this would be eminence for Him. God is very much exalted above it. . . . *The word "one" can be truly predicated only of God. . . . He is one in His sense, which does not resemble the senses by which a human being is described.*[17]

---

15. Al-Kindī in Netton, *Allah Transcendent*, 48 (with my minor modification).

16. Al-Kindī in Adamson, "Al-Kindī and the Muʿtazila," 60.

17. Al-Qāsim ibn Ibrāhīm, *Anthropomorphism and Interpretation of the Qurʾan*, 87–97 (my emphasis).

This causal form of apophatic theology was not uninformed by Plotinus. Indeed, parts of the *Enneads* were translated into Arabic and adapted to its vocabulary by al-Kindī's circle, probably under his very editorship. Al-Kindī also wrote an introduction to this Arabic adaptation, which began to be ascribed to Aristotle and came to be known as the *Theology of Aristotle,* while al-Kindī himself probably did not think it was by the Greek philosopher. Al-Kindī's major philosophical work, *On First Philosophy,* followed Plotinus' via negativa in placing God beyond discourse, but unlike Plotinus, al-Kindī avoided kataphatic statements on the true One, even if they would be metaphorical. Al-Kindī did not turn to the eminent, qualified names, or to the glorification of the One, even with a metaphorical language. Compared to Plotinus, al-Kindī makes very few positive assertions, and those only of a general sort. More importantly, al-Kindī resists Plotinus' move to a non-discursive connection with the divine. The Neoplatonic tradition, perhaps diverging from the doctrines of Plotinus, tended to supply its apophatic theology of the divine essence with an epistemology based on a non-discursive, but noetic, mystical union.[18] Al-Kindī not only negates discursive proofs of the divine essence, but he also closes the door of any non-discursive access to God, including mysticism. God becomes utterly apophatic, inaccessible, and the unknowable ultimate cause and agent.

The tension in early Arabic philosophy between presenting discursive proof for God as the ultimate source of existence and claiming that Her essence is beyond knowledge—that is, the Kindian dilemma—will persist in the later philosophical tradition. By the thirteenth century, the negative relation between God and creation will constitute a well-established philosophico-theological theme. Ibn Taymiyya's cynical report on the logicians of the time, including the famous Ibn ʿAbd al-Malik al-Khūnajī (d.1249), illustrates the philosophers' dilemma of the negative proof. Ibn Taymiyya narrates, "Just before he [al-Khūnajī] died he said: 'I die having known nothing except that the possible requires [*yaftaqir*] an agent.' " Then he added: " 'requirement' [*iftiqār*] is a negative attribute, thus I die knowing nothing."[19]

---

18. Ivry in al-Kindī, *Al-Kindī's Metaphysics: On First Philosophy*, 13, 41n20, 42n31; Adamson, *The Arabic Plotinus*, 256.

19. Ibn Taymiyya, *Against Greek Logicians*, 42. Also see ibid., 132–133.

The Kindian Dilemma in the Tenth Century

Al-Kindī's dilemma between presenting discursive proof for God and claiming that Her essence is beyond knowledge, according to the Khurasanian philosopher al-ʿĀmirī (d.992), goes back as far as Pythagoras and Empedocles. Accordingly, Empedocles claimed that God can be designated by the attributes of "knowledge," "generosity," "will" and "power," but this is not to say that these designations have particular meanings different from each other. On the contrary, these designations do not affirm different meanings because God is uniquely One [*aḥadan wāḥidan*]. Her being bears no similarity [*tashbīh*] to that of creation; the latter is possible being [*wujūd al-imkānī*], while the former is essentially necessary being [*dhātihi wājib al-wujūd*]. The unity [*waḥdāniyya*] of creation is dissimilar to the absolute unity of its source, the One. Therefore, reports al-ʿĀmirī, Empedocles argued that God can be designated with qualified attributes via eminentiae, but these attributes were not Her essence. What can be said of God's essence is that She is essentially real and essentially wise [*ḥaqq bi-dhātihi wa ḥakīm bi-dhātihi*], which respectively indicate Her necessary being and Her being the ultimate source of everything else.

According to al-ʿĀmirī, Pythagoras and Socrates debated on further reducing the divine essence into a single, negative meaning. They agreed with Empedocles that God is uniquely One, thus various designations cannot have different meanings. On the other hand, Pythagoras argued that "the wise" is a sufficient essential name, because God as the intentional agent of creation already entails Her necessary being. Socrates, however, went in the opposite direction: God's only essential name is "necessary being," while Her being the intentional, wise source of all possible beings can be derived from it. For al-ʿĀmirī, it is the great master Aristotle who settles the debate by reconciling both views, going back to Empedocles. Aristotle claimed that God's necessary being and Her being the ultimate cause of creation cannot be separated, because they are different expressions of the same reality: the absolute One is necessary being—that is, the cause of all possibilities, from which She categorically differs.[20] Divine attributes, however diverse they are, do not cause any plurality in the divine essence, because they unify in a single meaning, which is the negation of creation. No

20. Al-ʿĀmirī, *A Muslim Philosopher on the Soul and Its Fate*, 79–87.

similarity can be constructed on any basis whatsoever between the caused, possible beings and their cause: the absolute One, necessary being.

Traces of al-Kindī's apophatic theology can be found in the thought of al-Fārābī, who is closer to Plotinus in attributing qualified names to God. Al-Fārābī's work *On the One and Oneness* [*Kitāb al-Wāḥid wa-l-Waḥda*] is particularly reminiscent of al-Kindī's approach to divine oneness in *On First Philosophy* because of the *absence* of God in it. Al-Fārābī acknowledges that "one" is a homonymous term, which can indicate several different things: It might be employed for things that are of a shared type or have a shared accident. "One" can indicate the number of its object. It can mean something that is divisible. Or finally, something can be called "one" by its differentiation from other things. Carefully and extensively discussing the possible ways in which "one" can be said, al-Fārābī simply excludes its application to the divine essence. Every sense of "one" is analyzed except as a name or attribute of God: how "one" applies to God is not within the field of discursive analysis. The silence of *On the One and Oneness* about how oneness relates to God follows al-Kindī's apophaticism, in stark contrast to the Ashʿarite theologians such as Aḥmad ibn al-Ḥusayn al-Bayhaqī (d.1066), who were eager to ascribe oneness to God in rather *all* conceivable ways.[21]

The "One" of Al-Fārābī's *Perfect State* also manifests the Kindian dilemma in al-Fārābī's thought. The One is the necessarily dissimilar source of creation through emanation. Al-Fārābī's God is also the absolute One, the source to which the attributes apply only polysemously [*mustaʿār*]. This is not to say that the qualified attributes cannot apply; on the contrary, all attributes can be applied to Her eminently. Hence God is a mixture of a perfect being, which is necessarily dissimilar from beings substantially, and an apophatic One from all respects that merits the designation "the One" more than anything. It has no beginning, no need for anything, no cause, form, contrary, partner in anything, where-ness, substratum, genus, or magnitude; no purpose or aim can be attributed to its existence, and it is neither matter, nor divisible. These negations simultaneously mean that She is the pure, active intellect [*ʿaql bi-l-fiʿl*] from which intellects emanate and attain forms [*ṣūra*] in the lower levels of existence. Hence, as in the case of al-ʿĀmirī, the attributes apply to Her via a hermeneutics that

21. Al-Fārābī, *Kitāb al-Wāḥid wa-l-Waḥda*, 36–87. Cf., e.g., al-Bayhaqī, *Kitāb al-Asmāʾ wa-l-Ṣifāt*, 23–24.

underscores the divine oneness and indicates negation from creation. As the dissimilar, unknowable, negative cause of all, God is *true* being, love, intellect, wisdom, and living, glorious, beautiful, and so on. These attributes apply to God *eminently*, but how they relate to Her is not known except as negations of what we can know. In other words, unknowing is first and foremost a property of the via eminentiae among the early Muslim representatives of the Arabic philosophical tradition.[22]

On the one hand, al-Fārābī claims that the One is indescribable and unknowable; on the other, he gives demonstrations for Her being the perfect source of creation. Genuine knowledge of the absolute One is not possible, but Her proof is possible: al-Fārābī shows that we can discursively demonstrate that God is the absolute One, from which existence emanates. God as the actual intellect can be perfectly and completely represented, but our minds are weak as they are embodied, and intermixed with matter [*mādda*]. Al-Fārābī notes that a complete separation from matter would bring perfect mental apprehension of the First, but he shares al-Kindī's Aristotelian pessimism toward the possibility of ever completely separating the soul from the body for such a mystical experience. Hence we can neither fully understand [*fahm*] nor genuinely comprehend [*idrāk*] God, and we are left with employing analogies [*qiyās*] from ourselves and from creation.[23]

Discursive Thought and Non-Discursive Intellection

Ibn Sīnā's apophatic approach to the divine essence and attributes fits well into this philosophical context in Iraq. He adopts a negative theology of divine attributes most succinctly presented in his *Celestial Epistle* [*al-Risāla al-ʿArshiyya*], and detailed in his *Metaphysics of "The Healing"* [*Kitāb al-Shifāʾ*]. The *Celestial Epistle* focuses on three key philosophical-theological problems: (1) the proof of the necessary being [*ithbāt wājib al-wujūd*], (2) divine uniqueness [*waḥdāniyya*], and (3) the negation of effects of any kind

22. Al-Fārābī, *On the Perfect State.*

23. Al-Fārābī, *Kitāb al-Wāḥid wa-l-Waḥda*, 57–85.

In following this path, philosophers like al-Fārābī, Ibn Sīnā, and Maimonides are closer to the negative theology of Pseudo-Dionysius the Areopagite than that of Gregory of Nyssa (d.ca.395), who, like many Muslim scholars, prohibited the use of analogical reasoning on the divine nature. See Jones, *A Genealogy of Marion's Philosophy of Religion*, 51–52.

[*nafy al-ʿilal*] from God. After negating the four classical Aristotelian forms of causality from God as al-Kindī did, Ibn Sīnā adds a section on the divine attributes. Here Ibn Sīnā presents a negative theology of divine attributes in a Muʿtazilite fashion by considering the essential attributes as negations, and all relational attributes as divine actions.[24] Divine names address Her essence as long as they are negations. Once they contain a positive relation, they become non-essential attributes that express divine actions instead of the essence. This is also the case even for "the necessary being," apparently the essential name of God: it is a negation as much as it addresses the divine essence, and it is a positive relation as much as it indicates God's being the cause of all. Hence "necessary being" is not a purely essential name but rather is a combination of an essential negation and a relational affirmation as a *connection* that articulates a *distinction*. The essence itself is utterly apophatic:

> We have proven that He is the necessary being, unique from all possible aspects, and unaffected by causes [*munazzah ʿan al-ʿilal*]; that He does not have any cause [*sabab*] in any respect. It is also proven that His attributes are not added to His ipseity. . . . His attributes operate (1) as negations [*salb*], (2) as relations [*iḍāfa*], (3) as a composition of negation and relation. . . . Thus their plurality does not violate His oneness or contradict His necessary being. Negative attributes mean negations, such as "eternity" [*qidam*], which negates non-existence. Or they mean the negation of causality [*nafy al-sababiyya*] or the negation of precedence [*nafy al-awwal ʿanhu thāniyan*] to Him. "One," for example, is a general expression for His indivisibility in any possible way—be it discursively or practically. Or when we say "necessary being" this means that He is there without any cause, while He is the cause of everything; so it is a conjunction [*jamʿ*] of a negation and a relation. As for relational

24. Ibn Sīnā, "al-Risāla al-ʿArshiyya." Also see Adamson, *Interpreting Avicenna: Critical Essays*, 173.

The sixth chapter of Abū Ḥāmid al-Ghazālī's *Incoherence of the Philosophers* [*Tahāfut al-Falāsifa*], devoted to the divine attributes, argues that philosophers in general agreed on a negative theology of divine attributes, but it explicitly mentions only Ibn Sīnā throughout the chapter. "The philosophers have agreed, just as the Muʿtazilites, on the impossibility of affirming knowledge, power, and will for the first principle. . . . They reduce [referentially] to one essence. . . . They all agreed on the negation of the attributes [*nafy al-ṣifāt*]." (Ibid., 96 [with my modifications and emphasis].)

> attributes, they are such as His being "creator," "producer," "shape-giver"—His all attributes of action [*ṣifāt al-afʿāl*].[25]

The famous eighth book of Ibn Sīnā's *Metaphysics of "The Healing"* supports this negative theology of divine attributes with an apophatic divine essence. The first three chapters serve to discursively demonstrate the existence of the first cause [*al-ʿilla al-ūlā*], "showing that what is absolutely a first cause is a cause for the rest of the causes."[26] The only essential attribute of God is Her necessary being, which, as a conjunction of a negation and a relation, means that She is the ultimate cause of all beings. The first principle is the necessary being and has no quiddity other than Her very existence. No applicable quiddity except being the ultimate cause means no possibility of essential description:

> There is no quiddity for the necessary being other than its being the necessary being. . . . Everything that has a quiddity other than being is caused. . . . The First, hence, has no quiddity. Those things possessing quiddities have existence emanating upon them from Him. He is pure being with the condition of negating privation and [negating] all other description of Him [*salb al-ʿadam wa sāʾir awṣāf*].[27]

Ibn Sīnā does not see a contradiction between demonstrating that God is the first cause as the unique necessary being, and arguing that God is essentially undefinable. It can be discursively proven that God is essentially One, the necessary being, and the cause of creation. As Mānakdīm (d.1034)

---

25. Ibn Sīnā, "al-Risāla al-ʿArshiyya," 247.

In ch.9, *Interpreting Avicenna: Critical Essays*, Peter Adamson considers necessary being as an essential name of God that cannot be reduced to a negation, a relation, or a combination of the two. Hence he argues that necessary being is not just a negation but also an affirmative ground from which Ibn Sīnā derives the traditional positive and essential attributes of God. Our interpretations differ, as I consider Ibn Sīnā's necessary being as a combination of an essential negation and a relation, rather than an essential negation and an essential affirmation. My reading is also guided by Ibn Sīnā's *al-Risāla al-ʿArshiyya* quoted above, while Adamson's reading focuses on his strategy in the *Metaphysics of "The Healing."*

26. Ibn Sīnā, *Metaphysics of "The Healing,"* 270 (with my minor modification).

27. Ibid., 276 (with my minor modification). In other words, we can describe [*waṣafa*] God only by "negating features of Him that would be shared in common [with something else], and affirming relations of Him." (Ibn Sīnā in Adamson, *Interpreting Avicenna: Critical Essays*, 174.)

observes, divine dissimilarity and absolvement is the first knowledge one attains through theoretical reflection [*naẓar*] and argumentation [*istidlāl*] according to Ibn Sīnā. But this is a "negative proof," as the divine essence is proven through a long list of negations, which place God beyond any discursive spaces. Once God's essential, ineffable oneness without a quiddity is established, negations follow each other. Ibn Sīnā gives a succinct conclusion at the end of the chapter. What takes center stage is an apophatic theology with an ineffable God beyond all discursive spaces, Her necessary dissimilarity to all, and a negative theology of divine attributes with a Muʿtazilite differentiation of the essential, negative names from the relational names of action. He writes:

> Since He is devoid of all matter and its adherents, and of corruption—both being a condition of that which falls under contrariety—the first has no contrary. It has become clear, then, *that the first has no genus, no quiddity, no quality, no quantity, no "where," no "when," no equal, no partner, and no contrary—may He be exalted and magnified—[and] that He has no definition and [there is] no demonstration for Him. Rather, He is the demonstration of all things. . . . He is only described by means of negating all similarities of Him [salb al-mushābahāt] and affirming to Him all relations [ījāb al-iḍāfāt]*. For all things are from Him, and He shares *nothing in common* with what [proceeds] from Him. He is the principle of all things, and He is not any of the things that are posterior to Him.[28]

Ibn Sīnā argues for each attribute separately; he does not have a single argument or a consistent way of deriving all divine attributes. Yet, at least the key attributes that we have considered are essentially negative, because the very proof of Her essence is a negation of all relations that have a claim on Her essence. In the next chapters of the *Metaphysics of "The Healing,"* following al-Fārābī, Ibn Sīnā claims that we can still employ an affirmative language, not in the sense of essential attributes of God but *eminently*, as the logical conclusion of Her being the source of perfections. "He is *perfect-above-perfection* [*tām bi-l-fawq al-tām*]; good, bestower [of existence] on everything after Him; truth and pure intellect."[29] These attributes do not cause

28. Ibn Sīnā, *Metaphysics of "The Healing,"* 282–283 (with my minor modification).

29. Ibid., 283 (with my modification).

any plurality in the essence, because they are not essential to God. Beyond Her necessary being, which is still a causal yet negative relation, nothing is essential to Her. Hence attributes can be employed positively or negatively as long as they apply metaphorically or indicate this negative proof through Her difference. "God is a substance" can be said in the sense of God's necessary being with the negation of subjecthood from God. "God is willing" without a goal or purpose for Her causal efficacy. "God is One" means negating all quantitative and categorical divisions as well as any companionship. "*'The one' is only in Him in a negative manner.*"[30] God can be called "intellect" [*ʿaql*], "intellecter" [*ʿāqil*] and "intelligible" [*maʿqūl*], but this means negating "the possibility of mixing with matter and its attachments," insofar as She is their ultimate cause. Similarly, as Ibn Sīnā explains in the *Celestial Epistle*, God's necessary being proves that She is also essentially "all-knowing" and "intellecting," but these names are negations that are reducible to each other and thus do not violate divine oneness. He writes:

> He is all-knowing, knowledge, and that which is known, without these attributes causing any plurality. There is no difference between "all-knowing" and "intellecting" because *they are both expressing an absolute negation from materiality [salb al-mādda muṭlaqan].*[31]

In brief, various attributes can be employed, but they do not affirm different meanings. Instead, they either express divine actions distinct from the divine essence, or negative attributes all reducible to God's apophatic essence—that is, Her being the cause of creation, and paradoxically, Her removal from the discursive space and Her absolute dissimilarity from what can be known.

Finally, the discursive proofs for God's necessary being or absolute oneness do not in fact access God's essence, because they are already mediated by the temporal processes of the embodied, rational soul that apply only to divisible objects of thought. Ibn Sīnā points to the elusive difference between our discursive conception of God's oneness and Her essential

---

30. Ibid., 299.

31. Ibn Sīnā, "al-Risāla al-ʿArshiyya," 247; Ibn Sīnā, *Metaphysics of "The Healing,"* 296; al-Fārābī, *Kitāb al-Wāḥid wa-l-Waḥda*, ch.1; Maimonides, *Dalālat al-Ḥāʾirīn*, 1.68; E. R. Wolfson, "Via Negativa in Maimonides and Its Impact on Thirteenth-Century Kabbalah," 423.

oneness itself. Accordingly, all positive and negative attributes of the divine union, in the end, boil down to

> nothing but (1) union, where "union" is an idea in the intelligence rather than in the essence, or (2) negation [*nafy*] and denial. *In so doing they do not imply the existence of many characteristics, but rather an omission of many characteristics.*[32]

Ibn Sīnā, thus, makes a distinction between (1) essential divine unity and (2) human thought and discourse about it. On the basis of this distinction the apophaticism and kataphaticism of the philosopher operate in fact in two different spaces, if analyzed more closely, especially with the backdrop of Plotinus. The *Enneads* made a distinction between *dianoia* and *noēsis*—that is, discursive thought and intellection. Not only al-Kindī's circle but also Ibn Sīnā knew the work well, through the partial translation, the *Theology of Aristotle*. He even wrote a commentary on it titled the *Impartial Judgment* [*al-Inṣāf*]. Ibn Sīnā generally follows the *Theology of Aristotle* in employing the Arabic term *fikr* for discursive thought, as a rough analog to *dianoia*. *Fikr* involves the process of dividing up [*tafṣīl*] concepts or intelligible forms that are simple, to be unified [*tartīb*] in the intellect. *Fikr* as theoretical reasoning belongs to the rational soul and entails a process of "division and combination," or "analysis and synthesis" [*al-taḥlīl wa-l-tarkīb*].[33] Therefore, discursive proofs actually do not address God's indivisible essence insofar as they are already mediated by the temporal processes of the embodied, rational soul. Theoretical reasoning not only necessitates mentally divisible objects but also yields information solely in relational terms. Ibn Taymiyya's observation on the nature of logical proof and logicians' own perspective on its limits captures precisely this point:

> as for the necessary being, blessed and exalted may He be, the syllogism does not prove what is characteristic of Him; rather, *it proves a universal matter common to Him as well as to others. According to the logicians, what is proven by categorical syllogism is nothing but a*

32. Netton, *Allah Transcendent*, 154 (original emphasis).

33. Ibn Sīnā, *Metaphysics of "The Healing,"* 291; Plotinus, *Enneads*, 5.8.5:254–255; Adamson, "Non-Discursive Thought in Avicenna's Commentary on the *Theology of Aristotle*." The distinction has been intensively discussed by Sorabji, Lloyd and others. See Alfino, "Plotinus and the Possibility of Non-Propositional Thought."

> *universal, common matter having no bearing upon the necessary being,* the lord of beings, may He be glorified and exalted. Therefore, *their demonstration does not lead them to any knowledge of a matter which must be constant*—whether it belongs to the necessary being or to possible beings.[34]

The subtle distinction between discursive thought and non-discursive intellection, a key and nuanced continuation of the tradition of Plotinus, has three significant implications for Arabic philosophical apophaticism. First, God's simple and direct knowledge of things is independent from relations with the particulars. God knows Herself, God knows universals, and God knows particulars, but it is not permitted to say that "God apprehends [*idrāk*] them" for Ibn Sīnā. In other words, "to call intellection 'knowledge' in this lower sense would be to damn intellect with faint praise."[35] The neglect for this admittedly elusive epistemological distinction would provoke the infamous criticism that Muslim philosophers denied God's knowledge of the particulars. Second, Ibn Sīnā does not follow Plotinus in separating the soul from the body and attaining the non-discursive knowledge of higher intellects. In terms of the relationship between the body and the soul, the Arabic version of Plotinus' *Enneads*, the *Theology of Aristotle* is more Aristotelian than the *Enneads* itself. In the same vein, Ibn Sīnā is closer to Aristotelianism in that the human intellect is inseparably embodied until death; even non-discursive rational knowledge can be expressed syllogistically for him. Ibn Sīnā does not accept a non-syllogistic knowledge of God, following al-Kindī, and diverging from Plotinus. Third, not only Ibn Sīnā's followers from diverse backgrounds, but even his most staunch opponents confirm that the discursive proofs

34. Ibn Taymiyya, *Against Greek Logicians*, 71 (with my minor modification; my emphasis).

Arguably Ibn Taymiyya's description is a great summary of the role of demonstrative syllogism among the philosophers even beyond the Islamicate world. Such syllogisms, according to Thomas Aquinas, whose negative theological position closely aligns itself with Ibn Sīnā and Maimonides, only loosely indicates divine unity, "having no bearing upon the necessary being," to borrow Ibn Taymiyya's words. For Thomas Aquinas a syllogistic proof of God "does no more than indicate that the conclusion is not utterly irrational. The syllogism here clarifies and to some extent makes intelligible, teases out the implicit, and really nothing more." (Janz, "Syllogism or Paradox: Aquinas and Luther on Theological Method," 12–13.)

35. Adamson, "Non-Discursive Thought in Avicenna's Commentary on the *Theology of Aristotle*," 101; Ibn Sīnā, *Metaphysics of "The Healing,"* 283; Abū Ḥāmid al-Ghazālī, *Incoherence of the Philosophers: Tahāfut al-Falāsifa*, ch.11, 125–130.

of philosophers for God's necessary being do not violate divine unknowability due to this distinction.[36]

To sum up, Ibn Sīnā's negative theology of the divine attributes, hermeneutics, and approach to syllogistic reasoning boil down to a negative theology of the divine essence. Along with the *Celestial Epistle*, his *Glosses* [*Taʿlīqāt*], "a *reportatio* of Ibn Sīnā's comments and clarifications" compiled by his pupil Bahmanyār ibn al-Marzubān (d.1066) presents probably the best summary of Ibn Sīnā's position on divine unknowability and the inapplicability of any attributes, including "being," due to Her necessary dissimilarity. He writes:

> *We do not know the true nature of the first. All we know of Him is that He must either be necessary being or not. This, however, is not His true essence but simply one of His concomitants,* and by means of it we come to know some of His other concomitants, such as unity and the other attributes.
>
> In fact, the closest we can come to grasping His true nature is by thinking of Him as being per se; or in other words, that which exists solely by virtue of itself. By describing Him thus, however, we are, all told, merely referring to something the true nature of which eludes us. The fact is that *His true essence cannot be the same as being* [*nafs al-wujūd*], nor can it be a quiddity properly so-called, since being is extrinsic to quiddities as such, whereas He is intrinsically the very cause of being. . . . His essence should be regarded as *beyond-being* [*fawq al-wujūd*], such that the latter would be merely one of its concomitants.[37]

In other words, discursive processes prove God to only be that which eludes proof. Hence the distinction between discursive thought and non-discursive intellection partially explains the Kindian dilemma of negative proof for the unknowable divine essence. In addition to his immediate students like Bāhmanyār, Fakhr al-Dīn al-Rāzī, and Naṣīr al-Dīn Ṭūsī, from whom the two competing commentary traditions on Ibn Sīnā developed, critics like Ibn Taymiyya, Sufis like Ṣadr al-Dīn Qūnavī, and inquisitive

36. Plotinus, *Enneads*, 4.8.1:396–397; Adamson, *The Arabic Plotinus*, ch.3, 87–138; Wisnovsky, "Avicenna and the Avicennian Tradition," 93; Ibn Sīnā, *Metaphysics of "The Healing,"* 298.

37. Ibn Sīnā in Todd, *Sufi Doctrine of Man*, 212–213 (my emphases and minor modifications).

theologians like al-Qāḍī al-Bayḍāwī (d.1286) among others all agreed on this point.

Protectors of the Divine Oneness: Al-Tawḥīdī's Circle in Baghdad

The Aristotelian adaptation of the Neoplatonic distinction between discursive thought and immediate, non-discursive intellection became a key but elusive aspect of Muslim philosophers' approach to God, necessary being, and divine oneness. The distinction provided them, on the one hand, with logical proof that God is essentially the absolute One and the source of all existence as the necessary being. On the other hand, they could evoke God's unknowability, unlike the Muʿtazilites and other theologians, who did not make such a distinction. Thus, an analysis of Ibn Sīnā in the light of the distinction between *dianoia* and *noēsis* can be expanded to cover other philosophers in Kindī's line, who even preceded Ibn Sīnā. Al-Kindī himself was conversant with the distinction, and he describes "thought" [*fikr*] as a "function of soul that falls short of pure intellection."[38] Ibn Miskawayh's *On the Soul and Intellect* also makes the evident distinction between human intellects and simple, pure intelligence [*ʿaql*]. The epistemological distinction was far from obvious, and the inconsistent application of *ʿaql* and *fikr* by the philosophers partially explains the accusations they encountered in metaphysics.

Still, between al-Fārābī and Ibn Sīnā, we clearly observe that philosophers employed the distinction in the service of apophaticism. Abū Sulaymān al-Sijistānī (d.ca.985), for example, follows the same distinction. His student Abū Ḥayyān al-Tawḥīdī's *Book of Delightful and Intimate Conversations* [*Kitāb al-Imtāʿ wa-l-Muʾānasa*] records a debate between the shopkeeper al-Jarīrī and Abū Sulaymān al-Maqdisī (d.985), a leading name of the Brethren of Purity. The debate serves for al-Sijistānī to claim that both philosophy and religion are true in their own ways and that they should not be confused or blended with each other. Meanwhile, al-Sijistānī adopts the philosophical distinction between discursive and non-discursive thought—that is, between *fikr* and *ʿaql*—which serves to discursively prove

38. Adamson, *al-Kindī*, 141. "Al-Kindī seems to be following the Arabic Plotinus texts, which also use *fikr* for discursive thought that is inferior to intellection—what Plotinus himself called *dianoia*." (Ibid., 142.) Cf. Ibn Miskawayh in Marcotte, *Ibn Miskawayh's Concept of the Intellect (ʿAql)*, 100–101.

God's existence and oneness and simultaneously negate all discursive access to Her essence. In a night session on divine unity [*tawḥīd*], al-Sijistānī claimed as follows:

> Whoever points to the divine essence solely via *the simple, pure intellect* [*ʿaql*], without the dissemblance of a name [*tawriya bi-ism*] or the opaqueness of a symbol, purified and sanctified, they are recognizing divine unity [*ḥaqq al-tawḥīd*] to the utmost human capacity. Thus they have affirmed [*ithbāt*] the divine essence [*inniyya*] and negated spatiality [*ayniyya*] and howness [*kayfiyya*], and *transcended all thought [fikr] and discursivity [rawiyya].*[39]

The divine essence eludes all discursive spaces, but its non-discursive, simple vision is syllogistically possible, as it is received directly and intellectually by the intellect. On the other hand, al-Sijistānī makes it clear that only the prophets can achieve this level. He sharply rejects the proposal for a hierarchy of prophetic and philosophical forms of certain [*qaṭʿī*] knowledge. Only prophets can acquire certain knowledge and achieve such simple, non-discursive, immediate access, even if it is directed toward the active intellect and not to the divine essence itself. Compared to philosophical intellection, philosophers "engage in reasoned inquiries with their different intellects," and they can never attain the certainty that prophetic revelation brings. "Reason is a gift from God," submits al-Sijistānī, but it does not have the *immediacy* and *simplicity* of revelation. Thus God's necessary existence and unity can be discursively proven, while the discursive access to Her essence as well as the applicability of all attributes are simultaneously negated on the basis of the limitations of discursive thought. The theological speculation on God's essence negates itself at all discursive and non-discursive levels in favor of an apophatic divine essence. In al-Sijistānī's words, "Blessed is the one who says: 'if you want to describe [*waṣf*] it [i.e., the divine unity], it will be completely destroyed. If you try to deny [*juḥūd*] it, it will become most clear and manifest!' "[40]

Al-Sijistānī follows al-Kindī and Ibn Sīnā in negating the applicability of attributes to God in favor of Her absolute dissimilarity, hence, transcendence. Language can be employed either metaphorically or as a

39. Abū Sulaymān al-Sijistānī in al-Tawḥīdī, *al-Muqābasāt*, 259.

40. Abū Sulaymān al-Sijistānī in ibid., 259; Griffel and Hachmeier, "Prophets as Physicians of the Soul," 240–241.

negation. In an illustrative example, al-Tawḥīdī in private respectfully criticizes the kataphatic language that his master al-Sijistānī employed earlier in a heated session on astrology. Al-Sijistānī's response, which will be soon echoed in works of al-Baṭalyawsī and Moses Maimonides among others, emphasizes to his student that divine transcendence

> *annuls* [*yamḥaq*], *removes, rejects, and negates all of them.* However, when addressing Him, pointing to Him, naming His lordship [*rubūbiyya*], or explaining His godhead [*ilāhiyya*], there is no escape from these words. . . . But these words are *employed metaphorically, protecting the divine oneness and forbidding knowledge* [*mustaʿāran fī ḥimā al-tawḥīd wa ḥaram al-maʿrifa*].[41]

On other occasions as well, al-Sijistānī makes it clear that the qualified attributes apply to God only metaphorically, on the basis of customs or linguistic conventions, but in reality, these attributes only negate Her similarity or relationality with creation. For example, we customarily say that "God is agent," which in fact has the negative meaning of being "not acted upon" [*lā munfaʿāl*].[42] God's unity and existence are discursively proven, while the discursive or non-discursive accessibility of the divine essence is negated together with the applicability of the divine names and attributes.

Originally from a small town in Hamadan, Abū al-Fatḥ al-Nūshajānī from Abū Ḥayyān's circle was another known philosopher of the time, at least in Baghdad. Like other philosophers, he explicitly makes the distinction between discursive thought and non-discursive intellection. Accordingly, the divine essence is beyond the discursive field, because it is beyond simplicity—and thus, inaccessible through the processes of analysis and synthesis that discourse undergoes. Recalling the distinction between *dianoia* and *noēsis*, al-Nūshajānī argues that "the Producer is the real and the first, and the source of everything. They emanate from Him, and proliferate from Him, not through *discursive determination, which is formed by division and combination* [*faṣlan wa waṣlan*]."[43] The reason of God's transcendence of the discursive space is that He is "the first agent

41. Al-Tawḥīdī, *al-Muqābasāt*, 137. Cf. Maimonides, *Dalālat al-Ḥāʾirīn*, 1.59.

42. See al-Tawḥīdī, *al-Muqābasāt*, 149–151.

43. Ibid., 196. In his debate with Abū Sulaymān al-Maqdisī of the Brethren of Purity, al-Jarīrī cites al-Nūshajānī among the interconfessional group of philosophers. See al-Jarīrī in Griffel and Hachmeier, "Prophets as Physicians of the Soul," 244–245.

[*al-fāʿil al-awwal*], the cause [*ʿilla*] of everything visible, existing, intellected, and perceived. *His actions have no target, no purpose, no aim, no choice, no thought, no orientation, no decision, no interest, no direction, no experimentation, and no effort.*"[44] All of these negations serve to underline that the cause of all discursive spaces is necessarily beyond those spaces. All of these attributes are anthropomorphic constructs, and they indicate a deficiency from which She is far removed. In other words, positive attributes can operate only as similes [*mithl*], while their real meaning is decidedly negative. In al-Nūshajānī's words:

> *All forms, definitions in the language, and relations are negated from the realm of the divine.* However, they are symbols that stimulate the soul, and words that approximate to truth. They all transport their audience to what is beyond them [*mā warāʾ*]. The more complete and beautiful these symbols, and the more powerful and clear the words, the more subtle the stimulation.[45]

In brief, philosophers in Abū Ḥayyān's circle continue the distinction between divine revelation and philosophical reasoning. The former is not discursive, in the sense that it is directly and simply manifesting the divine will. It does not go through division or combination—a binary process that determines human thought. It is rather an immediate knowledge, with total adequacy and perfect clarity, of the active intellect, and not God. Reasoning cannot access the divine essence, while revelation—the way in which intellect unites non-discursively with the divine essence as the active intellect—is itself inaccessible in the post-prophetic age. The discourse on divine essence negates itself as God remains essentially unknowable.

To sum up, throughout the two centuries from al-Kindī to Ibn Sīnā, Muslim philosophers active in Iraq and Iran adopted a variety of theological positions on the divine essence and its accessibility. The strategic resemblances, referential continuities, and networks among these positions make it justifiable to talk about a tradition of "philosophical apophaticism" on the divine essence. Muslim philosophers since al-Kindī onward

---

"Nūshajān" should be a town around the hill of Nūsh-i Jān close to Hamadan. See Stronach et.al., "Excavations at Tepe Nush-i Jan."

44. Al-Tawḥīdī, *al-Muqābasāt*, 83. Here al-Nūshajānī resonates with Ibn Sīnā, who claimed in the *Metaphysics of "The Healing"* that God is willing without a goal or purpose.

45. Ibid., 196.

developed a peculiar apophatic theology of the divine nature—that is, a theological discourse that negates itself by employing the very tools of the discourse. The characteristics of this negative theology of the divine essence can be outlined as follows:

(1) God is necessarily dissimilar to creation, insofar as the cause must be dissimilar to the caused. God is essentially beyond discursive possibilities because of this decisive distinction between the cause and the caused, or the creator and the created.
(2) Due to the necessary distinction between God and anything that humans can know or imagine, philosophers are strong defenders of God's dissimilarity and transcendence [*tanzīh*], and bitter opponents of *tashbīh*—God's comparability to, and immanence in, creation. In line with this emphasis on divine transcendence, philosophers follow a negative theology of the divine attributes.
(3) A philosophical hermeneutics that, in Abū Sulaymān al-Sijistānī's words, "protects the divine oneness" is central to this theological approach. Not only Qur'anic verses and prophetic reports with corporeal implications but all attributes undergo a hermeneutical process lest they violate the absolute oneness and the necessary dissimilarity of the divine. This hermeneutics can contain (a) an active interpretation of the sacred sources, especially when they appear to address God anthropomorphically, (b) following via eminentiae, by distinguishing how an attribute appears present in creation and how it truly applies to God, and (c) claiming homonymy, arguing that terms are employed homonymously when applied to God and creation.
(4) The indivisible unity of God cannot be accessed discursively, but non-discursive paths, both mystical and philosophical, are also closed in the apophatic versions. Philosophers present discursive arguments to prove that God is the absolute one and the necessary being, from which creation emanates. Theological speculation on God's essence negates itself: theology leads to the demonstrative realization that God *is*, but only through a negative proof.[46] God's essence remains unknowable to theological discourse and non-discourse. Positive

46. In Muḥammad Iqbal's (d.1938) unfriendly words, the argument of philosophers "really tries to reach the infinite by merely negating the finite." (Iqbal, *Reconstruction of Religious Thought in Islam*, 23.)

theological discourse on the divine essence cancels itself, realizing the unknowability and inaccessibility of its excessive subject and, hence, its own incapacity.

Philosophical Apophaticism in Andalusia: Ibn Masarra

The key aspects of the philosophical apophatic tradition had already been set by the time of al-Kindī within a Muʿtazilite-dominated context, later to take different forms among philosophers, while preserving a shared vocabulary, hermeneutics, and theology. Still, it was not only philosophers who followed this form of apophaticism even in its early stage. The enigmatic, ascetic mystic and intellectual of Cordova, Ibn Masarra adopted it as well.

Ibn Masarra explains divine unknowability through the symbolism of letters. The divine essence is veiled behind the name "God," in the same way that the first letter of the alphabet and of the name "God" [Allāh], "A" [*alif*] is hidden by the long, wall-like letter "L" [*lām*], from which it stands decidedly disjointed, unlike most Arabic letters. Hence all divine attributes operate as veils separating God from creation, with the very name "God" acting as "the first veil and the concealed hiddenness" for Ibn Masarra. His *Epistle of Contemplation* is bold in defense of divine unknowability:

> Since the lofty and great One transcends direct contact with the limited, it also transcends resemblance to the limited and similitude with it. Therefore it is necessary that His encompassing should be above all encompassing, and His loftiness above all loftiness. He thus goes beyond the boundaries of imaginings, for the imaginings are the intellects, which resemble things that take the image of the models. The intellects are limited; the limited cannot contain or encompass whatever is above it, what does not correspond to it, what is loftier than it, or what contains it. . . . This implies necessarily that the lofty One has no similitude; He has no end; He has no beginning; He has no parts; and He has no limit, nor does [any of it] enter into His oneness and greatness. The supreme king transcends the entire species and is above it, except by means of the proofs which

give indication of Him and the traces which He imprinted in His creation, bearing witness to His lordship.[47]

Moreover, the unknowability of the divine ipseity in Ibn Masarra follows the paradox of philosophical apophaticism: negation of all imaginable attributes and God's dissimilarity are logical results of Her being the creator:

> *He has no partner, nothing is like His likeness* [Q.42:11]. He is greater than all things and He is the one who encompasses everything. The regions of the earth do not contain nor encompass Him. *Eyes do not perceive Him* [Q.6:103], for He has neither end nor beginning. He is the first, prior to everything that has limit and end. Everything but Him is created, restricted and hence disjoint.[48]

Ibn Masarra's unknowability of the divine essence seems to be supported by a negative theology of divine attributes. Among others, the intellectual historian al-Qifṭī defines Ibn Masarra as an "Esoteric" [Bāṭinī], and mentions of him as a follower of Empedocles. For al-Qifṭī, Empedocles was famous for being "the first to argue for the unity [*jamʿ*] of the attributes of God. All of them address one reality. The attributes of 'knowledge,' 'benevolence,' and 'power,' do not carry meanings specific to these different names. Instead, *they are of one reality*."[49] In his biography of sages, the Ishrāqī philosopher and historian Shams al-Dīn al-Shahrazūrī repeats the idea, and embeds a similar account of Ibn Masarra in a section on Empedocles. Al-Shahrazūrī depicts Empedocles in distinctly Sufi terms, and ascribes him ideas that also bear the signs of Ismāʿīlism, along with a negative theology of divine attributes as well as the necessary dissimilarity of God:

> Empedocles said: "Only the transcendent producer's He-ness is End-less [*Lam Yazal huwiyyatihi*]. He is knowledge essentialized

---

47. Ibn Masarra in Stroumsa and Sviri, "The Beginnings of Mystical Philosophy in al-Andalus," 223 (with my minor modification). For the Arabic text itself, see Ibn Masarra in Morris, *Ibn Masarra: A Reconsideration of Primary Sources*, 256. See also Ibn Masarra in Ebstein, *Mysticism and Philosophy in al-Andalus*, 86–87.

48. Ibn Masarra in Stroumsa and Sviri, "The Beginnings of Mystical Philosophy in al-Andalus," 224. For the Arabic text itself, see Ibn Masarra in Morris, *Ibn Masarra: A Reconsideration of Primary Sources*, 257–258.

49. Al-Qifṭī, *Taʾrīkh al-Ḥukamāʾ*, 16.

[*al-ʿilm al-mulkhaṣ*], pure will [*al-irāda al-maḥḍa*], generosity, majesty, power, justice, goodness, and reality, without these names bearing any power. Rather, they are He [*hiya huwa*], and He is simply all these creative attributes, not that He created from something, or co-existed with something. He originated the simple, which is the first of the simple intelligibles [*awwal al-basāʾiṭ al-maʿqūla*], I mean, the first element [*al-ʿunṣur al-awwal*]. Then, from that simple and single origination [*al-mabdaʿ al-basīṭ al-wāḥid*], elementary things [*al-ashyāʾ al-mabsūṭa*] were generated. Then the compounds were created from the elementaries. He is the originator of opposites and contraries, intelligible, imaginative or sensuous." . . .

Ibn Masarra al-Jabalī, the Esoteric, who came from Cordova, was fond of his [Empedocles'] philosophy and intent on its study. He was in general a great man, of high distinguished standing, dedicated to self-disciplinary practice [*al-riyāḍa*], deiformity [*taʾalluh*] and frugality, who abandoned the world and turned to the hereafter. He excelled in the knowledge of the soul and immaterial entities, their natures and order. I saw a book of his on philosophy, which reveals his mystical inclination, his powerful character and his preeminence in the metaphysical science and its wisdom.

He [Empedocles] was the first to argue for the unity of the meanings of God's attributes, and the fact that they all denote a single thing, rather than distinct meanings pertaining to each of these different attributes. For, He is truly the One in whom there is no plurality whatsoever, contrary to all other existing entities [bi-khilāf bāqiyy al-ashyāʾ]. For, the higher unities are susceptible of plurality, either in their parts, their meanings or their analogues. By contrast, the ipseity of the almighty and transcendent producer transcends all of this.

This idea is also expressed in the words of ʿAlī ibn Abī Ṭālib, may God be pleased with him, al-Ḥasan al-Baṣrī [d.728], a group of the Muʿtazilites and the majority of the Philosophers [Ḥukamāʾ].[50]

---

50. Shams al-Dīn al-Shahrazūrī, *Nuzhat al-Arwāḥ*, 83–84; Abrahamov, *Ibn al-ʿArabī and the Sufis*, 101. For an alternative translation by Majid Fakhry, see al-Shahrazūrī, "Excursion of Spirits and Garden of Delights (from *Nuzhat al-Arwāḥ wa Rawḍat al-Afrāḥ*)," 63–64. This translation, however, confuses Empedocles with Ibn Masarra. The section mentioning Empedocles becomes an account on Ibn Masarra in Fakhry's rendering.

Among these Muʿtazilites, al-Qifṭī specifically named Abū al-Hudhayl (d.841), who was famous for depicting different divine attributes as negations [*nafy*] of different imperfections that indicate a single meaning. It was exactly this negative theology of divine attributes that Abū al-Hudhayl borrowed from Aristotle, according to al-Ashʿarī.[51] Such a philosophical negative theology of divine attributes and an unknowable God, who is necessarily dissimilar to everything, was evidently associated with Ibn Masarra. His extant writings support this philosophical apophaticism with a hermeneutics that protects the absolute oneness from any positive attribute. He argues that the Qurʾanic verse that addresses "the throne of God," for example, should be interpreted as the prime matter from which the universe is created.

An ascetic intellectual who used to retreat to the mountains with his companions, Ibn Masarra presents an early mystical adoption of philosophical apophaticism. Andalusian historians as early as al-Ḥumaydī (d.1095) began associating Ibn Masarra with Sufism. Recent studies have underlined the probable influence of Ismāʿīlism on Ibn Masarra and also questioned whether Ibn Masarra can be properly called a "Sufi" or not.[52] While it is difficult to apply the term "Sufi" to Ibn Masarra or to the indigenous tradition of the Contemplators [Muʿtabirūn] in Andalusia, the later Andalusian Sufism flourishing at the end of the twelfth century adopted his views, including aspects of philosophical apophaticism. Ibn al-Marʾa (d.1214), a Sufi master of Ibn Sabʿīn and a commentator on Ibn al-ʿArīf (d.1140), preserves a section from Ibn Masarra's lost book on divine attributes, the *Certain Profession of the Divine Oneness* [*Tawḥīd al-Muqīnīn*]. The passage expresses a philosophical negative theology of divine attributes. Accordingly, the divine attributes are infinite, but they have a unity in meaning, which does not violate the ineffable divine oneness. Ibn al-ʿArabī not only praises Ibn al-Marʾa as "one of the greatest members of the [Sufi] path in terms of knowledge, spiritual state [*ḥāl*] and visionary power [*kashf*]" in his *Meccan Openings* [*al-Futūḥāt al-Makkiyya*] but also adopts similar theological positions on diverse topics including the hermeneutics of the "throne verse." Indeed, the context in which Ibn al-ʿArabī cites

---

51. Al-Qifṭī, *Taʾrīkh al-Ḥukamāʾ*, 16; al-Ashʿarī, *Maqālāt al-Islāmiyyin*, 1:225; 2:158.

52. His letter mysticism, for example, seems more directly related with Ismāʿīlism, even if it evidently associates itself with the Basran Sufi master Sahl al-Tustarī (d.896). See Ebstein, *Mysticism and Philosophy in al-Andalus*, 89–90; Morris, *Ibn Masarra: A Reconsideration of Primary Sources*, 22.

Ibn Masarra is also quite apophatic. In this section devoted to "knowledge of the station of the transcendence of divine unity" [*maʿrifat manzil tanzīhiyya al-tawḥīd*], Ibn al-ʿArabī makes the philosophical argument that God's transcendence entails Her exemption from all possible human definitions, attributions, and traits, including Her very unity. Hence, "*We can say nothing about the word 'unity' when applied to God.*" God is made free of any description through the word "unity"; in other words, "oneness" cannot qualify God if God is to be One. Divine unity is like a house that has no door, says Ibn al-ʿArabī; no one can enter this house, but some can merely peek inside via divine unveiling.[53]

Ibn Masarra's relationship with the Sufis of his time was not always friendly. Still, from the late eleventh century onward, we witness a continuous mystical tradition of study of Ibn Masarra's work in Andalusia. Sufism, once institutionalized in Andalusia, would reclaim this heritage. Philosophical apophaticism is a key component of this re-interpreted Sufi heritage. On the other hand, the main avenue by which philosophical apophaticism was transmitted to thirteenth-century Sufism was an internal transformation of philosophy itself in Andalusia.

Twelfth-Century Andalusia: From Philosophy to Sufism

Ibn Bājja's (d.1139) discussion on "one," like that of al-Kindī and al-Fārābī, explores all possible uses and applications of the term; yet it is silent about how it relates to, or describes God. His approach to the divine essence is close to that of Ibn Sīnā and al-Fārābī even if he is self-consciously more Aristotelian than his predecessors. Ibn Bājja argues that knowledge is a relation [*niṣba*] that correlates (1) to the quiddity [*mā huwa*], (2) to the particular essential qualities [*ʿilm lawāḥiqa al-dhātiyya al-khāṣṣa*], (3) or to the general essential qualities [*ʿilm lawāḥiqa al-dhātiyya al-ʿāmma*] of its object. The last one can be called "knowledge" only metaphorically, while knowledge of the quiddity, or the essence, deserves the priority. In each of these cases, notes Ibn Bājja, knowledge can be perfected only by attaining that which the definition of its object indicates. One should know the requirements of the definition of something in order to know what it is. The

53. See Abrahamov, *Ibn al-ʿArabī and the Sufis*, 100; Morris, *Ibn Masarra: A Reconsideration of Primary Sources*, 23.

definition, on the other hand, can be attained in three ways: "As explained in the *Posterior Analytics* there are three methods for the derivation of a definition: (1) the method of *division,* (2) the method of *composition,* and (3) the method in which *syllogism* is employed."[54]

Discursive thinking, with the *division* and *composition* it entails, cannot access divine oneness according to Ibn Bājja. Absolute oneness cannot be defined, or known, by these processes. Instead of discourse, it is non-discursive intellection that unites the elect few to the Active Intellect, "the second god, who is thought-thinking-itself." The highest knowledge that human intellect can attain, and even embody, is the active intellect, "represented not indeed as God, the One, the first mover, or any aspect of deity, but as an emanation of deity, ranking immediately below the separate intelligences which move the spheres. These higher forms are entirely beyond the comprehension of man in the sublunary sphere." This non-discursive, perfect knowledge of the active intellect is attained by philosophers, prophets and the elect. "[It] belongs to the category of particular spiritual forms, which do not pass through the common sense, but are received directly from the active intellect."[55] It is freed from conceptual intermediaries, and unites with the active intellect, unlike discursive thought. Ibn Bājja employs Plato's *Allegory of the Cave* to describe this epistemological difference. Accordingly, discursive knowledge "sees the intelligible but through an intermediary, just as the sun appears in the water." Non-discursive intellection is the highest rank:

> [Intellection] is the rank of the happy *who see the thing in itself*. . . . The [discursive] theorists step outside of the cave and so see light separated from colors and see all the colors according to their true nature. There is no equivalent in [the example of] seeing for the happy, since *they themselves become the thing.*[56]

Ibn Bājja adds here a higher level to Plato's famous vindication of philosophical discursive thought. Plato's philosopher attained the knowledge of

54. Ibn Bājja, *ʿIlm al-Nafs*, 22–23. For his discussion on "one," see Ibn Bājja, "Conjunction of the Intellect with Man," 269–270.

55. Montada, "Philosophy in Andalusia: Ibn Bājja and Ibn Ṭufayl," 163 (with my minor modification); Ibn Bājja in Ziyadah, *Ibn Bājja's Book: Tadbīr al-Mutawaḥḥid*, 74–75; Dunlop, "Ibn Badjdja."

56. Ibn Bājja, "Conjunction of the Intellect with Man," 279.

the active intellect discursively, after leaving the cave. For the elect, adds Ibn Bājja, an immediate, non-discursive conception of the active intellect is possible. This pure intellection of the active intellect means *becoming* it. The reason is obvious: the intellect [*ʿaql*], intellecter [*ʿāqil*], and intelligible [*maʿqūl*] cannot be different as there is no room for potentiality in the active intellect.[57]

The fact that non-discursive knowledge is received by "an infusion of a light which God casts into the heart of His elect" brings to the fore the issues of mysticism and Sufism that Ibn Bājja discusses in various works. Similar to the case in Ibn Sīnā, non-discursive intellection is still syllogistic, and not "mystical" in Neoplatonic terms, insofar as Ibn Bājja does not believe that body and soul can be separated before death. Nor does non-discursivity confirm a Sufi visionary union. Rather, Ibn Bājja is critical of some Sufi claims for a non-discursive, non-syllogistic, mystical union with God. His challenge toward Sufism shows familiarity with Abū Ḥāmid al-Ghazālī's famous autobiography *Deliverance from Error* [*al-Munqidh min al-Ḍalāl*]:

> [Sufis] used to say in their prayers "May God unite you and assign your unity" because, by falling short of the pure spiritual forms, they consider the previous spiritual forms instead of the pure one. . . . Al-Ghazālī says that he has attained high spiritual experience and that he has witnessed the spiritual substances. . . . That is why the Sufis claim that attainment of the ultimate happiness may occur without learning, but rather through devotion and dedication of one self to the continual remembrance of God. . . . All this is a matter of opinion. The effect of what the Sufis thought is unnatural phenomena. The end which they thought to be the ultimate end, if it were to be a true one and an end for the solitary man, then it should be obtained essentially and not accidentally, but it is in fact obtained accidentally (here) and not essentially. This means that the most honorable part of man is an appendage which has no role to play.[58]

57. Montada, "Philosophy in Andalusia: Ibn Bājja and Ibn Ṭufayl," 156. Ibn Khāqān (d.1134) denounces Ibn Bājja for stripping God of His attributes [*taʿṭīl*] which has strong political motivations according to the biographer Ibn Khallikān (d.1282). See Ibn Khallikān, *Kitāb Wafayāt al-Aʿyān*, 4.670: 429–431. For an English translation see Ibn Khallikān, *Biographical Dictionary*, 3:130–132.

58. Ibn Bājja in Ziyadah, *Ibn Bājja's Book: Tadbīr al-Mutawaḥḥid*, 79–80 (with my minor modification).

Ibn Bājja is claiming that Sufis mistake the particular spiritual visions that they acquire via Sufi practices for the universal forms that one can acquire only via pure intellection. They confuse non-discursive *intellection* with their own non-discursive *reflection*, wherein sense perception, imagination, and memory, and hence discursivity, are still active. Therefore, Sufis can attain union only accidentally, only for an instant, and without actually understanding its real noetic quality. Moreover, as opposed to their conviction otherwise, the union that Sufis can attain is in fact not with God but with the active intellect beyond which the human intellect cannot go.[59]

Ibn Bājja's critique of the Sufis, including the prominent Abū Ḥāmid al-Ghazālī, indicates that at least a strand of Sufism was seen to violate the incomprehensibility, unknowability, and inaccessibility of God, mistakenly assuming that their non-discursive mysticism was able to connect them with God Herself. Ibn Sīnā's non-discursive but intellectual union with the active intellect was easy to transform into a non-discursive and mystical union with God, especially once the elusive difference between *dianoia* and *noēsis* is overlooked. Ḥayy ibn Yaqẓān, Ibn Ṭufayl's (d.1185) *theologus autodidactus*, has such a Neoplatonic, non-discursive union [*wuṣūl*] with the active intellect that, unlike al-Fārābī and Ibn Bājja, displays a distinctly Sufi character. It not only overlooks the distinction between God and active intellect—that is, "the second god,"—but it also entails a non-discursive union that is not syllogistic and is safely mystical.

Ibn Yaqẓān's philosophical tale is a vast theological manifesto. The philosophical proof for God comes through the observation of creation and from discursive thinking. God as the necessary being is the cause of all things and necessarily dissimilar from them. Discursive thought indicates that the cause of all perfections should be devoid of any privation but that all attributes of perfection apply to Her eminently. Hence, Ibn Yaqẓān realizes that

> all belong to Him, and are more *truly* predicated of Him . . . [His] essence is necessary being, Who gives being to all that is. There is no being [*wujūd*] but Him. He is being, perfection and wholeness. He is goodness, beauty, power, and knowledge. He is He.[60]

---

59. Ibn Bājja, "Conjunction of the Intellect with Man," 282; Montada, "Philosophy in Andalusia: Ibn Bājja and Ibn Ṭufayl," 163. My reading is closer to Ziyadah and others, and differs from that of Majid Fakhry. Cf. Fakhry, *A History of Islamic Philosophy*, 273.

60. Ibn Ṭufayl, *Ibn Ṭufayl's Ḥayy ibn Yaqẓān*, 134.

Following al-Fārābī, Ibn Ṭufayl now applies all classical theological attributes to God by indicating that the necessary being is the cause of everything. This causality not only makes all perfections applicable to God but also entails a negative move beyond them, pushing God "beyond perfection," via eminentiae: "The existence of the noncorporeal Author of the universe remained unscathed: He is neither connected to nor separated from matter; neither within nor outside it—for 'connection' and 'separation,' 'inside' and 'outside' are merely attributes of physical things; and He transcends them all."[61]

Worldly attributes are created, and their creator must be eminently beyond them. The attributes of creation cannot be applied to God literally, but only via eminentiae—thus, homonymously. God does not have negative attributes; in Her decisive dissimilarity, She can rather be approached by negating worldly qualities. Ibn Yaqẓān's entire discursive process of the realization of the divine eminence is based on emulating the higher, positive qualities in creation, from which its ultimate cause is independent. Echoing Plotinus and Ibn Sīnā, Ibn Ṭufayl underlines that all of these discursive demonstrations are bound up with human thought and are decisively situated within the realm of "*separation and union, aggregation and distinction, agreement and difference.*" Discursive thought's limits are still drawn in Neoplatonic terms, and it follows the Arabic philosophical tradition. Ibn Yaqẓān's non-discursive level of union, however, is distinctly Sufi, as the terms he employs, "dying to oneself," "ecstasy" [*wajd*], and "witnessing," betray:

> Ḥayy made a concerted effort to purge his awareness-of-the-truth, die to himself. At last it came. From memory and mind all disappeared, . . . all forms of the spirit and powers of the body, even the disembodied powers . . . And with the rest vanished the identity that was himself. Everything melted away, dissolved . . . Not knowing how to speak did not prevent him from understanding. Drowned in ecstasy he witnessed "what no eye has seen or ear heard, nor has it entered into the heart of man of conscience."[62]

---

61. Ibid., 133.

62. Ibid., 148–149 (with my minor modification). For the depiction of Ḥayy as a Sufi saint [*walī*], see Ibn Ṭufayl, *Ibn Ṭufayl's Ḥayy ibn Yaqẓān*, 160. Cf. Q.56:6; 15:85; 78: 37.

Now, the non-discursive union that Ibn Yaqẓān attains follows that of Plotinus and diverges from the Muslim philosophers. First, it presupposes a total separation of the soul from the body via purification and self-abnegation. Second, the experience has a noetic content that is temporary, ineffable, and nonsyllogistic.[63] Third, these two moves toward mysticism accompany a clear turn to the Sufi vocabulary. In contrast to earlier philosophers, Ibn Ṭufayl's conception of mystical divine union follows Plotinus and adopts a Sufi vocabulary of non-discursive access to divine unity. But it also diverges from Plotinus as the latter's long-standing distinction between active intellect and God the apophatic One has disappeared in Ibn Ṭufayl's account. The discursively proven, but still unknown, God of philosophers turns into a God that can be non-discursively accessed by Sufi vision—and loses some of its key philosophical apophatic dimensions. In short, Ibn Ṭufayl's approach perfectly fits into the position that Ibn Bājja's critique attributed to Sufis.

Within the context of apophaticism on the divine essence, in other words, the relationship between Neoplatonism and Muslim philosophers is a complex one. Yet it is clear that there are serious problems in the associations of apophaticism with Neoplatonism, and in the widespread assumption that medieval monotheistic traditions became apophatic to the extent that they accommodated Neoplatonism. In the case of philosophical apophaticism, the development was quite the opposite of these associations. The non-discursive intellection of philosophical apophaticism in al-Kindī, al-Fārābī, Ibn Sīnā, and others was not properly "mystical" but also syllogistic, and the human visionary quests were limited with an emphasis on the inseparability of the body from the soul before death. Sufis were more inclined to associate non-discursive thought with mystical and visionary experience that cannot be expressed in syllogistic form at all. For them, vision [*kashf*] and experience [*dhawq*] form an independent epistemological source in addition (and superior) to reasoning.

---

63. "Now do not set your heart on a description of what has never been represented in human heart. For many things that are articulate in the heart cannot be described. How can I formularize something that cannot possibly be projected in the heart, belonging to a different world, a different order of being?" (Ibid., 149.)

Aristotle in Andalusia: al-Baṭalyawsī, Maimonides, and Ibn Sab^c^īn

The controversial Andalusian Sufi Ibn Sabʿīn claims to be the greatest expert on philosophical matters and questions. While hubris plays an evident role in his *Sicilian Questions*, the work is well-informed by major philosophical works. The *Epistles* of the Brethren of Purity, al-Fārābī's *Philosophy of Aristotle*, Abū Ḥāmid al-Ghazālī's *Purposes of the Philosophers* [*Maqāṣid al-Falāsifa*], Ibn Sīnā's *Book of Definitions* [*Kitāb al-Ḥudūd*], Ibn Bājja's *Book of Soul*, al-Baṭalyawsī's *Book of Gardens*, and various works of Ibn Rushd were among the visible firsthand philosophical sources for Ibn Sabʿīn's *Sicilian Questions*. Ibn Sabʿīn also evokes ancient philosophers in order to demonstrate his philosophical prowess and to support his theological positions. Among the four questions that he deeply engages, the one on the aims of metaphysics and its necessary premises [*muqaddamāt al-ḍarūriyya*] is key for understanding his conception of the divine essence and its apophatic dimensions. God is utterly unknowable, and Ibn Sabʿīn dismisses accusations of advocating access to the divine essence and an essential union with God, with the support of the Greek philosophers. Accordingly, Aristotle had argued that demonstrating something entails showing its causes [*ʿilal*], principles [*mabādīʾ*] and origin [*al-awwal*]. As none of these can be attributed to God, assumptions about the individual uniting with God are misplaced, as they allege to know the necessarily unknowable. Human incapability [*ʿajz*] to know God is a major theme that repeats itself throughout the *Sicilian Questions*:

> The person who supposes that he has connected with the first, supreme, unified [*mutawaḥḥida*] cause, and that he has been substantialized by Her [*yatajawhar bihā*] has in fact transgressed the limits of understanding. . . . Whoever says that he knows the essence of the first truth—transcendent as He is—has transgressed the limits of understanding [*fahm*].[64]

This position is very much in line with Ibn Bājja's critique of the supposedly experiential access to the divine essence. On the unknowability of the

64. Ibn Sabʿīn, *al-Kalām ʿalā al-Masāʾil al-Ṣiqilliyya*, 38.

first cause, Socrates and Plato were in agreement with Aristotle, according to Ibn Sabʿīn. He writes:

> The first, incomparable truth is transcendent; nothing precedes His being. But you are under the universals, and the universals are prior to you. On this point, Plato, the saved one, stated the following: "the inability [*ʿajz*] in [knowing] the essence of the first truth is essential [*bi-l-dhāt*] to us. For, we are relational [*maḥmūl*], caused [*muʿallal*] and subject to synthesis [*muʾallaf*]."[65]

The insistent depiction of Aristotle by al-ʿĀmirī, Ibn Sabʿīn, al-Qifṭī, and al-Shahrazūrī as a negative theologian per se reflects the popular Arabic texts and their Latin translations attributed to Aristotle. Al-Mubashshir Ibn Fātik's (d.ca.1087) influential compilation of maxims attributed to Aristotle titled the *Choicest Maxims and Best Sayings* [*Mukhtār al-Ḥikam wa Maḥāsin al-Kalim*] describes Aristotle as a powerful champion of negative theology of the divine attributes as well as the divine essence. The *Choicest Maxims* contains only a couple of sayings that address the nature of the divine, but they consistently buttress the key themes of philosophical apophaticism. The first one underlines the unknowable nature of God, the ineffability of Her praise, the impotence of the human faculties of estimation, reason, or imagination before Her transcendence, and the incapacity of language in Her description:

> "Praise to God who precedes how-ness and substance; and transcends all presences, definitions, and descriptions. . . . All praises of Him are inferior, all analogies [*qiyāsāt*] to His transcendence are vile. He is more elevated than all estimations, and loftier than all that which is praised."[66]

The second maxim attributed to Aristotle supplies this divine unknowability and ineffability with a negative theology of the divine attributes:

> Reasoning on God is difficult, and speaking [*tanṭiq*] of Him is not possible. *An affirmative discourse [al-khabar al-mawjib] is not applicable to Him, but it is applicable to anything but Him.* For example,

65. Ibid., 38.

66. Aristotle in Ibn Fātik, *Mukhtār al-Ḥikam*, 350–351.

> one can say "Socrates is the servant of God," but one cannot say that God is of someone or something among things that are attached. *But a negative discourse is applicable to Him, as in your saying "God has no attribute," "God has no definition," "God has no match." Other than this [negative discourse], nothing is applicable to Him.*[67]

In line with Ibn Fātik's portrayal of Aristotle, apophaticism of the divine essence in the Arabic philosophical tradition is a result of the categorical division between the necessary being and beings—or, the creator and the created realm wherein thought and discourse operate. "Being" applies truly and eminently only to God, while our engendered existence, with all the attributes that it is subject to, is an illusion that applies to us only metaphorically. Ibn Sabʿīn explains the point with reference to Themistius (d.ca.390), the peripatetic commentator whose works and orations had long been rendered into Arabic:

> Themistius said: "The being of the first, lofty cause is Her essence. Nothing except Her has being, except that which stretches from Her. Hence, nothing can be called a 'thing' except through Her, and nothing can be called 'being' except through Her, and nothing can be called 'truth' except through Her. . . . She [i.e., the first, lofty cause] . . . precedes everything. Thus, nothing else has being, and they have no ipseity, no attribute, and no reality except from Her. Their metaphorical existence [*al-wujūd al-mustaʿār*] is not being. . . . There is no being except Her." And I say: non-existence has no ipseity, and the ipseity is one as mentioned above, and there is no being except that ipseity.[68]

The existence of the engendered world, with all attributes in it, is in fact borrowed from the First Cause, to which these attributes apply via eminentiae. The perfection of divine knowledge, thus, lies in admitting the famous dictum of negativity attributed to Abū Bakr that "the incapacity in attaining understanding is understanding" and in negating attributes from creation. The names Ibn Sabʿīn cites here are al-Fārābī, Socrates, and Alexander Aphrodisias (fl.l.2nd-ea.3rd CE). Accordingly, "*being is realized*

---

67. Ibid., 388–389.

68. Ibn Sabʿīn, *al-Kalām ʿalā al-Masāʾil al-Ṣiqilliyya*, 40. Cf. Ibn Ṭufayl, *Ibn Ṭufayl's Ḥayy ibn Yaqẓān*, 134.

by negation [salb] from us. . . . When we say that it is ours, with us, and from us, we have not realized it. It is realized when we say that it is *not* ours, *not* from us, *not* with us."[69] Hence Ibn Sabʿīn follows a negative theology of attributes like earlier Muslim philosophers, but he adds a key Sufi dimension. Philosophers negated the attributes of God, while Ibn Sabʿīn negates the attributes of the self and creation.

The philosophical negative theology Ibn Sabʿīn propounds is similar to that of the well-known Jewish philosopher of the previous generation, Moses Maimonides. Per Maimonides, Ibn Sabʿīn claims that one's path to God follows a hierarchy beginning with reflecting (1) Her actions; then (2) the relationship between divine actions and the attributes to which they are related; and then, (3) the relationship between both positive and negative attributes and the divine essence. Both scholars share the necessary dissimilarity of creation from its source. Ibn Sabʿīn's removal of God from all relations is also similar to Maimonides. After introducing the classical fourfold causality of Aristotle, Ibn Sabʿīn argues that none of these possible causal relations, nor the nine Aristotelian categories, apply to God. Like Maimonides, he argues that Aristotle's position on the eternity of the world was ambivalent, and Ibn Sabʿīn's own skeptical approach on the question was parallel to that of Maimonides.[70] Also they share the claim that ultimately the prophets and philosophers agreed upon [*ijmāʿ*] the soul's survival of death. On the issue of philosophical apophaticism,

---

69. Ibn Sabʿīn, *al-Kalām ʿalā al-Masāʾil al-Ṣiqilliyya*, 40–41.

70. "There is . . . no way to apprehend Him except . . . through the things He has made." (Maimonides, *Dalālat al-Ḥāʾirīn*, 1.34; also quoted in E. R. Wolfson, "Via Negativa in Maimonides and Its Impact on Thirteenth-Century Kabbalah," 410.) For human perfection, see Maimonides, *Dalālat al-Ḥāʾirīn*, 3.51–54.

Ibn Sabʿīn, *al-Kalām ʿalā al-Masāʾil al-Ṣiqilliyya*, 23–24, 42, 60, 80; Maimonides, *Dalālat al-Ḥāʾirīn*, 1.1, 14, 1.70.

Maimonides shares the same skepticism. Indeed, he argues that even Aristotle himself did not see the argument for the eternity of the world as a conclusive proof [*ḥujja*] but rather as just an opinion [*raʾy*], or a working hypothesis. (Maimonides, *Dalālat al-Ḥāʾirīn*, 2.15.) Accordingly, it was the later philosophical tradition that dogmatized Aristotle's hypothesis. Instead, for Maimonides both the theory in favor of and against creation of the world are admissible. (Maimonides, *Dalālat al-Ḥāʾirīn*, 2.16.) Hence this is a "methodical skepticism," as trying to exceed the limit of human understanding is more imperfect than everything; and suspending the inaccessible is the human perfection [*kamāl insānī*]. Ibn Sabʿīn perceptively traces the skeptical position on the created or uncreated nature of the world back to Galen (d.216). (Ibn Sabʿīn, *al-Kalām ʿalā al-Masāʾil al-Ṣiqilliyya*, 7.) This skepticism on the origins of creation is found in Ibn Ṭufayl's *Ḥayy ibn Yaqẓān* and Zakariyyā al-Rāzī's (d.925) *Medicine of the Soul* [*Ṭibb al-Rūḥānī*], which also converses with Galen.

Maimonides was arguably more explicit than Ibn Sabʿīn. He argued that names apply to God eminently, and that the divine attributes were all negations in their meanings. This was very much parallel to what Ibn Sīnā pointed out in his works. For Ibn Sabʿīn, on the other hand, this process of perpetual negation focuses on one's self: one should negate one's own attributes in order to connect [*wuṣūl*] with God. This performance of self-negation is distinctly Sufi and focuses on one's transitory attributes, as all attributes truly and eminently belong to God. While Maimonides and Ibn Sabʿīn agree on all dimensions of philosophical negative theology and its method of negation, their divergence on the object of negation—that is, the attributes of God or the ego—defines the difference of philosophical and Sufi versions of negation, while they both engender an apophaticism on divine essence.

One of the major sources both for Maimonides and Ibn Sabʿīn was the *Book of Gardens* (or the *Book of Imaginary Circles*), written by the famous grammarian and philosopher of Badajoz, Ibn al-Sīd al-Baṭalyawsī. One of the most impressive yet underappreciated works in philosophical apophaticism, the book presents a few enigmatic dictums of Andalusian philosophers [*ḥukamāʾ*] of the time and explains in seven chapters what they mean by them. The sixth chapter is on the unknowability principle that widely circulated among prominent Sufis like al-Junayd, al-Kharrāz, al-Ghazālī and Ibn al-ʿArabī from early on: "*none knows God except Himself.*" The fifth chapter directly attests to the popularity of philosophical apophaticism among Andalusian intellectuals. It is titled "explaining their [i.e., philosophers'] statement: '*the attributes of the transcendent Producer cannot describe Him except through negation*'" [*fī sharḥ qawlihim: inna ṣifāt al-Bāriʾ Taʿāla lā yaṣihhu an yūṣaf bihā illā ʿalā wajh al-salb*].[71] Here al-Baṭalyawsī argues that descriptions aim at (1) either removing partnership or (2) praising or reviling its addressee. The first option does not apply to God, because She already has no similarity in any way to creation by being its transcendent creator. The second option, proceeds al-Baṭalyawsī in a rigorous logical manner, can be employed in three possible ways:

71. Al-Baṭalyawsī, *al-Ḥadāʾiq fī al-Maṭālib al-ʿĀliya al-Falsafiyya al-ʿAwīṣa*, 93.

Eliyahu argues that the authentic title of the work was the *Book of Imaginary Circles* [*Kitāb al-Dawāʾir al-Wahmiyya*], instead of its popular title, the *Book of Gardens* [*Kitāb al-Hadāʾīq*]. See Eliyahu, "Muslim and Jewish Philosophy in al-Andalus," 53–54; Ogren, *Renaissance and Rebirth*, 53.

(2.a) exaggeration: the praise is excessive for the praised,
(2.b) balance: the praise fits to the degree of the praised,
(2.c) incompetence: the praise cannot reach to the degree of the praised.

As God is utterly transcendent, no way except that of incompetence could possibly work in describing Her. Otherwise, the describer will violate divine dissimilarity [*mukhālafa*] and describe Her in accordance with one's own capacity. While describing God with terms employed for creation, one will necessarily fall into anthropomorphism [*tashbīh*]. Al-Baṭalyawsī's examples for such anthropomorphism are "all-living," "all-knowing," "all-hearing," "all-seeing"—all the attributes that fly in the face of the popular theological and traditionist positions. He further develops his assault by challenging the popular position:

> [They] claim: "We require for Him the attributes, and we add a negative clause [*ḥarf al-salb*] to remove that which is presupposed by the similarity to creation [*tashbīh*]. So we say: 'He is living unlike animates,' 'He is all-knowing unlike knowers,' 'He is existent unlike objects.'"[72]

Al-Baṭalyawsī undermines this popular position, arguing that adding a negative clause makes no logical difference at all, because it is already proven that God has no like. In other words, attributes already have no option other than the way of incompetence when applied to God. Hence the popular positions on the divine transcendence fall into the fallacies of anthropomorphism and of assuming that they already know the unknowable. Al-Baṭalyawsī's charge, of course, clearly resonates with the Ismāʿīlī dissatisfaction with the widespread forms of unsaying.

Al-Baṭalyawsī's own position, and the position of the philosophers as he describes it, is a negative theology of the divine attributes that strongly coheres with that of Aristotle presented by Ibn Fātik. Al-Baṭalyawsī explicitly positions himself and the philosophers against all affirmative languages:

> *[We] do not affirm any attribute via kataphasis [ʿala ṭarīq al-ījāb], because this will necessitate likening Him to creation. But we negate from Him the opposites of these attributes. So we do not call Him "all-knowing," but*

---

72. Al-Baṭalyawsī, *al-Ḥadāʾiq fī al-Maṭālib al-ʿĀliya al-Falsafiyya al-ʿAwīṣa*, 95.

> *we say "He is not ignorant"; we do not say "He is all-powerful," but we say "He is not incapable"; we do not say "He is existent," rather we say "He is not non-existent."*[73]

Al-Baṭalyawsī also claims that this via negativa does not violate divine unknowability or dissimilarity. A rival might argue that the negation "G is not A" has no superiority over the proposition "G is A," because saying what something is not implies that one already knows what it is. (Such a critique of the negative language was indeed prevalent among Sufis, as we will see in the next chapter.) Al-Baṭalyawsī responds to this possible logical challenge by recalling the first logical step that he took. Any divine attribute is employed only as an insufficient praise for Her, not in order to distinguish Her from something else. Distinction entails knowledge, but praise entails only one's own incapacity. As an expression of incompetence, negation does not contain any positive content [*ḥukm*] as it is directed toward discursivity itself. In other words, the negation of philosophers is not "G is not A," rather "not (G is A)." "The table is not white" implies that one knows the actual color of the table. But when it is applied to God, it does not affirm any positive content. It only indicates God through negation from what we can know, as the very transgression of human limits. Negation is praise, a performative that indicates one's own incapacity.[74]

In brief, al-Baṭalyawsī's account addresses (1) the unknowability of the divine essence, (2) a negative theology of divine attributes, and superiority of negative speech, (3) the necessary dissimilarity of God on the basis of the decisive distinction between the creator and the created. The fundamental similarities in the philosophical apophaticism of al-Baṭalyawsī and Rabbi Moses Maimonides are striking. Also, both of them distinguish the divine attributes in the fashion of Ibn Sīnā's appropriation of the Muʿtazilites. Essential names operate as negations of an unknowable God, while names of divine actions are not only non-essential, but also created.

---

73. Ibid., 95.

74. Ibid., 96–97. Cf. Maimonides, *Dalālat al-Ḥāʾirīn*, 1.59; Kars, "Two Modes of Unsaying in the Early Thirteenth Century Islamic Lands." Al-Baṭalyawsī's apophaticism of praise coincide with Marion's reading of Dionysius the Areopagite in *God without Being*. See Jones, *A Genealogy of Marion's Philosophy of Religion*, 29–35.

Jewish Mysticism and Arabic Philosophical Apophaticism: Eyn Sof and Lam Yazal

Clear parallels in the philosophical apophaticism of al-Baṭalyawsī, Maimonides, and Ibn Sabʿīn manifest the intellectual porosity between not only mysticism and philosophy but also Islam and Judaism in Andalusia. The interest of Sufis put aside, al-Baṭalyawsī's *Book of Gardens* remained an inconspicuous work among Muslim intellectuals, compared to its popular reception by and immense influence upon Andalusian Jewish scholars. The work has two complete Hebrew translations and three partial translations all produced between the thirteenth to fifteenth centuries. Al-Baṭalyawsī was cited by a plethora of Jewish and Christian scholars; these included the great polymath Abraham ibn Ezra (d.1164) as well as

> several commentators of his biblical commentary (such as Shem Tov ibn Shaprut and Samuel ibn Matut); philosophers such as Abraham ibn Daud, Maimonides, Jacob Anatoli, Nissim of Marseille, Joseph ibn Kaspi, Moses Narboni; Halachists or commentators such as Nissim Gerondi, Simeon ben Zemah Duran, Isaac and Juda Abrabanel; and Qabbalists such as the Gerona Qabbalists Jacob ben Sheshet and Azriel, Isaac ibn Latif, Abraham Abulafia, Moses de Leon, Johanan Alemanno and Eliezer ben Abraham Eilenburg, and many others.
>
> Through these translations and citations, and especially through the influence of Johanan Alemanno, al-Baṭalyawsī's ideas even reached Renaissance Christian thinkers such as Pico de la Mirandola, Johannes Reuchlin and Giordano Bruno.[75]

Al-Baṭalyawsī's approach to the universal soul, the median line, eschatology, and his connection of the image of the ladder with the ascent of dead souls had a lasting influence on Jewish thought in the medieval period as well as on some major Jewish Renaissance figures, as contemporary scholars like Alexander Altmann, David Kaufmann, and Moshe Idel

---

75. Eliyahu, "Muslim and Jewish Philosophy in al-Andalus," 59. Also see Akasoy, "Ibn Sabʿīn's *Sicilian Questions*"; özbalıkçı, "Batalyevsi," 139.

Rabbi Michael Balbo's (d.af.1484) "wise Ptolemy" (d.ca.170) and his "Book of Circles" is actually nothing but al-Baṭalyawsī and his *Book of Circles* (later called the *Book of Gardens*). See Ogren, *Renaissance and Rebirth*, 53. On the title of the book, see Eliyahu, "Muslim and Jewish Philosophy in al-Andalus."

have already highlighted.[76] Yet the prominence of philosophical apophaticism in al-Baṭalyawsī's context and work, and its reception in the later Jewish and Muslim mystical and philosophical traditions, are still understudied. The popularity of this apophaticism not only among western Jewish and Muslim philosophers but, more surprisingly, among mystics is attested by Judaism in the pre-Zoharic period. Particularly Azriel of Girona, probably a disciple of Isaac the Blind (d.1235) and a central figure in the development of Kabbalah, demonstrates not only the prominence of philosophical apophaticism among mystics but also its harmony with the early Kabbalistic theosophy in Catalonia. Azriel founded a new center for the Kabbalah in Girona, together with the elder Rabbi Ezra ben Solomon, and wrote the most important Kabbalistic works of the circle. In his influential *Explanation of the Ten Sefirot*, Azriel writes:

> The philosophers admit to this fact that *the cause of all causes* and the *origin of origins* is *End-less [Eyn Sof], unfathomable*, and *without limit*. . . . [I]f He is [truly] without limit, then nothing exists outside Him. . . . Furthermore, *the philosophers are in agreement with these statements that our perception of Him cannot be except by way of negative attribution.*[77]

This fascinating passage illustrates that Azriel adopted not only (1) an emphasis on divine unknowability but also (2) a negative theology of divine attributes and (3) a proof of the One as the negation of creation by being its ultimate cause.

The convergence of western Sufism, philosophy, and Kabbalah on philosophical apophaticism, especially Azriel's appeal to the now-famous phrase "End-less" [Eyn Sof], pulls us back to the ninth-century Muʿtazilites and Muslim philosophers. Early doxographical accounts noted that philosophers as well as the Muʿtazilites like al-Naẓẓām and ʿAbbād ibn Sulaymān of the ninth century consciously employed the Arabic phrase "End-less" [Lam Yazal], a negative designation in reference to the divine essence insofar as no name applied to Her. Al-Kindī's preferences for the cognate negative names Lam Yazal and al-Azalī confirmed these early doxographical depictions. This nominal form was novel, and admittedly

76. Especially see Idel, *Ascensions on High in Jewish Mysticism*, 167–203.

77. Azriel of Girona in Dan and Kiener, *The Early Kabbalah*, 89–90 (my slight modification, and my emphases).

problematic from a grammatical perspective. From a theological perspective, Lam Yazal was also an uncanny name for God that had no precedent in the Qur'an or the prophetic traditions. While the ninth-century Muʿtazilites and philosophers employed *lam yazal* both in adverbial and nominal forms, later philosophers like al-ʿĀmirī and Ibn Sīnā began employing "Lam Yazal" as well as its cognate "Azalī" exclusively in the nominal form. Ibn Miskawayh, for example, appeals to "Azalī" as the essential definition of God, saying, "If, as we asserted, being in Him is essential, He could not possibly be imagined to be non-being; thus He is necessary of being, and whatever is the necessary being will be perpetual of existence, and whatever is perpetual of being will be Eternal" (*wa idhā kāna al-wujūdu fīhi ka-mā qulnā dhātiyyan fa-laysa yajūzu an yutawahhama maʿdūman fa-huwa wājibu al-wujūdi wa-mā kāna wājiba al-wujūdi fa-huwa dāʾimu al-wujūdi wa-mā kāna dāʾima al-wujūdi fa-huwa azaliyyun*).[78]

Strikingly, Ibn Miskawayh's proof of God as the necessary being [*wājib al-wujūd*] is based on Her essentially Azalī ipseity. In the same vein, the Jewish scholar Moses Maimonides associates the unsayable divine name, "the Tetragrammaton" [*ism dhī arbaʿat ḥurūf*], with "but pure being" [*mujarrad wujūd lā-ghayr*] that does not denote any attribute. Accordingly, the unsayable essential name implies only absolute being [*al-wujūd al-muṭlaq*], which entails it be "*ceaseless, I mean, necessary being*" [*dāʾiman, āʿni, wājib al-wujūd*].[79] Indeed, in post-Avicennian philosophy as well as Sunnī theology, the names Azalī or Lam Yazal actually mean nothing but the essential philosophical name of God, the necessary being. While their masters were relatively reluctant, from the eleventh century onward Sunnī theologians like al-Rāghib al-Iṣfahānī (fl.ea.11th CE), Ibn al-Farrāʾ al-Ḥanbalī (d.1066), and Imām al-Ḥaramayn al-Juwaynī joined in this sweeping trend of defining the divine essence, applying Lam Yazal and Azalī in the nominal, rather than adverbial, forms.[80]

---

78. "Ibn Miskawayh in Wisnovsky, "One Aspect of the Avicennian Turn in Sunnī Theology," 67 (with my slight modification in the English translation).

79. Maimonides, *Dalālat al-Ḥāʾirīn*, 1:63, 160 (my emphasis). In other words, Maimonides employs the Arabic terms *azalī* and *dāʾimi* interchangeably, both of which are necessarily entailed in the designation "necessary being" that addresses the apophatic divine essence. As we saw above, *dāʾim* was interchangeable with *azalī* according to al-Kindī's definition as well.

80. "Post-Avicennian attempts . . . argue that when we define an eternal thing as 'that which has never ceased to be nor will ever cease to be' [*mā lam yazal wa lā yazālu*], what we really mean is that an eternal thing cannot possibly not exist, and that therefore an eternal thing is necessary of existence." (Wisnovsky, "One Aspect of the Avicennian Turn in Sunnī Theology," 67.)

The rise of Lam Yazal in the nominal form, and as a defining, negative designation for God in Arabic has strong parallels with the emergence of the nominal appeal to Eyn Sof in Jewish mysticism. In tenth-century Jewish mysticism that flourished around the commentaries on the *Book of Creation* [*Sefer Yesirah*], *eyn sof* curiously transformed from a Hebrew adverb to a negative noun addressing the divine essence. This nominal employment of the term can be observed first with the tenth-century physician and theologian Shabbatai Donnolo (d.af.982). Donnolo's nominal appeal "marks the integration of the philosophical transcendental description of God into Kabbalah and bears the mark of negative (apophatic) theology."[81] This linguistic change was accompanied with another shift in the understanding of infinity from a spatial dimension to an epistemological and vertical dimension and played an important theosophical role in Kabbalah. "The End-less" in Hebrew emerged as the apophatic designation of the divine essence, accompanied not only by a negative theology of divine attributes but also a negative proof of the creator:

> The Godhead itself is beyond all symbolic description and can therefore be described only by negative statements. The most frequently used negative appellation for the Godhead is Eyn Sof [End-less], but this term does not contain any specific meaning that renders it superior to any other negative term such as "no beginning" or "no color."[82]

The negative description of the divine essence, coupled with a negative theology of divine attributes, flourished not only among Muʿtazilites and the Muslim philosophers of the following centuries but also among Jewish philosophers and Kabbalists. Lam Yazal and Eyn Sof play a strikingly similar role within a philosophical apophatic context shared by Jewish and Muslim philosophical and mystical currents. Interestingly, while Kabbalah and Sufism are widely depicted today as twins in their theologies, the apophatic conception of God that early Kabbalists adopted is much closer to the philosophical apophatic path of Ibn Sīnā, al-Baṭalyawsī,

---

Sufis joined this Avicennian turn in associating the divine essence with *azaliyya*. See, e.g., Ibn al-ʿArabī in Chittick, *Sufi Path of Knowledge*, 64.

81. Valabregue-Perry, "The Concept of Infinity (*Eyn-sof*) and the Rise of Theosophical Kabbalah," 406.

82. Dan in Dan and Kiener, *The Early Kabbalah*, 8 (with my slight modification).

and Maimonides than to the more popular paradoxical apophaticism associated with Sufis. Particularly, Azriel's Hebrew *Eyn Sof* is virtually interchangeable with the *Lam Yazal* of Arabic philosophical apophaticism. Al-Kindī's apophatic End-less is in parallel with Azriel's depiction of *Eyn Sof*. Even more strikingly, the key passages of philosophical apophaticism in Azriel and in the Andalusian mystic Ibn Masarra, quoted below, are largely indistinguishable. Here is Azriel:

> Know that everything visible and perceivable to human contemplation is limited, and that everything that is limited is finite and that everything that is finite is insignificant. Conversely, that which is not limited is called "End-less" and is absolutely undifferentiated in a complete and changeless unity. And if He is without limit, then nothing exists outside Him. . . . Our perception of Him cannot be except by way of negative attribution.[83]

And here is Ibn Masarra:

> The intellects are limited; the limited cannot contain or encompass whatever is above it, what does not correspond to it, what is loftier than it, or what contains it. . . . This implies necessarily that the lofty one has no similitude; He has no end; He has no beginning; He has no parts; and He has no limit, nor does any of it enter into His oneness and greatness. . . . Nothing of what He has created resembles Him. He is distinct in essence and attribute from all that He has created, yet He is with all things.[84]

---

83. Azriel of Girona in Dan and Kiener, *The Early Kabbalah*, 89–90 (with my minor additions).

84. Ibn Masarra in Stroumsa and Sviri, "The Beginnings of Mystical Philosophy in al-Andalus," 223. For the Arabic text itself, see Ibn Masarra in Morris, *Ibn Masarra: A Reconsideration of Primary Sources*, 358.

This comparison also sheds light on Ibn Masarra's cosmological ideas that do not fit into Ismāʿīlism. Recent scholarship on mysticism in Andalusia underlines Ibn Masarra's Ismāʿīlī leanings. (See, e.g., Ebstein, *Mysticism and Philosophy in al-Andalus*.) Yet, Ibn Masarra's cosmology and his negative reading of the divine attributes makes him closer to philosophical apophaticism than to the Ismāʿīlī double negation—the difference between the two negative theologies of the divine attributes is elusive. Similarly, in the field of letter mysticism, which is often depicted as the most clearly Ismāʿīlī dimension of Ibn Masarra's thought, we do not find a clear overlap. For example, his interpretation of the letters of the Arabic name God [*Allāh*] has differences from that of Ismāʿīlī scholars like Nāṣir Khusrav. (Cf. Nāṣir Khusrav, *Six Chapters; or, Shish Faṣl: Also Called Rawshanāʾī-nāma*, ch.1; Ebstein, *Mysticism and Philosophy in al-Andalus*, 87).

Before its apophatic employment within the theosophic system developed by Isaac the Blind, Azriel, and the later Kabbalah, *Eyn Sof* was used in this new apophatic sense by Juda ben Barzillai (fl.12th CE), Shlomo ibn Gabirol (d.ca.1058), and Shabbatai Donnolo. Hence Donnolo plays a key role in the puzzle of the emergence of *Eyn Sof* as the apophatic designation for the divine essence in Hebrew language. The connections between tenth-century Muslim thought and Donnolo, one of the founders of Hebrew culture in medieval Europe, is of particular importance in analyzing possible convergences in the apophatic philosophical and mystical employments of *Lam Yazal* and *Eyn Sof*.[85]

It should be no surprise that philosophical apophaticism can transcend religious boundaries. Thomas Aquinas, as a famous example, referred to Ibn Sīnā and Maimonides in his discussion of negative theology. However, its adoption by Kabbalists like Azriel and Sufis like Ibn Sabʿīn, and the key role early mystic Ibn Masarra plays in Andalusian philosophical apophaticism, is surprising. After Ibn Masarra, al-Baṭalyawsī serves as an even more obvious crossroad role for philosophical apophaticism in Andalusia. Ibn Sabʿīn quotes lengthy paragraphs from the *Book of Gardens* without, however, citing al-Baṭalyawsī's name. Ibn al-ʿArabī mentions al-Baṭalyawsī a few times with appreciation, and the writings of another mystic, Ibn Barrajān (d.1141), display traces of al-Baṭalyawsī's thought. On the other side of the coin, Muslim Sufis were familiar with Maimonides' work as

---

Another elusive yet important difference appears in the cosmology of the philosophical apophaticism of Azriel and the Ismāʿīlī apophaticism of Nethanel al-Fayyūmī. Nethanel has a negative theology of divine attributes as well, and he cites Q.42:11 in the same context with Ibn Masarra. On the other hand, in the very next sentence, al-Fayyūmī follows the Ismāʿīlī cosmology claiming that the first creation of God was the Universal Intellect via Divine Word. (al-Fayyūmī, *The Bustan al-Ukul*, 2 [(English text], 2 [Judeo-Arabic text].) Ibn Masarra's next sentence, on the other hand, is that "the first to be created were the throne and the water, and within the throne He inscribed all His decrees and rulings and that upon which His will is borne." (Ibn Masarra in Stroumsa and Sviri, "The Beginnings of Mystical Philosophy in al-Andalus," 224. For the Arabic text, see Ibn Masarra in Morris, *Ibn Masarra: A Reconsideration of Primary Sources*, 258. For Ibn Barrajān (d.1141) on water created under the throne, see Casewit, *The Mystics of al-Andalus*, 194–195.) Azriel argues that "if you claim that the first limited being that is brought into existence from Him is this world—lacking in perfection—then you ascribe imperfection to the force which stems from Him." (Azriel in Dan and Kiener, *The Early Kabbalah*, 90.)

85. Donnolo's intellectual journey began with an apprenticeship to "a Gentile scholar from Babylon," probably a scientist named "al-Baghdādī," after he fell captive to the Fāṭimids. On the other hand, except for a couple of Arabic terms that appear in his writings, there is no cogent proof that Donnolo had extensive knowledge of Arabic. (Mancuso in Donnolo, *Shabbatai Donnolo's Sefer Hakhmoni*, 13–35.)

well. Ibn Sabʿīn mentioned Maimonides as "the author of the *Guide to the Perplexed*" in his *Treatise on the Illuminative*, and his mystic student Ibn Hūd al-Judhāmī (d.ca.1300) is said to have taught the *Guide*, a controversial book among Jews at that time, in a multifaith circle in Damascus. The historian Ibn Shākir al-Kutubī (d.1363) mentions the ascetic Ibn Hūd as one of the great authorities of a distinctly "monistic" form of Sufism [*aḥad al-kubbār taṣawwuf ʿalā ṭarīqat al-waḥda*], which was associated with Ibn Sabʿīn as well. Al-Kutubī also notes that Ibn Hūd wrote a poem that began with a paradox, and underlined the unknowability of God:

> The knowledge of My folk is for Me ignorance:
> My dignity is well beyond.[86]

As philosophy transcended disciplinary and religious borders, the negative theology of the divine essence that developed with it also found expression across traditions. The negative theology of divine attributes occasionally shared among Sufis and philosophers of Andalusia in the thirteenth century well illustrates this porosity. For example, Ibn al-ʿArabī's incorporation of Ibn Masarra in order to develop his exquisite apophaticism was similar to Maimonides' negative theology of divine attributes. They share the radical theme that even the name "one" cannot apply to God as it will violate that very oneness. The idea was first articulated in *Parmenides*, one of Plato's most difficult yet influential dialogues. Plato wrote:

---

86. Al-Kutubī, *Fawāt al-Wafayāt*, 197; Eliyahu, "Muslim and Jewish Philosophy in al-Andalus," 58.

A surprising variety of non-Jewish scholars of the thirteenth century had access to Maimonides. The Ḥanbalī jurist and theologian Najm al-Dīn al-Ṭūfī (d.1316) discusses an anonymous polemical work by a Christian author that attacked Islam and quoted several Arabic sources, the latest apparently being Ibn Rushd and Maimonides. (Shihadeh, "Three Apologetic Stances in al-Ṭūfī," 2.)

Al-Kutubī notes:

> Under his [Ibn Hūd] guidance the Jews were wont to occupy themselves with the study of the [*Book of the Guide*]: this is a work upon the principles of their religion by [the Master] Mūsā [Maimonides]. . . . [ʿImād al-dīn] al-Wāsiṭī [d.1311] came to him (Ibn Hūd) and begged him to undertake to guide [him] in spiritual things. He asked: "Upon which road? the Mosaic, the Christian, or the Mohammadan?" At sunrise he turned towards the sun, and crossed himself. (Goldziher, "Ibn Hûd, the Mohammedan Mystic, and the Jews of Damascus," 220; al-Kutubī, *Fawāt al-Wafayāt*, 196–197; with my minor modifications.)

> [If the one is one, then] the one in no sense is. It cannot, then, "be" even to the extent of "being" one, for then it would be a thing that is and has being. . . . Consequently, it cannot *have* a name or be spoken of, nor can there be any knowledge or perception or opinion *of* it.[87]

Not only philosophers but also Sufis like Ibn al-ʿArabī and Awḥad al-Dīn al-Balyānī (d.ca.1284) toyed with Plato's hypothesis and argued that even "oneness" cannot apply to God as it will violate that very oneness. Indeed the idea that "God is one without possessing the attribute of oneness" can be traced within Sufism itself as powerfully as among philosophers. The phrase appears as early as in al-Ḥallāj's enigmatic *Book of Ṭ and S* [*Kitāb al-Ṭawāsīn*], and recurs as a theme in Rūzbihān Baqlī's (d.1209) thought, among other Sufis. Maimonides' philosophical negative theology of divine attributes follows the same line of apophaticism. Nothing should compromise God's necessary oneness and absolutely dissimilar transcendence. No predicates apply to God in the way they apply to creation, as this would result in anthropomorphism. Even the essential attributes of "unity" or "being" (as understood by human beings) cannot apply to Her literally. Hence Maimonides writes that "*He is one without oneness*" [*wāḥid lā bi-waḥda*].[88] Its influence was not limited to later Jewish philosophy, and the same expression would also appear in the works of later Kabbalists. The key aspects of philosophical apophaticism, like other theological ideas and currents, were shared across disciplinary and religious traditions in Andalusia.

Sufis and Genies: Philosophical Apophaticism within Sufi Epistemology

Mysticism and philosophy in Andalusia engaged in creative encounters around philosophical apophaticism. Mystics like Ibn Sabʿīn employed it with Sufi adaptations, such as revising the negative theology of divine

87. Plato in Franke, *On What Cannot Be Said*, 1:45; Franke's emphasis. Cf. Plato, *Plato's Parmenides*, 137b–144e.

88. "He is the One without oneness [*al-wāḥid bilā waḥdāniyya*], and the single without singleness [*al-fard bilā fardāniyya*]." (Awḥad al-Dīn al-Balyānī [misattributed to Muḥyī al-Dīn Ibn al-ʿArabī], *Whoso Knoweth Himself*, 3.) Also see Maimonides, *Dalālat al-Ḥāʾirīn*, 1.57, 135; Abrahamov, *Ibn al-ʿArabī and the Sufis*, 100; al-Ḥallāj, *Kitāb al-Ṭawāsīn*, 68; E. R. Wolfson, "Via Negativa in Maimonides and Its Impact on Thirteenth-Century Kabbalah," 403; Kars, "Two Modes of Unsaying in the Early Thirteenth Century Islamic Lands," 266.

attributes into a negative theology of worldly attributes. The exchange of letters between two Persian Sufis in the gradually emerging Kubrawī network, Majd al-Dīn Baghdādī and his disciple Sharaf al-Dīn Balkhī, witnesses a similar, visionary version of the philosophical path of negation. In an interesting vision, what seems to be a circle of learned *jinns* was unveiled to Sharaf al-Dīn Balkhī. Quite surprisingly, the *jinns* were discussing nothing other than Plato's hypothesis, ending with an experiential version of philosophical apophaticism:

> The spirits, words and questions of the *jinns* became manifest: "what is the meaning of saying 'there is no god but God?' *If your saying 'there is no god but God' is correct, then you cannot say 'there is no god but God.'* "
>
> They said: we have a master from Alexandria, and he says: "*the wayfaring of all wayfarers happens in 'there is no God'* [i.e., in negation]. No one is allowed to transgress it, or depart from it. And *no one among the wayfarers can access 'but God'* [i.e., the affirmation], because eternity [*qidam*] is not to be entered by the originated [*ḥadas̱*]. *When the wayfaring ends in 'there is no God,' which is the negation* [*nafy*], *the negator and the wayfarer are negated* [*intafā al-nāfī va-l-sālik*]. *If so, then who will wayfare thereafter?*"[89]

The perplexing question of the master of genies dragged Sharaf al-Dīn Balkhī to endless deserts, with the vision getting even more baffling for him and his reader as it unfolds. This brief but dense conversation of the circle of learned *jinns* is composed of three key aspects of philosophical apophaticism in a Sufi context: (1) the discursive inapplicability of any attribute to God, including oneness—a glaring appropriation of Plato's hypothesis, (2) the inaccessibility of the divine essence based on the decisive distinction between the creator and the created realm, and (3) negation as the most suitable, and indeed, only possible path of approaching God.

Majd al-Dīn is keenly aware of the import of the dream of Sharaf al-Dīn. His sophisticated interpretation of the dream has two parts, both of

---

89. Sharaf al-Dīn Balkhī in Meier, *Essays on Islamic Piety and Mysticism*, 269. (The letter is in Persian, while the quotation from the Alexandrian master of genies is in Arabic.)

The following translation of this difficult sentence is also legitimate: "when the wayfaring ends in *lā ilāh*, which is the negation that negates the negator and the wayfarer, who will wayfare after that?"

which lay bare the harmonious mixture of Sufi principles and philosophical apophaticism. Majd al-Dīn writes:

> "*If your saying 'there is no god but God' is correct, then you cannot say 'there is no god but God.'*" This is a correct statement. It is the truth, because the validity of the saying "there is no god but God" is based on the negation of human presence [*nafy-e bashariyyat*]. As long as their human attributes are extant, the claimers are not sincere. For, divine unity is the negator of ego and presence. . . . For this reason, this poor one [i.e., Majd al-Dīn himself] chooses the invocation [*ẕikr*] "There is no god but God" and prefers it over the invocation "God." *As long as you are a wayfarer, you need negation. As long as the attributes (of the self) are not negated, one's need is affirmed* [*s̱ābit*]. As long as the need for negation is extant, the phrase [i.e., "There is no god but God"] shall be present [*bar kār ast*].
>
> As for the saying of the master from Alexandria, "*the wayfaring of all wayfarers happens in 'there is no God' [i.e., in negation]. No one can access 'but God' [i.e., the affirmation].*" This is a correct statement, because this world . . . which is the realm of wayfaring, is bounded with . . . human attributes. *The completion of this wayfaring is "there is no God."*[90]

In the exchange of letters between the two Persian wayfarers, we find an exquisite, sophisticated employment of the components of philosophical apophaticism in a Sufi epistemological context. Approaching the unknowable one, in its ineffable oneness, is possible only within the realm of the perpetual negation of attributes. What is negated is *not the divine attributes, but the attributes of the human self.* Unlike with the philosophers, perpetual negation is non-discursive and experiential, as the purported access of mystics to the divine essence is non-discursive and visionary. Majd al-Dīn and Sharaf al-Dīn are undermining the claims for discursive as well as mystical, non-discursive access to the divine essence. Their bias toward the negative aspect of the *tahlīl*, "There is no god but God," in favor of negative speech on God was quite rare among thirteenth-century Sufis who inclined toward a balanced approach.

---

90. Majd al-Dīn Baghdādī in Meier, *Essays on Islamic Piety and Mysticism*, 274.

Their preference for negative over positive language was, still, not without precedent among Sufis. Abū Ḥāmid al-Ghazālī most famously had a distinctly negative approach to language concerning God. In the *Highest Aim* [*al-Maqṣad al-Asnā*], al-Ghazālī adopts all the principles of a philosophical apophaticism. The unknowability of the divine essence is strongly emphasized, again and again underlining that the highest knowledge concerning God is one's own incapacity to know—docta ignorantia. Not only divine essence but even divine attributes cannot be known to us as much as they relate to the divine essence. We can only imagine divine attributes through comparison with their created counterparts, but their reality is beyond human conception, imagination, and intellection. Contrasting negative and positive language concerning the divine essence, al-Ghazālī finds the former superior. Accordingly, negations contain a latent praise of God more powerful and correct than positively describing Her with qualified attributes:

> Since there is no likeness of Him, none knows His essence other than He. So al-Junayd . . . was right when he remarked: "*none knows God except God.*" For that reason, He gave even His noblest creature a name, with which He veiled Himself, as He said: "Praise the name of your Lord Most High" [Q.87:1]. *So, by God, none knows God except God, in this world, or the next.*
>
> On his deathbed, Dhū al-Nūn was asked, "What do you long for?" He replied: "That I knew Him before I die—be it for an instant." Now, this confuses the hearts of most of the weak, and leads them to the delusion of negation [*nafy*] and ineffectualism [*taʿṭīl*]. . . . I say: if someone were to say "I do not know God," that would be true. And if they were to say "I know God" that would also be true. . . .
>
> This would be the case were a person to ask another, "Do you know Abū Bakr, the faithful one?" . . . If one replied, "Who does not know Abū Bakr, or is ignorant about him? Given the visibility, fame, and renown of his name, is it conceivable that anyone in the world doesn't know him? . . ." This reply would be true. . . .
>
> But if another were asked, "Do you know him [Abū Bakr, the faithful one]," and replied: "Who am I to know the faithful one? Alas, far from it! None knows him except himself, or someone who is like him or above him. Who am I to claim to know him or even hope for that? People like me hear his name and attributes, but as for claiming to know him—that is impossible." *This is also*

> *true—indeed, this proposition has an aspect, which comes closer to the due glorification and homage.*[91]

In the following discussion, al-Ghazālī gives other examples as well, in order to point out that the negative language is superior to positive language concerning the divine essence. His association of the negative language with praise, and the principle of unknowability, *none knows God except God,* clearly resonate with al-Baṭalyawsī, Maimonides, and the Arabic Aristotle among others. Yet these main principles of philosophical apophaticism are now native speakers of the language of Sufism through the mouth of al-Junayd of Baghdad and Dhū al-Nūn of Egypt.

Later, the Naqshbandī master Muḥammad Pārsā (d.1420) quotes Majd al-Dīn's preponderance of negation over affirmation in the declaration of faith [*tahlīl*]. While Pārsā's work as well as Majd al-Dīn's original letter to Sharaf al-Dīn are in Persian, the quotation from Majd al-Dīn is in Arabic. Hence, it appears that Majd al-Dīn's bias toward negation in the *tahlīl* was testified in different sources associated with him. Still, the philosophical preference for negative speech in al-Ghazālī, or its personalized, experiential version in Majd al-Dīn Baghdādī, and Sharaf al-Dīn Balkhī's asymmetrical approach to the *tahlīl* did not find immediate followers among Sufis. Najm al-Dīn Kubrā's students kept their master's tradition of using the *tahlīl* as their common invocation, but they did not adopt the preference of negation over affirmation that Majd al-Dīn, Sharaf al-Dīn, and his Arabic *jinn*-master from Alexandria have. The asymmetry of negation and affirmation disappears in the writings of later Kubrawīs—Najm al-Dīn Dāya Rāzī, Nūr al-Dīn Isfarāʾīnī (d.1317), Sharaf al-Dīn Ḥanawayh (fl.l.13th CE), and ʿAlāʾ al-Dawla Simnānī—as well as in the writings of Farīd al-Dīn ʿAṭṭār and of ʿAzīz Nasafī, the latter of whom may have associated with early Kubrawīs. Najm al-Dīn Kubrā's own approach is very similar to that of Dāya Rāzī and Simnānī, and it underlines the balance of affirmation and negation, as in non-Sufi sources. Pārsā himself is following the same practice of invoking "There is no god but God," established by Yūsuf Hamadānī (d.1140), who was a student of Abū ʿAlī al-Fārmadhī (d.1084) together with Abū Ḥāmid al-Ghazālī. While Pārsā is familiar with Majd

91. Al-Ghazālī, *al-Maqṣad al-Asnā*, 33–34; al-Ghazālī, *Ninety-Nine Beautiful Names of God*, 35–36. Also see Shehadi, *Ghazali's Unique Unknowable God*, 38.

al-Dīn's negative interpretation of the *tahlīl,* he follows the more popular, balanced version of Najm al-Dīn Dāya Rāzī.[92]

Abū Ḥāmid al-Ghazālī, Majd al-Dīn Baghdādī, and Sharaf al-Dīn Balkhī have a rare negativist emphasis on the binary of transcendence and immanence in the declaration of divine unity. Their negativist reading of the *tahlīl* is a philosophical variation on the stronger line of paradoxical apophaticism, developed by the Persian Sufis Aḥmad al-Ghazālī (d.1126), Abū al-Ḥasan Bustī (d.af.1077), ʿAyn al-Qużāt Hamadānī, and Najm al-Dīn Dāya Rāzī, among others. However brief, the negativist departure from the more common, balanced Sufi approach is a significant case to assess the prominence of philosophy in early thirteenth-century Persia and Central Asia. Majd al-Dīn Baghdādī hailed from Khuwarazm, a terrain not really hospitable for Sufis at the time, as a result of the prominence of the philosopher Fakhr al-Dīn al-Rāzī at the Khwārazmshāhī court.[93] Similarly, Sharaf al-Dīn's hometown was captured by Muḥammad Khwārazmshāh from the Ghūrids in 1206, and it remained under their control until 1220, when Chingiz Khān destroyed the city. As the correspondence belongs to the first two decades of the century, Majd al-Dīn and Sharaf al-Dīn's shared bias toward a negative language might be a direct result of the political eminence of philosophical theology under Khwārazmshāhī rule. By the time of Muḥammad Pārsā, however, the asymmetry between negation and affirmation had given way to a symmetrical balance that creates paradoxical statements and resists propositional logical analysis. Pārsā himself promoted paradoxes, and he was an exponent of influential Sufi masters like Ibn al-ʿArabī and Rūmī, who were champions of paradoxes in the thirteenth century. Accordingly, the declaration of faith is composed of the perfect balance of negation and affirmation, which creates the fascinating principle of "healing with paradoxes" for Sufis in Kubrā's lineage.

Summary

The apophatic tradition of the Arabic philosophers on the divine essence had a set of distinguishing marks, composed of (1) a negative theology of

92. Muḥammad Pārsā, *Qudsiyya: Kalimāt-i Bahāʾ al-Dīn Naqshband,* 44; Kubrā in Mole, "Traites Mineurs de Nagm al-Dīn Kubrā," 27; Yūsuf Hamadānī, "Seyyid Yusuf-i Hemedani'nin Tasavvufa İlişkin Bir Risalesi"; Elias, *Throne Carrier of God,* 24; Dāya Rāzī, *Path of God's Bondsmen,* 269–277.

93. Algar in Dāya Rāzī, *Path of God's Bondsmen,* 9–10.

divine attributes, (2) the unknowability the divine essence, closely connected with an Aristotelian version of Plotinus' distinction between discursive thought [*dianoia*] and non-discursive intellection [*noēsis*], (3) the necessary dissimilarity of God as the First Cause of everything else, (4) and a philosophical hermeneutics that protects divine oneness and dissimilarity. As ideas moved flexibly, philosophical apophaticism found representatives among mystics or Sufis from early on. Especially in Andalusia, we find that philosophical apophaticism transcended religious and disciplinary borders, and it circulated among Sufis from Ibn al-Marʾa to Ibn Sabʿīn. The strikingly powerful philosophical apophaticism circulating among early Kabbalists beyond the Islamicate world suggests that the surprising parallels in the rise of nominal employment of the negative names of God, *Lam Yazal* and *Eyn Sof*, are more than a coincidence.

While other components of philosophical apophaticism were found among many Sufis of the thirteenth century, the negativist approach to the divine attributes was its most important barrier for them. The majority of Sufis challenged a negativist reading of the divine attributes from the ninth century onward in favor of paradoxes, as discussed in the next chapter. Yet Ibn Sabʿīn and al-Ghazālī's writings, and the correspondence between two Kubrawī Sufis of the thirteenth century, indicate that a negative theology of divine attributes could and did flourish among Sufis, with fine-tunings in order to confirm the superiority of vision and unveiling in Sufi epistemology. For the vast majority of Sufis of the thirteenth century, it was a sustained epistemological principle that no discourse or intellect could apprehend God by any means. Instead, Sufi epistemology, and mysticism at large, underlined non-discursive forms of access, as we saw in the case of Ibn Ṭufayl. Insofar as accessing deity via discourse was already out of the question, it was the discussions about and approaches to the visionary, experiential connection with God that determined a negative theology of divine essence among Sufis. In other words, negative theology of divine essence within a Sufi framework relied not only on canceling discursive knowledge about God but also on non-discursive, visionary possibilities.

With the epistemological shift from discourse to vision, the negative theology of divine attributes also underwent a Sufi fine-tuning, parallel to the experientializing shift in the negative theology of divine essence. For Peripatetic philosophers, a negative theology of divine attributes entailed the discursive negation of the attributes, or the negative interpretation of affirmative predicates, following Wāṣil ibn ʿAṭāʾ (d.748), al-Najjār (d.836),

Ḍirār, and al-Naẓẓām, if not earlier Ibāḍī theologians like al-Fazārī.[94] Such negative theology of divine attributes was key for the divine transcendence [*tanzīh*], and for their critique of divine comparability [*tashbīh*]. It was also their performative way of praising God and was a key component of the intellectual perfection of the soul. For Sufis, as in the case of Ibn Sabʿīn, Majd al-Dīn Baghdādī, and Sharaf al-Dīn Balkhī, the negative theology of divine attributes had to relate to their visions and self-disciplinary practices as well. What should be negated is not divine attributes, but one's own human, created attributes. The negation of divine attributes by the Muʿtazilites and philosophers turns into the performative negation of one's own attributes, and relates to human apotheosis defined by the Sufi path and epistemology.

94. Al-Najjār and Ḍirār were among the earliest to introduce negative interpretation of affirmative predicates. Accordingly, the meaning of the statement that God is knowing or powerful is that He is not ignorant and not powerless. (See H. A. Wolfson, *Philosophy of the Kalām*, 223.) For al-Naẓẓām's negative theology of divine attributes, see Abrahamov in al-Qāsim ibn Ibrāhīm, *Kitāb al-Dalīl al-Kabīr*, 24. Harry A. Wolfson's evaluation should be revised in the light of the recent discovery of earlier Ibāḍī theological texts; see al-Fazārī, *Early Ibāḍī Theology*, 172–176.

PATH THREE

"Yes and No"

PARADOXICAL APOPHATICISM AND DIALECTICAL LOGIC

THIS CHAPTER INTRODUCES paradoxical apophaticism on the divine essence and tests the common association of paradox and Sufism, with a particular focus on the self-contradictory phrases and statements in the "X-not-X" forms. I argue that neither the employment nor the celebration of paradoxes were uniquely Sufi phenomenon. Yet it was primarily Sufis from early on who consciously adopted paradoxical apophatic approaches to the divine essence. While other theological positions sought to show that their self-contradictory statements could be explained within propositional logic without violating logical meta-principles, Sufis employed them to show how propositional logic fails when addressing the divine essence. Apophaticism here is performed via the self-negating binaries of a dialectical logic that shows the incapacity of propositional discourse before an inscrutable divine excess. In other words, the employment of paradoxes follows a rule-governed set of strategies in order to negate propositional discourse on God. These strategies entailed (1) a balanced, or symmetrical, attitude that finds affirmative and negative language equally disqualified, (2) a balanced take on the binary of divine incomparability and immanence, while the vast majority of Muslim scholars hold the former superior, and (3) a dialectical logic that performs divine trans-discursivity by uniting the irreconcilable opposites that constitute a specific propositional discourse.

Paradox in Literature and Sufism: An Overview

Paradox as *para-dox*, or "inverted doxa" as Jean-Luc Marion, Denys Turner, and other contemporary scholars find in negative theology, is irreducible to religious discourses. Indeed, *para-dox*—that is, "going against the received beliefs" [*taghāyur*]—is one of the favorite practices of Arabic literature since its emergence. The ability "to beautify the ugly and uglify the beautiful" has been a desired skill from at least the seventh century. Abū Hilāl al-ʿAskarī (d.af.1005) attributed examples of this poetical skill to Ibn Muqaffaʿ (d.ca.755), while Abū al-Faraj al-Iṣfahānī (d.967) and Ibn Durayd (d.933) gave examples from even earlier poets, Labīd (d.661) and Ḥasan ibn Thābit (d.680), respectively. Such literary paradoxes were widely employed early on in diverse arenas of Arabic scholarship, no less than the scowling field of law. Just to give an example, the distinguished Ḥanafī jurist Abū Yūsuf al-Anṣārī (d.798) grumbled that knowledge through speculative theology [*kalām*] is ignorance, and ignorance of it is knowledge. A key figure in the long historiography of Arabic literary and poetical paradox was the famous polymath al-Jāḥiẓ (d.869), yet he was not the first person to spill ink on paradox, describing it as a poetical and literary skill. Al-Jāḥiẓ himself quoted the poet Kulthūm Ibn ʿAmr al-ʿAttābī (d.823 or 835), who had already listed "rendering what is false in the form of what is true" as one of the elements of eloquence.[1]

In some cases, the poetical virtuosity to represent things against conventional beliefs could also entail the joint truth of two contrary statements, or opposite phrases. The famous literary critic Ibn Rashīq of Qayrawan (d.1063 or 1070) commended Abū Nuwās (d.813) for his eloquence in describing the wine maiden, who brings love-sickness, which she herself cures through serving wine. The same Ibn Rashīq introduced the term "*taghāyur*" exactly for the purpose of conceptualizing such self-contradictory statements. He wrote that *taghāyur* (or *para-dox*) "is that two opinions are contrary [*yataḍāddu*] in meaning, so that they are opposed to each other, while both are correct."[2] In this sense of the employment of

---

1. See Van Gelder, "Beautifying the Ugly and Uglifying the Beautiful"; al-Tawḥīdī, "Essayistic Prose: Al-Tawḥīdī on the Superiority of the Arabs," 198; Abrahamov, *Islamic Theology*, 28.

Abū Hilāl al-ʿAskarī employed the term *takhyīl* to address the rhetorical figure [*badīʿ*] of "giving the impression of praising while lampooning, and *vice versa*." See Heinrichs, "Takhyil: Make-Believe and Image Creation in Arabic Literary Theory," 2, 10–11.

2. Van Gelder, "Beautifying the Ugly and Uglifying the Beautiful," 328; Cowell and Ibn Rashīq, "On the Ancients and the Moderns," 72.

contradiction [*taḍādd*] in apparent violation of the law of non-contradiction, paradox embodied a key poetical device, with Abū Tammām (d.846) and Ibn al-Rūmī (d.896) as its famous early representatives. The greatest Arab court poet, al-Mutanabbī (d.965) liked employing such paradoxes as well. One of his poems is cited by Abū Manṣūr al-Thaʿālībī (d.1038), one of his most critical commentators, as an example for his paradoxical employment of contrasting propositions:

> Beloved,
> you are the world to me,
> so my leaving you
> is but my return![3]

Sufism somewhat unexpectedly comes into play exactly with the coexistence of the opposites in al-Mutanabbī's poetry. Al-Thaʿālībī dislikes the verse quoted above, arguing that al-Mutanabbī is here "imitating the expressions of the Sufis and using *their tangled words [kalimātihim al-muʿaqqada] and abstruse meanings*."[4] The employment of paradox, or tangled words with opaque meanings, for al-Thaʿālībī, is a Sufi gesture that he does not really appreciate. The example of verse by al-Mutanabbī that al-Thaʿālībī gives is unmistakably paradoxical:

> When the cup startles my hands
> I sober up—
> it won't part
> me from myself!

Yet al-Thaʿālībī was certainly not alone in associating paradox with Sufism. An earlier commentator on al-Mutanabbī's *Dīwān* (and the poet's friend), Ibn Jinnī (d.1002), claimed more vocally that al-Mutanabbī adopted a specifically Sufi style in some of his poems, saying that Al-Mutanabbī

> "took this from the style . . . of Sufi speech, like the statement of one of them:

3. Al-Thaʿālībī in Stetkevych, *Reorientations: Arabic and Persian Poetry*, 195.

4. Al-Thaʿālībī in ibid., 194 (my emphasis).

I am amazed by you and me—
you annihilated me
in you from me!

You stood me in a station
where I supposed
that you were me!"[5]

A version of the latter poem that Ibn Jinnī compares with that of al-Mutanabbī is ascribed to al-Ḥallāj. The phrase "you stood me in a station" [*aqamtanī bi-maqāmin*] is also strikingly similar to the *Book of Stations* [*Kitāb al-Mawāqif*] of his contemporary, the legendary mystic al-Niffarī. The *Book of Stations* entails seventy-seven (or more) poems, all of which begin with the phrase "he stood me in the station," of a mystical theme that changes in each poem. One can easily claim that al-Niffarī's work is one of the most exquisite books of paradoxical poems ever written. While al-Niffarī's identity is foggy, historians of the later Islamic tradition such as al-Shaʿrānī (d.1565) and Kātib Çelebī (aka Ḥajji Khalīfa) (d.1657) defined al-Niffarī as a Sufi. Himself a Sufi master [*al-shaykh al-ʿārif*], ʿAbd al-Raḥmān al-Ṣaqalī (fl.l.10th CE) directly transmitted from Sahl al-Tustarī (d.896) on the authority of al-Niffarī.[6] It is the western Sufis of the thirteenth century, Ibn al-ʿArabī, al-Shushtarī (d.1269), Bint al-Nafīs (d.1288), and ʿAfīf al-Dīn al-Tilimsānī (d.1291) who not only popularized al-Niffarī's *Book of Stations* but also firmly situated it within Sufism.

Almost contemporaneous with al-Mutanabbī, al-Ḥallāj, and al-Niffarī, the collections of Sufi teachings began emerging in the late tenth century. The manuals of al-Sarrāj, al-Kalābādhī (d.990), al-Makkī (d.996), al-Kharkūshī (d.1016), al-Sīrjānī, al-Ṭabarī, al-Qushayrī, and al-Sulamī (d.1021) contained a plethora of Arabic Sufi poems and anecdotes with dense paradoxes attributed to the earliest Sufis and their forebears. These Sufi compilations employ self-contradictions quite comfortably. Even Abū Ṭālib al-Makkī, with his conservative position in terms of Sufi language, writes that God is "last in His firstness, first in His lastness," or "first without first [*awwal bilā awwal*]; not from any first; last not to any last."[7] In

5. Ibn Jinnī in ibid., 196.

6. Böwering, *Mystical Vision of Existence in Classical Islam*, 14; also see Arberry's introduction in al-Niffarī, *Mawāqif and Mukhāṭabāt*.

7. Abū Ṭālib al-Makkī, *Qūt al-Qulūb*, 3:1171, 1173.

the same vein, amusing literary compilations of paradoxical anecdotes like Abū al-Qāsim al-Nisābūrī's (d.1016) *Wise Fools* [*ʿUqalāʾ al-Majānīn*] were already filled with Sufi themes, and narratives about the earlier Sufi masters when they emerged. These Sufi and literary compilations also provide us with a large body of evidence on early Sufi employment of a strange, unclear language, and abandonment of the customary one. Al-Kalābādhī, Farīd al-Dīn ʿAṭṭār, and others cite a theologian who accused Sufis exactly of this unhappy departure from norms in his conversation with the Baghdadian Sufi, Ibn ʿAṭāʾ (d.922). Their conversation very much reflects the issue of the "tangled words and abstruse meanings" that al-Thaʿālibī associated with Sufism:

> A certain theologian asked Abū al-ʿAbbās Ibn ʿAṭāʾ: "What is it with you, Sufis? You have spun language so that it is strange to the ears of its listeners, and you departed from customary speech." . . . Abū al-ʿAbbās replied: "We only did this because we were jealous of His power over us" [*ʿizzatihi ʿalaynā*].[8]

This brief overview resists the temptation to depict the paradoxes of Sufis as mere borrowings from Arabic poetry. A similar observation can be made on the development of paradox in Persian literature as well. The earliest extant compendium of rhetorical rules in Persian poetry was written by Rashīd al-Dīn Vaṭvāṭ (d.ca.1182). The only form of paradox that he discusses is "contrast" [*mutażādd*]—the proto-Sufi al-Ḥasan al-Baṣrī (d.728) and al-Mutanabbī are among the names that he cites. Later Shams-i Qays (fl.1204–1230), the author of the next standard manual of rhetoric, explores the art of juxtaposing contrasting things, calling it *mutābaqa*. The employment of such forms of paradox in Persian poetry preceded these

---

8. Al-Kalābādhī, *Kitāb al-Taʿarruf*, 102; al-Kalābādhī, *Doctrine of the Ṣūfīs*, 77–78; ʿAṭṭār, *Muslim Saints and Mystics*, 321; al-Suyūṭī, *Taʾyīd al-Ḥaqīqa al-ʿAliyya*, 34.

Al-Mawṣiliyya penned by al-Murtaḍā Ibn al-Shahrazūrī (d.1117) is another witness to this typical association of paradoxes with Sufism. *Al-Mawṣiliyya* is among the earliest Arabic odes [*qaṣīda*] on Sufism, and it follows earlier Sufi poetic precedents by using several prepositions to establish a paradox suggesting the spiritual nature of love:

"People of passion," I said, "Peace be upon you!
My heart's attraction to you distracts it from you."

The famous bibliographer Ibn Khallikān describes *Al-Mawṣiliyya* as an "excellent ode on the Sufi path" and praises its language as "the finest expression of the mystic way." (Homerin, "A Distant Fire," 27–39.)

compilations of the rhetorical rules. More importantly, the presence of paradox in Persian poetry coincides not only with mysticism but, more specifically, with the history of Sufi poetry. Paradoxes are densely employed in the quatrains [*rubāʿīs*] attributed to Ibn Abī al-Khayr (d.1049). Ibn Abī al-Khayr is not only counted among the pioneers of mystical Persian poetry, but he is also known to have established the first known Sufi convent in eastern Iran. The authenticity of his quatrains are debated, but at least such early examples of paradoxes were either his own, or of his associates. Aḥmad-i Jām (d.1141), whose lyrics [*ghazals*] show patterns strikingly similar to those of Rūmī, is another early Sufi poet to make use of paradoxes in his Persian quatrains.[9] Together with Ibn Abī al-Khayr, Abū al-Ḥasan Bustī is one of the earliest poets to write *rubāʿīs*. A Persian Sufi of Nishapur, Bustī was a student of Abu ʿAlī al-Fārmadhī together with Aḥmad al-Ghazālī. Bustī's famous paradoxical quatrain on the "black light" [*nūr-e siyāh*] was quoted and requoted by Persian mystics and philosophers from the time of Aḥmad al-Ghazālī and his student ʿAyn al-Qużāt Hamadānī onward.

The case of Persian prose is not different from the case of lyrics insofar as the earliest instances of paradoxes appear in unmistakably Sufi contexts. Notably, the earliest examples of paradoxes in Persian prose are al-Bisṭāmī's ecstatic sayings [*shaṭaḥāt*]—the theologically transgressive outbursts of the Sufi master. Also the hagiography of Ibn Abī al-Khayr already contained paradoxical phrases and statements by the time it took its final shape in the hands of his descendant Ibn al-Munavvar (d.1202). Accordingly, when mentioning his perpetual meditations and invocations of God in his youth, Ibn Abī al-Khayr said: "*In my seeing I was blind, in my hearing deaf, in my speaking dumb.*"[10] This is a key paradox in al-Shiblī's line, the theological importance of which cannot be overstated, for Ibn al-ʿArabī's creative and controversial hyper-literalist hermeneutics on Noah

9. Keshavarz, *Reading Mystical Lyric: The Case of Jalāl al-Dīn Rūmī*, 43; Vaṭvāṭ, *Ḥadāʾiq al-Siḥr fī Daqāʾiq al-Shiʿr*, 24–25.

Wolfhart Heinrichs notes that *takhyīl*, which might embody literary paradoxes in various context, indicates "amphiboly, double entendre" for Vaṭvāṭ. (See Heinrichs, "*Takhyil*: Make-Believe and Image Creation in Arabic Literary Theory," 2, 14.) Hence he sees *takhyīl* interchangeable with *tawriya*, and introduces *takhyīl* under *īhām*. (Vaṭvāṭ *Ḥadāʾiq al-Siḥr fī Daqāʾiq al-Shiʿr*, 39–42.) As Heinrichs notes, the encyclopedist al-Nuwayrī (d.1332), and authors like Shihāb al-Dīn al-ḥalabī, Ibn Mālik al-Ruʿaynī, Ibn ḥijja, and Ibn Maʿṣūm listed these three terms as synonyms, which differed from the speech figures that signify paradox.

10. See Nicholson, *Studies in Islamic Mysticism*, 12.

employs the subversion of the same terms in the Qur'an.[11] Briefly, Persian Sufism was already a wellspring of paradoxes in the twelfth century even before the compilation of the Persian rhetorical rules. The early development of paradox in Persian literature and poetry, very much like in Arabic, is strongly tied to Sufism.

Paradox of Human Apotheosis: From Sufism to Philosophy?

An explicit and intriguing case of Sufi paradoxes adopted by others can be shown in the case of one of the most important philosophers in history. Ibn Sīnā's labor on logic was so significant that by the end of the twelfth century, Aristotle ceased to be a significant coordinate for logicians writing in Arabic—that place having been filled by Ibn Sīnā. Ibn Sīnā devoted volumes to logic, and he strictly followed logical meta-principles, including the laws of exclusive bivalence and non-contradiction, in the demonstration of proofs or refutations. Yet there is one context wherein the joint presence of opposites, hence the apparent transgression of the law of non-contradiction, did not indicate a violation of logic for him. This is the penultimate section of Ibn Sīnā's *Pointers and Reminders* [*al-Ishārāt wa-l-Tanbīhāt*] where he explained "the Stations of the Gnostics" [*maqāmāt al-ʿārifīn*] with a densely Sufi terminology. According to Fakhr al-Dīn al-Rāzī, the key figure in the establishment of the commentary tradition on the *Pointers and Reminders*, this was the most important section of the monumental work insofar as it explained "the path of Sufis."[12] As Ibn Sīnā described it, the stations of the gnostics began with their remaking into "an aspirant" [*murīd*] via a transformation in their volition [*irāda*]. Then the purification of their souls could begin with self-disciplinary practices [*riyāḍa*]. At an advanced level, the gnostic-aspirant was donated a stable attainment of gnosis via her self-disciplinary practices. At this level, the aspirant's constantly changing states transformed [*inqilāb*] into non-transformation [*sakīna*] where apparently exclusive binaries unified. In Ibn Sīnā's words, "the stolen prize [*makhṭūf*] becomes the commonplace

11. Anonymous, *ʿIlm al-Taṣawwuf*, 199. See Ibn al-ʿArabī, *Fuṣūṣ al-Ḥikam*, ch. 3, 68–74. Ibn al-ʿArīf's *Assemblies* employed the same subversion of meaning in these binaries. See Ibn al-ʿArīf, *Maḥāsin al-Majālis*, 93. For a new French translation, see Ibn al-ʿArīf, *Splenderus des Enseignements Soufis*, 40.

12. Ṭūsī in Ibn Sīnā, *al-Ishārāt wa-l-Tanbīhāt*, 4:47. Cf. Ibn Sabʿīn, *Budd al-ʿĀrif*, 144.

[*ma'lūf*]. The twinkling one [*al-wamīḍ*] becomes a fixed star [*shihāb*]."[13] Not only what she is witnessing but also the aspirant-gnostic herself becomes the coincidence of opposites—the *embodied paradox*: "Up to this point, [the gnostic-aspirant] was maybe manifesting whatever he was undergoing. Once he is immersed in this gnosis, his presence will dwindle. *So he becomes absent-present* [*ghā'ib ḥāḍir*], *and moving-stable* [*ẓā'in muqīm*]."[14]
Ibn Sīnā's unusual employment of an X-not-X form of paradox in relation to human perfection is significant on the basis of three immediate observations.

(1) First, one of the most influential logicians of his times, Ibn Sīnā adopts paradoxical self-contradictory phrases, without immediately assuming that this is violating logical principles—a position unlike many contemporary scholars of religion. Instead, philosophers paid utmost attention to logical principles, and their employment of paradoxes followed these principles. Indeed, in his commentary on Aristotle's *Metaphysics*, Ibn Sīnā claims that one should threaten the "obstinate" opponent of the law of non-contradiction with being thrown into a fire, as it should not make any difference for that person. "Let him be beaten, since suffering and not suffering are the same. Let him be deprived of food and drink, since eating and drinking are identical to abstaining." For Aristotle himself, one had nothing to talk about with such a fool who asks for a proof for the law of non-contradiction, "for, insofar as he does not engage in any rational discourse, *he is like a plant*."[15] In brief, there is no reason to argue that Ibn Sīnā calls for canceling, queering, or transgressing logical principles in employing self-contradictory statements in describing human perfection.

ʿAyn al-Qużāt reports another instance of Ibn Sīnā's appeal of paradoxes. In this case too, the context is the perfection of the human soul, and it relates to the popular Sufi master of the time, Ibn Abī al-Khayr. Accordingly, Ibn Abī al-Khayr wrote a letter to Ibn Sīnā, asking for a proof of God. Ibn Sīnā responded with a treatise where he claimed that the proof is "entering into real infidelity [*al-kufr al-ḥaqīqī*] and leaving behind metaphorical Islam [*al-islām al-majāzī*]. It is that you do not orient yourself toward anything . . . until you *become one who submits to God and is an*

13. Ibn Sīnā, *al-Ishārāt wa-l-Tanbīhāt*, 4:88.

14. Ibid., 4:89.

15. Aristotle, *Selections*, 253 (1006a, ll.14–15) (my emphasis); Ibn Sīnā in Horn, "Contradiction." Al-Māturīdī also claimed that the person who denies reasoning has nothing but reasoning itself to support their claim. (Al-Māturīdī, *Kitāb al-Tawḥīd*, 73.)

infidel." In other words, ʿAyn al-Qużāt situates Ibn Sīnā within the sustained tradition of love mysticism, and describes him appealing to paradoxes in the context of human perfection. The apotheosis of the human soul is its turning into an embodied paradox. Within this clearly mystical context, the Sufi master Ibn Abī al-Khayr naturally responds that "I have received more benefit from these words than I would have from a hundred thousand years of worship."[16]

Ibn Sīnā was not the only Muslim philosopher of his time to employ such paradoxical statements in the context of human perfection. The great Muʿtazilite polymath al-Jāḥiẓ, who had a fundamental role in the development of paradoxes in Arabic literature, employed self-contradictory statements within this very context. Transmitting the late Khārijite rebel Abū Ḥamza's (d.747) description of the piety of his own radical sect, al-Jāḥiẓ wrote that "these are young men who are *old in their young age.*"[17] But Ibn Sīnā had more immediate precedents from within Islamic philosophy. Just a couple of decades before Ibn Sīnā, Abū Ḥayyān al-Tawḥīdī's teacher, Abū Sulaymān al-Sijistānī adopted the X-not-X form of paradox as well, with a careful logical explanation reminiscent of Aristotle's critique of the violations of the principle of non-contradiction. Al-Tawḥīdī reports that a nightly session gathered in the learned circle of Ibn Saʿdān (d.986), the vizier of the Būyid Grand Amīr in Baghdad. The topic of the group of lovers [*muḥibb*] of philosophy in the session was whether temperament [*akhlāq*] is changeable or fixed. Abū Sulaymān al-Sijistānī points to the perspective-dependency of the human temperament. Accordingly, the same person might appear to have opposite qualities, depending on this perspectival difference:

> The knowledge of our own temperament is generally not transparent to us. Our companions [*ṣāḥib*], neighbors [*jār*], and friends [*ʿashīr*] might know us better [than we know ourselves], even though we might assume the opposite. Hence, *we are knower-ignorant, aware-neglectful, coward-brave, gentle-severe.*[18]

16. See Safi, *Politics of Knowledge in Premodern Islam*, 178–179.

17. Al-Jāḥiẓ in Zaman, "The Relevance of Religion and the Response to It," 273 (my emphasis).

18. Al-Tawḥīdī, *al-Muqābasāt*, 141.

Al-Sijistānī's employment of the self-contradictory phrases strictly follows the principles of Aristotelian logic rather than lacking, transgressing or canceling it. Indeed, not only the pivotal role of friendship but also the immediately following discussion in the session displays the heavily Aristotelian context, insofar as al-Sijistānī defends the idea that a "golden mean" [*al-mizāj al-muʿtadil*] is the key to a virtuous human temperament. Self-contradictory statements are not seen as a violation of the law of noncontradiction but rather as perfectly consistent with it, if one follows logical principles and uncovers the unstated categories in such a compound statement. A person might be simultaneously absent (at a certain given moment, in a specific location, in one sense, from one perspective, etc.) and present (at another moment, in another location, in another sense, from another perspective, etc.).[19] Abū Ḥayyān himself stresses the necessity of following logical principles in any speculation. Aristotelian logic is not a rival to be challenged with paradoxes; rather, it is the remedy for solving apparent contradictions according to Ibn Sīnā and other philosophers.

(2) The second observation is in support of the widespread association of Sufism with paradox. The same paradox in Ibn Sīnā's *Pointers and Reminders*, with a strikingly similar word choice and in the same context, appears in the famous Sufi manual of Ibn Sīnā's fellow countryman, al-Kalābādhī. Al-Kalābādhī had employed the same paradoxical binary of "absent-present" in the introduction to the *Disclosure of the Path of the Sufis* [*Kitāb al-Taʿarruf*], where the term "Sufi" appeared for the first time in the book:

> [The elects] were spiritual-bodily, ordinary-divine, silent-observing, absent-present, kings in rags, outcasts from every tribe, possessors of all virtues and lights of all guidance; their ears attentive, their hearts pure [*ṣāfiya*], their qualities concealed—chosen [*ṣafawiyya*], "Ṣūfīs," illuminated, pure [*ṣafiyya*].[20]

---

19. Al-Tawḥīdī, *al-Muqābasāt*, 141. Al-Sijistānī's explanation finds literary repercussion in Najm al-Dīn Abū Rajā' Qummī's (d.1188) description of the ill-tempered Saljūqī vizier Dargazīnī (d.1133). The historian wrote that Dargazīnī was like "a lightning in which there is both the possibility of merciful rain, and the fear of the fire caused by lightning. *In him there was both loss and benefit.*" (Qummī in Safi, *Politics of Knowledge in Premodern Islam*, 193 [my emphasis].)

20. Al-Kalābādhī, *Kitāb al-Taʿarruf*, 6. Here I followed Arberry's translation with slight modifications; see al-Kalābādhī, *Doctrine of the Ṣūfīs*, 2.

A possible influence of al-Kalābādhī on Ibn Sīnā, and even their personal encounter, has long been postulated, yet the evidence was rather feeble. One major point of theoretical convergence between the two is the distinction between "ontological" and "cosmological" approaches to God that Ibn Sīnā makes use of in his proof. The distinction is based on the dichotomy between "disclosure" [*taʿarruf*] and "making known" [*taʿrīf*], firmly rooted in Sufi theory pre-dating Ibn Sīnā.[21] The distinction is evident from the very title of the Sufi manual of al-Kalābādhī, who himself attributes the *taʿrīf-taʿarruf* dichotomy further back to the Sufi master al-Junayd. Al-Kalābādhī and Ibn Sīnā also cite the same Qurʾanic verse on the dichotomy. Al-Kalābādhī's situation of the *taʿrīf-taʿarruf* dichotomy within mysticism finds further support in al-Niffarī's enigmatic *Book of Stations*. The distinction, indeed, appears within the context of a paradox on divine proximity and distance, which Ibn al-ʿArabī, among other later Sufis, intensively employed. Al-Niffarī wrote:

> I am the near, but not as one thing is near to another.
> And I am the far, but not as one thing is far from another.
> Thy nearness is not thy farness, and thy farness is not thy nearness.
> *I am the near-far, with a nearness which is farness, and a farness which is nearness.*
> The nearness which *thou knowest* [*taʿrīf*] is distance,
> And the farness which *thou knowest* [*taʿrīf*] is distance: *I am the near-far without distance.*
> . . .
> *I disclosed* [*taʿarruf*] *Myself unto thee, and thou knewest Me not*: that is farness.
> Thy heart saw Me, and saw Me not: that is farness.[22]

The *taʿrīf-taʿarruf* distinction was employed by the mystic al-Niffarī within a densely paradoxical context. The distinction that Ibn Sīnā appealed to was already situated within the field of mysticism by the tenth century.

21. Mayer, "Theology and Sufism," 279.

22. Al-Niffarī, *Mawāqif and Mukhāṭabāt*, 28 (English translation), 2–3 (Arabic text) (my emphases; with my slight modifications).

For the Arabic original with al-Tilimsānī's commentary, see al-Tilimsānī and al-Niffarī, *Sharḥ Mawāqif al-Niffarī*, 73–76.

In addition to this distinction, we can now postulate another continuity between the Bukharan author of a Sufi manual and his polymath townsman: the adoption of an X-not-X form of paradox within the context and vocabulary of Sufi wayfaring.

Al-Kalābādhī is by no means the first Sufi to employ self-contradictory statements to describe the apotheosis of the soul. Indeed, if we follow al-Tilimsānī, the paradox of the "near-far" in al-Niffarī's *Book of Stations* is actually a reference to the Sufi wayfarer's attainment of perfection. While al-Niffarī's affiliation with Sufism is dubious, we can still safely postulate that the Sufi employment of self-contradictory statements within the context of the soul's perfection precedes that of philosophers by almost a couple of centuries. Al-Junayd himself, introducing the ones who have attained the degree of "gnostic" [*ʿārif*], employs self-negating binaries closely related to the ones that al-Kalābādhī and Ibn Sīnā adopted. Accordingly, the gnostics are at once present and absent, absent and present: "*[The gnostic] is found-lost [mawjūd mafqūd], and lost-found; he is as he is not, and he is not as he is.*"[23] The Persian Sufi manual of Hujvīrī (d.1077), the *Unveiling of the Hidden* [*Kashf al-Maḥjūb*] even reports a debate among some Sufi masters on the paradoxical nature the soul attains during daily prayer [*namāz*]:"One group said: 'Prayer is a means to attain presence.' Another group said: 'It is a means to attain absence.' The group that was in absence became present in the prayer; and those who were present became absent."[24] But our sources trace paradoxes on the perfection of the human soul even further back among Sufis. Al-Kharkūshī reports an exquisite example from Bāyazīd al-Bisṭāmī, the famous master of ecstatic utterances:

> Al-Bisṭāmī was asked: "When does one know whether he is on track to the reality of gnosis?" He said: "When he becomes annihilated [*fāniyan*] under divine knowledge, and persistent [*bāqiyan*] in the divine realm without ego, without causality, and without engendering. So he is *annihilated-persistent, dead-alive, alive-dead, veiled-manifested, manifested-veiled.*[25]

---

23. Al-Junayd, *Rasāʾil al-Junayd*, 58. Cf. ibid., 54. Also see Abdel-Kader, *The Life, Personality and Writings of al-Junayd*, 103.

24. Hujvīrī, *Kitāb Kashf al-Maḥjūb*, 387. For English translations, see Hujvīrī, *A Persian Treatise on Sufism*, 301; Hujvīrī, *Kashf al-Maḥjūb*, ch.19, 398.

25. Al-Kharkūshī, *Tahdhīb al-Asrār*, 46.

Similarly, the attainment of ultimate knowledge, which is eventually a negative one, the docta ignorantia, is one of many cases in which al-Bisṭāmī appeals to dizzying paradoxes: "The servant continues to know so long as he remains unknowing, but when he leaves his unknowing his knowing departs" [*lā yazālu al-ʿabdu ʿārifan mā dāma jāhilan fa-idhā zāla ʿan jahlihi zālat maʿrifatuhu*].[26]

Such paradoxical descriptions of human perfection became a widespread Sufi theme well before the rise of Ibn al-ʿArabī, whose school saw the human being as the coincidence of opposites that mirrors the paradox of the divine essence. Ibn al-ʿArabī's own teacher ʿAbd al-ʿAzīz al-Mahdawī (d.1221), according to Ibn al-Qunfudh (d.1407), wrote a panegyric poem for his master and the pole of Sufis of the West, Abū Madyan (d.1198), praising him with paradoxes: "*You are present and not present, absent and not absent.*" The oldest Persian treatise on love theology that we know, Aḥmad al-Ghazālī's *Incidents of Lovers* [*Savāniḥ al-ʿUshshāq*] also intensively employs paradoxes not only in verse but also prose to describe the apophatic perfection that the soul attains through being consumed in divine love:

> Love should devour both separation and union. As long as the reality of union is in love's crop, the possibility of separation is removed. And this is something that not everyone understands. Since union is partition, partition is nothing other than union. Therefore, parting from one's self is the same as union. At this level, food is foodlessness, being is non-being, attainment is non-attainment, and having a share is having no share.[27]

The eponym of the Rifāʿiyya, a major Sufi order in Iraq and Anatolia, described those who have attained gnosis as "*dead-living, living-dead, veiled-unveiled, and unveiled-veiled.*" Rūmī's Bukharan master Sayyid Burhān al-Dīn (d.1244) employed self-contradictory phrases in his description of the soul's perfection in the daily prayer, echoing Hujvīrī. Accordingly, the faithful see creation through divine lenses during the prayer. In this condition, they are *absent-present, drunken-wine.* The binary of "absent-present" follows that of al-Kalābādhī and Ibn Sīnā, and the "drunken-wine" binary Abū Nuwās' description of the wine maiden—both, however,

26. Al-Bisṭāmī in Frank, "'Lam Yazal' as a Formal Term in Muslim Theological Discourse," 244–245.

27. Aḥmad al-Ghazālī, *Sawāniḥ: Inspirations from the World of Pure Spirits*, 24.

now in Persian instead of Arabic. His student, Rūmī is the poet of paradoxes, but his discourses and conversations also witness his appeal to self-contradictory statements on human perfection. During an audition [*samāʿ*] assembly, when a drunken dervish at the height of ecstasy questions the theological veracity of an utterance of Rūmī, the master declares that it was not an unintentional outburst. Instead, the ecstatic saying was perfect both from esoteric and exoteric perspectives. Accordingly, the dervish was drunken, but Rūmī himself was "sober-drunken." He celebrates his perfect mirror-companion, Shams Tabrīzī, via similar paradoxes, such as "mature-immature" (or "cooked-raw") [*pukhta tūyi khām tūyi*], "droplet-ocean" [*qaṭra tūyi baḥr tūyi*], "blessing-anguish" [*lutf tūyi qahr tūyi*], and "sweet-poison" [*qand tūyi zahr tūyi*]. Farīd al-Dīn ʿAṭṭār's description of the wayfarer at the valley of perplexity [*ḥayrat*] employs a wide array of apparently self-contradictory binaries, like Rūmī. The one who arrives at the valley of perplexity messes with many binaries, including day and night, absence and presence, and sobriety and drunkenness—she becomes a "frozen fire." Per Rūmī, ʿAṭṭār himself follows a sustained tradition that depicts human nature as the coincidence of the opposites. She is the soul and the body, the raised and the lowly, the pure and the impure—both the very Sulṭān herself as well as her vicegerent.[28]

(3) The third observation: these abundant cases of paradoxical human perfection are irreducible to self-contradictory statements. Rather than nullifying or canceling logical principles, the transcendence of binaries presents a subtle, still logical, twist. For example, ʿAmmār al-Bidlīsī (d.1207) summarizes the most popular explanation of the self-contradictory descriptions of Sufis as the "dead-living." He writes that "they are 'dead' in terms of humanity and habits; 'alive' with the attributes of lordship and witnessing."[29] In other words, such self-contradictory propositions actually embody intended performative challenges to the propositional discourse, and instead follow the principle of non-contradiction at the dialectical level. They are performative gestures that indicate the transcendence of propositional discourse through a rather rigorous, systematic,

28. Ibn al-Qunfudh in Elmore, "Shaykh ʿAbd al-ʿAzīz al-Mahdawī, Ibn al-ʿArabī's Mentor," 604; Aḥmad al-Rifāʿī, *Ḥālat Ahl al-Ḥaqīqa maʿa Allāh Taʿāla*, 9; Sayyid Burhān al-Dīn, *Maʿārif*, 48; Aflākī, *Ariflerin Menkıbeleri*, 1:283. Rūmī, *Kulliyyāt-i Dīvān-i Shams*, 64. (Shahram Nazeri [b.1950], the famous Iranian musician, performs this poem in his album *Flames in the Reedbed* [*Ātash Dar Nayastān*].) ʿAṭṭār, *Manṭiq al-Ṭayr*, verse 4125, verses 135–140.

29. ʿAmmār al-Bidlīsī, "Bahjat al-Ṭāʾifa," 59 (Arabic text).

logical employment of carefully chosen binaries that sustain it. Within the context of human apotheosis, if X-not-X statements or phrases do not adopt a systematic dialectical logic and stay merely at the propositional level, they cannot go beyond outright contradictions for many medieval Sufis. In other words, the coincidence of opposites is acceptable only on dialectical grounds. The Andalusian Sufi Ibn Sabʿīn's discussion of paradoxes and self-contradiction within the context of his explanation of Aristotle's *Categories* [*Maqūlāt*] is particularly helpful. Here Ibn Sabʿīn introduces the ten categories that define the logical possibilities in which a subject can relate to its predicate. If these categories are ill-defined, then apparent self-contradictions might arise due to vagueness. In other words, self-contradictions emerge because one does not understand or apply logic rigorously enough at the propositional level. Ibn Sabʿīn's fierce critique of the prominent polymath Abū Ḥāmid al-Ghazālī is another exemplary case. The Andalusian mystic accuses al-Ghazālī of inconsistency, as he joins irreconcilable opposites in his body:

> Al-Ghazālī—a discourse lacking explanation [*lisān dūna bayān*], a voice lacking remark [*ṣawt dūna kalām*], *a hodgepodge that unites the opposites* [*takhlīṭ yajmaʿ al-aḍdād*], *a breath-taking confusion* . . . Now he is a Sufi, now a philosopher, now an Ashʿarī, now a jurist, and now, *puzzle-headed*![30]

ʿUmar al-Suhrawardī's Sufi manual the *Guidance of the Aspirants* [*Irshād al-Murīdīn*], which is based on al-Qushayrī's famous *Epistle on Sufism*, shares Ibn Sabʿīn's distaste with the coincidence of the opposites in the propositional level. Accordingly, praised and reviled attributes are opposites [*ḍiddān*]. One should disappear if the other emerges, insofar as two opposite attributes cannot exist in the same locus in the same sense.[31] If we limit them to the realm of propositional logic, X-not-X phrases are nothing but self-contradiction for these prominent Sufis. They become indicators

30. Ibn Sabʿīn, *Budd al-ʿĀrif*, 144; Ibn Sabʿīn, *al-Kalām ʿalā al-Masāʾil al-Ṣiqilliyya*, 54–57.

Ibn Rushd directed a parallel critique toward al-Ghazālī, adorning it with an old Arabic poem. (Cf. Ibn Rushd, "The Decisive Treatise," 178.) Ibn Taymiyya later cites the same poem, reporting Ibn Rushd's distaste with al-Ghazālī's supposed duplicity. See Hanif, *Biographical Encyclopaedia of Sufis: Central Asia and Middle East*, 179.

31. ʿUmar al-Suhrawardī, *Irshād al-Murīdīn*, MS Şehit Ali Paşa 1397, 7b.

of a deeper truth only if understood from a dialectical perspective that aims to take the reader beyond these self-contradictory binaries.

Bābā Afżāl, the Avicennian philosopher and mystic explains this dialectical logic in employing self-contradictory statements, again, within the context of human flourishing. The marks of the soul's perfection are, for Bābā Afżāl, distinctly paradoxical, similar to the statements of al-Kalābādhī and Ibn Sīnā: "[The perfected ones] are patient in trial and grateful in comfort. *They are the absent-present, the far-near, the evident-hidden*, the lamp in darkness and obscurity, the clarification in bewilderment and bafflement."[32] Do these paradoxical binaries violate the law of non-contradiction, or invalidate logical analysis? Not at all, according to Bābā Afżāl, because the unregulated breaking of the law of non-contradiction indicates the logical failure of that statement. Self-contradictory statements on human apotheosis, for Bābā Afżāl, do follow logical meta-principles. The contraries in such statements are either about different states of the body or about the states of the soul, which can coexist because they are not contraries, as the knowledge of two opposites is not self-contradictory. Bābā Afżāl argues:

> Two incompatibles, two contraries, and two opposites can exist together in the soul, and from the one's existence the other's existence is not nullified or made deficient—such as movement and rest, life and death, white and black. From the existence and knowing of movement, the existence and knowing of rest are neither nullified nor weakened and made deficient, for the soul knows both together. So also are life and death, white and black, and the other contraries. But in the body, the existence of movement nullifies the existence of rest, and so also rest movement, and *both cannot be found within it together in one state*.[33]

Bābā Afżāl's explanation, like that of Abū Sulaymān al-Sijistānī, follows Aristotle's response to Heraclitean paradoxes and moves to clarify the different conditions under which the predication is made. The perfected ones transcend the logical binaries in propositional logic, but their

---

32. Bābā Afżāl in Chittick, *The Heart of Islamic Philosophy*, 267 (my emphasis).

33. Bābā Afżāl in ibid., 265 (my emphasis). Bābā Afżāl's argument strikingly follows the same logic with Imām Riḍā's (d.818) challenge to the Muʿtazilite theologian in al-Maʾmūn's court. See the section below, "Paradox in Theological Questions."

transcendence itself follows a dialectical rule that complies with the principle of non-contradiction.

Najm al-Dīn Kubrā's emphasis on the law of non-contradiction is another excellent illustration of the role of logical principles in the dialectical employment of paradoxes in Sufi wayfaring. Kubrā claims that a Sufi can be in the state of "fear-hope," or "contraction-expansion," at a given time. His explanation carefully follows the meta-principles of logic. First, Kubrā explains that the states of fear and hope are not logical opposites, and they can co-exist in the same state of the soul. Hence the state of "fear-hope" does not really violate logical meta-principles. The case is different with the binary of contraction and expansion. According to Kubrā, contraction and expansion are indeed opposites that cannot be united [*ḍiddān lā yajtamiʿān*] in one state of the soul. Here Kubrā perceptively adds another dimension that specifically clarifies the logical employment of this binary. Accordingly, "the station of transformation" [*maqām al-talwīn*], very much like ʿAṭṭār's "valley of perplexity," is a peculiar level of the soul, in which opposite states can coexist without violating the law of non-contradiction. If one clarifies the exact station of the soul, the apparent contradictions in the coexistence of temporary states will be solved. [34] In the *Stations of the Sufis* [*Maqāmāt al-Ṣūfiyya*] Yaḥyā al-Suhrawardī (d.1191) makes the same point. After stating that "gnosis has primacy over love, and love has primacy over gnosis" on the Sufi path, he explains how this apparent self-contradiction is solved when the terms of primacy are clarified.[35]

Even medieval scholars directly treating Ibn al-ʿArabī's paradoxical views did not accept the coincidence of opposites in contexts where it meant unregulated self-contradiction. Quṭb al-Dīn Shīrāzī's exposition of Ibn al-ʿArabī's cosmological and eschatological position exemplifies such an excellent appeal to logic to solve apparent contradictions. In a letter written to Quṭb al-Dīn at the end of thirteenth century, a certain scholar named Aḥmad expressed his concern over the fate of human soul in the afterlife:

> If misery is real, then the soul must descend. This, however, is contrary to what we hope for from the divine mercy. If it goes neither to bliss nor to misery, a suspension will occur. Its going to

34. Hence Kubrā does not support Sviri's assumption that fear and hope were necessarily opposite, "antithetical states" for Sufis. Cf. Sviri, "Between Fear and Hope," 333–344. Najm al-Dīn Kubrā, *Fawāʾiḥ al-Jamāl wa Fawātiḥ al-Jalāl*, 189.

35. Yaḥyā al-Suhrawardī, *Maqāmāt al-Ṣūfiyya*, 82.

> both together will combine two opposites [*fa-yakūn jamʿan bayna ḍiddayn*].[36]

Aḥmad is questioning here whether the human soul can attain opposite qualities that survive death. The response of Quṭb al-Dīn Shīrāzī is strongly Akbarī and logical at the same time. In his response to the questions on eschatology, he gives a long exposition of Ibn al-ʿArabī's cosmology, quoting the *Bezels of Wisdom* [*Fuṣūṣ al-Ḥikam*] for pages, and answering each question within this framework. When he comes to the question of whether the human soul can combine opposites in the afterlife, Quṭb al-Dīn's answer, again, underlines the categorical differences in the two statements: "man's being *happy in one respect* and *in misery in another* only implies *the conjunction of two opposites only in speech, and not in reality*."[37] No contradiction remains once we follow Aristotle's advice and clarify that contradictory phrases apply to the same subject but in different respects.

None of these paradoxical cases of human apotheosis advocate the overturning of the law of non-contradiction. Instead, they all emphasize the incapacity of propositional logic on issues that transcend its nomenclature with its distinct discursive binaries. They indicate the transcendence of propositional logic via the employment of paradoxes that specifically target the key binaries of the discourse on human perfection. Paradox follows a rule-governed, dialectical logic: it systematically cancels the endemic binaries that ground a specific discourse, in order to show its incapacity in the propositional level.

Paradoxes of Late Antiquity in Philosophy

The presence of al-Kalābādhī's contradictory phrases in the influential works of subsequent philosophers in the same context of human apotheosis is arresting, because such statements are otherwise fiercely opposed by philosophers. The Arabic terms that Muslim philosophers employed to refer to such self-contradictory phrases were normally quite negative: "sophistry" [*safsaṭa*] and "contradiction" [*tanāqudh*] were depicted as kinds of fallacy production [*mughālaṭa*]. The evidence goes back to

36. Aḥmad in Walbridge, *The Science of Mystic Lights*, 203 (English text); 236 (Arabic text).

37. Quṭb al-Dīn Shīrāzī in Walbridge, *The Science of Mystic Lights*, 227 (English text); 265 (Arabic text); my emphases.

al-Kindī. He was the first scholar to frame a logical study of "infinity" as a mathematical concept. Al-Kindī showed that an infinite object would lead to its own negation and result in the simultaneous truth of a statement and its negation. This, for al-Kindī, was a violation of the law of non-contradiction. Hence, a statement in the form of "X-not-X" derived by syllogism was nothing but self-contradiction. The popular logical argumentations known as *reductio ad absurdum* [*al-khulf*], conversion [*al-ʿaks al-mustawī*], or full contraposition [*ʿaks al-naqīḍ*] relied on the idea that self-contradictory statements were violations of the law of non-contradiction, hence logically false, as al-Kindī, Ibn Sīnā, Yaḥyā al-Suhrawardī, Athīr al-Dīn al-Abharī (d.1266), and others explained.[38]

The popular paradoxes of Late Antiquity were familiar to Arabic philosophers, particularly through the unfriendly lens of Aristotle. His *Sophistical Fallacies* was already among the books translated into Arabic commissioned by the ʿAbbāsid Caliph al-Mahdī (r.775–785), while another version of the book was also produced by the circle of al-Kindī. From this prevailing Aristotelian perspective that would shape the madrasa system, these ancient paradoxes embodied unpleasant logical mistakes. When introducing the two famous ancient paradoxographers, Zeno and Parmenides, Ibn Fātik wrote that they followed "*the path of paradoxes*" [*madhhab al-ghawāmiḍ*], and he does not hide his dislike for this path in describing Zeno's work: "a book of his written in the African language was found after his death. It was inundated with filṭh on the issue of metaphysics." The Paradox of Inquiry, or the question of how unknown things can be apprehended, also known as the Meno Paradox [*al-majhūl al-muṭlaq*] was sharply criticized by al-Fārābī and later by Ibn Sīnā. Both of them refused Plato's original solution—that is, the doctrine that "learning is a recollection"—in favor of the construction of a "rule-governed art," which follows nothing but syllogism. The final answer to the Paradox of Inquiry was, for al-Fārābī, circumscribed by the canons of Aristotelian demonstrative science. In approaching the Paradox of Inquiry, like al-Fārābī, Ibn Sīnā emphasized the distinction between conceptualization [*taṣawwur*] and

38. Ibn Sīnā, *al-Ishārāt wa-l-Tanbīhāt*, 1:403–431; Yaḥyā al-Suhrawardī, *Majmūʿa-yi Muṣannafāt*, 2:40; al-Abharī, *Hidayetü'l-Hikme'nin Tenkitli Neşri*, 159–160 (for an English translation, see al-Abharī, *A Guide to Philosophy*, 113–115); Ibn Taymiyya, *Against Greek Logicians*, 141–142; Garro, "The Paradox of the Infinite by al-Kindī"; Street, "Arabic and Islamic Philosophy of Language and Logic."

assent [*taṣdīq*].[39] As Socrates did not distinguish between the two concepts, he falsely fell into the fallacy in which a person can simultaneously know and not know something. "This is not logical discourse," claimed Ibn Sīnā. As a logical weakness, the Meno Paradox arose because the premises were ambiguous. Once they were more clearly framed by the distinction between conceptualization and assent, it would become evident that we can conceptualize something that we do not exactly know. We have the Meno Paradox not because it transcends and challenges the principle of non-contradiction, but because the categories that determine the truth value of the statement are not well-stated.[40]

The Liar Paradox [*al-jadhr al-aṣamm*] was also known at least since the late ninth century to the Muʿtazilite theologians according to Sayf al-Dīn al-Āmidī (d.1243). But it was two philosophers contemporary with al-Āmidī, Athīr al-Dīn al-Abharī and Naṣīr al-Dīn Ṭūsī, who represent the first substantive work on the Liar Paradox in the Arabic tradition. Al-Abharī stated the Liar Paradox as a "difficult fallacy" [*mughālaṭa*] in the X-not-X form:

> One of the difficult fallacies is the conjunction of the two contradictories [*jamʿ al-naqīḍayn*] when someone says, "All that I say at this moment is false." This sentence is either true or false. If it is true, then it must be true and false. And if it is not true, then it is necessary that one of his sentences at this moment is true, as long as he utters something. But, he says nothing at this moment other than this sentence. Thus, this sentence is necessarily true and false.[41]

For al-Abharī, the Liar Paradox was an instance of a self-contradictory statement, which was nothing but a logical fallacy. Al-Abharī's *Guide to Philosophy* [*Hidāyat al-Ḥikma*] clearly manifested the Aristotelian lens in

---

39. Ibn Fātik, *Mukhtār al-Ḥikam*, 96v97; Black, "Al-Fārābī on Meno's Paradox." Ibn Taymiyya also recognizes that the distinction lies at the very foundation of logic: "They have held that, inasmuch as knowledge is either a concept [*taṣawwur*] or a judgment [*taṣdīq*], the means by which a concept is formed is a definition, and that by which a judgment is formed is a syllogism." (Ibn Taymiyya, *Against Greek Logicians*, 5–6.)

40. Ibn Sīnā in Marmura, "Avicenna on Meno's Paradox," 55. By replacing Plato with Socrates, Ibn Sīnā saves Plato from inconsistency.

For Abū Ḥāmid al-Ghazālī's (and later, al-Rāzī's) indirect way of dealing with Meno Paradox through a logical analysis of al-Ashʿarī's circular definition of knowledge, see Fakhr al-Dīn al-Rāzī, *Munāẓarāt*, 46–47.

41. Al-Abharī in Alwishah and Sanson, "The Early Arabic Liar," 107.

this judgment. Accordingly, an X-not-X compound statement is derived in the case of unity of the predicate, subject, relation, time, place, condition, potentiality or actuality, and particularity or universality categories. In other words, if one does not clearly state the categories that determine the conditions under which a statement is given, then the statement will be ambiguous enough to give rise to such self-contradictory statements. Naṣīr al-Dīn Ṭūsī was the first intellectual in history (of whom we know) to approach the Liar Paradox as a problem of self-reference that can be better understood and solved by logic. Ṭūsī's innovative approach to the Liar Paradox was critical to that of al-Abharī, yet his solution depicted it as a logical fallacy as well. Ibn Sabʿīn also discussed a couple of paradoxes with reference to Zeno ["*Zīzi*"], labeling them as logical fallacies [*mughālaṭa*] and sophistries that emerge due to the lack of rigorous application of logic. After the thirteenth century, with the increasing contributions of Ottoman and Indo-Muslim logicians, the interest in paradoxes, particularly in the Liar Paradox, Meno's paradox, and certain apparent paradoxes of conditional logic (such as the *consequentia mirabilis*) intensified. Yet the negative attitude toward self-contradictory statements prevailed. Such statements were considered instances of logical fallacies for philosophers and logicians, as long as it is others who utter them.[42]

Their unfavorable approach to paradoxes did not mean that Muslim philosophers' own doctrines were free of paradoxes, and they were certainly not.

Paradox in Theological Questions

The Qurʾan was one of the key sources of the paradoxes in medieval Muslim theology, as rhetoricians like Rashīd al-Dīn Vaṭvāṭ reminded their readers. Yet Muslim theologians were familiar with older philosophical paradoxes as well. The earliest Muʿtazilite theologians, for example, knew the paradoxes of antiquity. Both Abū al-Hudhayl and al-Naẓẓām employed Zeno's paradoxes to challenge the atomist conception of space as discrete. Al-Āmidī discusses, though briefly and with some hostility, the

42. Al-Abharī, *Hidayetü'l-Hikme'nin Tenkitli Neşri*, 153–154 (for an English translation, see al-Abharī, *A Guide to Philosophy*, 100–101); Alwishah and Sanson, "The Early Arabic Liar," 113–127; Ibn Sabʿīn, *al-Kalām ʿalā al-Masāʾil al-Ṣiqilliyya*, 54; El-Rouayheb, *Relational Syllogisms and the History of Arabic Logic, 900–1900*, 9–10. On paradoxes in later Arabic and Persian philosophy, see Ziai, "Recent Trends in Arabic and Persian Philosophy," 416–418.

responses of Abu ʿAlī al-Jubbāʾī, Abū Hāshim al-Jubbāʾī (d.933), al-Qāḍī ʿAbd al-Jabbār, and Abū ʿAbd Allāh al-Baṣrī (fl.10th CE) to the Liar Paradox. Also Al-Naẓẓām's theory of jump recalls the famous paradox known as Aristotle's Wheel, a problem discussed for the first time in Pseudo-Aristotle's *Mechanics*. Indeed, Hero of Alexandria's account of this paradox survives only in Arabic translation.[43]

Theological discussions containing self-contradictory statements and their relation to the law of non-contradiction had already taken a sophisticated form by the second Islamic century. One of the earliest instances of such paradoxical phrases and their logical status comes within the context of an early debate on divine nature and its relationship with plural attributes. A surviving fragment from an early primary source, *Remembrance of the Assemblies of al-Riḍā* [*Dhikr Majālis al-Riḍā*] by al-Ḥasan al-Nawfalī (fl.l.8th–ea.9th CE), contains the debate of ʿAlī ibn Mūsā, aka Imām Riḍā (d.818) with the Khurasanian theologian Sulaymān al-Marwazī before the ʿAbbāsid Caliph al-Maʾmūn (r.813–833). Al-Marwazī, most probably a Muʿtazilite, does not accept Imām Riḍā's claim that God can have real attributes like wise, all-knowing, or all-powerful, insofar as She is one [*wāḥid*]. God's having real attributes means that God is one and many at the same time, which is impossible [*muḥāl*]. In Socratic style, Imām Riḍā employs self-contradictory phrases when he gives examples indicating that one can have the will, knowledge, and ability to do contradictory things at the same time.

AL-RIḌĀ: Sulaymān, can a person know that he is created, but he does not want to be a creature? That he will die one day, and he does not want to die?

AL-MARWAZĪ: Yes.

AL-RIḌĀ: Can a person know that he is becoming something he wanted to become? Or, can he know that he is becoming what he doesn't want to become?

AL-MARWAZĪ: He can know if he becomes both.

AL-RIḌĀ: Then he could know when he is *living-dead, standing-sitting, blind-seeing in one state—but this is impossible.*

43. Vaṭvāṭ, *Ḥadāʾiq al-Siḥr fī Daqāʾiq al-Shiʿr*, 24; Van Ess, *Flowering of Muslim Theology*, 96–104; Alwishah and Sanson, "The Early Arabic Liar," 100, 124; Sviri, "Between Fear and Hope," 322–324.

AL-MARWAZĪ: That's right; then a person can know only one of them without the other in one state.

AL-RIḌĀ: So there is no problem if one becomes either what he wanted to become or what he did not want to become?

AL-MARWAZĪ: Only if he becomes what he wants to become.

AL-RIḌĀ, AL-MAʾMŪN, and the people present in the assembly laughed.

AL-RIḌĀ: You have stumbled, and departed from truth.[44]

Al-Marwazī finds the one-manyness of the divine essence against the principle of non-contradiction, while Imām Riḍā disarms his opponent by steering him into self-contradictory statements. Both scholars and their audience have an unquestioning trust in the principle of non-contradiction and have distaste for self-contradictory statements in the theological context, unlike the literary one. Arrivals at such statements indicate simple fallacies in reasoning that mark the decisive victory of their adversary and humiliate those who uttered them. In other words, even in early times when logic [*manṭiq*] was actually not evoked as a full-fledged discipline, the principle of non-contradiction was still, at least intuitively, known to Muslim theologians. The great theologian of Samarqand, al-Māturīdī, argues that "two opposites cannot join to each other" [*lā yajūz ijtimāʿ al-ḍiddayn*]. He employed this principle in support of his claim that the world is created. Accordingly, movement and stillness, beautiful and ugly, evil and good, excess and inadequacy coexist in the world. Yet, as two opposites cannot coexist in one place and time, they should have an ultimate Agent that creates them in sequence [*taʿāqqub*]. Ibn Ḥazm employs the same principle in his book on legal methodology, where he argues that consensus [*ijmāʿ*] and disagreement [*ikhtilāf*] are two opposites that cannot join together. The Ismāʿīlī scholar al-Qāḍī al-Nuʿmān (d.974), on the other hand, applies the same principle that "truth cannot lie in two contradictory answers at the same time" in refuting those who refute legal reasoning [*ijtihād*]—probably Muḥammad ibn Dāwūd (d.909), a key figure in the formation of the Ẓāhirī School.[45]

Still, the very debate of Imām Riḍā with Sulaymān al-Marwazī on divine unity indicates that medieval philosophy and theology were neither

---

44. Al-Nawfalī in Ansari, *al-Mutabaqqī min Kutub Mafqūda*, 289.

45. Al-Māturīdī, *Kitāb al-Tawḥīd*, 79. Also see ibid., 82–89; Muḥammad Ibn Tūmart, *Aʿazz mā Yuṭlab*, 213; Ibn Ḥazm, *al-Nubadh fī Uṣūl al-Fiqh al-Ẓāhirī*, 18, 26. See Osman, *The Ẓāhirī Madhhab*, 39.

immune to logical fallacies nor free from paradoxes. We have already seen the paradox of the negative proof for God among Muʿtazilites and philosophers as early as with al-Kindī, who adopted the proof of the Muʿtazilites. It was God's very relationship with the world as its unique creator that removed Her from all possible relations. Neither their critics nor philosophers themselves defended any paradoxicality at this point. Critics like Ibn Ḥazm, al-Shahrastānī, Abū Ḥāmid al-Ghazālī, or Fakhr al-Dīn al-Rāzī accused the philosophical position of being incoherent, while philosophers like Ṭūsī tried to prove otherwise by showing that their negative proof is not reducible to self-contradictory statements. Other philosophers like Ibn Rushd preferred to distance themselves from such statements and to whitewash their own versions of philosophy.[46] For all of these camps, it was a matter of proving (or from the critics' perspective, disproving) the logical consistency of the philosophical position on God's negative relation with creation. The impartial referee was the law of non-contradiction; the X-not-X statements, for both sides of the debate, marked logical failure and disgrace.

This reduction of self-contradictory statements to logical fallacies was the popular view not only among logicians but also among those who were uneasy with the discipline of logic. Skeptical approaches to logic occasionally focused on paradoxes in order to challenge logical principles and the applicability of logic to religious sciences, or beyond the Greek language. For al-Āmidī, the Liar Paradox is a counterexample to the universal appeal of the law of exclusive bivalence and a key component of his refutation against the philosophers and the Muʿtazilite theologians. Accordingly, paradoxes and tautologies are among four exceptional cases in which the law of exclusive bivalence does not work. One of these exceptions is the Liar Paradox. According to al-Āmidī, it is a simultaneously true and false statement, hence a clear contradiction that indicates an exceptional problem—but still a challenge for the Muʿtazilites. A simultaneously true and false statement is not a *transgression* but a *weakness* of logic—an embarrassment to al-Āmidī's mind. Another Ashʿarite theologian ʿAbd al-Qāhir al-Baghdādī, saw the Liar Paradox as an exception to the law of exclusive bivalence as well. He wrote:

46. Ibn Rushd, *Tahāfut al-Tahāfut*, ch.3, 104–108.

> *There is no declarative sentence that is both true and false together, except one*: namely, the declaration by he who has not lied at all, about himself, that he is a liar, and this declarative sentence, from him, is false. And a liar who declares that he is a liar says the truth. And therefore this one declarative sentence is true and false, and it has one subject.[47]

The Liar Paradox is both true and false and is an instance that violates the rule of exclusive bivalence, according to al-Baghdādī. Still, like al-Āmidī, he depicts the paradox as an embarrassment, and an exceptional, isolated case. Paradoxes were not indicators of "paraconsistency," but rather were disgraceful inconsistencies employed for attacking intellectual rivals.

Even the most famous opponents of logic in the thirteenth century do not welcome paradoxical or self-contradictory statements. One of the most prominent skeptics on logic was Ibn Taymiyya. Having written a few refutations of logic, Ibn Taymiyya argued that statements in the X-not-X form were self-contradictory. This was a "pure rational matter" as he put it—one did not need to know Aristotelian logic to refute such statements:

> With respect to all other things which are known to be contraries, if two particulars are known to be contrary to each other it will be known that they cannot simultaneously exist. . . . *Arriving at the conclusion, that these are two contrary meanings and thus cannot be both true, is possible without knowing the major premise, namely, that "no two contraries can be both true." In order to know this, there is no need for a syllogism.*[48]

Hence paradoxes served Ibn Taymiyya's more general claim that one does not need to learn Greek logic in order to intuit that statements in X-not-X form are contradictory. (This self-evidence was in fact exactly Aristotle's point in claiming that the person who asks for a logical proof for the law of non-contradiction is "like a plant!") Ibn Taymiyya's argument for the self-evident contradictoriness in all X-not-X statements followed the earlier attack of Ibn al-Ṣalāḥ al-Shahrazūrī (d.1245) on logic. The Shāfiʿī jurist

47. ʿAbd al-Qāhir al-Baghdādī in Alwishah and Sanson, "The Early Arabic Liar," 101 (my emphasis).

48. Ibn Taymiyya, *Against Greek Logicians*, 36–37 (my emphasis).

had argued that "the use of the terminology of logic in the investigation of religious law is despicable and one of the recently introduced follies. Thank God, the laws of religion are not in need of logic."[49] The ground of logic is shaky, hence one should follow simple "common sense" in order to avoid paradoxes. Accordingly, this common sense already entails the law of non-contradiction and the excluded middle. Skeptics attacked logic precisely because it led to self-contradictions, divergences, and "non-sense" that abound among philosophers. Not only logicians but also their opponents were skeptical of self-contradictions, which were indicators of logical fallacies of one's adversaries.

Yet theology and philosophy were fields saturated with self-contradictions. It is again Ibn Taymiyya's diatribe on logic that most succinctly displays and criticizes the ubiquity of paradoxes in these fields. Dramatically, it was this fiercest opponent of logic who "refused to use ambiguous or equivocal language that either asserts two opposites or negates two opposites." The doctrine of states [*aḥwāl*] was one of those theological issues that Ibn Taymiyya vehemently targeted. This philosophical doctrine, developed by Abū ʿAlī al-Jubbāʾī and Abū Hāshim al-Jubbāʾī, if not by earlier Muʿtazilites, stated that the intellectual universals or universal concepts were neither existent nor non-existent. Ashʿarites too followed the doctrine, as Ibn Ḥazm grumbled:

> One of the stupidities of the Ashʿarites is their assertion that [it is possible] for men [to believe in] states and [universal] concepts [*al-maʿānī*] which are neither existent nor non-existent, neither known nor unknown, neither created nor uncreated, neither beginningless nor originated, and neither real nor unreal.[50]

The philosopher Ibn Sīnā and his followers joined Ibn Ḥazm in the critique of the theory of states as it violated the law of the excluded middle. In his *Treatise on Existence* [*Risāla fī-l-Wujūd*], the mathematician and poet ʿUmar Khayyām (d.1123) followed "the best of the modern philosophers"

49. Street, "Logic," 253; Street, "Arabic and Islamic Philosophy of Language and Logic."

50. Ibn Ḥazm in H. A. Wolfson, *Philosophy of the Kalām*, 215–216. Also see Wisnovsky, "Essence and Existence in the Eleventh- and Twelfth-Century Islamic East (Masriq): A Sketch," 39; Ajhar, *The Metaphysics of the Idea of God in Ibn Taymiyyah's Thought*, 54–55. Al-Shahrastānī depicts al-Naẓẓām and Abū al-Hudhayl as their forerunners with regard to the problem of modes. (H. A. Wolfson, *Philosophy of the Kalām*, 229.)

[*afḍal al-muta'akhkhirīn*] Ibn Sīnā in underlining that the theory of states contradicted the law of the excluded middle, one of the "greatest first principles" of logic. The paradoxical doctrine of states remained current among prominent Ashʿarite theologians such as al-Bāqillānī and Imām al-Ḥaramayn al-Juwaynī. While its prominence dwindled after Abū Ḥāmid al-Ghazālī, it was still in circulation among later Ashʿarites such as Abū ʿUmar al-Sakūnī (d.1317).[51]

The theory of states was connected to another paradox that Ibn Taymiyya saw as inconsistent. Philosophers, as Abū Ḥāmid al-Ghazālī and Moses Maimonides corroborate, adapted the doctrine of states to the created attributes that are not firmly rooted [*ghayr rāsikha*] in their subject. Accordingly, an acquired state of an existent thing could later become aptitudinal [*malaka*] and inseparable from that thing. Such a state was in itself *neither existent nor non-existent*. Ibn Taymiyya defines this philosophical doctrine as a clear self-contradiction that can be refuted without any appeal to formal logic, as it already violates common sense. Common sense itself, again, dictates the law of non-contradiction:

> If one wishes to refute the argument of those who adhere to the doctrine of states and who argue that these states are neither existent nor non-existent, one will say: "These two are contradictories, and any two contradictory matters can neither be both true nor both false, for this would render one thing simultaneously existent and non-existent. . . . In order to arrive at this conclusion, demonstration is not needed."[52]

Yet another theological paradox that Ibn Taymiyya, now more politely, criticizes is the well-known Kullābite doctrine of the divine attributes. In

---

51. Ibn Sīnā, *Metaphysics of "The Healing,"* 27–29. Khayyām (in Wisnovsky, "Essence and Existence in the Eleventh- and Twelfth-Century Islamic East [Masriq]: A Sketch," 38) says,

> Some reckless moderns . . . posit colorness and accidentality and existence and similar states as modes that obtain in what can be characterized by neither existence nor non-existence. The doubt that makes them fall into this grave mistake pertains to the greatest of first premises: that there is no middle ground between negation and affirmation, the self-evident nature of which needs no discussion by us, nor is there any way for idiots to contradict it or explain it away.

Groff argues that later Ashʿarites like Abū Ḥāmid al-Ghazālī and Fakhr al-Dīn al-Rāzī adopted the paradoxical theory of modes as well. (Groff, *Islamic Philosophy A–Z*, 57.)

52. Ibn Taymiyya, *Against Greek Logicians*, 37.

order to solve the dilemma of ascribing attributes to God while preserving Her absolute unity, Ibn Jarīr al-Zaydī (fl.785), Hishām ibn al-Ḥakam, and Ibn Kullāb developed a paradoxical doctrine with sustained impact on later Muslim theology, including Sufis. Ibn Kullāb asserted that the divine attributes have a positive meaning, but they are inseparable from God. Hence he refused more prevalent Muʿtazilite positions and argued that the divine attributes, including Her Speech, are *"neither God nor other than God."*[53] By the twelfth century, the Kullābite formula had already become a standard Ashʿarite as well as Māturīdite doctrine. The paradoxical formula was adopted even by later Muʿtazilites. Abū Hāshim al-Jubbāʾī, for example, co-opted the Kullābite formula in support of his doctrine of states by employing the term "state" as a new name for divine attributes. Al-Māturīdī also argued that al-Kaʿbī's (d.931) approach to the divine attributes was actually convertible to the Kullābite formula. Although the Kullābite formula became dominant not only among the Ashʿarites but also among Sunnīs in general and even some Shīʿī intellectuals, Ibn Taymiyya dismissed the paradoxical claim that God's attributes are neither God nor other than God for violating basic common sense.[54]

The debates on predestination and free will, to give a final example, also witnessed abundant self-contradictory statements made and solved by logical clarification in Aristotelian fashion. The Ḥanbalī jurist Najm

---

53. See H. A. Wolfson, *Philosophy of the Kalām*, 207–209. Benjamin Jokisch argues that "by using formulations such as *lā hiya huwa wa lā hiya ghayruhā*, Ibn Kullāb depends on the old Christian compromise between 'unionists' (Monophysites) and 'separatists' (Nestorians) confirmed in all Ecumenical Councils since 451." (Jokisch, *Islamic Imperial Law*, 363.)

54. Pellat, "Nābita"; Aḥmad al-Rifāʿī, *Kitāb al-Burhān al-Muʿayyad*, 111; ʿAbd al-Razzāq Kāshānī in Hamza, Rizvi, and Mayer, *An Anthology of Qurʾanic Commentaries*, 1:550; al-Kalābādhī, *Kitāb al-Taʿarruf*, 36; al-Qushayrī, *al-Risāla al-Qushayriyya fī ʿIlm al-Taṣawwuf*, 38; Hujvīrī, *Kitāb Kashf al-Maḥjūb*, 15 (for English translations, see al-Kalābādhī, *Doctrine of the Ṣūfīs*, 16; al-Qushayrī, *Epistle on Sufism*, 14; Hujvīrī, *A Persian Treatise on Sufism*, 14; Hujvīrī, *Kashf al-Maḥjūb*, 83; al-Bayhaqī, *Kitāb al-Asmāʾ wa-l-Ṣifāt*, 112; al-Juwaynī, *Kitāb al-Irshād*, 138; Ajhar, *The Metaphysics of the Idea of God in Ibn Taymiyyah's Thought*, 54–55; H. A. Wolfson, *Philosophy of the Kalām*, 174, 215.

The famous *Sharḥ al-Fiqh al-Akbar* asserts that the divine attributes are "neither Him nor other than Him" [*lā huwa wa lā ghayruhu*]. El-Bizri, like many scholars, assumes that the text is written by Abū Manṣūr al-Māturīdī (see el Bizri, "God: Essence and Attributes," 127), but H. Daiber has convincingly shown that the authorship of al-Māturīdī is very improbable (see Daiber, *Islamic Concept of Belief in the 4th/10th Century*). Instead, the *Sharḥ al-Fiqh al-Akbar* was written in, if not reworked by, the late eleventh century (see Rudolph, *Al-Māturīdī and the Development of Sunnī Theology in Samarqand*, 325–328). Hence it presents us with important insights to the Transoxanian Māturīdism. Al-Māturīdī himself did defend the Kullābite paradox. See, e.g., al-Māturīdī, *Kitāb al-Tawḥīd*, 119, 122.

al-Dīn al-Ṭūfī (d.1316) claimed that human acts cannot be at once both voluntary and determined by God in the sense of being produced by God and by the human agent *in the same respect*. The emphasis on, or the lack thereof, such categorical clarifications were vital in debates on free will. A thirteenth-century Christian polemic accused the Qurʾanic and Sunnī theological emphasis on divine omnipotence of being reducible to self-contradiction. Accordingly, "God prohibits things that He does not will, and creates things that He wills; therefore, if He creates something that He prohibits, *then He both wills and does not will the same thing, which is inconceivable.*"[55] In response, al-Ṭūfī differentiated the various ways in which "will" is employed by Muslim theologians. Accordingly, Sunnī theologians typically distinguish between God's cosmogonic will [*irāda takwīniyya*] and Her normative will [*irāda taklīfiyya*]. There is no contradiction, thus, if God both prohibits certain acts and creates them, or commands certain acts, yet determines that some humans omit them. In addition, against his opponent's claim that the Qurʾan contains self-contradictory statements, al-Ṭūfī appeals, again, to the categories:

> Where Qurʾanic statements appear contradictory in the broadest sense (*muṭlaq al-ikhtilāf*), none of these cases satisfy all the conditions (*shurūṭ*), or restrictions, of real incoherence (*al-tanāquḍ al-maḥḍ*), i.e. contradiction in the pure formal, logical sense. . . . Once analysed, these statements, or the propositional doctrines that follow once they are interpreted, do not affirm and negate exactly the same thing in exactly the same respect; hence the reference to the conditions of contradiction, which have to be fulfilled in two propositions for them to be contradictory. It follows that Qurʾanic ayas [verses] may be only *prima facie* contradictory, and do not violate the Aristotelian laws of non-contradiction and the excluded middle.[56]

Logical rigor was essential in such debates in pointing to, or solving, self-contradictory statements—the Achilles' heel in rival teachings.

These debates show that theology was indeed a field full of paradoxes. Yet they were either instances of outright inconsistency for their adversaries

55. Shihadeh, "Three Apologetic Stances in al-Ṭūfī," 8.

56. Ibid., 15.

or valid arguments that could be expressed in propositional logic for their exponents. Their truth in the very self-contradictory format, in violation of the law of non-contradiction, was not defendable. Instead, scholars defended their positions by using logic, particularly by clarifying the categorical dimensions of compound statements. In refuting al-Ghazālī's attack, for example, Ibn Rushd appealed to Aristotle's categories. Al-Ghazālī's first accusation held that philosophers fell into self-contradiction by defending that a thing's existence and its non-existence, in their system of emanations, are the same. Ibn Rushd concurs that this would be contradictory but adds that "the time of the possibility of its existence is different from the time of the possibility of its non-existence." Hence the X-not-X statement is only an apparent self-contradiction, which disappears once we clarify that the category of temporality is different in two components of the compound statement.[57]

Sufis were not an exception to the adherence to formal logical principles in philosophical or theological matters. The Kullābite formula, for example, was very prominent among Sufis, and naturally they explained the doctrine through logical principles instead of surrendering to self-contradiction. Again, Aristotle was a big help. ʿAbd al-Razzāq Kāshānī, for example, follows the formula that "*His attributes are not Him nor other than Him.*" Then he demonstrates that there is no self-contradiction in this compound statement by clarifying the categorical differences of the opposite predicates. Accordingly, "His attributes are not Him" with respect to human intellect, and "His attributes are not other than Him" with respect to His reality.[58] Sufis not only dissociated themselves from arguments reducible to self-contradictory statements, but they also appealed to the law of non-contradiction in their arguments, and they criticized others for falling into such error, which in most contexts was self-contradiction.

To sum up, paradoxes in the explicit self-contradictory form circulated widely in the fields of Muslim philosophy and theology. The opponents of such paradoxical doctrines described them as sophistry and contradictions violating the law of non-contradiction or the excluded middle. Nor were the exponents of such controversial ideas advocates of violating the law of non-contradiction. Instead, they attempted to explain that the apparent self-contradictory statements were convertible to logically valid

---

57. Ibn Rushd, *Tahāfut al-Tahāfut*, ch.1, 31.

58. ʿAbd al-Razzāq Kāshānī in Hamza, Rizvi, and Mayer, *An Anthology of Qurʾanic Commentaries*, 1:550.

statements, as in the case of the paradoxes inherited from late antiquity, the Kullābite formula, or the doctrine of states. Nobody seems to really defend paradoxes as a challenge to the principle of non-contradiction or the excluded middle. For their champions, doctrines would not appear in the self-contradictory form if logical analysis were applied more rigorously. One could question the veracity of logic as a discipline, but not that of the logical meta-principles. In other words, there were those who rejected Aristotle, but nobody who opposed the common-sense law of non-contradiction.

It is in this theological atmosphere hostile to, yet also saturated with, paradoxes that Sufis intensively and intentionally employed self-contradictory statements to describe the divine essence. Like paradoxes of human apotheosis, Sufi paradoxes on the divine essence negated propositional discourse and worked within a *dialectical logic.* While discourse on God was negated in the level of propositions, the addition of a new, logical rule-following dimension structured this apophatic mode. It was necessary to find the right terms, create the right binaries, and employ them in the right dialectical context and moment to perform the self-cancellation of propositional discourse on an unknowable God. Instead of a break, lack, or transcendence of logic, paradoxical apophasis demanded additional logical regulations, hence rigor, in order to negate propositional theological discourse.

The Divine Paradox: When Incomparability and Immanence Are Balanced

The appeal to paradoxes on the essence of God can be traced back to the earliest Sufi masters. Al-Bisṭāmī and al-Ḥallāj were probably the most exquisite paradoxographers among them. In the fundamentally important and influential section on divine incomparability in his *Orchard of Gnosis* [*Bustān al-Maʿrifa*], al-Ḥallāj employs a plethora of negations in relation to God, which he eventually adorns with self-contradictory phrases as they address the divine essence:

> "Before" does not outstrip Him, "after" does not interrupt Him, "of" does not root Him, "from" does not accord with Him, "to" does not attach to Him, "in" does not inhabit Him, "when" does not stop Him, "if" does not consult with Him, "over" does not overshadow

> Him, "under" does not support Him, "opposite" does not face Him, "with" does not press Him, "behind" does not take hold of Him, "before" does not limit Him, "previous" does not manifest Him, "after" does not extinguish Him, "all" does not unite Him, "is" does not bring Him to being, "is not" does not deprive Him of being. Concealment does not veil Him. His pre-existence preceded time, His being preceded not-being, His eternity preceded limit. If thou sayest "when," His existence has outstripped time. If thou sayest "before," before is after Him. If thou sayest "He," "H" and "e" are His creation. If thou sayest "how," His essence is veiled from description. If thou sayest "where," His being preceded space. If thou sayest "ipseity," His ipseity is apart from things. *Other than He does not unite two opposite attributes at the same time; yet they do not create any opposition [taḍādd] in Him. He is hidden in His manifestation, and manifest in His concealment. Hence He is the Manifest-Hidden, the Proximate-Distant.* He is removed from being comparable [*tashbīh*] to creation through this.[59]

Here al-Ḥallāj is following the earlier Baghdadian Sufis, Abū Saʿīd al-Kharrāz and al-Junayd, on divine unknowability, which is marked by paradoxicality. For al-Kharrāz, "none knows God but God," and the only characteristic of God "known" to human beings is Her transcending of what we know—a negative knowledge. For al-Kharrāz, this means God's transcendence of all human speculations with their binaries, and Her unique joining of contraries [*jamʿ bayna al-ḍiddayn*]. The exposition of divine unity by al-Ḥallāj also depicts God as the ultimate coincidence of opposites—God's unique mark is the overturning of our binaries. Al-Ḥallāj's entire passage, including the paradoxes, is quoted verbatim in al-Kalābādhī's section on divine unity as the saying of "one of the great Sufis."[60]

---

59. Al-Ḥallāj, *al-Aʿmāl al-Kāmila*, 224.

60. Abrahamov, *Ibn al-ʿArabī and the Sufis*, 64; al-Kalābādhī, *Kitāb al-Taʿarruf*, 33–34. For Arberry's translation, see al-Kalābādhī, *Doctrine of the Ṣūfīs*, 15–16.

Mayer's analysis overlooks the fundamentally Ḥallājian origin of al-Kalābādhī's creed and tries to situate al-Kalābādhī's approach exclusively to the Sunnī *kalām* schools that emerged in his time. It also confuses al-Kalābādhī's Sufi creed on the *divine unity and essence* with that on the *divine attributes*. It is correct that al-Kalābādhī adopts specific Ashʿarī and Māturīdī *kalām* doctrines in his chapter on the divine attributes, but his chapter on the divine essence is simply a long excerpt from al-Ḥallāj, as Arberry already realized in his translation

What is going on logically in the creed of al-Ḥallāj, hence of al-Kalābādhī? First, we observe that the same attribute both belongs and does not belong to God; hence, at least apparently, we have a violation of the law of non-contradiction. Besides, the paradox of the divine essence seems to violate the law of the excluded middle, that one thing must be either affirmed or negated of a subject, as defined by Aristotle. Therefore, at the propositional level, al-Ḥallāj's statements do violate logical meta-principles. Yet the construction of the self-contradictory statement is by no means the result of an illogical procedure. On the contrary, the joint employment of X and not-X places the divine essence not only beyond knowability, as well as all binaries, but also beyond the very discursivity that is composed of binaries given in the theological discourse. Abū Ḥāmid al-Ghazālī explains this dialectical logic in uniting contradictories in an Aristotelian manner, immediately after employing a paradox on (un) knowing the divine essence. Al-Ghazālī will eventually find the negative language superior to the positive one, but he indicates that the path of paradox, with its balance of negative and positive languages on God, still follows the law of non-contradiction:

> If someone were to say "I do not know God," that would be true. And if they were to say "I know God," that would also be true. *Now it is known that negation and affirmation (of the same proposition) cannot both be true,* but rather split truth and falsity. If the negation is true then the affirmation is false, and vice versa. However, *if the aspects of the proposition are different, then the negation and affirmation can be both true.*[61]

Al-Ghazālī points out that any statement concerning God can be as true as its negation, due to Her simultaneous incomparability and excessive

(al-Kalābādhī, *Doctrine of the Ṣūfis*, 15n2). The Sufi doctrine on divine unity and divine attributes are clearly separated in al-Kalābādhī's work, and his approach to the divine nature is informed by, yet irreducible to, the Ashʿarī or Māturīdī *kalām* positions, which fully developed after the Sufi exposition of the divine essence quoted by al-Kalābādhī. (Cf. Mayer, "Theology and Sufism," 269–270.)

Notably, the section quoted by al-Kalābādhī under the heading of "divine unity [*tawḥīd*]" is actually al-Ḥallāj's exposition of divine incomparability [*tanzīh*], even though al-Ḥallāj's work had a section titled "divine unity." (Cf. al-Ḥallāj, *al-Aʿmāl al-Kāmila*, 227–229.)

61. Abū Ḥāmid al-Ghazālī, *al-Maqṣad al-Asnā*, 3. Cf. Shehadi, *Ghazali's Unique Unknowable God*, 38.

immanence. Hence it is only such self-contradictory structures that can point to this simultaneity through their dialectical negation of propositional binaries. These paradoxes are *real* rather than mere rhetorical tools or "seeming contradictions"; they do violate the law of non-contradiction, yet only at the propositional level. They are not illogical. They rather point out that "rules of non-contradiction and excluded middle apply specifically to delimited language reference."[62] The paradox performs the unsayability, unknowability, and non-discursivity of its subject in its own propositional failure, which is achieved by a dialectical rule-governed procedure. Instead of an illogical "anything goes" where logical meta-principles have been canceled or ignored, we arrive at a dialectical logic that operates only through a systematic matching of the binaries endemic to the discourse. This dialectical logic plays against and upon the linear logic of delimited reference, and resists an illogical depiction.

Second, the paradoxical approach to divine unknowability has a markedly balanced approach to the binary of divine incomparability and immanence. The negativist theological strands developed by Ibāḍīs, Ismāʿīlīs, Muʿtazilīs, traditionists, and philosophers followed the Qurʾanic discourse on divine incomparability as opposed to immanence. The binary Arabic technical terms through which they discussed the problem were *tanzīh* and *tashbīh*. *Tanzīh* referred to God's transcendence, dissimilarity, and incomparability—Her being beyond any possible conception of man. *Tashbīh*, having the distinct connotation of "similarity," indicated God's being comparable to creation, or Her ubiquity and immanence in creation, depending on the context. God's immanence welcomed the ascription of certain qualified attributes, and in certain interpretations, all possible attributes and names, widening the already open (and never-closing) door of anthropomorphism. God's incomparability, on the other hand, aimed to strip away from Her every predication and positive attribute in favor of Her supreme ipseity, which human mind and language cannot circumscribe.[63] It was lowering *tanzīh* to the same level with *tashbīh*, a term marked with negative meaning for others, which grounded paradoxical apophaticism.

---

62. Sells, *Mystical Languages of Unsaying*, 20–21.

63. Q.50:16. For an introduction to the Qurʾanic basis of the paradox, see Renard, *Islamic Theological Themes*, 4–7. On the other hand, the Qurʾan employs the term *mithl* instead of *tashbīh*. For the irreducibility of *tashbīh* to "anthropomorphism," see Williams, "Aspects of the Creed of Imām Aḥmad Ibn Ḥanbal."

This symmetry is evident in the popular, balanced approach to *tanzīh* and *tashbīh* among Sufis, as expressed by Naṣīr al-Dīn Qūnavī (fl.ca.1262):

> "Eyes perceive Him not" [Q.6:103] and "Thou shalt not see Me" [Q.7:143] allude to the properties of the name "Nonmanifest." This is called the "position of asserting incomparability" [*tanzīh*]. But "Upon that day faces shall be radiant, gazing upon their Lord" [Q.75:22-23] and "I saw my Lord in the most beautiful form" allude to the properties of the name "Manifest." This is called the "position of asserting similarity" [*tashbīh*]. "Glory be to God above *tanzīh* and *tashbīh*!"[64]

Third, the balanced view toward divine immanence and dissimilarity accompanies a symmetrical approach to language. The paradox in these cases not only undermines the kataphatic discourse that underlines divine comparability but also the negative discourse that underlines divine transcendence. Accordingly, the negative discourse that different Muslim groups employed is itself limiting God. Hence what makes the key difference between paradoxical apophaticism and other apophatic forms is their approach to language. Muʿtazilīs, philosophers, Ismāʿīlīs, and Ibāḍīs, as we have seen, often preferred a negative language over kataphatic language in escaping divine immanence in favor of Her incomparable transcendence. Therefore, their approach to language tended to be *asymmetrical*, as they argued that employing negative language is more appropriate than positive language when addressing God. But the approach to language in the path of paradox is *symmetrical*; negative speech has no superiority over positive speech, as God is beyond both sides of this binary. In other words, not a hierarchy but a symmetry marks the binaries such as "negation-affirmation," "transcendence-immanence," "absent-present," "dead-alive," "ignorant-knower," "hidden-manifest." These binaries sustain discourse on the divine essence, and it is their joint failure that negates propositional discourse and performs the divine unknowability beyond the discursive field through its own incapacity.

What, then, demarcates paradoxical apophaticism is (1) its balanced take on the binary of divine comparability and incomparability before unknowability, while the vast majority of theologians and philosophers have

64. Naṣīr al-Dīn Qūnavī in Chittick, *Faith and Practice of Islam*, 40.

a negative view of the former; (2) a symmetrical approach to discourse on divine essence, while prominent schools of thought prefer negation over affirmation; and (3) the employment of a dialectical logic that negates the propositional discourse on divine essence and indicates divine trans-discursivity by uniting the binaries that constitute propositional discourse. The discourse on God is negated at a dialectical level via paradoxes that performatively indicate divine excess and unknowability.

The thirteenth century continued and strengthened the apophatic paradoxical line inherited from ninth-century Sufism. Thanks to its adoption by the influential eponyms of the Sufi orders as well as by the "ecumenical master" Ibn al-ʿArabī, paradoxical apophaticism would have a sustained career, arguably, inseparable from Sufism.

Symmetrical Approach to Language, and Dialectical Logic

Ibn al-ʿArabī opens the third chapter, "the Wisdom of Exaltation in the Word of Noah" of his *Bezels of Wisdom* with an enigmatic sentence: "The doctrine of incomparability [*tanzīh*] is on par with that of limitation [*taḥdīd*] and restraint [*taqyīd*] of God."[65] Ibn al-ʿArabī is succinct; his claim is that God cannot be limited even with non-delimitedness, which is still anthropomorphic. Therefore, negative and positive speech are equally insufficient; all ascriptions are symmetrical in front of the divine excess. To give examples, the negativist propositions such as "God has no fingers," or "God does not sit on a throne," "God does not get angry," or "God is not similar to anything" defended by Muʿtazilites and philosophers still imply the accessibility of God's essence and violate rational transcendentalism. Maybe God has fingers, or maybe She sits on a throne; who knows? Indeed, She does have fingers and does get angry, as entities in creation have fingers and get angry, while She ceaselessly manifests Herself in and via these phenomena. Here, Ibn al-ʿArabī is criticizing nothing less than the main hypothesis of philosophical apophaticism—the *necessary* dissimilarity [*mukhālafa*] of God. Claiming that God is necessarily dissimilar assumes that we can actually access Her divine essence. In other words, the fact that language is anthropomorphic does not necessarily prove that

65. The discussion in this section is adapted from my comparative study of Ibn al-ʿArabī and Maimonides. See Kars, "Two Modes of Unsaying in the Early Thirteenth Century Islamic Lands."

the absolutely transcendent *is not* in the way we imagine or think. Rather, the transcendent *is* also fully and excessively the engendered. Thus, true *tanzīh* must take a further step, and negate itself. From Ibn al-ʿArabī's perspective, the prevalent negative theological currents are not radical enough; they still make essentialist claims implicitly about the absolute, and presume to access its ipseity. The apophatic step he takes aims to free the absolute from being limited to our own conception of non-delimitedness.[66]

Ibn al-ʿArabī, while carrying incomparability further through negation, supplies it with an existential immanence via his cosmology. Accordingly, the world wherein we dwell is nothing but God's finite, temporal, and spatial manifestations [*tajallī*]. Creation and God are thus in a seemingly paradoxical relationship. On the one hand, God is so transcendent that nothing can be said about Her ipseity. The term "God" is nothing but a word of negation. Our affirmations of Her incomparability are still binding for Her. On the other hand, all things are the tongues of God; creation is the unveiling of God; and neither can be alienated from the other. Thus, *tanzīh* and *tashbīh* both must be pursued to their limits, which produce the dynamic of the famous "paradox of the veil." *Tanzīh* (pushed to the extreme) dictates that God is always inaccessibly veiled from us however we affirm Her incomparability. *Tashbīh* pursued courageously suggests that it is God's "face" that appears through all phenomena. "All veils are He. Yet, none are He. This simultaneous identity and difference is the paradox."[67] Once the two modes are unified, existence and God present themselves within apparent paradoxes, as he writes:

66. Ibn al-ʿArabī, *Fuṣūṣ al-Ḥikam*, ch.3, 68. See also Ibn al-ʿArabī, "Kitāb Naqsh al-Fuṣūṣ," 395; Ibn al-ʿArabī in Chittick, *Sufi Path of Knowledge*, 75–76.

Citing Ibn al-ʿArabī and Ṣadr al-dīn Qūnavī, Muḥammad Mahdī Narāqī (d.1794) explains this radical non-delimitedness as follows:

> Whatever is known to us is known through its effects and concomitants but here there are no effects or concomitants, therefore it is unknown in every respect and *absolutely free of all bonds, even from the absoluteness which is the opposite of particularity*. The absoluteness which is applicable to this stage is a negative feature that represents the negating of all attributes, qualities, names and effects from Its essence. Rather, *this necessitates the negation of every intellectual characterization, even these negations, from Its essence*. (Narāqī, "The Delight of the Eyes [from Qurrat al-ʿUyūn]," 434 [my emphasis].)

67. Chittick, *Sufism: A Beginner's Guide*, 178. See Ibn al-ʿArabī, "Kitāb al-Azal," 119; Ibn al-ʿArabī, "Kitāb al-Jalāla, wa Huwa Kalimat 'Allāh,'" 48; Ibn al-ʿArabī, *Fuṣūṣ al-Ḥikam*, 69.

> Every entity qualified by existence is it-not-it. The whole cosmos is He-not-He [*huwa-lā-huwa*]. The Real manifest through form is He-not-He. He is the limited who is not limited, the seen who is not seen.[68]

From the subjective point of view, the paradox manifests itself in the very nature of one's self [*nafs*]: "You are not He" [*mā anta huwa*] and "you are He" [*anta huwa*] simultaneously. The face of truth is nothing but its veils. The veil of truth is nothing but its face.

Two important aspects of Ibn al-ʿArabī's position are worth underlining briefly. First, his objection is not based on a mystical or anti-intellectualist negativist schema. The objection raised here is based on a rational argument and refers to an elusive intellectual problem. It accuses the theologians and philosophers of avoiding the logical conclusions of reasoning. In this sense, his critique does not attack reason and does not rely on mystical intuition per se. On the contrary, his reasoning is working in the same paradigm of intellectual negativity with his contemporaries. Second, the objection does not rely on a simple negation of everything predicated to God, which yields an infinite regress. Instead, it reaches a resting point (or more accurately, an unresting, continuous dialectic) in the symmetry of positive and negative attributes ascribed to God. Accordingly, no defense of negative vis-à-vis positive language can be made without essential claims on the absolute. This rigorous objection is radically intellectualist and negativist insofar as it pushes both negativist reasoning and anthropomorphism to an extreme.[69]

Negation is a purely rational process for Ibn al-ʿArabī: reason approaches God only "from the aspect of negation, not from the aspect of affirmation." Affirmation of the divine is more challenging to defend, because of its very excessive, inalienable immediacy. *Tanzīh* is the function

---

68. Ibn al-ʿArabī in Chittick, *Sufi Path of Knowledge*, 116. See also Ibn al-ʿArabī, "Kitāb al-Fanāʾ fī al-Mushāhada," 20; Ibn al-ʿArabī, *Fuṣūṣ al-Ḥikam*, 70; Ibn al-ʿArabī, "Kitāb al-Yāʾ," 109–113. "You veil yourself from you, and you are His curtain over you." (Ibn al-ʿArabī in Chittick, *Sufism: A Beginner's Guide*, 193.)

69. Challenging the scholarly stereotypes about Sufism, Ibn al-ʿArabī's works are philosophically rigorous and precious. His Sufism and philosophy are "neighbors," which "visit each other." (See Rosenthal, "Ibn al-ʿArabī Between 'Philosophy' and 'Mysticism.'") The scholarly, stereotypical, mutually exclusive categories such as "philosophers" and "mystics" evidently do not do justice to the great many-faceted minds. "The element of transcendence in Islamic mysticism" is pursued "to its extreme," instead of being destroyed by Ibn al-ʿArabī. (Sells, *Mystical Languages of Unsaying*, 113.)

of the rational faculty, and it must be audaciously pursued to its limits in a radically intellectualist spirit. *Tashbīh*, on the other hand, is the faculty of our imagination [*takhayyul*] and also has to be pursued to its limits, until the divine presence is affirmed in every entity and divergent belief systems. Ibn al-ʿArabī does not surrender to the widespread philosophical superiority of reason to imagination that was defended by Aristotle and accepted by al-Fārābī, Ibn Sīnā, Ibn Rushd, Maimonides, Ṭūsī, and many others. Instead, they are two distinct faculties, which have to operate in harmony and complement each other. Wisdom and divine knowledge rely on the dialectic of reason and imagination, which are irreducible to each other.[70] As complementary faculties, they should operate independently and fully to achieve highest knowledge. The two faculties are "blind" alone, and best operate together. Ibn al-ʿArabī uses the metaphor of binocular vision to explain their unity: transcendence and immanence are like two lenses through which we relate ourselves to divine reality. Two eyes actually do not contradict but instead testify and accord with each other. "Ontologically speaking, one eye sees being and the other perceives nothingness. Through the two eyes working together, man perceives that he himself and the cosmos are He-not-He."[71] One has to become a "possessor of two eyes" [*dhū-l-ʿaynayn*], which means to unify these two faculties, and hence, incomparability and immanence. *Tanzīh* must be unified [*jamʿ*] with *tashbīh*.

> If you insist only on His incomparability, you restrict Him,
> And if you insist only on His immanence, you limit Him.[72]

---

70. Ibn al-ʿArabī, "Risāla ilā al-Imām al-Rāzī," 185; Ibn al-ʿArabī, "Kitāb al-Aʿlām bi-Ishārāt Ahl al-Ilhām," 78. As Stelzer points out, this issue would be the major divergence between Ibn al-ʿArabī and Ibn Rushd, who firmly believed in the supreme authority of reason. Old Ibn Rushd's meeting with the young Ibn al-ʿArabī in Cordova has a symbolic significance as it dramatizes the meeting (and separation) of two distinct positions of epistemology and worldviews. In his *Meccan Openings*, Ibn al-ʿArabī narrates this enigmatic meeting as follows:

> He [Ibn Rushd] said, "How did you find the situation in unveiling and divine effusion [*fī al-kashfi wa-l-fayḍ al-ilāhī*]? Is it what rational consideration [*al-naẓār*] gives to us?" I replied, "*Yes and no*. Between the yes and the no spirits fly from their matter and heads from their bodies." (Ibn al-ʿArabī in Chittick, *Sufi Path of Knowledge*, xiii.)

For an alternative translation, see Ibn al-ʿArabī, in Stelzer, "Decisive Meetings: Ibn Rushd, Ibn al-ʿArabī, and the Matter of Knowledge," 35.

71. Chittick, *Sufi Path of Knowledge*, 362.

72. Ibn al-ʿArabī, *Fuṣūṣ al-Ḥikam*, 70.

Scholars widely use the solemn term *coincidentia oppositorum* [coincidence of the opposites] to refer to Ibn al-ʿArabī's paradox. Even if inspiring, the term might be misleading if we do not clarify what it means, for the visible and the invisible, or immanence and transcendence, are actually not opposites for Ibn al-ʿArabī. Defining the unity of God's manifestation with the world as the coincidence of the opposites means to assume that the two are opposites. However, the world is the manifestation of God not in the sense that God remains always veiled as the essential (un)ground of being. God is neither the essential truth veiled behind the material un-truth nor the being of beings according to Ibn al-ʿArabī. Phenomena are not un-truth but rather are the truth *of* the deeper truth, the visible *of* the invisible, the surface *of* a deeper reality. The visible is not only the veil of the invisible but also the way in which the invisible shows itself (as an absence). The face of God is not hidden behind infinite veils. On the contrary, relying on a dizzying perspective shift, the face *is* the veil, *and* the veil *is* the face. The vessel and the wine it contains, the content and the form wherein the content appears, are not opposites; but they are "the two daughters of a single father" who cannot be separated.[73] In favor of a dialectical logical system, the law of non-contradiction is violated—and this violation is real in the propositional level.

Ibn al-ʿArabī's critique of the asymmetry in the *tanzīh* versus *tashbīh* binary is not an additional negation deepening the already infinite asymmetry, but a step toward the (un)resting (dialectical) balance of apophasis and kataphasis—that is, to a different mode. His position does not simply add a negation to the perpetual negation of philosophical apophaticism; it adopts a different apophatic approach that reduces into blatant paradoxes intolerable within the propositional logico-philosophical standards of philosophers. Hence it would be a grave error to assume that the paradoxical path rises to a higher, more critical level of thinking on the divine essence than does the philosophical apophatic path. Philosophical and paradoxical negative theologies of medieval Islamicate world were interconnected yet distinct apophatic modes with different ontological claims, performative dimensions, and methods of manipulating discourse on the divine essence, in order to point to its beyond.

73. Chodkiewicz, *An Ocean without Shore: Ibn al-ʿArabī*, 10; Chittick, *Sufism: A Beginner's Guide*, 178; Ibn al-ʿArabī, "Risāla ilā al-Imām al-Rāzī," 187–188.

Logic and Nomenclature in Paradoxical Apophaticism

The presence of paradoxical statements on the divine essence in the popular works of Ibn Sīnā and al-Kalābādhī already had an immense effect among Sufis before the rise of Ibn al-ʿArabī's school. Al-Kalābādhī's paradoxical exposition of the divine essence, which originally belonged to al-Ḥallāj, was also preserved in the popular Sufi manual of al-Qushayrī, which, unlike al-Kalābādhī, explicitly acknowledged the authorship of al-Ḥallāj.[74] Hence, a paradoxical approach to the unknowability of the divine essence was available to a variety of intellectualist, sober, and more ecstatic varieties of Sufism. Al-Ḥallāj's paradox of the divine essence, for example, appears later in ʿUmar al-Suhrawardī's work on creed, *Signposts of Right Guidance* [*Aʿlām al-Hudā*]. Al-Suhrawardī quotes the controversial master a few times in the *Gifts of Gnosis* [*ʿAwārif al-Maʿārif*] and the *Sealed Nectar* [*al-Raḥīq al-Makhtūm*] on various topics, such as divine providence and the primordial tension between Adam and Satan. More importantly, al-Suhrawardī's interpretations of al-Ḥallāj on the thorny issues of his ecstatic sayings [*shaṭaḥāt*] and his theory of unity between man and God are quite constructive. *Signposts of Right Guidance* follows al-Ḥallāj's explanation of the divine unity, sometimes quoting him verbatim without giving his name. After a page-long list of negative statements and removal of all relationalities, paradoxes irrupt in order to indicate God's transcendence of all binaries: "If you ask for explanation for Him, the particles of creation explain and prove Him: *He is first-last, manifest-hidden—all 'firsts' and 'lasts' vanish in His preeternity and everlastingness.*"[75]

Penned around a century later, ʿIzz al-Dīn Maḥmūd Kāshānī's Persian *Lamp of Guidance* [*Miṣbāḥ al-Hidāya*] follows a version of the same Ḥallājian paradoxical apophaticism on the divine essence. In its introduction, Kāshānī claims to be translating al-Suhrawardī's *Gifts of Gnosis*, but the section on the divine essence is actually an adaptation of al-Suhrawardī's *Signposts of Right Guidance*, which was clearly influenced by the creed of al-Ḥallāj. After negating a long list of propositions, Kāshānī writes:

---

74. Al-Qushayrī, *al-Risāla al-Qushayriyya fī ʿIlm al-Taṣawwuf*, 27–28. For the English translation, see al-Qushayrī, *Epistle on Sufism*, 6–7. Also see Michot, "Ibn Taymiyya's Commentary on the Creed of al-Ḥallāj."

75. ʿUmar al-Suhrawardī, *Rasāʾil Aʿlām al-Hudā*, 54. Also see ʿUmar al-Suhrawardī, *ʿAwārif al-Maʿārif*, 58; Salamah-Qudsi, " 'The 'Sealed Nectar.' "

> There is no beginning to His endless ipseity, and no ending to His countless attributes. Pre-eternity and infinity are under His enclosing sway. Existence and space are enveloped in His carpet. *All "firsts" are "last" in His pre-eternity. All "lasts" are "first" in His infinity. Their "manifestnesses" are hiddenness in His manifestness. The "hiddennesses" in creation are manifestness in His hiddenness. All "eternals" are posterior in His eternity. All "infinities" are successors in His infinity.* Ultimately, compared to whatever is contained in the intellect, understanding, estimation, perception or analogy, the essence of the glorious Lord is more transcendent and holy than that.[76]

The balance of *tanzīh* and *tashbīh*, and equivalence of positive and negative discourse in front of the divine unknowability, produce an intensive employment of paradoxes that do not cancel, nor annul, but follow logical meta-principles in a dialectical system that rather carefully chooses its binaries. This system indicates the helplessness of propositional discourse before divine excess. In other words, paradoxes follow a dialectical logic in systematically negating the binaries given in a discourse on the divine essence. Even well-known paradoxographers illustrate that the paradoxes on the divine essence are not negating logical principles but following them in a dialectical form. Rūmī explains in one of his discourses:

> *God is neither present, nor absent.* But He is the creator of both. In other words, He is beyond both presence and absence. For, if He were present, then absence would not exist, but it does. Also He is not present, because absence exists on par with presence. Therefore, He cannot be described by presence or absence. Otherwise, an opposite should emerge from its opposite, because absence requires His creation of presence, while presence is the opposite of absence. Ditto in the case of absence. Then, it is not possible that an opposite emerges from its opposite, and that God creates His analogous. As it is said, "He has no match."[77]

---

76. ʿIzz al-Dīn Kāshānī, *Miṣbāḥ al-Hidāya*, ch.1.2, 17–18 (my emphasis). See Ohlander, *Sufism in an Age of Transition*, 257–258.

77. Rūmī, *Kitāb-i Fīhi mā Fīhi*, 219. Arberry's translation does not have this passage, as he did not have access to the manuscripts Furūzān-far had.

This is yet another clear statement of the logic behind the negation of binaries or the appeal to paradoxes. On the other hand, Sufis rarely explain this dialectical logic of paradoxical apophasis in explicit, propositional terms in the way Rūmī does here. Such explanation would undermine the performative power of the paradox and go against its very apophatic raison d'être to negate propositional discourse on God in the first place. Hence paradoxes might burst unexpectedly in a discourse on the divine essence in order to express God's transcendence of all binaries. Rūmī's *Dīvān-i Shams*, in which his selfhood has already been negated in that of Shams Tabrīzī, provides exquisite examples of the paradox of the divine essence as well as human apotheosis. Paradoxes of the divine essence appear in the *Maṣnavī* as well—they irrupt unexpectedly, such as in the following couplets:

> O you whose attributes are those of the sun of gnosis,
> While the sun of the heavens is confined to a single attribute.
>
> Now you become the sun, now the sea,
> Now mount Qaf, now the ʿAnqa.
>
> *In your essence, you are neither this nor that,*
> *O greater than all that can be imagined, and more than all "more"!*
> . . .
> *Both the one who asserts your incomparability, and the one who asserts your immanence are*
> *Bewildered by you, O you who, being without image, have countless forms!*[78]

The rule-following employment of self-contradictory statements or phrases negate the propositional discourse on God, indicating divine excess beyond incomparability and immanence. Paradoxical apophaticism of the divine essence via dialectical negations of propositional discourse can by no means be confined to Rūmī or Ibn al-ʿArabī, as its seeds were already sown by al-Kharrāz, al-Ḥallāj, and al-Junayd on Qurʾanic soil. Yet Ibn al-ʿArabī's school plays an undeniable role in the momentum that paradoxical apophaticism gained in the thirteenth century. The symmetrical binaries that Ibn al-ʿArabī subverted in favor of divine unknowability

78. Rūmī, *Maṣnavī-ya Maʿnavī*, 2: 53–55, 57.

were intensively employed by Sufis who were familiar with his work. His son-in-law, Ṣadr al-Dīn Qūnavī, for example, adopts the same symmetrical approach to the *tanzīh* and *tashbīh* binary. The divine unknowability engenders the paradox of the veil, with the balance of *tanzīh* and *tashbīh*: "There is nothing in existence to be described by nondelimitation without having a face toward delimitation. . . . In the same vein, there is nothing in existence to be ruled by delimitation without having a face toward nondelimitation."[79] The divine unknowability is not the result of Her necessary dissimilarity from creation, as philosophers would argue. Conversely, God is so unknowably transcendent that one cannot really know whether She is dissimilar or not. As opposed to the convictions of the Muʿtazilites, philosophers, and Ismāʿīlīs, unknowability cancels discourse not through negative speech but through the balanced insufficiency of negation and affirmation. Qūnavī writes:

> Given that there can be no real conformity between man's discursive intellection of God and the latter's true nature, it follows that all the judgments derived through man's reasoning and which consist in attributing things to God by way of negation or affirmation [*salban aw ithbātan*], ultimately pertain to nothing more than this intellection itself—that is, the determinate concept arrived at through the operation of the intellect.[80]

Ibn al-ʿArabī and Qūnavī were not unique in approaching this self-cancellation of positive and negative discourse on God as a self-projection of human judgment to an unknowable infinity. Abū Ḥāmid al-Ghazālī and al-Kalābādhī had already claimed that our discourse on God in fact "returns back to us." In the act of naming, the name returns to the one who gives the name, not to the named. The name contains nothing essential of the named, but it represents the judgment of the one who gives the name. The discourse on the named does not really touch it. Farīd al-Dīn ʿAṭṭār, among others, pronounces the same reversive approach to naming the unnamable in his *Conference*:

---

79. Ṣadr al-Dīn Qūnavī, *al-Nuṣūṣ fī Taḥqīq al-Ṭawr al-Makhṣūṣ*, 66. I used Chittick's translation with minor modifications. See Ṣadr al-Dīn Qūnavī, *The Texts (al-Nuṣūṣ)*, 22.

80. Ṣadr al-Dīn Qūnavī in Naṣīr al-Dīn Ṭūsī and Ṣadr al-Dīn Qūnavī, *al-Murāsalāt*, 54. I followed Todd's translation; see Ṣadr al-Dīn Qūnavī in Todd, *Sufi Doctrine of Man*, 211–212.

If they talk about Him—either good or bad,
Whatever they say on Him is rather on themselves.[81]

For Ṣadr al-Dīn Qūnavī, God's transcendence of discursivity, very much like in Ibn al-ʿArabī's thought, follows Her transcendence of all binaries. Quoting al-Kharrāz, whom Ibn al-ʿArabī himself cited, Qūnavī depicts the divine essence in his *Key to the Arcane* [*Miftāḥ al-Ghayb*] as the prime coincidence of the opposites [*jamʿ bayna ḍiddayn*].[82] The human soul, once perfected, becomes a mirror of the divine coincidence of the opposites—an embodied paradox: "hidden-manifest, lofty-lowly, created-preeternal" and so forth.

The intensely philosophical vocabulary in Qūnavī's labors gives way to a moving love letter with his associate Fakhr al-Dīn ʿIrāqī (d.1289), yet preserving the paradoxical apophaticism of the divine essence. ʿIrāqī claims that "Love" is the essential name of God. He uses *ʿishq* and *ḥubb* interchangeably in this context: "embodied love" and "compassionate love" are both expressions of the divine ipseity—"a reality purified of all entification."[83] All forms of love, faith, and desire emanate from this excessive essence and manifest Her through the never-lifting veils of creation—or "entifications" [*taʿayyun*], in technical terms popularized by Ibn al-ʿArabī. It is the paradox of the veil that is played out on this divine essence, as ʿIrāqī writes eloquently: "He Himself is His own veil, for He is hidden by the very intensity of His manifestation and occulted by the very potency of His light."[84] The paradox of the veil is a popular way of breaking the superiority of divine incomparability over immanence in favor of their symmetry. In ʿIrāqī's *Flashes* [*Lamaʿāt*], the popular paradox of the veil is performed in the language of love:

> How high is Love, too high for us to circle the Kaba of its Majesty on the strength of mere understanding, mere words; too exalted for us to gaze upon its real beauty with eye unveiled and vision direct:

81. ʿAṭṭār, *Manṭiq al-Ṭayr*, verse 102. Cf. Thiele, "Abū Hāshim al-Jubbāʾī's (d. 321/933) Theory of 'States,'" 367.

82. Qūnavī, *Miftāḥ Ghayb al-Jamʿ wa-l-Wujūd*, MS 236.

83. ʿIrāqī, *Divine Flashes*, 72.

84. Ibid., 97.

Removed is Love above man's aspiration,
above the tales of union and separation;

for that which transcends the imagination
escapes all metaphor and explication.[85]

Love transcends human language and understanding: it cannot be defined, or grasped by reason or mystical vision. The binaries of creation only come into existence after the entification of the divine attributes that emanate from the apophatic essence. Hence Love is beyond all binaries—"Love upon Its mighty throne is purified of all entification, in the sanctuary of Its reality *too holy to be touched by inwardness or outwardness.*"[86] Instead, the entification of Love, by looking at itself through the mirror of "lover" and "beloved," creates binaries. Love itself transcends binaries such as "hidden-manifest," "lover-beloved." It is through self-contradictory phrases that ʿIrāqī negates propositional discourse on the divine essence, which is Love:

> How could anything else veil Him? For veils belong only to the limited, and He has no limits. All you behold in the world of form and meaning is His Form—but He is unbound by any form. . . .
>
> *Hidden, manifest,*
> *both at once:*
> *You are not this, not that*
> *yet both at once.*[87]

At the end of the century, ʿAbd al-Razzāq Kāshānī's disciple Dāwūd al-Qaysarī (d.1350) followed ʿIrāqī's apophatic approach to Love/God in his Arabic *Treatise on the Gnosis of True Love* [*Risāla fī Maʿrifat al-Maḥabbat al-Ḥaqīqiyya*]. Indeed, the two Arabic couplets that al-Qaysarī quotes are the same as ʿIrāqī's above quoted couplets:

> Essential love [*al-maḥabbat al-dhātiyya*] arises from God's comprehension of His ipseity and the perfections of His ipseity through His ipseity. This rank is higher than that of knowledge. This love

85. Ibid., 70–71 (my emphasis).

86. Ibid., 73 (my emphasis).

87. Ibid., 97–98 (my emphasis).

is in the rank of "exclusive unity" [*aḥadiyya*]. This rank has no plurality in it in any sense, no multiplicity in it of any sort—so there is no name, no description, no attribute of it added to the ipseity. The entification of the ipseity of the exclusive unity [*ʿayn al-dhāt al-aḥadiyya*] is never separate from her [the ipseity]. No intellect or thought can comprehend her reality. No eyes or beholders can grasp Her. None can encompass Her. None can encircle the reality of her rank. Hence it is said:

> Removed is Love above man's concerns,
> above the tales of union and separation;
>
> for that which transcends the imagination
> escapes all metaphor and explication.[88]

Qaysarī adopts the paradox of the veil in the vocabulary of love, with the balanced transgression of *tanzīh* and *tashbīh*, and negation and affirmation. This is a significant move, considering Qaysarī's headship at the first Ottoman university at Iznik and his influential role as a key commentator on Ibn al-ʿArabī's dense works. Not only paradoxical apophaticism but also the language of love that ʿIrāqī and Qaysarī adopt became a pivotal dimension of the Sufi heritage of what would become the Balkans-to-Bengal cultural complex.

Thirteenth-century Sufism witnesses an intensive performance of self-contradictory statements on the nature of the divine essence. In addition to the figures introduced above, many Sufis of the time adopted such paradoxes to develop apophatic positions on the divine essence. Badr al-Dīn al-Ḥabashī (d.1221), ʿUmar Ibn al-Fāriḍ (d.1235), Naṣīr al-Dīn Qūnavī, Bint al-Nafīs, ʿAfīf al-Dīn al-Tilimsānī, Saʿd al-Dīn al-Farghānī (d.ca.1299), and ʿAbd al-Razzāq Kāshānī are just some of these figures. Due to the prominence of Ibn al-ʿArabī's followers or associates in this list, it is worth asking whether Ibn al-ʿArabī was the decisive reason of this fondness of paradoxes. Sufis of the previous centuries already resorted to paradoxes intensively on the divine essence, yet the cosmology laid out by Ibn al-ʿArabī systematizes the paradoxes and their dialectical logic developed by the earlier masters. Al-Niffarī's paradox of the veil, al-Kharrāz's divine coincidence of opposites, al-Ḥallāj's theory of unity between man and God, al-Bisṭāmī's paradoxical human apotheosis are now the wheels of a

88. Al-Qaysarī, *al-Rasāʾil*, 138–139.

tremendous dialectical apophatic juggernaut.[89] Ibn al-ʿArabī lays out the dialectical logic behind the appeal to a variety of paradoxes, making it immediately available to his followers and readers. In this system, the binaries that construct the specific discourse on God are carefully matched and united in order to perform the unsayability and unknowability of the divine essence through the self-negation of the discourse. Such statements embody a self-canceling theology—they systematically and powerfully demonstrate that the excessive object of the discourse cannot be contained within its own limits. The paradox not only states the unsayability and unknowability but also performs it through negating its own act of saying on knowing. Hence it is praise in its self-negation: echoing the Qurʾan, self-contradictory phrases dwell predominantly within the contexts of praise or prayer, which intensify their performativity. Naṣīr al-Dīn Qūnavī's paradoxes powerfully manifest the multidimensional performativity of the paradoxes on the divine essence:

> "Glory be to Him who is *high in His lowness, low in His highness, nonmanifest in His manifestation,* and *manifest in His nonmanifestation.*"
>
> It is He that is He, and the he-ness of all things derives from Him. "Nothing is like Him, and He is the seeing, the hearing" [Q.42:11]. . . .
>
> The heart knows only the temporal,
> the lips speak only words—
> How can I know Thee in my heart,
> how can I call Thee with my tongue?
>
> Glory be to your lord, the lord of inaccessibility, above what they describe![90]

Here discursivity is canceled in the balance of affirmation and negation; unknowability and unsayability are performed through this self-cancellation

89. Al-Niffarī was mostly forgotten until he was reclaimed as a Sufi master by Ibn al-ʿArabī and his circle. Ibn al-ʿArabī's circle plays also a significant role in the transmission of al-Kharrāz's work, *Book of Truthfulness* [*Kitāb al-Ṣidq*]. Indeed, as far as we know, only one copy of the book has survived, that by the hand of the well-known pupil of Ibn al-ʿArabī, Ismāʿīl ibn Sawdakīn (d.1248). (al-Kharrāz, *The Book of Truthfulness [Kitāb al-Ṣidq]*, 83 [Arabic text].) For Ibn al-ʿArabī's reclaim of al-Bisṭāmī, see Ernst, "The Man without Attributes," 1–14.

90. Naṣīr al-Dīn Qūnavī in Chittick, *Faith and Practice of Islam*, 41 (my emphasis).

of the theological discourse. Unsayability is the praise. Still, the performative dimensions of paradoxical apophaticism cannot be limited to these panegyric self-negations. Depending on the normative institutions that regulate the discourse, and the repertoire of terms and binaries that sustain it, a paradoxical apophatic act may dress or undress unique performative dimensions. The healing power of paradoxes in thirteenth-century Kubrawī network is an excellent example of this contextual specificity of apophatic performances on the divine essence.

Healing with Opposites: Performativity in Paradoxical Apophaticism

Al-Kharrāz explained that remedy and sickness will turn into their opposites if one is not truthful [*ṣādiq*] in her reliance on God [*tawakkul*]. One should not hope for a cure nor fear sickness, but rather turn one's eyes beyond the binary—to "*the lord of sickness and cure.*" If the cure is desired for itself, and mistaken for the real, divine agent of healing, then it turns into poison. The remedy proves to be one's sickness, and many die of the "remedy." "Many have sought to be healed, and have hoped to be helped by the very thing which has proved their undoing, or have feared to be harmed by the very thing that may have saved them."[91]

A Persian hagiography of Avḥad al-Dīn Kirmānī (d.1238) narrates a parallel paradoxical incident in which the shaykh caught a terrible and painful eye infection when he was in Kayseri, Central Anatolia. Without letting his doctors and disciples know, he went to the Baṭṭal Mosque for the afternoon prayer. Kāmil Tabrīzī, apparently a lunatic who had become Avḥad's associate after he was warned in a dream, filled the mosque with ten to fifteen quintals of melons upon Avḥad's request. Avḥad ate all of the melons that ten persons could barely finish. When his doctors and disciples arrived at the mosque, they began crying and grieving, because melon was medically notorious for being the worst substance for his eye disease. Quite undisturbed, Avḥad ignored the protests of his doctors and disciples, put a slice of melon on each eye, wrapped them carefully, and rested for a while in the mosque. When he removed the wraps, the obstinate illness was already cured, and the infection had miraculously disappeared. In Avḥad's own

91. Al-Kharrāz, *The Book of Truthfulness (Kitāb al-Ṣidq)*, 38 (Arabic text); 31 (English, with slight modification of mine).

words, he had made "*the quintessence of remedy from the substance of disease*" [*mādda-yi dard rā ʿayn-i davā sāzīm*].[92]

Al-Kharrāz's replacement of the cure and disease, and Kirmānī's self-treatment with the opposite of the remedy, recall a wider paradoxical theme that embraces theology and Sufi practice. Accordingly, the realization of the paradox of the divine essence is a key component of human perfection. The practice of invoking the divine coincidence of the opposites helps the healing of the soul in the same paradoxical way Kirmānī was healed by the very substance of disease. The performance of the divine paradox has an irreducible transformative and therapeutic aspect. The Kubrawī and Naqshbandī Sufi lines, both of which inculcate the declaration of faith [*tahlīl*] "*There is no god but God*" as their invocation [*dhikr*], pointedly call this performative dimension of the paradoxical apophaticism "healing with opposites."

The idea that paradoxes on the divine essence heal the soul has a distinct Persian lineage, and an orientation toward love mysticism. It can be traced back to the two disciples of Abu ʿAlī al-Fārmadhī: Abū al-Ḥasan Bustī and Aḥmad al-Ghazālī. For Aḥmad, the first half of the *tahlīl*—that is, the negation—is not only of all discourses on the divine but also of one's selfhood. Through the move of negation, one removes all assertions from the divine beloved and annihilates all states of selfhood in the beloved. As contradictory binaries [*ażdād*], these states are the source of all maladies of the soul. The negation "there is no" in the *tahlīl*, hence, frees the wayfarer from the created binaries and transports one to the divine beloved, which is the realm of paradoxes. In Aḥmad al-Ghazālī's words:

> Once the lover comes in himself to the (real) self from the beloved, his way to the (real) self starts from Her and leads to Her. Since his way to the self starts from Her and leads to Her, he will not be subject to those states. What could the states of *separation and union* do here? How could *acceptance and refusal* tie him down? When could *contraction and expansion*, and *sorrow and delight*, circumambulate around the pavilion of his empire?[93]

92. Avḥad al-Dīn Kirmānī, *Manāqeb-e Owḥad al-Dīn Ḥāmed Ibn-e Abi al-Fakhr-e Kermānī*, 265–266.

93. Aḥmad al-Ghazālī, *Savāniḥ al-ʿUshshāq*, 13–14 (my emphases). For Pourjavady's translation, see Aḥmad al-Ghazālī, *Sawāniḥ: Inspirations from the World of Pure Spirits*, 38–39.

The movement beyond the negation of binaries is the paradoxical yet unending quest "from and in" the divine beloved. This is the "secret depth" of the second half of the *tahlīl*, "but God [*illā Allāh*],"—that is, the apophatic affirmation of the unknowable divine paradox. Once the threshold of the realm of negating all binaries is transcended, the lover enters the realm of affirmation through, and of, the paradox. The beacon of the experiential realm of paradoxes is itself a visionary self-contradiction: the "*black light*" [*nūr-e siyāh*]. It is a paradox as only the divine beloved can affirm Herself—no kataphatic discourse is possible on the beloved. The affirmation in, hence the completion of, the *tahlīl* is a move within the realm of paradoxes. The utterance of the paradox carries the lover to maturity—to the *healing* of the soul through going beyond the binaries:

> and with ease we got over spiritual sickness and defect.
> Know, that black light is beyond the mystery of the negation [lā].
> We passed beyond even that black light,
> and now neither this nor that remains.[94]

This popular poem in Aḥmad al-Ghazālī's *Incidents of Lovers* was originally penned by Abū al-Ḥasan Bustī, and it was also cited by later mystics in the paradoxical line, including Aḥmad al-Ghazālī's ill-fated student, ʿAyn al-Qużāt Hamadānī, and Kubrā's pupil, Najm al-Dīn Dāya Rāzī. It uses the symbol of black light as the experiential marker of the transition from the realm of negation to the realm of paradoxes—a realm where light and darkness, faith and infidelity, affirmation and negation unite, as ʿAyn al-Qużāt explains:

> You have heard of the cheek and mole of this beauty, but do you know what this beauty's tress and eye and eyebrow are? Alas, doubtless they have not shown you the black light, high above the canopy! That is the light of Satan, which they symbolize by that tress of this beauty, and which, in relation to the divine light, they call darkness; but in any other (comparison), it is light. Alas, doubtless Abū al-Ḥasan Bustī has never said to you, and you have never heard from him, these verses:

94. Aḥmad al-Ghazālī, *Savāniḥ al-ʿUshshāq*, 14. For Pourjavady's translation, see Aḥmad al-Ghazālī, *Sawāniḥ: Inspirations from the World of Pure Spirits*, 39.

We saw the hidden world, and the people
of both spheres, and we easily passed
beyond accident and reproach.

Know that the black light is higher than the
unpointed word; even this we passed by.
Neither this (world) nor the
other remained.[95]

Bustī wrote a short treatise titled *On the Explication of the Reality of "There is no god but God"* [*Dar Bayān-e Ḥaqīqat-e Lā Ilāha Illā Allāh*]. The treatise narrates the perfection of the soul through the ascent from the negation "there is no" to the paradoxical transcendence of the binary of negation and affirmation in the word "but God."[96] Aḥmad al-Ghazālī follows the same paradoxical interpretation of the *tahlīl*, yet with a language of love mysticism. Like Bustī, he argues that this move "from and in" the beloved through paradoxes does not cater to an ontological unification between the lover and the beloved or to an epistemological access to the ipseity of the beloved. On the contrary, the lover is defined by incapacity before the divine beloved, and "when the lover thinks he is closer to Her and considers Her to be closer to himself, he is (actually) farther away (from Her)." Yet it is not in vain that one negates the created binaries and plunges into endless paradoxes. The path of love of the unattainable beloved is paved with paradoxes, which negate the artificial binaries and asymptotically draw the lover closer to the beloved. Again, Aḥmad al-Ghazālī employs terms of healing to express this quest in paradoxes: "A patient is in need of medicine, but the medicine has no need of the patient, because the patient suffers deficiency when he does not take the medicine while the medicine is free from the patient. . . . What loss to the idol if it has no idolater?"[97] His exposition of the paradox in the *tahlīl* is especially detailed, and associated with a complex cosmology in his Arabic *Excursus Regarding the Expression of Unity* [*al-Tajrīd fī Kalimat al-Tawḥīd*]. Accordingly, what

95. ʿAyn al-Qużāt in Ernst, *Words of Ecstasy in Sufism*, 77. For a rich section on the role of the notion in ʿAyn al-Qużāt's thought, see Rustom, *Inrushes of the Spirit*, ch.10.

96. See Pourjavady, "El-Büstî, Ebüʾl-Hasen Alî b. Muhammed," 496; Papan-Matin, *Beyond Death*, 160.

97. Aḥmad al-Ghazālī, *Savāniḥ al-ʿUshshāq*, 19–20. For Pourjavady's translation, see Aḥmad al-Ghazālī, *Sawāniḥ: Inspirations from the World of Pure Spirits*, 52.

follows the negative expression "there is no god" is the "affirmation" of the divine transcendence of all binaries—a performative paradox that heals:

> *"There is no god" is the poison, and "but God" is the remedy.* This is like somebody who drinks only the poison without drinking the remedy—he will perish. In the same way, if somebody drinks the poison of "there is no god" and does not drink the remedy of "but God," he will perish.[98]

Not only the binary of negation and affirmation in the *tahlīl* but also the theme of healing with paradoxes, and even the "black light" as the marker of the threshold, appears in ʿAyn al-Qużāt's theology as well. Again, the move from the invocation of the negation "there is no god" to the paradoxical affirmation "but God" marks not only God's transcendence of binaries but also human apotheosis through self-annihilation. One cannot be said to possess a perfected soul unless one passes beyond the level of "there is no god" and reaches the level of "but God." This idea of being caught up in the realm of negation was exactly the starting point for the negativist emphasis of Majd al-Dīn Baghdādī and Sharaf al-Dīn Balkhī. In contrast, Aḥmad al-Ghazālī, ʿAyn al-Qużāt, and others emphasize the balance. As ʿAyn al-Qużāt puts it:

> Alas! How do you know what thought the circle of "No" [*lā ilāha*] has? In the circle of No, the world is captive. One hundred thousand souls are made soul-less, and have become soul-less. In this path, there is a soul that reaches "but God" [*illā Allāh*]. That soul whose passing is not given to "but God" will not have perfection of soul.[99]

Here, the realm of affirmation is not that of the kataphatic discourse on God but instead the negation of both the kataphatic and apophatic discourse on God in the "unthinkable conjunction of opposites"—in paradoxes. Binaries vanish here, but not in vain. "*The people of insight learn a lesson from the coincidence of opposites,*" as ʿAyn al-Qużāt is told in a dream by the inhabitants of the canopies of the unseen.[100]

---

98. Aḥmad al-Ghazālī, *al-Tajrīd fī Kalimat al-Tawḥīd*, ch.5, 55.

99. ʿAyn al-Qużāt in Rustom, *Inrushes of the Spirit*, ch.10. Also see ʿAyn al-Qużāt in Lewisohn, *Heritage of Sufism*, 1:306; Papan-Matin, *Beyond Death*, 158–161.

100. Papan-Matin, *Beyond Death*, 77; Böwering, "Ideas of Time in Persian Sufism," 227.

The paradox of the divine essence not only embodies a theological position, which keeps divine unknowability beyond the "black light," but also performs the treatment and perfection of the soul as a transformative speech-act.

Najm al-Dīn Kubrā's description of the *tahlīl* as a remedy to the maladies of the soul fits neatly into this Persianate Sufi theological context. Invocation, or literally, "anamnesis" [*dhikr*], is forgetting the remembrance of all-but God and performing the speech-act "There is no god but God." This is a healing coincidence of the opposites. The negation removes all binaries, and the affirmation indicates the paradoxical nature of the divine essence though a dialectical logic which breaks propositional discourse. What is affirmed is the balanced incapacity of both negative and positive discourse before the unknowability of the divine paradox. The paradoxical poem Kubrā cites in this context, unsurprisingly, belongs to al-Ḥallāj:

> ["There is no god but God"] is an electuary composed of negation and affirmation. With negation, corrupt substances disappear, those in which are engendered the malady of the heart, the fettering of the spirit, and the rise in potency of the self along with the fostering of its attributes . . . Through the affirmation "but God," soundness of the heart results, as well as the heart's safety from the vile character traits that come from disorder in its essential temperament. A rebalancing of the heart's temperament by means of its light occurs . . . The state of remembering is exchanged for the state of being remembered, and the state of being remembered is exchanged for the state of remembering. He who remembers becomes annihilated in remembrance, and the one remembered remains, standing in as a vicegerent for the one who remembers. Thus, when you seek the one who remembers, you find the one remembered, and when you seek the one remembered, you find the one who remembers.
>
> "And when you behold me, you behold him,
> and when you behold him, you behold me."[101]

101. Kubrā in Mole, "Traites Mineurs de Nagm al-Dīn Kubrā," 18–19 (Arabic text). For an impeccable translation to English, see Kubrā in Zargar, "The Ten Principles: Theoretical

In the thirteenth century, the inheritors of this performative paradoxical apophaticism on the divine unity were connected to the nascent network of Kubrā who promoted the *tahlīl* as the best daily invocation. In Farīd al-Dīn ʿAṭṭār's *Conference of the Birds*, similarly, divine unknowability leads to paradoxes that indicate the balanced incapacity of negative and positive discourse by removing all binaries. Incomparability and immanence as well as positive and negative language are balanced in the paradoxical excess of the divine essence:

> When you seek Him in hiddenness, He is manifest,
> When you seek Him manifest, He is hidden.
>
> He is hidden when you seek Him manifest,
> Manifest, when you seek Him hidden.
>
> When you seek Him in both,
> He is beyond both of them.
>
> You haven't lost anything—do not seek.
> Whatever you say isn't that—don't say.
>
> Whatever you say, whatever you know—that's *you*.
> Recognize who you are—*you* are a hundred times beyond.
>
> Know Him with *Him*—not with *you*.
> His path to Him begins from Him—not from your reason.
>
> Descriptions of describers don't reach Him,
> It's not in everyone's capacity.
>
> Failure to describe Him goes hand in hand with His gnosis,
> For, He is neither utterable nor describable.
>
> . . .
>
> He is so transcendent to knowledge, and beyond vision that
> He is traceless in His eminence.

Implications of Volitional Death in Najm al-Dīn Kubrā's *al-Uṣūl al-ʿAshara* (a Study and Translation)," 128.

For Ottoman commentary by Ismāʿīl Ḥaqqi Bursawī (d.1724) on the section, see Kubrā and Ismāʿīl Ḥaqqi Bursawī, *Tasavvufi Hayat*, 58–62. Bursawī's creative reading of Kubrā is firmly situated on the background of Ibn al-ʿArabī as well as Ottoman Sufism, as his Turkish quotation from Yunus Emre (d.ca.1320) clearly indicates.

One cannot find a trace of Him, except tracelessness,
Or a remedy except leaving the soul.

No one, conscious or ecstatic, has a share from Him,
Except this transcendence.

Even if you seek Him in every atom, in this and the next world,
Whatever you find or say is your understanding—God is beyond.[102]

This early section on divine unknowability and ineffability occupies pages of the *Conference* and sets the stage of the entire allegory. In these pages, discourse on the divine essence is negated in favor of a paradoxical approach wherein divine incomparability and immanence are equally incapacious. In the following couplets, ʿAṭṭār connects this move beyond the binaries to the move beyond the negation of the *tahlīl:*

Whoever failed to find this pearl in this ocean
Became "there is no," and has found nothing of tracelessness, except "there is no."

That which can be described—how can it be He?
How on earth can one chat about Him so easily?

He cannot be indicated—don't utter a word.
He cannot be expressed—don't converse.

Neither indication is allowed, nor a signal.
No one has knowledge about Him, nor a signal.[103]

There are various theories on ʿAṭṭār's spiritual lineage, none of which are conclusive; the evidence for a Kubrawī link appears weak.[104] On the other hand, ʿAṭṭār's performative paradoxical apophaticism on the *tahlīl,*

102. ʿAṭṭār, *Manṭiq al-Ṭayr,* verses 98–105; 107–110.

103. ʿAṭṭār, *Manṭiq al-Ṭayr,* verses 123–126.

104. Jāmī's (d.1492) *Breezes of Intimacy* [*Nafaḥāt al-Uns*] seems to mistake the Kubrawī shaykh Majd al-Dīn Baghdādī with Majd al-Dīn Khwārazmī, who is praised in the introduction of ʿAṭṭār's hagiography. Majd al-Dīn Baghdādī's name does not appear in any of ʿAṭṭār's authentic works. See Daadbeh and Melvin-Koushki, "ʿAṭṭār Nīsābūrī." For ʿAṭṭār's link to Majd al-Dīn Baghdādī via a certain Imām Aḥmad Khuwārī, a disciple of Majd al-Dīn, see Lewisohn and Shackle, *ʿAṭṭār and the Persian Sufi Tradition,* xix, 9–10.

shared with other contemporary Persian associates of Kubrā, at least demonstrates ʿAṭṭār's acquaintance, if not association, with his circle. These convergences can be extended to textual and doctrinal overlaps, such as the "annihilation of annihilation" [*fanāʾ al-fanāʾ*] found both in the works of Kubrā's network and in ʿAṭṭār's *Conference.*[105] For ʿAṭṭār, the station of annihilation in annihilation marks the passing of the seventh and last valley of the soul, "the valley of destitution and nothingness" [*vādi-ye faqr-u fanāʾ*], where the binaries of theology, logic, and discourse are transcended in favor of their dialectical subversion in paradox. The station of annihilation of annihilation indicates the same threshold for Najm al-Dīn Dāya Rāzī, and it is symbolized by the now-familiar "black light." The black light is the union of opposites, hence discursive reasoning cannot access its paradoxical meaning, or move beyond it. Dāya Rāzī also connects the *tahlīl* to the performative shift from the negation of the self to the therapeutic affirmation of the paradox. The *tahlīl* is the best invocation, as it performs the healing of the self through this apophatic theology. Accordingly, the malady of forgetfulness of the lower soul has the reverse structure of the *tahlīl*—it is composed of the negation of remembering God and the affirmation of remembering all-but-God. The invocation "There is no god but God" is its opposite, and thus a perfect cure: "*A potion mixed like oxymel out of the vinegar of negation and the sugar of affirmation.*" By "there is no god," everything one can imagine or conceive is negated, while the second part, "but God" affirms the paradox.[106] The invocation of the divine *tahlīl* is "*the cure through the opposites*" [*ʿilāj bi-ażdād-hā*]—a performance that transforms the human soul. "The scissors of negation" in "there is no god" severs all attachments, and the beauty of divine might become manifested with the affirmation of paradoxical unknowability in "but God." This is the paradoxical, performative, and experiential interpretation of the *tahlīl*,

---

105. Both Dāya Rāzī and ʿAṭṭār, for example, use the imagery of a moth diving into a candle flame to depict the erasure of the ego before ultimate reality. (See Ridgeon, *Cambridge Companion to Sufism*, 143–144.) Dāya Rāzī, *Mirṣād al-ʿIbād min al-Mabdaʾ ilā al-Maʿād*, 169; Dāya Rāzī, *Path of God's Bondsmen*, 302. For Sayyid ʿAlī Hamadānī (d.1385) on annihilation of annihilation, see Hanif, *Biographical Encyclopaedia of Sufis: South Asia*, 344–345. For Lāhījī (d.1506), see Corbin, *Man of Light in Iranian Sufism*, 118. For ʿAzīz Nasafī, see Ridgeon, *Cambridge Companion to Sufism*, 139; ʿAṭṭār, *Manṭiq al-Ṭayr*, verses 4282, 4291; Papan-Matin, *Beyond Death*, 168.

106. Dāya Rāzī, *Mirṣād al-ʿIbād min al-Mabdaʾ ilā al-Maʿād*, 148–149; Dāya Rāzī, *Path of God's Bondsmen*, 269–270.

and the hidden meaning of the cryptic statement of the Sufi master Yūsuf ibn al-Ḥusayn al-Rāzī that *"none says 'God' but God."*[107]

ʿAzīz Nasafī is yet another Persian mystic who established links with Kubrā's Sufi circle. At a relatively young age, he associated with Najm al-Dīn Kubrā's prominent student Saʿd al-Dīn Ḥammūya (d.1252), whom he served in Khurasan. While Nasafī's relation to the Kubrawīs and Ismāʿīlīs is a complex one, his writings bear the mark of the former group on his paradoxical approach to the divine essence. Nasafī connects the binary of negation and affirmation in the *tahlīl* to the performance of human apotheosis. The opening of Nasafī's *Unveiling of Realities* [*Kashf al-Ḥaqāʾiq*] sets the stage of wayfaring with reference to the *tahlīl*, with a striking similarity to Najm al-Dīn Dāya Rāzī's word choice:

> For the People of the Truth, the wayfarer is the individual who negates and affirms while wayfaring is negation and affirmation, in other words, negating the self and affirming the Truth Most High. This is the meaning of *there is no god but God.*[108]

Other writings of Nasafī, such as the popular *Furthest Goal* [*Maqṣad al-Aqṣā*], reverberate with the same theme of the symmetrical binary in *tahlīl* with transformative power on the human soul. Hence Nasafī's approach to the symmetry of negative and positive language is closely connected with those of his contemporaries who associated with Kubrā.[109]

The symmetrical incapacity of positive and negative discourse is coupled with the symmetry of divine incomparability and immanence for Nasafī. On the one hand, following full *tanzīh*, Nasafī asserts the unknowability of the divine essence as a "Sufi principle." Accordingly, "the Sufis

---

107. Dāya Rāzī, *Mirṣād al-ʿIbād min al-Mabdaʾ ilā al-Maʿād*, 150; Dāya Rāzī, *Path of God's Bondsmen*, 270.) For further on Dāya Rāzī's reading of the profession of faith, see Waley, "Contemplative Disciplines in Early Persian Sufism," 532–533. This is also quite parallel to the ineffability of the *tahlīl* in the exchange of letters between Majd al-Dīn Baghdādī and Sharaf al-Dīn Balkhī.

108. ʿAzīz Nasafī, *Persian Metaphysics and Mysticism*, 191.

109. "Renunciation and gnosis of God is the testament of Islam, and the testament of Islam is affirmation and negation. Negation is the renunciation of idols and affirmation is the gnosis of God. . . . Negation is not witnessing the self, and affirmation is witnessing God." (ʿAzīz Nasafī, *Persian Metaphysics and Mysticism*, 58–59.) ʿAzīz Nasafī employs the phrase "annihilation of annihilation" like the Kubrawī Sufis of his time. (See Ridgeon, *Cambridge Companion to Sufism*, 139.) Also see ibid., 135–136; ʿAzīz Nasafī in Rippin and Knappert, *Textual Sources for the Study of Islam*, 171.

say that there is no road from man to God, because *the nature of God is illimitable and infinite, without beginning or end or even direction.*" He repeats the idea in the *Book of the Descent* [*Kitāb al-Tanzīl*]. On the other hand, along with this unknowability and hiddenness comes divine proximity, manifestness, and immanence—that is, divine *tashbīh*: "Since the nature of God is infinitely subtle, nothing can ever veil or conceal it, for the more subtle a thing is the greater is its capacity for penetration." This subtle unity of divine immanence and transcendence permeates phenomena, rendering them both veils and face of the divine excess. The paradox of the veil manifests itself immediately in the human self. What you assume to be "you," therefore, is actually a locus of divine unveiling entified as "you." The self, like every entity, is a veil that produces the illusion that "you" have an independent existence, while in fact there is only God manifesting Herself to Herself through Herself. Ibn al-ʿArabī described the self as the foundation of all veils and the immediate locus of divine manifestation, writing in *Meccan Openings* that "He may speak to you from you, since you veil yourself from you, and you are His curtain over you." Nasafī's description is identical, yet in Persian verse:

> Don't wrap yourself in your own veil,
> You are your veil, remove it from yourself.[110]

This simultaneous pursuit of divine incomparability and immanence is coupled with a symmetrical distance to the negative and positive discourse on the divine essence. Nasafī negates propositional discourse on the divine essence in favor of a dialectical logic that operates via the cancellation of all binaries:

> [Sufis assert that] He is infinite and illimitable, by which they mean not only without beginning or end, but also without determinate position of time, place, or direction. The nature of God, according

110. Ibn al-ʿArabī in Chittick, *Sufism: A Beginner's Guide*, 193; ʿAzīz Nasafī, *Persian Metaphysics and Mysticism*, 192.

The prominent and prolific Khalwatī Sufi master Niyāzī Mıṣrī (d.1694) would reverberate the paradox, now in Turkish: "*It is God who is saying 'I' in 'you' and in everything*" [*sende ve cümlede ben diyen oldur*]. (Niyāzī Mıṣrī, *Risāle-yi Tevḥīd*, MS 06 Mil Yz A 853/3, f.8b.) The application of the paradox of the veil to the self was a key theme of Ibn al-ʿArabī's heritage, and had a sustained impact on Ottoman Islam.

> to them, is an infinite and illimitable light, a boundless and fathomless ocean . . . There is no single atom of existent beings which God does not pervade, comprise, and comprehend. God is always near to man, but man is always far from God, because he is not aware of His proximity.[111]

The markers of paradoxical apophaticism—(1) the symmetry of divine incomparability and immanence, (2) the symmetry of negative and positive discourse, (3) the divine unknowability that transcends these binaries and produces paradoxes that negate propositional logic via its dialectical logic—all are present in Nasafī's corpus. Moreover, the connection of the binary of negation and affirmation to the perfection of the human soul in Nasafī's thought adds to the invocation of the profession of faith a performative dimension that was promoted primarily by Kubrā's associates in Nasafī's time.

The performative paradoxical apophaticism on the profession of faith, shared by nascent Kubrawīs of the thirteenth century, takes complex forms in the following centuries. ʿIzz al-Dīn Kāshānī, whom modern scholars tend to situate under Suhrawardī Sufism, connects the invocation of the *tahlīl* to the binaries of negation and affirmation, and annihilation and subsistence. His account is virtually the same as that of Nasafī, and hence, of Dāya Rāzī.[112] Muḥammad Pārsā, the Bukharan follower of Bahāʾ al-Dīn al-Naqshband (d.1389) and a key figure in the organization of the Naqshbandiyya, quotes almost verbatim the words of Najm al-Dīn Dāya Rāzī on the binary in the profession of faith, and attributes them to his own master. Pārsā even adopts Kubrā's and Dāya Rāzī's concept of "*cure through the opposites*" [*ʿilāj bi-aẓdād-hā*]—a performance associated with the *tahlīl*, wherein all binaries are negated and the paradox of the

111. ʿAzīz Nasafī in Rippin and Knappert, *Textual Sources for the Study of Islam*, 172. The argument that Ibn al-ʿArabī introduced when negating "thingness" from God is identical with Nasafī's passage. Ibn al-ʿArabī wrote, "He is with the things, but the things are not with Him, since 'withness' follows from knowledge: He knows us, so He is with us. We do not know Him, so we are not with Him." (Ibn al-ʿArabī in *Sufi Path of Knowledge*, 88.)

112. ʿIzz al-Dīn Kāshānī, *Miṣbāḥ al-Hidāya*, ch.5.7, 169:

> The masters have chosen "There is no god but God" among all formulae of recollection. This is because it is composed of negation and affirmation. . . . On the side of the negation, the wayfarer perceives the being of all creation through the lens of annihilation. On the side of the affirmation, the wayfarer witnesses the preeternal being via the eye of subsistence.

ineffable essence is dialectically indicated. Pārsā reports from the master al-Naqshband:

> The finest invocation is the profession of faith—that is, "There is no god but God." The form of this invocation is composed of negation and affirmation. In reality, only this word can be the path to the Supreme Majesty–glorious and transcendent He is. The veils before the wayfarers are due to forgetfulness. The truth of the veil is the reification of the worldly forms in their hearts. In this reification, the Real is negated, and all-but-Him is affirmed. Yet, according to the principle of "*healing with oppositions*" [*al-muʿālaja bi-l-ażdād*] in the declaration of faith, there is a negation of all-but-God and an affirmation of the Real–glorious and transcendent He is.[113]

The lineage of al-Naqshband that Pārsā introduces not only overlaps with that of the Kubrawiyya, but it also follows the same invocation "There is no god but God," at least from the time of Yūsuf Hamadānī.[114] Yet the convergences go beyond the lineages and invocation preferences and expand to the performative apophasis of the divine essence. Most prominently Pārsā's description of the realm of paradox clearly follows that of Dāya Rāzī and ʿAṭṭār. Pārsā calls the threshold of the ascent from the realm of negation of all binaries to the realm of paradoxes "annihilation of annihilation," as they did. Again, it is the performance of the invocation of the *tahlīl* that breaks the binaries of negation and affirmation and leads to the gates of divine paradoxes. Here propositional discourse ends and dialectics rules. At that threshold, in his words:

> The wayfarer is annihilated from his intellection, and from his soul. And he is annihilated even from that annihilation. In this quintessence of annihilation [*ʿayn-e fanā*ʾ], his tongue actually begins to speak, while his body is serene and meek. Perplexity and tracelessness is in this quintessence of annihilation.

113. Muḥammad Pārsā, *Qudsiyya: Kalimāt-i Bahāʾ al-Dīn Naqshband*, 34.

114. Yūsuf Hamadānī, "Seyyid Yusuf-i Hemedani'nin Tasavvufa İlişkin Bir Risalesi," 27. The *Litany of the Lovers* [*Awrād al-Aḥbāb*] penned by Abū al-Mafākhir Yaḥyā (d.1335), a grandson of the Kubrawī master Sayf al-Dīn Bākharzī (d.1231) through Burhān al-Dīn Aḥmad (d.1296), also underlines the importance of the declaration of faith as the Kubrawī *dhikr*. (See DeWeese, *The Kashf al-Huda of Kamal ad-din Husayn Khorezmi*, 34–36.)

Nobody acquires a trace from you,
This is the trace of the traceless![115]

The paradoxical poem on divine tracelessness [*bī-nishānī*] that Pārsā adds in this context is impossible to distinguish from the one that ʿAṭṭār uttered on the divine unknowability. It is not just Pārsā who inherits the performative paradoxical apophaticism on the profession of faith. Shams al-Dīn Lāhījī (d.1506) represents an outstanding case of incorporating ʿAṭṭār within the threshold of the divine paradox, "the black light." The prominent master of the Nurbakhshiyya branch of the Kubrawiyya in Shiraz, Lāhījī describes black light as the final visionary marker before losing one's consciousness, in the way Bustī, Aḥmad al-Ghazālī, and ʿAyn al-Qużāt did. He also repeats the phrase "none knows God but God"—the catchword for divine unknowability from al-Kharrāz, al-Junayd, and Yūsuf ibn al-Ḥusayn al-Rāzī to Najm al-Dīn Dāya Rāzī, Sharaf al-Dīn Balkhī, Majd al-Dīn Baghdādī, Farīd al-Dīn ʿAṭṭār, and ʿAzīz Nasafī. Moreover, Lāhījī is clearly influenced by ʿAṭṭār when mentioning the self-negation of the wayfarer (and binaries) in order to approach the affirmation of the divine paradox. Al-Lāhījī calls this station "the seventh valley of destitution and nothingness"—the exact name ʿAṭṭār employed in the *Conference*.[116]

To sum up: the balance of incomparability and immanence before divine unknowability, and the symmetry of negative and positive discourse before the paradoxical transcendence, were key strategies of paradoxical apophaticism in thirteenth-century Sufism. By connecting the binary of negation and affirmation to the daily self-disciplinary practice of invocating the profession of faith, many Sufis in Kubrā's network added a performative aspect that did not exist in more theoretical paradoxical approaches to divine incomparability and immanence or in other Sufi circles. The paradox of the divine essence heals just by being uttered, however silently. The ritual act of utterance manifests the paradox, hence the fundamental problem, of the divine excess, which, in turn, solves the essential problem of the soul just by being chanted in the correct, institutionalized, context and moment. Through the declaration of faith, Persian Sufis in Kubrā's circle make "the quintessence of all remedies from the

115. Muḥammad Pārsā, *Qudsiyya: Kalimāt-i Bahāʾ al-Dīn Naqshband*, 40.

116. Lāhījī in Corbin, *Man of Light in Iranian Sufism*, 112, 118.

cause of all maladies," like Avḥad's paradoxical self-healing with melons, and the wine maiden of the poet Abū Nuwās:

> Don't get the wrong impression of
> Her who brought about both
> *The illness of the healthy and*
> *The cure of the illness.*[117]

Summary

Among medieval Sufis, paradoxical apophaticism on the divine nature follows a loosely defined set of strategies: (1) It has a markedly balanced take on the binary of divine incomparability and immanence, while the vast majority of Muslim scholars hold the former superior. Various contemporary scholars of religion or constructive theologians have depicted this dialectic as the only path of apophaticism. However, the dialectic of divine incomparability and immanence is the hallmark of paradoxical apophaticism, not that of other apophatic approaches to the divine essence. (2) A symmetrical approach to discourse on the divine essence is a key dimension of this path, while most of the Muʿtazilites, Peripatetic philosophers, and Ismāʿīlīs prefer negative speech over the positive one. (3) Paradoxical apophaticism employs a dialectical logic that negates propositional discourse on divine essence and performs divine trans-discursivity by uniting the irreconcilable opposites that constitute propositional discourse. It performs the divine unknowability and unsayability by self-negation of its own discursive variables. Yet the invocation [*dhikr*] theory and practice of Kubrā's circle indicate the context-specificity of the apophatic paradoxical performances. The repertoire of terms and binaries define the discursive space; the apophatic act is performed within an existing field in order to negate that discourse. Depending on the normative institutions and practices that regulate the negated discourse, the apophatic act elicits or forfeits diverse performative dimensions. Apophatic paradox is a rule-following, discourse-dependent performance—far from being an infinite or illogical negation presented in its popular postmodern depictions.

117. Ibn Rashīq in Cowell and Ibn Rashīq, "On the Ancients and the Moderns," 72 (my emphasis).

Do these intense performances of paradoxical apophaticism corroborate the common associations of Sufism with paradoxes, at least within the scope of the divine ipseity? Al-Junayd, al-Ḥallāj, and al-Kharrāz had already pointed out that "God" is a term that essentially signifies a paradox. Later Sufis like Ibn al-ʿArabī and Ṣadr al-Dīn Qūnavī, most notably, pursue the claim that the divine essence is in itself the ultimate coincidence of opposites [*jamʿ al-aḍdād*].[118] Yet, the overview of paradoxes in poetry, literature, philosophy, and theology indicate their currency beyond Sufism. The field of theology, even with reference to the specific question of the divine nature, was full of paradoxical positions, such as the Kullābite doctrine, and the negative causality of philosophers. What is peculiar to the apophatic paradoxes of Sufis was their performative dimension largely absent in other theological paradoxes. Second, they aim to undermine propositional discourse through targeting its binaries in a dialectical system. The speech-act of self-negation performs divine unknowability and divine transcendence that is beyond all conceptions of incomparability. Naṣīr al-Dīn Qūnavī, for example, directly problematizes the discursivity of divine essence and negates both positive and negative discourse via paradox:

> "He is the first and the last, the manifest and the
> nonmanifest."
> Because of hiddenness
> He is totally apparent,
> Because of apparentness
> He is totally hidden.
> . . .
> *Since you call Him manifest and hidden,*
> *Know for certain that He is neither this nor that!*[119]

God is neither X nor not-X precisely because both can be the subject of theological speculation. With its dialectical logic, paradox negates the propositional discourse on God on the basis of the balanced incapacity of negative and positive statements before the divine excess. Paradoxes simultaneously perform the incapacity of propositional discourse, logical binaries, and human understanding, and they play a fundamental role in

---

118. Ibn al-ʿArabī, "Kitāb al-Tajalliyāt," 342. Also see Chittick, *Sufi Path of Knowledge*, 59.

119. Naṣīr al-Dīn Qūnavī in Chittick, *Faith and Practice of Islam*, 52–53 (my emphasis); Q.57:3. Also see Kars, "Sufis and Muʿtazilites: Theological Engagements of Ibn ʿArabī."

the attainment of the soul's perfection. The connection of apophatic performance to human apotheosis renders paradoxes an important dimension of Sufi wayfaring.

One should avoid, however, extending paradox-philia to Sufism in general. We have seen the sway of paradoxes far beyond. In most contexts Sufis saw such statements as self-contradictions—we saw how Ibn Sabʿīn criticized al-Ghazālī for uniting the opposites in his ambidextrous scholarship. Paradoxes were welcomed to challenge propositional logic only in limited fields, such as the nature of divine attributes, the relationship between divine essence and attributes, and human perfection. Second, we have examples of Sufis who not only distanced themselves and their schools from paradoxical apophaticism on the divine essence but also actively censured them. Such intriguing counterexamples come from al-Qushayrī's *Epistle* and Jalāl al-Dīn al-Suyūṭī's (d.1505) *Affirmation of the Sublime Truth* [*Taʾyīd al-Ḥaqīqa*]. These major works on Sufism quote the entire portion on the Ḥallājian creed but carefully censor the self-contradictory statements. Al-Ḥallāj's own work as well as its version in al-Kalābādhī entail the statements "*He is hidden in His manifestation, and manifest in His concealment. Hence He is the manifest-hidden, the proximate-distant.*" First, al-Qushayrī quotes the entire passage but specifically cuts out the sentence "*He is hidden in His manifestation, and manifest in His concealment.*" He also tampers with the paradox "*He is the manifest-hidden*" by adding a conjunction between the two terms, converting it into the well-known Qurʾanic "He is the manifest, and the hidden."[120] Only the paradoxical "*proximate-distant*" remains intact. Al-Suyūṭī goes further. He had access to al-Kalābādhī's faithful quotation from al-Ḥallāj, and his extended exposition and subtle defense of al-Ḥallāj might be informed by direct familiarity with his work. Yet al-Suyūṭī is careful to remove all of the paradoxes in the deeply negativist section on divine nature. He not only removes the phrase "*He is hidden in His manifestation, and manifest in His concealment,*" as al-Qushayrī did, but also the binary "*proximate-distant.*" It is only the Qurʾanic transcendent discourse that remains after al-Suyūṭī's removals and modifications: "He is the first, and the last, and the manifest, and the hidden."[121] Al-Suyūṭī undermines the paradoxical emphasis

---

120. Al-Qushayrī, *al-Risāla al-Qushayriyya fī ʿIlm al-Taṣawwuf*, 28. For the English translation, see al-Qushayrī, *Epistle on Sufism*, 6–7.

121. Al-Suyūṭī, *Taʾyīd al-Ḥaqīqa al-ʿAliyya*, 52.

of the passage and successfully shifts it to the affirmation of the sacred, Qur'anic, transcendent discourse.

Al-Qushayrī and al-Suyūṭī's careful censure of paradoxical statements might have been intended to deflect the accusation of departing from daily speech for a convoluted and baffling language. The threat of such accusations was real: al-Suyūṭī himself was one of those who narrated the complaints of theologians to Abū al-ʿAbbās Ibn ʿAṭāʾ that Sufis strayed from ordinary speech and used "*tangled words.*"[122] Yet the move of al-Qushayrī, al-Suyūṭī, and many Sufis away from paradoxical apophaticism cannot be explained merely by a defensive rhetoric or such external and circumstantial factors. Their consistent gesture toward the Qurʾanic transcendent discourse indicates an alternative theological approach that affirms the sacred scripture *amodally*, or *without asking "how"* [*bilā kayfa*], instead of appealing to paradoxes to remove God from discursive spaces.

122. Ibid., 34.

PATH FOUR

Against Discourse

AMODAL APOPHATICISM

SINCE ITS EMERGENCE as a systematic discipline in the ninth century, the scholarship on prophetic traditions depicted itself as the heir of a mainstream apophaticism, which cancels itself in favor of the unknowability of the divine nature and the incomprehensibility of the sacred Qurʾanic discourse on it. The main features of this tradition were as follows: (1) the conviction that the Qurʾan is the uncreated, eternal word of God. In other words, the scripture was the transcendent discourse. (2) This premise was fundamental in canceling out human discursive constructs, since they cannot grasp the meaning of the transcendent discourse on God's nature, specifically in the case of Her anthropomorphic depictions. (3) Any interpretive inquiry is doomed to fail before the unknowable divine nature and the transcendent discourse on it. Theological discourses nullify themselves in favor of a non-cognitive position, where neither the divine ipseity nor the meaning of the transcendent discourse on it can be known. This non-cognitive, anti-interpretive position played an important and rather exceptional role in the canonization of Sufism in the tenth and eleventh centuries and in the formation of the nascent Sufi orders in the late twelfth and early thirteenth centuries.

The Background: "Bilā Kayfa" *as a Theological Concept*

The previous chapters have displayed a rich variety of apophatic approaches on the nature of the divine essence. These approaches embodied self-negating theologies: they were discursive constructs that ended up targeting all forms of discursive or non-discursive access to their very subject—the divine essence. A widespread self-cancellation of discourse on divine nature, on the other hand, is another approach to Muslim theology that has been associated with strict literalism. Known in the literature as the principle of accepting the literal reading of scripture "without [asking] how," the principle of *bilā kayfa* circulates widely in contemporary scholarship. Yet, studies devoted to this principle were, until recently, surprisingly rare. The phrase flourished in Western scholarship with Ignaz Goldziher (d.1921) and Joseph Schacht (d.1969) as *balkafa*, having later appeared in diverse forms like *balkafiya, bi-lā kayf,* and *bilā kayfa,* all being different transliterations of the same Arabic phrase, which can mean "without howness," "amodally," or "without asking the reason why," depending on the context.[1]

The unquestioning acceptance and affirmation of scriptural authority at the expense of theological discourse as an apophatic, self-negating discursive construct is in stark contrast with the postmodern depictions of apophasis in terms of intellectual rigor and critical thinking. After all, in Goldziher's words, *bilā kayfa* does not go beyond a "primitive conception of God," as it supposedly demands but a "blind belief in the literalness of the text." Associating intellectually conservative or dogmatic theological positions with apophaticism also goes against the perennialist paradigms that link it with mysticism or wisdom traditions. On the other hand, various scholarly works depict *bilā kayfa* with a clear negative theological bent, describing it as "apophatic assertion," or "amodal affirmation." Indeed, the only phrase that appears under the term "apophatic theology" in the index of the *Cambridge Companion to Classical Islamic Theology* is *bilā kayfa*.[2]

The prominence of *bilā kayfa* as bowing before the incomprehensible and unknowable is a general dogmatic theological gesture that grows out of its sacred textual sources and pervades modern Islam. Very much like Mālik ibn Anas (d.796), many contemporary scholars associate *bilā*

1. Goldziher, *Mohammed and Islam*, 113. Most recent works devoted to the topic are Abrahamov, "The 'Bi-lā Kayfa' Doctrine"; Williams, "Aspects of the Creed of Imām Aḥmad Ibn Ḥanbal," Williams, "A Body Unlike Bodies"; Ali-Shah, *Anthropomorphic Depictions of God: The Concept of God in Judaic, Christian, and Islamic Traditions*; Holtzman, "Accused of Anthropomorphism"; Shihadeh, "Three Apologetic Stances in al-Ṭūfī." The most significant contribution in the field, Holtzman's recent book *Anthropomorphism in Islam* (especially see ch.5) and her forthcoming works are expanding and refining the role of *bilā kayfa*, also shedding new light on the performative dimensions of the utterance.

2. Winter, *Cambridge Companion to Classical Islamic Theology*, 326; Goldziher, *Mohammed and Islam*, 113.

kayfa with the problem of anthropomorphism. Accordingly, the anthropomorphic descriptions of God in the Qur'an should not be interpreted to mean something else but should be accepted as they appear, because their meaning is known only to God. In other words, *bilā kayfa* marks the self-cancellation of theological discourse, and the ultimate unknowability of the meaning of the sacred sources when they address the divine nature. Instead of understanding the sacred sources literally, it marks one's *inability* to understand or interpret them. Such an apophatic response to anthropomorphism has been dominant in Sunnī theology for many contemporary scholars. A doctoral dissertation on evangelical missiology published in 2013 recommends that prospective missionaries appeal to *bilā kayfa* if they want to be theologically palpable in Arab Muslim contexts:

> The Ḥanbalite and Ashʿarite resorting to accepting revealed (Qur'anic) truth without understanding how [*bilā kayfa*] can be applied to Muslim objections to Christian theological difficulties such as the Trinity or sonship of Christ. We should explain that in as much as these doctrines have a basis in the scripture we must accept them as true, even when we cannot really understand how [*bilā kayfa*].[3]

The author claims that Muslim theologians appealed to *bilā kayfa* in settling the problems that emerge from God's apparently anthropomorphic connections with creation, such as Her "establishment on the throne" [*istiwā' ʿalā al-ʿarsh*] in various verses of the Qur'an. Hence, the argument goes, the core Christian doctrines that are prone to similar problems, such as the suffering and crucifixion of God, can be transmitted to Arab Muslims in the same way: "The hypostatic union of Christ's two natures is a *bilā kayfa*."[4]

Is the *bilā kayfa* anti-interpretive position so widespread among contemporary scripturalists? The famous Egyptian Salafī, Sayyid Quṭb (d.1966), rather preferred to interpret the apparently anthropomorphic reports of the Qur'an. On the other hand, the *bilā kayfa* anti-interpretivism is appealed to in the contemporary scripturalist attitudes not only toward anthropomorphism but more broadly toward the divine nature and the

3. Harlan, *A Model for Theologizing in Arab Muslim Contexts*, 315.

4. Ibid., 167.

divine attributes. Violent political ideologies have no genuine interest in the nature of God, or in any purely intellectual question of classical Islamic theology.[5] But movements that nourish such ideologies do apply *bilā kayfa* on divine nature. Following Ibn Taymiyya's tripartite rubric on God's unity, later Salafis differentiate the unity of God's lordship [*tawḥīd al-rubūbiyya*], the unity of God's divinity [*tawḥīd al-ulūhiyya*], and the unity of divine names and attributes [*tawḥīd al-asmāʾ wa-l-ṣifāt*]. They accept all divine names that are given in the scripture and the prophetic traditions, without further interpretation, however anthropomorphic they might appear. Rather than falling into anthropomorphism, this acceptance indicates the unknowability of the subject and the constructed hence limited capacity of speculation. Quoting Ibn Taymiyya and Mālik ibn Anas, Ibn Khalīfa al-Tamīmī argues that Salafis negate any knowledge of God's essence insofar as "none knows the howness [*kayfiyya*] of His ipseity and attributes except Himself." Thus many Salafi scholars appeal to *bilā kayfa* in favor of unknowability and anti-interpretivism—affirming that the divine attributes are "utterly unlike those of any creature, and that one should not inquire into their precise nature." In such a scripturalist context, *bilā kayfa* is employed not only in eschewing anthropomorphism on divine ipseity but also on the nature of divine attributes. The Ḥanbalī scholar Ibn Badrān al-Dimashqī (d.1927), for example, writes that "those curious about the nature of the divine attributes should reverently recognize that such matters are necessarily veiled from the workings of reason. In addition, no questions like 'why?' or 'how?' [*kayf?*] may apply in this context."[6]

Precolonial theologians adopted non-cognitive positions on diverse themes by suspending the ordinary meanings of scriptural statements, or declaring their unknowability. Hence, they could discuss not only the divine essence and attributes but also other theological issues with a *bilā kayfa* anti-interpretive attitude. Scripturalist approaches appealed to this principle especially in relation to questions that were seen to transcend the realm of reason, such as the question of destiny. Another Ḥanbalī jurist of Ibn Taymiyya's times, al-Ṭūfī, for example, accepted the scriptural account

5. See Quṭb in Renard, *Islamic Theological Themes*, 31–32. The "creed and path" [*ʿaqīda wa manhāj*] of the jihadist group called Islamic State, for example, has no reference to the divine nature or divine attributes. See Bunzel, *From Paper State to Caliphate*, 38–42.

6. El-Bizri, "God: Essence and Attributes," 126; Al-Tamīmī, *Muʿtaqad Ahl al-Sunna wa-l-Jamāʿa fī Tawḥīd al-Asmāʾ wa-l-Ṣifāt*, 64–65; Lav, *Radical Islam and the Revival of Medieval Theology*, 42–43.

of destiny *prima facie*, as any discursive inquiry can be easily, and rationally, falsified in this transcendent field:

> The problem of destiny is one of the *divine mysteries*, the nature and reality of which no human being has a route to realize, except by the will of God . . . [One has to] revert to what revealed religion stipulates, namely having faith [*īmān*] and acquiescent assent [*taslīm*] in a heart that is sound and unadulterated by fallacies . . . Even Abū ʿAbd Allāh [Fakhr al-Dīn] al-Rāzī, despite his great learning in *Kalām* and his knowledge of the methods of proof and refutation . . . said, "if it is said, 'what then is to be done?' One should say, 'what should be done is to abandon doing anything.' "[7]

Al-Rāzī's reported claim that "*what should be done is to abandon doing anything*" [*al-ḥīla tark al-ḥīla*] concerning the transcendent discourse on the destiny indicates that al-Ṭūfī and al-Rāzī situate *bilā kayfa* within the question of our ultimate fate after death, or one's destiny. When introducing the question of destiny, the *Creed III* attributed to Ibn Ḥanbal had employed the exact phrase that al-Ṭūfī later used: "It is necessary to have faith in it and acquiescent assent in it." In other words, scholars employed broad terms like "divine mystery," "faith," and "acquiescent assent" in adopting anti-interpretive positions, even if they did not explicitly use the formula *bilā kayfa*.[8]

This brief observation suggests that Muslim traditionists of different generations, Mālik, al-Ṭūfī and Ibn Badrān, and modern Western Islamicists appeal to *bilā kayfa* on a variety of questions no less than the nature of divine names and attributes, destiny, the problem of Qurʾanic verses with anthropomorphic passages, or the nature of the divine essence itself. Yet, two aspects of this anti-interpretive, non-cognitive position should be highlighted for theoretical clarity. First, it marks the unknowability of the divine nature, and the inaccessibility of the meaning of the

---

7. Al-Ṭūfī in Shihadeh, "Three Apologetic Stances in al-Ṭūfī," 6–7 (my emphasis and my minor modifications).

8. Williams, "Aspects of the Creed of Imām Aḥmad Ibn Ḥanbal," 459.

A couple centuries before al-Rāzī, the principle "what should be done is to abandon doing anything" was already associated with Sufi approaches to destiny and reliance on God. According to al-Kharkūshī, it was the great Sufi master of Baghdad, al-Junayd, who uttered the principle. (Al-Kharkūshī, *Tahdhīb al-Asrār*, 139.)

sacred discourse, instead of following a literal interpretation. Second, the non-cognitive, anti-interpretive position applies only to some, not all, theological questions—specifically, those within the field of metaphysics. Both of these nuances are generally neglected in reductive depictions of Islamic theology, Ḥanbalism in particular. Depictions over the last centuries of *bilā kayfa* as a general anti-rational Islamic doctrine of submission to the literal reading, irrespective of the theological question under scrutiny, still haunt the scholarship. Recently, an objectivist student of philosophy described *bilā kayfa* as a general, immoral principle of Islam as it demands unquestioning submission to the arbitrary will of its despotic God:

> If God slays thousands of human beings for worshipping a golden calf instead of Him . . . then this is good simply because He wills it. God's will be done—or, alternatively, *Allāhu Akbar*, God is great, *bilā kayfa*, without inquiring how, as Islam states.[9]

The mistake in such quick connections between theology and violence is twofold, at least. First, the *bilā kayfa* anti-interpretive position that the Salafo-Wahhābī scholars reclaim is dominantly a non-cognitive one. It focuses on the unknowability of the interpretation of the sacred sources concerning the divine nature, divine attributes, the verses with anthropomorphic appearances, or the enigmatic disjointed letters [*al-ḥurūf al-muqaṭaʿāt*] in the Qurʾan, instead of their literal interpretation. Second, the *bilā kayfa* anti-interpretivism has not been appealed to in *all* theological questions, but specifically in the field of transcendence in Kantian sense: metaphysics. The theological question discussed here is a rather new field—the determination of what is good and evil [*al-taḥsīn wa-l-taqbīh*]—or broadly, ethics. The author is critical of the position that supposedly "Islam," in its essence, states—the determination of good and evil via a strictly unquestioning submission to the literal reading of their scripture. However, the term *bilā kayfa*, as opposed to the author's essentializing, sweeping generalization, did not appear in the context of *al-taḥṣīn wa-l-taqbīh* in Islamic theologies. Ethics has, rather, been an actively interpretive field, even in its most conservative sense. The continuities with the representations of Islam in the last centuries are striking in such uncontextual and politicized appeals to the phrase *bilā kayfa*.

9. Berstein, "Religion versus Morality," 40.

On the other hand, the term *bilā kayfa* was not the only term to mark anti-interpretive, self-canceling discourses. Rather, theology provided a variety of terms that were employed in defense of non-cognitive positions. Theologians appealed to the terms *tafwīḍ* ["delegation"] and *taslīm* ["acquiescent assent"] in suspending the ordinary meanings of terms, and hence discursive constructs or interpretation, concerning sacred reports on God. Instead of *bilā kayfa,* alternative formulae for negating modalities [*kayfiyya*], ineffectualism [*taʿṭīl*], or comparability [*tashbīh*], and affirming [*ithbāt*] the sacred reports without interpretation [*taʾwīl*] were used to express non-cognitive positions on different theological questions. Al-Māturīdī appealed to *tawaqquf,* literally, "stoppage," or "discontinuation," which indicated suspending judgment and interpretation where human knowledge reached its limits. Al-Ṭūfī informs us of another metaphor to indicate a similar position: he rather grumbled that one of the Qurʾanic verses, Q.21:23 is known among Sunnīs as "the verse of mace" [*āyat al-dabbūs*]—a phrase that indicates transcendence of discursive fields regarding its content. Al-Bayhaqī cited this verse, which states that "God does what He wills," as a corroboration for the impossibility of knowing God's modality. Other terms that were appealed to in the exposition of such positions described the report in question as a "divine mystery" [*sirr*] that only God knows; sometimes the phrase "as He deserves" [*yalīqu bihi*] was added after an apparently anthropomorphic description to indicate the discursive inaccessibility of its meaning. Also the phrase "I do not know" [*lā adrī*] acquired among the critics of traditionism something near the status of slogan to avoid any discursive construction. Abū Ḥāmid al-Ghazālī's *Restraining the Lay Public from Approaching Speculative Theology* [*Iljām al-ʿAwāmm ʿan ʿIlm al-Kalām*] introduced seven different ways of approaching the corporeal descriptions of God, all of which directly or roughly correspond to taking *bilā kayfa* positions. Neither *bilā kayfa* positions were applied indiscriminately to all theological questions, nor was the term *bilā kayfa* explicitly employed when such positions were adopted.[10]

Hence, studying the apophatic dimensions of non-cognitive positions regarding the divine essence poses challenges that demand careful contextualization. First are terminological difficulties: the term *bilā kayfa* does

10. Al-Māturīdī, *Kitāb al-Tawḥīd,* 122; Shihadeh, "Three Apologetic Stances in al-Ṭūfī," 7, 11, 22; Abrahamov, "The 'Bi-lā Kayfa' Doctrine," 368; Dickinson, *The Development of Early Sunnite Hadith Criticism,* 8; Dickinson, *The Development of Early Muslim ḥadīth Criticism,* 13; Abū Ḥāmid al-Ghazālī, *A Return to Purity in Creed,* 23–24.

not appear in various theological discussions, even if the specific positions adopt similar non-cognitive, anti-interpretive positions that cancel themselves in favor of the unknowability of the divine excess. Second, *bilā kayfa* positions might be easily confused if the theological question is not specifically defined and contextualized. The anti-interpretive position marked by *bilā kayfa* did not apply to all theological questions, as opposed to rather reductive or hostile depictions of Islamic theology. A final difficulty is related to the diverse meanings of *bilā kayfa* in historical context, especially in the first six centuries of Islam. During this period, the principle of *bilā kayfa* could indicate two different anti-interpretive positions: (1) literalist anthropomorphism in the ancient Mesopotamian tradition or (2) non-cognitive approaches to the divine essence that are non-anthropomorphic and self-negating, hence, apophatic.

Divine Nature Uninterpreted: Between Anthropomorphism and Apophaticism

The notion that the divine cannot be understood via human conceptual and modal thinking goes back to the Qur'an and the prophetic reports. We have seen how ʿAlīd traditions that adopt a negative reading of the divine attributes proliferated under Ismāʿīlī rule as a corporate project wherein even Sunnī traditionists like al-Quḍāʿī played their part. The *Scripture of Sajjād* [*Ṣaḥīfat al-Sajjādiyya*] and the *Way of Eloquence* [*Nahj al-Balāgha*] contain not only negations of the knowability of the divine essence or the applicability of the divine attributes, but they also deny that any modality or human category applies to God. A famous supplication of the grandson of ʿAlī, Zayn al-ʿĀbidīn (d.712), denies the accessibility of the modality, or literally, "howness" of God:

> It is Thou
> Before whose selfness [*dhātiyya*] imaginations fall short,
> Before whose howness [*kayfiyya*] understandings have no capacity,
> And the place of whose whereness [*ayniyya*] eyes perceive not.[11]

11. ʿAlī ibn al-Ḥusayn, *Psalms of Islam*, Supplications, 47:166 (Chittick's translation says "understandings have no incapacity" rather than "capacity" which is a typo). The dense appeal to terms with philosophical significance indicates that the supplication might be added a few centuries after Zayn al-ʿĀbidīn passed away.

Scholars of the eighth century appealed to such non-cognitive positions in the face of questions that concerned anthropomorphic depictions of God. The Qurʾanic description of God's "establishment" on a "throne" was one of the topics where early exegetes, traditionists, and jurists preferred to cancel discursive thought in favor of unknowability. The most famous report of the archetypal *bilā kayfa* apophaticism comes from the early jurist Mālik ibn Anas. Accordingly, asked about the meaning of the verse Qurʾan 20:5, which mentions of God as "established on a throne," Mālik famously defended the inapplicability of modalities:

> God's establishment [*istiwāʾ*] on the throne is known [*maʿlūm*], but its modality is unknown [*al-kayf majhūl*]. The belief in the establishment is obligatory [*al-īmān bihi wājib*], and the inquiry about it is an innovation [*al-sūʾāl ʿanhu bidʿa*].[12]

As the repugnant term "innovation" signals, Mālik saw the endeavor to use discursive modes in approaching the revelation as inauthentic and theologically erroneous. Later scholars like Ibn al-Jawzī (d.1200) and Ibn Taymiyya would trace Mālik's non-cognitive approach back to the early companions of the Prophet. The doxographer al-Shahrastānī, on the other hand, extrapolated the position to a wide group of scholars of the next generation. Accordingly, Mālik's position dispensed with any interpretive inquiry, which eventually could not escape human terms, modal categories, and hence, comparability and knowability. His position, al-Shahrastānī argued, was followed by the later traditionists and pietists like Ibn Ḥanbal, Sufyān al-Thawrī (d.778), Dāwūd al-Iṣfahānī (d.883) and his Ẓāhirī School, and, more recently, Ibn Kullāb, al-Muḥāsibī (d.857), and al-Qalānisī (d.970). Aḥmad al-Rifāʿī described all eponyms of the four Sunnī legal schools and the Imāmī school of Shīʿism as unanimous proponents of an amodal, *bilā kayfa* approach to the divine nature, who fell neither into anthropomorphism nor ineffectualism.[13]

Such monolithic descriptions of a homogeneous block of pious ancestors, however, overlooked major differences between various early positions concerning anthropomorphism. Later scholars underplayed the prominence of what Ronald S. Hendel calls "transcendent anthropomorphism"

---

12. Mālik ibn Anas in Abrahamov, "The 'Bi-lā Kayfa' Doctrine," 336.

13. Al-Shahrastānī, *al-Milal wa-l-Niḥal*, 80–81; al-Shahrastānī in Renard, *Islamic Theological Themes*, 146; Aḥmad al-Rifāʿī, *Kitāb al-Burhān al-Muʿayyad*, 19–20.

in some earlier *ḥadith* folk, particularly in association with Ibn Ḥanbal. Many among Ibn Ḥanbal's followers rather seemed to accept the literal appearance of the sacred sources in favor of transcendent anthropomorphism in the ancient Near Eastern type. Such anthropomorphism, which depicted God as a divine anthropos with a "body unlike bodies" and with an inscrutable form too holy for human eyes, was a Mesopotamian heritage that Islam inherited in different forms.[14] Some of these clearly anthropomorphic strands among early Muslims were recorded, with a fascinating variety, by the doxographers like al-Ashʿarī. Yet, the literal acceptance of anthropomorphic depictions of God could not be easily separated from the more overt forms of anthropomorphism. Such inclinations were rather more common than being associated with some "radical" groups. In addition to traditionists, a rich variety of mystical and pietist groups seem to share anthropomorphic sentiments, particularly when it comes to the vision of God. Abū ʿĀṣim al-Naṣāʾī (d.867) mentions an early antinomian group called the "pneumatics" [*rūḥāniyya*], who claimed direct vision of and communication with God. Al-Ashʿarī introduces a group called "renunciants [*nussāk*] among Sufis" who believed in incarnation, and some held it possible to see Her, to accompany Her, and to sit with Her. Al-Bisṭāmī was associated with the claim to have a vision of God as a beardless young man, and Abū Bakr al-Qaḥṭabī (fl.9th-10th CE) even claimed to have seen God in the form of his mother. ʿAbd al-Wāḥid ibn Zayd (d.793) believed God would be seen in this world according to one's pious acts, and Kahmas (d.766) was indicted for believing that God could be touched. Some of these names found their place in prominent Sufi hagiographies, although prominent Sufis criticized such positions from early on.[15]

At least from the ninth century onward, the phrase *bilā kayfa* could be called upon for more agnostic, self-canceling discursive positions as well as for transcendent anthropomorphism. Prominent traditionists Ibn ʿUyayna (d.814) and al-Dāraquṭnī (d.995), for example, were closer to the latter group as they affirmed the reports on the vision of God literally, without further interpretation. Similarly, Ibn ʿUyayna accepted the reports that described God as surprised and laughing [*yuʿajjib wa yaḍḥak*]. Asked

---

14. See Williams, "A Body Unlike Bodies"; Hendel, "Aniconism and Anthropomorphism in Ancient Israel," 223.

15. Al-Naṣāʾī in Karamustafa, "Antinomian Sufis," 102; Massignon, *Essays on the Origins on the Technical Language of Islamic Mysticism*, 79–81; Coppens, *Seeing God in This World and the Otherworld*, 196–204; Karamustafa, *Sufism: Formative Period*, 102–106.

about these depictions, he appealed to *bilā kayfa*, which means in this context the literal acceptance of anthropomorphism rather than non-cognitive, apophatic unknowability: "They are revealed in this way; we acknowledge them, and transmit them without asking how [*nuḥaddith bihā bilā kayfa*]."[16] Hence the presence of the term did not always mean the negation of knowability and modality, nor did it guarantee non-anthropomorphism. Nevertheless, those traditionists who deliberately avoided the term *bilā kayfa* were particularly prone to accept the sacred reports on the vision of God—or Her throne, body, face, or form—literally. According to the Muʿtazilite polymath al-Jāḥiẓ, one of the differences between the recently grown group scornfully called "Weeds" [Nābita] and the larger Sunnīs [Ahl al-Sunna] was that the former succumbed to anthropomorphism precisely because they refused to use *bilā kayfa* as a marker of amodality. A careful observer of the Inquisition [*Miḥna*] (833–847), al-Jāḥiẓ compared the wider Ahl al-Sunna with the group of "the Weeds":

> One group among them [Sunnīs] asserted that God will be seen, without adding any explanation. If it feared being suspected of anthropomorphism [*tashbīh*], it explained, "He will be seen *bilā kayfa*," thus avoiding corporeality [*tajsīm*] and attributing God a form [*taṣwīr*]. But the Weeds sprouted, and the secessionist group insisted: He is a body; and it ascribed form and limits to Him and declared anyone who believes in the beatific vision without *tajsīm* and *taṣwīr* to be a heretic.[17]

Echoing al-Jāḥiẓ, the Ḥanbalī scholar of the following century, Abū Bakr al-Ājurrī (d.971) would state that the acceptance of anthropomorphic accounts must be accompanied by the expression *bilā kayfa* in order to emphasize non-cognitivism.[18] A key name in the Inquisition period, Ibn Ḥanbal has been depicted as a central figure within the general lens of *bilā kayfa* non-cognitivism. Yet he does not seem to have applied the term. He showed no reservations about attributing a form [*ṣūra*] to God. He not only acknowledged the soundness of the report on the Prophet's vision of

16. Al-Dāraquṭnī, *Kitāb al-Ṣifāt*, 119, 116.

17. Al-Jāḥiẓ in Williams, "Aspects of the Creed of Imām Aḥmad Ibn Ḥanbal," 452 (my minor modification).

18. Holtzman, "Anthropomorphism."

God "in the form of a young man, beardless [*amrad*] with short curly hair [*jaʿd*] and clothed in a green garment" but also made belief in it obligatory. He committed to taking this prophetic report of the young man [*ḥadīth al-shābb*] *prima facie* [*ʿalā ẓāhirihi*], without disputing it, or qualifying with *bilā kayfa*. On the other hand, far from being a simple literalist, he did not shy away from interpreting the seemingly anti-anthropomorphic descriptions of God allegorically [*taʾwīl*], while he accepted the literal meaning of anthropomorphic verses and prophetic reports without interpretation or qualification. The *Creed I*, which Abū Jaʿfar Muḥammad ibn ʿAwf (fl.9th CE) claims Ibn Ḥanbal dictated to him, might contain the latter's authentic ideas, which have a clear transcendent anthropomorphic bent. Accordingly, Ibn Ḥanbal took straightforward anthropomorphic positions in much-debated issues such as the vision or speech of God:

> The people of paradise will see God with the eyes. . . . God speaks to human beings, and there is no interpreter between Him and them. The messenger of God has a basin, whose vessels are more in number than the stars in the sky.[19]

Ibn Ḥanbal claimed that the vision of God will be via the mediation of the standard human organs, and Her speech can be directly heard by human beings in this world. He said: "I heard ʿAbd al-Raḥmān ibn Muḥammad al-Muḥāribī (d.810), who had it on the authority of Sulaymān ibn Mihrān al-Aʿmash (d.765), on the authority of Abū al-Ḍuḥā, on the authority of Masrūq (d.682), on the authority of ʿAbd Allāh [ibn Anīs al-Juhanī (d.673)], say: 'When God gives utterance to revelation [*waḥy*], people of heaven hear His voice.' "[20] Abū Naṣr al-Sijzī (d.1052) supported the claim that the dwellers of paradise will hear God's actual voice, arguing that its chain of transmission is a valid one. Ibn Qudāma (d.1223), in the same vein, accused ʿAlī al-Baghdādī (d.1119) of heresy [*zandaqa*] as the latter denied that God's voice will be literally heard by the believers, and interpreted it as a burst, and a crack in the air. The report that "the messenger of God has a basin" is also curious, as it literally accepts a popular divine saying [*ḥadīth*

---

19. Ibn ʿAwf in Watt, *Islamic Creeds*, 31. Cf. Ibn al-Jawzī, *Virtues of the Imām Aḥmad ibn Ḥanbal*, 306–307, 312–313; Williams, "Aspects of the Creed of Imām Aḥmad Ibn Ḥanbal," 443–450.

For a discussion on the authenticity of the work, see AlSarhan, *Early Muslim Traditionalism*.

20. Ibn Qudāma in Renard, *Islamic Theological Themes*, 197.

qudsī] on the afterlife without further explanation.[21] In other words, Ibn Ḥanbal adopts an anti-interpretive approach not only to the Qurʾan but also to the prophetic reports, when it comes to anthropomorphic depictions of God in particular. The *Creed I*, however, adds a bent of unknowability and amodality to Ibn Ḥanbal's anti-interpretivism:

> *Ḥadīths* are sound and preserved. We submit to them even if we do not know their interpretation. We do not discuss them or argue about them, and we do not interpret them, but we relate them as they have come (to us).[22]

In oscillating between literal acceptance of a transcendently anthropomorphic God and the admission of the unknown, incomprehensible surface of the eternal word, Ibn Ḥanbal demonstrates that anthropomorphism and *bilā kayfa* apophaticism could not be easily separated in the formative period of Islamic thought. The same ambivalence can be observed in al-Ashʿarī's approach to the anthropomorphic depictions of God. He employs the phrase *bilā kayfa* after such anthropomorphic depictions, but it can mean unquestioning acceptance of the literal Qurʾanic readings, instead of their unknowability:

> God is on His throne; as He said: "The Merciful on the throne is seated" [Q.20:5]. God has two hands *bilā kayfa*; as He said: "(what) I created with my two hands" [Q.38:75], and: "Nay, His two hands are spread out (in bounty)" [Q.5:64]. God has two eyes *bilā kayfa;* as He said: "Which sailed before Our eyes" [Q.54:14]. God has a face; as

---

21. This famous anthropomorphist *ḥadīth* widely circulated among traditionists, including the canonical collections such as the *Saḥīḥ* of al-Bukhārī (d.870), and the *Sunan* of al-Nasāʾī (d.915):

> One day when he—the Prophet—was still among us, he took a nap, then he raised his head, smiling. We said to him: "Why are you smiling, O Messenger of God?" He said: "Just now this chapter [*sūra*] was revealed to me: In the Name of God, the Most Gracious, the Most Merciful. Verily, We have granted you (O Muḥammad) *al-Kawthar*. Therefore turn in prayer to your Lord and sacrifice (to Him only). For he who hates you, he will be cut off." Then he said: "Do you know what *al-Kawthar* is?" We said: "God and His Messenger know best." He said: "It is a river that my Lord has promised me in Paradise. Its vessels are more than the number of the stars. My community will come to me, then a man among them will be pulled away and I will say: 'O Lord, he is one of my community' and He will say to me: 'You do not know what he did after you were gone.'"

22. Ibn ʿAwf in Watt, *Islamic Creeds*, 30.

> He said: "the face of your Lord endures, full of majesty and honor" [Q.55:27].[23]

Al-Ashʿarī also declared that God will be seen by our physical eyes on the day of resurrection, and he accepted the reports on the afterlife, such as the basin and bridge, as realities that should be accepted without further comment. Accordingly, the Sunnīs "do not say 'how?' or 'why?'" on these metaphysical questions. Once again, it is ambiguous whether *bilā kayfa* expresses the unquestioning acceptance of transcendent anthropomorphism or an apophaticism that emerges from the unknowability or inaccessibility of such sacred discourses.

Al-Ashʿarī's *Creed* had strong similarities with the Ḥanbalī creeds of his time, which more clearly embraced the simultaneous corporeality and otherness of God in transcendent anthropomorphism. The popular Ḥanbalī creed, which was written probably after the ninth century, clearly defended such a theological position:

> God is hearing undoubtedly, and seeing undoubtedly. He is knowing and not ignorant, generous and not mean, forbearing and not hasty, remembering and not forgetting, awake and not sleeping, near (with His favor) and not neglectful. He moves and speaks and considers (or observes); He sees and laughs; He rejoices and loves and dislikes; He shows loathing and good pleasure; He is angry and displeased; He is merciful and pardons; He impoverishes and enriches and is inaccessible. He descends every night to the lowest heaven as He wills. "There is nothing like Him, and He is the hearing and seeing" [Q.42:11].[24]

---

23. Al-Ashʿarī in Watt, *Islamic Creeds*, 41. For the original Arabic, see al-Ashʿarī, *Maqālāt al-Islāmiyyin*, 1:320.

In his defense of an unnamed Ḥanbalī scholar—most probably his teacher Ibn Taymiyya—who was persecuted by Ashʿarites on grounds of anthropomorphism, Ibn al-Qayyim al-Jawziyya (d.1350) would quote al-Ashʿarī himself:

> He [al-Ashʿarī] affirmed that God sits on His throne, and proved this by Qurʾanic verses.
> He beautifully proved God's aboveness, so go and read his books with diligent eyes!
> I swear that the so-called anthropomorphist said exactly what this scholar of divine knowledge has already said!
> So accuse him, woe unto you! Let this anthropomorphist be put to trial, you hateful people! (Ibn al-Qayyim al-Jawziyya in Holtzman, "Accused of Anthropomorphism," 580.)

24. Watt, *Islamic Creeds*, 37.

In stunning contrast to the vast majority of theological schools, such traditionists employed the verse Q.42:11 in defense of transcendent anthropomorphism, instead of divine otherness. Indeed, a review of the exegetical history of this verse indicates that it was employed by the advocates of transcendent anthropomorphism in support of their position early on. Ibn Abī Ḥātim al-Rāzī (d.938) cited this verse after affirming that God is established on Her throne without adding further comment other than a list of prominent traditionists who defended the same literalist position. The notorious advocates of transcendent anthropomorphism, Muqātil (d.767) and Dāwūd al-Jawāribī (fl.8th-9th CE), who affirmed that God is composed of flesh and blood, and has organs, also cited Q.42:11 in support. (Muqātil, as opposed to his popular depictions as an "extreme" or radical anthropomorphist, squarely fit into his context.) Fakhr al-Dīn al-Rāzī's critique of anthropomorphism also highlight that the divergent readings of Q.42:11 were at the core of these controversies. The verse was still used in the service of transcendent anthropomorphism when Ibn al-Jawzī wrote his influential insider critiques of anthropomorphism within Ḥanbalism, and when Ibn al-Qayyim al-Jawziyya (d.1350) was defending Ḥanbalism against the outsider charges of anthropomorphism. Ibn al-ʿArabī also testifies the prevalence and tension of these opposite readings of Q.42:11. Accordingly, the rationalists interpret it as a declaration of divine dissimilarity, and the common people understand it anthropomorphically, while his own group, "the people of unveiling," embraces both—the paradox. Hence the famous Andalusian scholar of jurisprudence and prophetic traditions, Muḥammad ibn Saʿdūn, better known as Abū ʿAmir al-ʿAbdarī al-Qurashī (d.1130), was not an exceptional figure in arguing for an anthropomorphic reading of Q.42:11, in line with this traditionist anthropomorphism:

> *The [anti-anthropomorphist] heretics cite in evidence the Qurʾan verse "Nothing is like Him,"* but the meaning of that verse is only that nothing can be compared to God in His divinity. *In form, however, God is like you or me.*[25]

---

25. Holtzman, *Anthropomorphism in Islam*, 268, 303–304; Williams, "A Body Unlike Bodies," 35; Dickinson, *The Development of Early Muslim ḥadīth Criticism*, 43; Sirry, "Muqātil b. Sulaymān and Anthropomorphism"; Abrahamov in al-Qāsim ibn Ibrāhīm, *Anthropomorphism and Interpretation of the Qurʾan*; Madelung, *Religious Trends in Early Islamic Iran*, 41; Holtzman, "Accused of Anthropomorphism," 568; Ibn al-ʿArabī in Chittick, *Sufi Path of Knowledge*, 75–76.

Probably the most surprising defense of transcendent anthropomorphism at the level of general public comes from the philosopher and Mālikī jurist of Andalusia, Ibn Rushd. According to his theological work penned in 1179, the *Exposition of the Methods of Proof* [*al-Kashf ʿan Manāhij al-Adilla*], the belief in God's corporeality and His comparability to pure light too glorious to see is valid for the general public. The scripture suggests that the attributes shared [*mushtarak*] between God and Her creation are not just abstract capacities, but also physical qualities, such as having a face, two hands, and so on. God possesses these attributes in their most complete existence [*atamm wujūdan*]. Ibn Rushd then cites Q.42:11 and continues, "many among Muslims believe that *the creator has a body unlike bodies.* And this is the belief of the Ḥanbalīs and many among those who follow them." Ibn Rushd prefers this over interpretivism, while at the elite level he follows incorporealism. Yet, in both levels, he affirms the directionality [*jiha*] of God above the world. She *is* above the world, beyond the outermost sphere, while this is beyond place and corporeality. It is striking that Ibn Taymiyya and his pupil Ibn al-Qayyim al-Jawziyya would both quote Ibn Rushd's *Exposition* to argue that the most skillful philosophers [*ḥudhdhāq al-falāsifa*] refuted interpretivist approaches to anthropomorphism.[26]

There were, then, at least three different hermeneutical takes on the apparent anthropomorphism in the sacred sources in the ninth century. One way was to follow rationalist or mystical allegorical readings to respond to anthropomorphism; dialectical theologians, Sufis, and philosophers often adopted such positions. Transcendent anthropomorphism would be removed discursively, via interpretive responses to the sacred sources.

Second, one could accept the anthropomorphic verses as they are, with their literal meaning. This position, "transcendent anthropomorphism" as some scholars call it, fit into the larger ancient Near Eastern theological models in general, and embraced both divine otherness and corporeality, wherein God is a super anthropos that has a face and body too glorious and luminous for human gaze. To use the words of Ibn Rushd that al-Ashʿarī had also ascribed to the early Imāmī theologian Hishām ibn al-Ḥakam, God is "a body [*jism*] unlike bodies." In this context, *bilā kayfa* resists the description of "traditional agnosticism about anthropomorphism," as widely defended in the contemporary scholarship and by Salafis. Instead of an agnosticism that shies away from interpretation and

---

26. Ibn Rushd, *al-Kashf ʿan Manāhij al-Adilla*, 138–139; Ovadia, *Ibn Qayyim al-Jawziyya and the Divine Attributes*, 252–265.

declares unknowability of the meaning of verses with anthropomorphic appearance, we have their literal acceptance mixed with divine otherness. Some extreme versions of this literalism were recorded in doxographical works, but its milder versions were also quite widespread among traditionists. While the Shīʿite theologians more readily adopted the Hellenistic emphasis of late antiquity on divine otherness by the ninth century, Sunnism had rather a large, however mild, anthropomorphist strand in the ancient Near Eastern tradition well into the twelfth century. While many of these scholars criticized the more blatant ascriptions of human attributes to God, they adopted a transcendent anthropomorphism wherein God has a sublime form, a face too luminous to see, a heavenly location too lofty to reach, and a body unlike bodies. Transcendent anthropomorphism could attack divine comparability [*tashbīh*], yet it did not hesitate to describe God as a super anthropos.[27] Such anthropomorphist literalism expressed itself sometimes in association with phrases like *bilā kayfa*.

The third way was to follow the apophatic non-cognitive and amodal reading of *bilā kayfa*—that is, to confirm the forms of scriptural theological statements with the unknowability of their meaning and the modalities of their referents. In other words, scholars in this line abandoned hermeneutical inquiry altogether as it entails the accessibility of the divine speech, attributes, and ipseity. Not everybody who explicitly employed the phrase *bilā kayfa* adopted non-cognitive positions instead of anthropomorphism. Similarly, not everybody who took non-cognitive positions on the divine nature used the phrase *bilā kayfa*, as there was a rich variety of concepts that played that role.[28]

In the post-Inquisition period, we find among the followers of both Abū Ḥanīfa and Ibn Ḥanbal those who defend a form of apophaticism associated with amodality that cancels theological discourse. This development was somewhat unexpected on both sides. First, Ibn Ḥanbal himself,

---

27. For example Ibn Abī Ḥātim al-Rāzī himself penned a critique of those who overtly ascribed God human attributes and comparability, *al-Mujassima*. As they widely saw the use of analogical reasoning in theology as a form of rendering God comparable, even the overtly anthropomorphist traditionists could accuse more rationalists of *tashbīh*.

Dickinson, *The Development of Early Muslim ḥadīth Criticism*, 58; Dickinson, *The Development of Early Sunnite Hadith Criticism*, 36n97; Williams, "A Body Unlike Bodies," 22–23.

28. Holtzman's forthcoming studies will bring further nuance to these briefly introduced hermeneutial camps, particularly to the diversity within the second, anti-interpretive group. My study here is particularly interested in the third camp due to its emphasis on unknowability.

as opposed to his later portrayal, was probably closer to literal reading of anthropomorphic depictions of God than he was of declaring the unknowability of these depictions. Second, we are told that al-Maʾmūn, the caliph who oversaw the Inquisition, "excelled in jurisprudence according to the school of Abū Ḥanīfa," and the latter scholar, for at least part of his career, had taught that the Qurʾan had been created.[29] We observe a gradual distancing from transcendent anthropomorphism among the students of Ibn Ḥanbal, and the quick popularization of the uncreated, transcendent depictions of the divine word among the students of Abū Ḥanīfa. In the following centuries, both camps would widely adopt an apophaticism wherein human discursive activities on the divine ipseity cancel themselves by the amodal acceptance of the unknowability of the transcendent discourse.

Bilā Kayfa *Apophaticism and Early Ḥanafism*

The spread of *bilā kayfa* apophaticism is widely testified in the post-Inquisition period theology, particularly among Ḥanafīs. The *Testimony* [*Waṣiyya*], attributed to Abū Ḥanīfa but penned probably in the late ninth century, adopts such a strategy concerning the vision of God in the afterlife:

> We confess that the meeting [*liqāʾ*] of God with the inhabitants of paradise will be *a reality, without modality, comparison or spatiality* [*bilā kayfiyya wa lā tashbīh wa lā jiha*].[30]

The *Testimony* also accepts the Qurʾanic depiction of God as sitting on a throne but underlines that this transcendent discourse should not be understood in human terms as She transcends [*taʿāla*] these depictions. The Ḥanafī scholar al-Ṭaḥāwī (d.933), who lived mainly in Egypt, exemplifies the key aspects of this rising form of apophaticism at the expense of both anthropomorphism and discursive inquiries. The first and indispensable

29. Hinds, "Miḥna."

30. For the Arabic text, with the commentary of the Anatolian jurist, Akmal al-Dīn al-Bābartī (or al-Bayburtī) (d.1384), see Abū Ḥanīfa and al-Bābartī, *Sharḥ Waṣiyyat al-Imām Abī Ḥanīfa*, 132–136. For alternative English translations, see Wensinck, *The Muslim Creed*, 130; Watt, *Islamic Creeds*, 60. Abū Ḥanīfa in Abū Ḥanīfa and al-Bābartī, *Sharḥ Waṣiyyat al-Imām Abī Ḥanīfa*, 87.

aspect of this *bilā kayfa* apophaticism is its emphasis on the divine nature, hence otherness, of the sacred scripture. In al-Ṭaḥāwī's words:

> The Qur'an is the Speech of God; it proceeded from Him *amodally* as words; He sent it down upon His servant by revelation; the believers truly counted it true in accordance with that (description); they were certain that it was truly the Speech of God. It is not created like the speech of the creature. . . . *Human speech does not resemble it. Whoever attributes to God any of the characteristics belonging to humanity is an unbeliever.*[31]

Its uncreated nature transcendentalizes the scripture and its meaning. Therefore, the meaning of consimilar [*mutashābih*] verses and sacred reports cannot be accessed by creation—only God knows them. The sacred sources cancel all efforts for discursive access as they embody the transcendent discourse:

> The vision (of God) is a reality for the people of Paradise, *without comprehension or modality*. (It is) as the book of God expresses it, "faces on that day bright, looking to their Lord" [Q.75:22-23]; and *the interpretation of this is according to what God intended and knew*. Every sound *ḥadīth* reported from the Messenger of God is *as he said*, and *its meaning is what he intended*. We (refrain from) introducing anything (false) into that by interpreting it according to our own ideas or imagining it to be according to our fancies. *Only he is safe in his religion who submits to God and His messenger and refers back the knowledge of what is doubtful to the knower of it [i.e., does not interpret but admits that only God knows the interpretation].*[32]

The divine discourse itself is incomprehensible when it addresses the divine ipseity. When it gives us an anthropomorphic image, its meaning remains rather unknowable to us, like the divine ipseity Herself. In al-Ṭaḥāwī's words, the transcendent discourse is simultaneously clear and incomprehensible:

---

31. Al-Ṭaḥāwī in Watt, *Islamic Creeds*, 50 (my emphasis).

32. Al-Ṭaḥāwī in ibid., 49–50 (my emphases).

> The throne and the footstool are a reality, as *God made clear in His glorious book*. He is independent of the throne and what is below it; *He comprehends everything above it, and has made His creation unable to comprehend (that)*.[33]

Al-Ṭaḥāwī's theological position depicts scripture as the transcendent discourse on divine nature essentially beyond comprehension. Human discourse retreats from the scriptural fields that transcend its limits. These fields are the human destiny after death, the nature of the divine essence, and its relationship with the attributes. Nobody has access to these fields—hence there is no possibility to understand the mystery of the transcendent discourse on these topics. One can neither negate the attributes expressed in the incomprehensible transcendent discourse nor assume that they are anthropomorphic, comparable, or comprehensible. As a self-negating theological gesture, al-Ṭaḥāwī challenges all interpretive and speculative inquiries on the divine nature and its relationship with the divine attributes:

> He who does not guard (both) against denial (of God's attributes) and assimilation (of them to human attributes, or anthropomorphism) is mistaken and has not attained purity of conception [*tanzīh*]. For our lord is characterized by the attributes of oneness and the properties of uniqueness; *none of the creation has what is characteristic of Him. God is exalted above limits, ends, elements, members, instruments; the six directions do not comprise Him as they do all creatures.*[34]

"Negation," "denial," or "ineffectualism," expressed in Arabic terms like *nafy, salb,* or *taʿṭīl,* are rejected simultaneously with terms that indicate divine comparability, incarnation, or anthropomorphism, such as *tashbīh* and *tajsīm*. Al-Ṭaḥāwī's *bilā kayfa* non-cognitive position cancels both positive and negative speculative constructs in favor of the incomprehensibility of the transcendent discourse on the unknowable divine excess.

Not only the later Ḥanafī creeds, such as The *Greatest Insight II*, but also Abū Muṭīʿ al-Makḥūl al-Nasafī's *Refutation* [*Kitāb al-Radd ʿalā Ahl al-Bidaʿ wa-l-Ahwāʾ*], al-Māturīdī's *Book of Unity* [*Kitāb al-Tawḥīd*], and al-Ḥakīm al-Samarqandī's (d.953) *Book of the Greatest Abode* [*Kitāb al-Sawād*

33. Al-Ṭaḥāwī in ibid., 52 (my emphases and my minor modifications).

34. Al-Ṭaḥāwī in ibid., 50 (my emphasis).

al-Aʿẓam] demonstrate that it was eastern Iranian and Central Asian Ḥanafism where the *bilā kayfa* attained such self-canceling apophatic dimensions early on. Especially the *Book of the Greatest Abode*, very much like al-Māturīdī's slightly later *Book of Unity*, showed a clear break from, and even explicit condemnation of, Karrāmī anthropomorphism on the divine nature. Still we find parallels: for example, al-Samarqandī argues that all attributes of God, including the essential ones and those that express actions are uncreated and unchangeable. He also considers divine contentment [*riḍā*] and anger [*ghaḍab*] among these attributes. (The Mālikī-Ashʿarī theologian of his time, al-Bāqillānī, who inclined toward transcendent anthropomorphism as we will discuss below, saw contentment and anger as essential attributes of God as well.) Still, al-Samarqandī's approach to the divine essence was strongly negativist, as it removes all modalities from God. In line with the *bilā kayfa* apophaticism of al-Ṭaḥāwī, he depicted the Qurʾan as the transcendent discourse, the meaning of which cannot be accessed, hence interpreted:

> One must not ascribe to God location, nor speak of His presence, nor of His coming and going, nor describe Him by anything resembling created things. This is because the perfection of faith is that one should know, and strive to know, God, but not to know in Him modality [*kayfiyya*]. . . . As for the verses in which God has mentioned coming and arrival, and the tradition from the Prophet concerning the "descent" of God and suchlike, *he must believe in it but not explain it; for he who explains it enters into the doctrine of ineffectualism* [*taʿṭīl*] and becomes a heretic. If you explain coming, going, eye, hand, self, etc., you become an anthropomorphist. If you see an ambiguous verse or tradition, leave it to God, and do not (try to) explain it, that you may escape giving a wrong explanation.[35]

Al-Māturīdī's *Book of Unity*, written in the last decade of his life, follows the *bilā kayfa* apophaticism of earlier Ḥanafīs. The work embodies "the

35. Al-Ḥakīm al-Samarqandī in al-ʿOmar, *Doctrines of the Māturīdīte School with Special Reference to As-Sawād al-Aʿẓam*, 167–169.

Penned in early tenth-century Transoxania, the *Book of the Greatest Abode* served as a "public text" that expressed the theological consensus of the "greatest mass." It played a crucial role, as it was designed as the fixed, official catechism under the Sāmānid rule. By the end of the century, it was already translated into Persian under Nūḥ ibn Manṣūr (r.976–997).

oldest theological summa extant from Islamic civilization" and also plays a significant role in drastically changing the Ḥanafī outlook on various theological questions while at the same time successfully giving the deceptive appearance of a continuity. Al-Māturīdī indicates that the attributes apply to God in a way that is unknown to us. For that reason, he employs them in a way that simultaneously affirms the transcendent discourse amodally, and negates comparability as well as knowability. His phrases like "God is knower unlike knowers" [*ʿalīm lā ka-l-ʿulamāʾ*] affirm the transcendent discourse, with clear proof of rational demonstration, but also indicate that neither the nature of the divine essence nor how divine attributes relate to the essence is knowable, describable, or open to human discourse.[36]

Ulrich Rudolph argues that for al-Māturīdī, in line with Ḥanafī rationalism and similar to the Muʿtazilite position, the divine essence is knowable. He claims that "the Ḥanafites had always held a rationalistic position on this issue and claimed that God was knowable by natural means." He focuses on al-Māturīdī's appeal to creation as a "witness" to its invisible creator [*dalālat al-shāhid ʿalā al-ghāʾib*]. In conclusion, he asserts that "al-Māturīdī teaches the possibility of rational knowledge of God. Thus al-Māturīdī positions himself contrary to other Sunnī doctrines such as those of the Ashʿarites, and outwardly would seem to take his place alongside the Muʿtazilite theologians."[37]

Although Rudolph's study is probably the most erudite analysis of al-Māturīdī and early Ḥanafism, his evaluation of this specific point harbors at least two problems. First, his categorization of the Ashʿarites, as we will see below, has problems. In the eleventh century Ashʿarites were already accepting reason and nature as legitimate means to derive knowledge about God, in contrast to Rudolph's suggestion that "the possibility of rational knowledge of God" was in opposition to Ashʿarism. Notwithstanding their differences, later Ashʿarites defend divine knowability as well.[38] Second, Rudolph's depiction of al-Māturīdī as a defender of divine knowability does not accurately reflect his approach to the divine essence. It is correct that al-Māturīdī describes creation as containing accessible signs of its creator, and that reasoning provides us a variety of strong arguments

---

36. Al-Māturīdī, *Kitāb al-Tawḥīd*, 106; Rudolph, *Al-Māturīdī and the Development of Sunnī Theology in Samarqand*, 189.

37. Rudolph, *Al-Māturīdī and the Development of Sunnī Theology in Samarqand*, 265–268.

38. See Kars, "What Is 'Negative Theology'? Lessons from the Encounter of Two Sufis"; Kars, "Sufis and Muʿtazilites: Theological Engagements of Ibn ʿArabī."

that there should be a singular agent that governs creation. Philosophers provided similar arguments as well, but they also explicitly defended divine unknowability. In other words, "signs," analogy from creation, or the witnessing of the visible to what is beyond, are only bottom-up gestures toward, or indicators of, the unknowable creator, rather than direct claims that He can be known or comprehended. Instead, al-Māturīdī provides important evidence that he thinks otherwise. Most clearly, concerning the divine ipseity and its relationship with attributes, al-Māturīdī follows the principle of "stoppage" [*waqf*]—that is, stopping short of comprehension. As a critical metaphysician, he appeals to this principle whenever he thinks that reason cannot progress:

> God probes the believers with stoppage concerning that which is received about the promise and threat (in the afterlife) [*al-waʿd wa-l-waʿīd*], about the disjointed letters, and issues like those, where man is tested [*miḥna*] with belief as there is stoppage and no certain knowledge.[39]

As there is no clear, demonstrable proof in such metaphysical topics, opposing arguments can be defended on similar grounds. Scholars should rather admit their incapacity to reach a final, certain knowledge in such issues, and be rather prudent beyond their reach. Such prudence is expressed by *bilā kayfa*, concerning the verses on the "vision" of God, or Her "establishment" on a throne. Stoppage dictates that these scriptural truths actually transcend the human mind; one should negate all similitudes and comparisons in relation to God, and defer the final interpretation to Her. The intended meaning of such verses cannot be known, except as a negation of what we can actually comprehend.

The divine nature, with its relationship to the divine attributes, is one of the fields where al-Māturīdī appeals to stoppage. He adopts the Kullābite formula that the essential attributes of God are neither Her nor other than Her. This very paradoxical formula, accordingly, entails the unknowability of the way in which these attributes relate to the divine essence. We can rationally and speculatively prove that the universe has a creator, who cannot lack knowledge, speech, or power. But this does not mean that we actually

39. Al-Māturīdī, *Kitāb al-Tawḥīd*, 138. *Al-waʿd wa-l-waʿīd* was one of the famous five principles [*al-uṣūl al-khamsa*] of Muʿtazilism, which are commonly traced back to Abū al-Hudhayl.

know the way in which She is so. Al-Māturīdī associates the Kullābite formula with rational prudence—the stoppage: "To say: *it is neither Him nor other than Him*. This means to stop short of knowledge, and it is true as it is confirmed for [divine] knowledge and power [in addition to speech]."[40] Al-Māturīdī's description of the essential names of God is a strongly negative theological one. "God," "One," and "all-merciful," according to al-Māturīdī, are among Her essential names, which express the same ipseity in different forms. Unlike the attributes, which differ in their meaning, the essential names of God differ only in expression, but not in their meaning, insofar as "He transcends the words through which He could be understood."[41] These essential names themselves, on the other hand, resist being understood in positive terms. In al-Māturīdī's description, the philosophical rigor of which is evident, "oneness" is anything but knowable:

> "One" [*wāḥid*] has four meanings: (1) The totality that cannot be doubled. (2) The part that cannot be halved. (3) That which is in-between them, insofar as it carries the [former] two aspects: it is larger than that which cannot be halved, but smaller than that which cannot be doubled, as there is nothing beyond a totality. (4) That through which the other three [definitions of "one"] exist [*qāma bihi*]. *"He"; and He is not "He"; hidden from "He." Of whom the tongue is muted [inkharasa]. About whom declaration dries up. From whom estimations [awhām] recede. In whom understandings are perplexed—He is God, the lord of both worlds.*[42]

"He; and He is not He" [*huwa wa lā huwa huwa akhfā min huwa*] is a strongly apophatic self-negation that we find among Sufis like al-Kalābādhī, and Ismāʿīlī theologians of eastern Iran contemporary with al-Māturīdī—such as Abū Yaʿqūb al-Sijistānī, the chief of the Ismāʿīlī *daʿwa* in Khurasan following Muḥammad al-Nasafī (d.943). The analysis of the ways in which "one" is applied also recalls the works of philosophers like al-Kindī, al-Fārābī, and Ibn Bajjā. Similarly, al-Māturīdī adds

40. Ibid., 122.

41. Al-Māturīdī's position here follows Abū Muṭīʿ al-Makḥūl, who maintained that God possesses distinct attributes not identical with His being. See Rudolph, *Al-Māturīdī and the Development of Sunnī Theology in Samarqand*, 276–279; al-Māturīdī, *Kitāb al-Tawḥīd*, 129.

42. Al-Māturīdī, *Kitāb al-Tawḥīd*, 107. For an alternative translation of this ambivalent passage, see Rudolph, *Al-Māturīdī and the Development of Sunnī Theology in Samarqand*, 275–276.

that divine oneness is not a numerical oneness, as he repeats on different occasions such as under the "negation of comparability" [*nafy al-tashbīh*].[43] Accordingly, divine oneness can neither be comprehended nor depicted, except as a unique category.

The same unknowability applies to the problems of anthropomorphism for al-Māturīdī. In both issues of God's "establishment" on the throne, and Her "vision" in the afterlife, al-Māturīdī is quite consistently following a *bilā kayfa* apophaticism. In the case of the "throne," for example, he enumerates all interpretations that he finds reasonable, precisely because all of them negate divine comparability. But his eventual position in terms of interpretation is to cancel it entirely, in favor of stoppage:

> For us, the principle here is, as God says, "Nothing is like unto Him" [Q.42:11]—*to negate similarity to creation from Himself.* We have clarified that He also transcends similarity in His actions and attributes. The verse "The all-merciful, established on the throne" [Q.20:5] *should be understood as it is revealed,* and negate from Him similitude to creation. For, revelation came down about this, and proven by reason. Then, we do not go to any interpretation [*la naqṭaʿa fī taʾwīlihi ʿalā shayʾ*], as it is possible to be different than what we have mentioned. It is also possible that it might have an interpretation other than comparing to creation that is unknown to us. We believe in what God willed in it [i.e., in negating similitude]. In all such issues that are established in the revelation, such as the vision of God and other issues, one should negate similarity, and *believe in it without affirming [ghayri taḥqīq] one [interpretation] over another.*
>
> The principle here is that *the person is narrow-fitted [yuḍayyiq] to the issue, as their effort for understanding is [based on] existing creation.* As discourse on God must be uplifting from similitude in essence or action, relations regarding Him should not be understood in terms of existents other than Him.[44]

Concerning the "vision" of God in the afterlife, al-Māturīdī adopts a similar position. He employs the phrase "*bilā kayfa*" in terms of beatific vision, consistent with his general anti-interpretive apophaticism on the

---

43. Al-Māturīdī, *Kitāb al-Tawḥīd*, 89; cf. Abū Yaʿqūb al-Sijistānī, *Kitāb al-Yanābīʿ*, 69.

44. Al-Māturīdī, *Kitāb al-Tawḥīd*, 138.

unknowable divine nature.[45] First, "His vision is real, without comprehension, and without interpretation [*tafsīr*]."[46] The very possibility of vision in the afterlife, for al-Māturīdī is actually the negation of Her knowability, as it is a negation of understanding Her [*nafy al-idrāk*]:

> "Eyes do not apprehend Him" [Q.103:6]; He is praised with the negation of apprehension [*idrāk*], not with the negation of vision. He also said: "they do not comprehend Him in knowledge" [Q.20:110]. Here is an affirmation of knowledge, and a negation of comprehension [*iḥāṭa*]. The same with apprehension. . . . Besides, "apprehension" is to comprehend something limited. God transcends this, and being described by limitation.[47]

Al-Māturīdī emphasizes the Qur᾽anic distinction between "apprehending" God, which is impossible, and Her "vision," which preserves Her ultimate unknowability. The distinction was employed by later Ashᶜarites such as al-Juwaynī, and became a key principle for Sufis who adopted *bilā kayfa* approaches to beatific vision. Ibn al-ᶜArabī, for example, argued in the *Meccan Openings* that we witness God in creation and in each object of knowledge both through our eyes and insight, but witnessing does not mean apprehending the unknowable.

Eleventh-century Māturīdite creeds also preserve the *bilā kayfa* apophaticism of the earlier centuries. An important text for Transoxania's subsequent Māturīdite theological development, the *Greatest Insight II*—probably written in the late eleventh century—extensively employs *bilā kayfa* in amodal affirmation of God's physical descriptions and cancellation of human understanding and interpretation.[48] Briefly, from the tenth

---

45.

> If it is said: how is He seen? It is said: Without "how" [*bilā kayfa*]. Howness applies to what which has a form [*ṣūra*]. Rather He is seen without standing or sitting, leaning or relating, connection [*ittiṣāl*] or separation [*infiṣāl*], confrontation or turning, short or long, light or darkness, stillness or movement, tangent or distant, outside or inside—no meaning is taken by estimation [*wahm*], or afforded by reason; He transcends them. (ibid., 151.)

46. Ibid., 141.

47. Ibid., 145.

48.

> He is without body, without substance, and without accident. He has no limit, no opposite, no rival, none similar to Him. He has a hand, a face, and a self, as he mentioned in the Qur᾽an. When God mentions in the Qur᾽an His "face," His "hand," and His "self,"

century onward, Ḥanafism rapidly differentiated itself from Karrāmism and followed an anti-interpretive and non-cognitive approach toward the transcendent discourse on the divine nature.

Early Ashʿarism: From Anti-Interpretivism to Anti-Anthropomorphism

Imāmī theologians widely distanced themselves from transcendent anthropomorphism by the ninth century. Ibn Bābawayh's *Epistle on Imāmī Beliefs* [*Risālat al-Iʿtiqādat al-Imāmiyya*], and his student Shaykh al-Mufīd's (d.1022) *Correction of the Treatise on Beliefs* [*Taṣḥiḥ al-Iʿtiqādat*] both strongly underline divine otherness and criticize the "ignorant" anthropomorphism of the Sunnī traditionists. Ibn Bābawayh's creed, very much in line with Muʿtazilite rationalism, begins with a focus on divine otherness. The page that describes God has around thirty Arabic negative particles in different forms. Ibn Bābawayh immediately begins with criticizing anthropomorphic readings of the Qurʾan and prophetic reports, and he interprets them with a focus on divine transcendence. Against al-Bāqillānī's protests, he reads God's "face" [Q.28:88] as Her religion; Her "leg" [*saq*] [Q.68:42] as the unfolding of events; Her "side" [*janb*] [Q.39:56] as obedience to Her; Her "hands" [Q.5:64] as Her blessings in this world and the next, or alternatively, as Her power; Her footstool as Her knowledge, and so on. Ibn Bābawayh adopts a negative theology of divine attributes, reading all

these are His attributes *amodally* [*bilā kayfa*]. It is *not said* that His hand is His power or His grace, because that would abolish the attribute; such is the view of the Qadariyya and the Muʿtazila. On the contrary, *His hand is His attribute amodally*, and *His anger and His good pleasure are two amodal attributes.* . . . His decree, His predetermination and His will are His attributes from eternity *amodally*. (Watt, *Islamic Creeds*, 63–64. with minor modifications of mine. For an alternative translation, see Wensinck, *The Muslim Creed*, 190.)

Besides, *The Fiqh al-Akbar II* [*The Greatest Insight II*] adopts this approach to other anthropomorphic descriptions as well:

> God's being near or far is not to be understood in the sense of a shorter or longer distance, but in respect of (a person's) being honored or not honored. The obedient (person) is near God *amodally* and the disobedient (person) is far from Him *amodally*. Nearness, distance and coming closer apply to a person's intimate relation with God, as does God's being near in paradise, and a person's standing before Him; all are to be understood *amodally*. (Watt, *Islamic Creeds*, 67. For an alternative translation, see Wensinck, *The Muslim Creed*, 196.)

essential attributes as negations of their opposites.[49] With a strong rationalism, Ibn Bābawayh is committed to interpretive and discursive solutions to anthropomorphism instead of *bilā kayfa* apophaticism.

The wide variety of cases that the occupied Ibn Bābawayh were also discussed among the Ashʿarite theologians of his time. Late-tenth-century Ashʿarism still embodied an anthropomorphist resistance to an apophaticism that stressed the inaccessibility of the divine discourse. The Mālikī jurist of the Maghrib, Ibn Abī Zayd (d.996), demonstrated the ambivalence of the context wherein Sufi creeds on the divine essence emerged. Ibn Abī Zayd's *Epistle* presented a detailed creed, which, accordingly, addressed a wide audience, including children. The *Epistle* opened with a group of negations concerning the divine nature, where he declared:

> Those who describe do not achieve the reality [*kunh*] of his attributes. Those who think do not encompass anything [about Him]; they learn [something] from His signs, but they do not reflect upon the nature of His ipseity [*māʾiyyat dhātihi*]. "They do not encompass anything from His knowledge except as He wills" [Q.2:255].[50]

Ibn Abī Zayd also accepts the Qurʾanic descriptions of God as established on [*fawq*] a throne, and speaking [*kallama*] to Moses "with His speech, which is an attribute of His ipseity, not one of His creatures. He appeared to the mountain and it became leveled at His majesty. The Qurʾan is the speech of God; it is not a created thing." God's friends [*awliyāʾ*] will look at "His noble face" [*naẓar ilā wajhihi al-karīm*] in the afterlife.[51] While his negations on the divine essence were powerful, Ibn Abī Zayd's approach to the problems of anthropomorphism was mixed with the literal reading of these sacred reports without further explanation.

Ibn Abī Zayd embodies a transitional point in the West between the Mālikī theological literalism and Ashʿarism proper. He never attacked Ashʿarism outright, but he shared a traditional Mālikī distaste for divisive disputation [*jadal*] and futile theological speculation. Al-Bāqillānī, another Mālikī scholar with great importance for later Sunnī theology, who

---

49. Ibn Bābawayh, *al-Iʿtiqādāt fī Dīn al-Imāmiyya*, 22–44. His student Shaykh al-Mufīd does not follow this negative reading of the divine attributes. See Shaykh al-Mufīd, *Taṣḥīḥ Iʿtiqādāt al-Imāmiyya*, 28–41.

50. Ibn Abī Zayd al-Qayrawānī, *al-Risāla al-Fiqhiyya*, 75.

51. Ibid., 76–78. Also see Watt, *Islamic Creeds*, 68–69.

presented one of the earliest systematic statements of Ashʿarism, embodies a similar negotiation of anthropomorphism with *bilā kayfa* apophaticism. In his famous *Prolegomena* [*Tamhīd*], al-Bāqillānī argues that the creator should be necessarily dissimilar [*mukhālif*] to creation "in kind [*jins*] or form [*ṣūra*]."[52] Here al-Bāqillānī explains that God actually does not have a kind, type, shape [*shakl*], and more importantly, form, which anthropomorphists were reluctant to negate. Al-Bāqillānī's ascriptions of the essential attributes of God are all justified in rational, rather than dogmatic, grounds. He adds a set of questions—"what is He" [*mā huwa*], "how is He" [*kayfa huwa*], "where is He" [*ayna huwa*], and "when was He" [*matā kāna*]—in order to negate all these categories of space, time, and form from God.

Yet transcendent anthropomorphist dimensions of al-Bāqillānī's theology are obvious. Most surprisingly, al-Bāqillānī adds "face," "eyes" and "hands" to the list of God's essential attributes. His justification for these anthropomorphic ascriptions are purely scriptural. He fiercely attacks the Muʿtazilite claim that God has no face, or hand, even if the transcendent discourse says so. He criticizes al-Naẓẓām, as the latter argued that the Prophet did not have a vision [*raʾa*] or witnessing [*shahāda*] of God. Then he targets the Muʿtazilites in general, saying they negate the vision of God in the afterlife, in contrast to the scriptural and prophetic statements. He criticizes those who interpret God's "hands" as Her power and blessing—the Imāmī theologians of the time were following this line of interpretation. Al-Bāqillānī's own exposition of the divine "countenance" and "hand" disallows any interpretive inquiry—yet not due to unknowability, but rather to anthropomorphist literalism. He does allow the literal vision of God in the afterlife with our physical eyes. In line with the Muʿtazilites and later Ashʿarites, he claims that God can actually be known, and apprehended [*idrāk*]. More tellingly, like the earlier Ḥanbalī creeds and Muḥammad ibn Saʿdūn, al-Bāqillānī cites Q.42:11 in support of transcendent anthropomorphism—the vision of God. His appeal to the term *bilā kayfa* on the question of the vision of God is in the service of a literal acceptance of the anthropomorphic verse rather than apophaticism.[53]

---

52. Al-Bāqillānī, *Tamhīd al-Awāʾil*, 44.

53. Al-Bāqillānī, *Tamhīd al-Awāʾil*, 296–305, 315; Ibn Bābawayh, *al-Iʿtiqādāt fī Dīn al-Imāmiyya*, 23; al-Bāqillānī in Renard, *Islamic Theological Themes*, 210.

Early Ashʿarites were as close to transcendent anthropomorphism as they were to *bilā kayfa* unknowability in terms of the divine essence. Al-Shahrastānī's genealogy of the phrase "Attributionists" [Ṣifātiyya] shows that the phrase was invented by their Muʿtazilite adversaries, but he also acknowledges that many who fall under this category from early on were actually anthropomorphists. "Attributionists" was the name of a broad, heterogeneous spectrum of theological approaches; only some of them were overtly anthropomorphist, while all of them accepted the reported [*khabarī*] attributes of "two hands," or "face" of God *prima facie*, without interpretation. Al-Shahrastānī acknowledges that the Ashʿarites, along with the overt Anthropomorphists and Karrāmites, embodied the three groups of "Attributionists."[54] Briefly, the Ashʿarites of the tenth century were as susceptible to transcendent anthropomorphism as the traditionists were. But the later Ashʿarites emphasized the importance of interpretivism and reasoning [*ʿaql*] much more strongly than al-Bāqillānī and al-Ashʿarī, who adhered solely to the sacred reports [*naql*] in approaching anthropomorphic depictions of God. From the eleventh century onward, Ashʿarite theological texts instead begin with reasoning as the most important source of theological speculation. Hence Ashʿarism gets increasingly discursive and interpretive on the issue of the divine nature. ʿAbd al-Qāhir al-Baghdādī's *Principles of Theology* [*Uṣūl al-Dīn*] documents this significant change toward discursive, interpretive approaches among the Ashʿarites:

> "His 'establishment' is among the consimilar verses: *'none knows its interpretation except God'* [Q.3:7]." This was what Mālik ibn Anas and the Medinan jurists said. . . . Among his followers are those who claim that His "establishment on the throne" means His "being above [*fawq*] the throne without touching." And this is what al-Qalānisī said, and ʿAbd Allāh ibn Saʿīd [Ibn Kullāb] mentioned in his *Book of Attributes* [*Kitāb al-Ṣifāt*]. *For us, the correct way is to interpret* [*taʾwīl*] *the "throne" in this verse to mean His "dominion"* [*mulk*]; the intention [*irāda*] is that "none except He is established in the dominion."[55]

54. Al-Shahrastānī, *al-Milal wa-l-Niḥal*, 80–81. For an English translation, see al-Shahrastānī in Renard, *Islamic Theological Themes*, 145–146.

55. ʿAbd al-Qāhir al-Baghdādī, *Kitāb Uṣūl al-Dīn*, 112–113.

By literally accepting God's being established *above* the throne, al-Qalānisī and Ibn Kullāb actually joined a still-powerful Sunnī transcendent anthropomorphist line. Indeed, Ibn al-Nadīm (d.af.990) listed Ibn Kullāb among the main exponent of the "Riff-Raff Weeds" [Nābitat al-Ḥashwiyya]—a twice-pejorative designation for anti-intellectual literalism and simplistic traditionism. Similarly, the infamous Ashʿarite Qurʾan reciter and doxographer Ibn ʿAbd al-Raḥmān al-Malaṭī (d.987) accepted God's being above [*fawq*] the throne in literal terms, along with Her hand, face, footstool, veil, leg, and foot, as well as Her laughing, descent, ascent, and arrival, without adding any signifier of amodality. He also denounced anybody or any school of thought—obviously a large and diverse group of approaches—who interpreted these verses in non-corporeal ways as heretics. Despite this strong tradition of anti-interpretivism of early Ashʿarism, ʿAbd al-Qāhir al-Baghdādī self-consciously turned toward discursive strategies on the divine essence, disagreeing with the traditionist literalism.

From the early eleventh century onward, Ashʿarites increasingly adopted rationalistic, interpretive approaches to the divine essence instead of anti-interpretivist anthropomorphism or *bilā kayfa* apophaticism. Like ʿAbd al-Qāhir al-Baghdādī, Ibn Fūrak (d.1015), al-Bayhaqī, Abū Isḥāq al-Shīrāzī (d.1083), and Imām al-Ḥaramayn, al-Juwaynī refused the anti-interpretive acceptance of the transcendent discourse on the divine essence. Abū Isḥāq al-Shīrāzī directly criticized the position of amodality and unknowability associated with Mālik ibn Anas as quoted by ʿAbd al-Qāhir al-Baghdādī. According to Abū Isḥāq al-Shīrāzī, as Ibn Rushd will later argue, "*None knows its interpretation except God*" is actually an erroneous reading of the verse Q.3:7. The *bilā kayfa* position mistakenly reads the verse as follows: "None knows its interpretation except God. And those firmly rooted in knowledge say, 'We have faith in it; all is from our Lord.'" For Abū Isḥāq al-Shīrāzī, this reading cannot be correct, because "Faith [*īmān*] indicates verification [*taṣdīq*], and the verification of something cannot happen without knowing it." One should rather add the full stop a couple of words later, and read the verse as "None knows its interpretation except God *and* those firmly rooted in knowledge. They say, 'We have faith in it; all is from our Lord.'" Hence, as Abū Isḥāq puts it, "*The verse [Q.3:7] is a proof [dalīl] for interpretation [taʾwīl], rather than the negation of interpretation [nafy al-taʾwīl]!*"[56]

56. Abū Isḥāq al-Shīrāzī, *al-Ishāra ilā Madhhab Ahl al-Ḥaqq*, 161. Cf. Ibn Rushd, "The Decisive Treatise."

Al-Bayhaqī and al-Juwaynī were even more inclined to active interpretation than were Abū Isḥāq al-Shīrāzī. Al-Bayhaqī interpreted God's "hands" as two divine attributes that are not a part of the body [*jāriḥa*], God's two "fingers" as Her power and rule, God's "face" as Her mercy. While al-Juwaynī interpreted [*ḥaml*] the "hands" as divine power, "eyes" as vision, and "face" as existence, he supplied his interpretation with a long dialectical section, which suggests that the controversy still raged among the Ashʿarites.[57] He criticized the "Riff-Raff," the vulgar among the anthropomorphists [*al-ḥashwiyya al-raʿāyat al-mujassima*], for their literal understanding of the self-declared allegory [*ḍarb al-mathal*] in Q.24:35: God as the "Light of the heavens and the earth." We know that well-known Sunnī scholars of Nishapur, where al-Juwaynī himself served as a teacher in the famous Saljūqī Niẓāmiyya madrasa, had adopted a literal reading of the Light Verse in previous generations. One of the most prominent judges of the time in Nishapur, Ibn Khuzayma had declared:

> *God has affirmed for Himself a splendid and venerable face, which He declares is eternal and non-perishable.* We and all scholars of our path from the Hijaz, the Tihama, Yemen, Iraq, Syria, and Egypt affirm for God (the) face, which He has affirmed for Himself. We profess it with our tongues and believe it in our hearts, without likening [*ghayr an nushabbiha*] His face to one from His creatures. May our lord be exalted above our likening Him to His creatures. . . . We and all our scholars in all our lands say that *the One we worship has a face. . . . And we say that the face of our lord [radiates] a brilliant, radiant light. . . . The face of our lord is eternal.*[58]

In support of his anthropomorphic reading of the Light Verse, Ibn Khuzayma did not hesitate to provide logical arguments. He argues: "Is it not but reasonable that the Prophet would not have asked his Lord the impossible? Concluding from the Prophet's wish to experience the joy of

57. Al-Juwaynī, *Kitāb al-Irshād*, 155–164; Holtzman, "Anthropomorphism."

58. Ibn Khuzayma in Williams, "A Body Unlike Bodies," 39 (my emphasis). The prominent theologian Fakhr al-Dīn al-Rāzī would call Ibn Khuzayma's *Book of Monotheism* [*Kitāb al-Tawḥīd*] the *Book of Polytheism* [*Kitāb al-Shirk*]. On the other hand, Ibn Khuzayma's book was warmly embraced by the Ḥanbalites as its public reading in Baghdad in 1068 indicates. See Holtzman, *Anthropomorphism in Islam*, 294–308.

seeing His face, *it is perfectly clear that God has a face.*"[59] Accordingly, God has a glorious, luminous face unlike faces. The reading that al-Juwaynī criticized was this transcendent anthropomorphist position that adopted a literal *bilā kayfa* understanding of a verse, which the Qur'an described as a metaphor. (Such an anthropomorphist reading was common not only among the Ḥanbalites as noted by Ibn al-Jawzī but also the Ashʿarites.) Al-Juwaynī, in the same line, introduced a variety of themes, such as the "establishment" on the "throne," "leg" [*saq*]" in Q.68:42, "descent," and "coming," insisting on anti-anthropomorphic, interpretive solutions.[60] From the eleventh century onward, Ashʿarites increasingly appealed to such interpretive approaches to the divine nature. Al-Ghazālī's complaint in the *Decisive Criterion* [*al-Fayṣal al-Tafriqa*] is an excellent witness to this rapid change and the related theological conflicts:

> The Ḥanbalite brands the Ashʿarite an unbeliever, claiming that the latter deems the Prophet to be a liar in the Prophet's attribution of God's "aboveness" [*al-fawq*] and "establishment" on the throne. The Ashʿarite brands the Ḥanbalite an unbeliever, claiming the latter to be an anthropomorphist who deems the prophet to be a liar when the Prophet says about God, "Nothing is like unto Him" [Q.42:11].[61]

By the time of al-Ghazālī, Ashʿarites were now appealing to Q.42:11 in order to criticize the anthropomorphic position that earlier Ashʿarites like al-Bāqillānī adopted by using this very verse. Besides, ʿAbd al-Qāhir al-Baghdādī's interpretive divergence from depicting God as "above" the

---

59. Ibn Khuzayma in Holtzman, "Anthropomorphism"; Holtzman, *Anthropomorphism in Islam*, 305–306.

60. Only the vision of God in the afterlife remained as a *bilā kayfa* possibility. It was not knowable how the beatific vision will happen, but it remained open as it was not possible to negate it logically. Al-Juwaynī was deliberately inclusive on the vision of God in this world, allowing divergences. Accordingly, divine omnipotence may allow it as another logical possibility, but one can also interpret the verses on the vision of God, as in the case of Moses, as disallowing it in this world. Al-Juwaynī's tolerance was understandable, because the Ashʿarites in his time predominantly adopted non-interpretive approaches to the beatific vision, in opposition to the Muʿtazilite protests. Notwithstanding his tolerance, al-Juwaynī aligned with the latter, discursive, interpretive position that eliminates Her "vision" in this world. In this discussion, al-Juwaynī benefited from the Qur'anic distinction between apprehension [*idrāk*] and vision, in the exact way al-Māturīdī did in his *Book of Unity*. (Al-Juwaynī, *Kitāb al-Irshād*, 165–186; Ibn al-Jawzī, *Attributes of God*, 42, 88, 110.)

61. Abū Ḥāmid al-Ghazālī in Jackson, *On the Boundaries of Theological Tolerance in Islam*, 93. For the original Arabic, see Abū Ḥāmid al-Ghazālī, *Fayṣal al-Tafriqa*, 27.

throne had already become their dominant position. At the end of the century, after reviewing various interpretations, Fakhr al-Dīn al-Rāzī cited the famous Shāfiʿī exegete al-Qaffāl (d.976) with approval, claiming that "the words, 'His throne encompasses the heavens and the earth:' are meant to describe God's greatness and exaltation through images."[62] In Shams Tabrīzī's Sufi discourses, the Anatolian theologian Asad-i Mutakallim (fl. ca.13th CE) fiercely defended the interpretive position on anthropomorphism. For Tabrīzī, a typical Sunnī theologian would fiercely accuse anthropomorphic positions of heresy and would ardently interpret the sacred sources in order to remove all anthropomorphic implications.[63]

In the tenth and eleventh centuries, Sufi manuals broke out in these theologically rich and ambiguous landscapes. By that time, Shīʿīs at large, philosophers, and Muʿtazilīs had already adopted interpretive approaches to the corporeal depictions of God in the sacred sources. Ḥanafism dominantly followed a non-cognitive, anti-interpretive apophatic approach to these depictions, declaring the incomprehensibility of such reports and the unknowability of the divine nature. Ḥanbalīs, and traditionists at large, were on the anti-interpretive side, oscillating between transcendent anthropomorphism and non-cognitivism. Ashʿarīs were moving within a wider range of theological positions. We find both anthropomorphist and non-cognitive versions of anti-interpretivism, but also an intensive movement toward interpretivist approaches from the eleventh century onward. Unlike the Ḥanafīs, non-cognitive Ashʿarī positions did not always entail apophaticism, because many Ashʿarīs defended the discursive knowability of the divine essence, like many Muʿtazilīs.

It is in conversation and negotiation with these diverse theological positions that Sufi manuals emerged. These manuals would fundamentally contribute to, and pave the road for, the formalization of Sufism, the inclusion or exclusion of various indigenous mystical or ascetic trends under its banner, the establishment of idiosyncratic methods, and eventually orders, associated with charismatic doctors of the soul.

---

62. Fakhr al-Dīn al-Rāzī in Renard, *Islamic Theological Themes*, 31.

63. Shams Tabrīzī, *Me and Rūmī*, 61, 156–157; Q.57:4. For Asad, see Aflākī, *Ariflerin Menkıbeleri*, 2:255. Cf. Maybudī, *Unveiling of the Mysteries*, 402.

Anti-Interpretivism among Early Sufis?

Islam in the tenth century displayed a rich variety of opinions on the nature and accessibility of the divine essence in terms of its physical descriptions. Among those who admitted the uncreated nature of the Qurʾan as the transcendent discourse, we find three prominent approaches: (1) traditionists and early Ashʿarī positions that side with transcendent anthropomorphism by accepting the literal reading of the sacred sources and rejecting interpretivism on such issues, (2) *bilā kayfa* apophaticism that negates speculative access to divine nature by admitting the inaccessibility of the divine nature and the meaning of the transcendent speech, and (3) speculative paradigms that eschew anthropomorphism through active interpretation.

Since its early formation, Sufism associated itself predominantly with the latter two positions. Prominent Sufis active in Baghdad like al-Ḥallāj and al-Junayd were strong critics of the traditionist or literalist proneness to anthropomorphism. Sufi activity in Basra was also quite anti-anthropomorphic and inclined to interpret the scripture and prophetic reports through that lens. A clear example is the *Book of Exegesis* by Sahl al-Tustarī, one of the most influential mystics of the formative period. Here, al-Tustarī interprets the "vision" of God, even in the afterlife as narrated in Q.19:61, as nearness to Her.[64] His readings of the divine love and "throne" are similarly non-literal, and accordingly the verse "the hand of God is above their hands" indicates that "the power [*ḥawl*] of God and His strength [*quwwa*] is above their strength and their action [*ḥaraka*]." This interpretivism is couched in a strong emphasis on the unknowability of divine essence and its relationship with divine attributes. While faithfully

---

64. [Q.19:61] "Gardens of Eden, which the Compassionate One has promised to His servants in the unseen . . ." This means the "visual" beholding [*muʿāyana*] of God, in the sense of nearness that He appointed between Him and them, so that the servant sees his heart in the proximity of God, witnessed [*mashhūd*] in the unseen of the unseen [*ghayb al-ghayb*]. The unseen of the unseen is the spiritual self [*nafs al-rūḥ*], the understanding of the intellect [*fahm al-ʿaql*], and the discernment of meaning by the heart [*fiṭnat al-murād bi'l-qalb*]. The spiritual self is the seat of the intellect [*ʿaql*], which is the seat of the Holy [al-Quds]. This Holy is linked with the throne [*ʿarsh*], and is one of the names of the Throne. (al-Tustarī, *Tafsīr al-Tustarī*, 120.)

Similarly, al-Tustarī interprets divine love in terms of obedience. (Hujvīrī, *Kashf al-Maḥjūb*, 408.) On the two forms of beatific vision in the afterlife, as *rūʾyat al-janna* and *rūʾyat al-Ḥaqq*, see al-Tustarī, *Tafsīr al-Tustarī*, 170 [Q.39:7], 181 [Q.42:20]. As narrated by Abū Khalaf al-Ṭabarī, al-Tustarī interpreted *mushāhada* as servanthood [*ʿubūdiyya*]. (See Abū Khalaf al-Ṭabarī, *Khalwat al-ʿākifīn*, 76.)

transmitting al-Tustarī's emphasis on divine unity and its unknowability, al-Qushayrī's celebrated Sufi manual the *Epistle* [*al-Risāla*] does something elusive yet significant. Al-Qushayrī adds another sentence, ascribing to al-Tustarī the corporeal vision of God in the afterlife: "*In the hereafter eyes will see it manifested in His dominion and omnipotence.*" An important difference between al-Tustarī's own reading of Q.19:61 and his depiction by al-Qushayrī is the latter's Ashʿarization of the former's metaphorical, anti-anthropomorphic interpretation of the vision of God. As opposed to the anti-interpretivism that al-Qushayrī ascribes him, al-Tustarī was rather insistent on interpreting such verses in anti-anthropomorphic ways. Even the Prophet's vision of God, for him, was a metaphorical reference to his primordial adoration in pre-existence during an unfathomable aeon of time. Still, this was a "witnessing of the unseen within the unseen," where God's attributes became manifest via Her signs. In other words, al-Tustarī was far from adopting the literalist hermeneutics that al-Qushayrī's Sufi manual would ascribe him.[65]

Al-Tustarī's appeal to interpretive strategies in eschewing anthropomorphism instead of their *bilā kayfa* acceptance followed the theological approach of Dhū al-Nūn, who clearly preferred to interpret the throne verses in anti-anthropomorphic ways.[66] He was also the first editor of the Qurʾanic exegesis attributed to Jaʿfar al-Ṣādiq, which was strongly pro-interpretation instead of *bilā kayfa* around any description of God. A great polymath and cornerstone for Shīʿī theologies, Jaʿfar al-Ṣādiq was incorporated into various Sufi lineages, manuals, and encyclopedias. His Qurʾanic exegesis was preserved in al-Sulamī's *Truths of Qurʾanic Exegesis* [*al-Ḥaqāʾiq fī-l-Tafsīr*], a popular compilation of Sufi exegesis. Authors of Sufi manuals like al-Qushayrī and al-Kharkūshī narrate how strongly Jaʿfar al-Ṣādiq disagreed with the *bilā kayfa* acceptance of the reports about the "vision" of God (even by the Prophet), Her "descent," or "throne." A similarly strong, anti-anthropomorphic preference of early Sufis for interpretive paradigms was also recorded in these popular manuals. Indeed, such interpretive

65. Hujvīrī, *Kashf al-Maḥjūb*, 408; al-Tustarī, *Tafsīr*, 176, Q.48:10, 197, Q.7:180, 78; xlvii, fn.204; Q.53:13–18, 213; Böwering, *Mystical Vision of Existence in Classical Islam*, 150–151, 165–175.

66. Someone asked Dhū al-Nūn al-Miṣrī about God's words: "The all-compassionate established Himself upon the throne." He answered: "The all-compassionate asserted His essence, while denying [His location] in a specific place. He exists through His own essence, whereas all other things exist through His command, as He wished [them to be]." (Al-Qushayrī, *Epistle on Sufism*, 12–13.)

solutions to anthropomorphic reports, instead of their amodal acceptance, was the dominant position among Baghdadian Sufis of the late ninth and early tenth century. A plethora of Sufis active in Baghdad, such as al-Kharrāz, al-Junayd, al-Ḥallāj, Abū ʿAlī al-Rūdhabārī (d.934), Jaʿfar al-Khuldī (d.959), and Abū ʿUthmān al-Maghribī (d.983) undertook interpretive anti-anthropomorphic solutions to the issues of God's "throne," "vision," "descent," or physical attributes and actions in general.[67] Such speculative anti-anthropomorphism seems particularly strong among Sufis in Baghdad—the seat of the ʿAbbāsid caliphate and the hub of rich theological debates. Abū ʿUthmān al-Maghribī's account not only speaks more generally to the interpretivist theology in tenth-century Baghdadian Sufism, but it also suggests the currency of transcendent anthropomorphism in his times:

> I used to believe in the teaching [that postulated] that God is located in a certain direction. However, when I arrived in Baghdad, this [idea] disappeared from my heart. I then wrote to my companions in Mecca, saying: "I have become Muslim once again."[68]

Al-Sulamī's *Truths of Qurʾanic Exegesis* is an excellent source as it shows how early Sufis adopted interpretive strategies against anthropomorphism. Here "the Baghdadians" play an important role in insisting on the anti-anthropomorphic interpretations of verses that could otherwise indicate divine corporeality. As it testifies, the verses that mention the "throne," or the "face" of God, were interpreted by Abū Bakr al-Wāsiṭī (d.932), among others, with an emphasis on divine otherness. Even if vision and unveiling play fundamental roles in Sufi epistemology, many early Sufis chose to interpret the sacred reports on the vision of God in anti-anthropomorphic, metaphysical ways instead of accepting them literally. Al-Kharkūshī of Nishapur explains that many scholars understood the vision of God in non-corporal, non-literal ways. Accordingly, there were Sufis who said that "the reality of gnosis is the witnessing of the Real with the innermost heart [*sirr*], without any means, without modality [*bilā wāsiṭa wa lā kayfa*], and without similarity." As al-Sarrāj reports, al-Nūrī (d.908) negated the

67. Al-Qushayrī, *Epistle on Sufism*, 4–13; al-Kharkūshī, *Tahdhīb al-Asrār*, 44–46; Hujvīrī, *Kitāb Kashf al-Maḥjūb*, 360 (for English translations, see Hujvīrī, *Kashf al-Maḥjūb*, 377; Hujvīrī, *A Persian Treatise on Sufism*, 281); al-Sīrjānī, *Sufism, Black and White*, 52, 528.

68. Al-Qushayrī, *Epistle on Sufism*, 8–9; Abū Khalaf al-Ṭabarī, *Salwat al-ʿĀrifīn*, 20.

knowability of God and the applicability of any attributes ascribed to Her. Al-Nūrī also held the vision of God to be an impossibility because the distinction between creation and its creator is decisive. The content of direct vision is rather the realities of faith in the unseen [*ḥaqāʾiq al-īmān bi-l-ghayb*], and such witnessing belongs to the heart [*qalb*], instead of the physical eye. Al-Shiblī similarly interprets "throne" and "footstool" as high cosmological levels that can be visited by the heart through attaining higher levels on the Sufi path.[69]

As we approach the end of the tenth century, Sufism as a pietist movement developing in Baghdad was predominantly adopting an interpretivist approach toward the anthropomorphic depictions of God. We should not only leave Baghdad and Basra but also adopt looser definitions of "Sufism" to find exceptional deviations from early interpretivism. One such case is Ibn al-Mubārak (d.797) of Khurasan, a pioneer in writing on piety, who was incorporated in Sufism through the later Sufi manuals. First and foremost a celebrated traditionist, he was an active proponent of scripturalist theological hermeneutics regarding anthropomorphism. Muḥammad al-Bukhārī's (d.870) polemical work against the Jahmīs cites Ibn al-Mubārak within the context of a debate on the depiction of God established on Her throne:

> We do not say as the Jahmiyya have said, that He [God] is here on earth.
> "Verily He is above His throne."
> And it was said to him [Ibn al-Mubārak] "How do we know our Lord?"
> He replied, "He is above the heavens on His throne."
> . . . "Who says that He with whom there is no other deity is created, has disbelieved."[70]

Here, Ibn al-Mubārak defends an anti-interpretive position, which is depicted by al-Bukhārī as a critique of rendering God a created, comparable entity. On the other hand, Ibn al-Mubārak's anti-interpretivism was an

69. Abū ʿAbd Allāh al-Sulamī, *Ḥaqāʾiq al-Tafsīr*, Q.2:115, Q.55:27, Q.27:26, Q.85:15, Q.75:22–23. al-Kharkūshī, *Tahdhīb al-Asrār*, 46; al-Sarrāj, *Kitāb al-Lumaʿ*, 38 (Arabic text); Avery, *Shiblī: His Life and Thought in the Sufi Tradition*, 23–24, 56, 73, 96, 103.

70. Salem, *Emergence of Early Sufi Piety and Sunnī Scholasticism*, 30; Holtzman, *Anthropomorphism in Islam*, 295.

anthropomorphist one that empowered Ibn Khuzayma's defense of God's aboveness according to Ibn Qayyim.

Early Sufism manifests a similar deviation from its common interpretivism also within early Ashʿarī context. One of the best-known Sufis of his time and a student of al-Ashʿarī, Ibn Khafīf al-Shīrāzī, is credited with bringing Baghdadian Sufism to Shiraz. In his *Major Creed*, cited by Ibn Taymiyya, as well as in his *Minor Creed*, Ibn Khafīf adopts al-Ashʿarī's anti-interpretive, literalist position on the divine nature. Ibn Khafīf's creeds were essentially the same articles of belief as those of al-Ashʿarī and Ḥanbalīs of his time, such as al-Barbahārī (d.940) and Ibn Baṭṭa (d.997), at times using precisely the same traditional wordings. Ibn Khafīf underlined that the "two hands" of God was not an allegorical reference to Her power but referred to one of Her actual attributes. Her "descent," similarly, was a genuine attribute of God. Ibn Khafīf did not qualify these short maxims with any marker of amodality, such as *bilā kayfa*.[71]

If Ibn Khafīf brought Shiraz something from Baghdad, it was obviously not only Sufism but also an anti-interpretive traditionist hermeneutics of the divine essence that was widely seen as anthropomorphist rather than non-cognitivist. His biographer and pupil, Abū al-Ḥasan al-Daylamī (fl.10th-11th CE) seems to have followed his approach to God's "hands," "throne," and the creation of Adam in Her "likeness."[72] Such anti-interpretivism would later have a substantial effect on the formation of Sufism as orders. With its anti-interpretivism, Ibn Khafīf's *Minor Creed* [*al-ʿAqīdat al-Ṣughrā*], for example, would make its mark on Abū al-Najīb al-Suhrawardī's creed in the influential *Sufi Etiquette for Novices* [*Ādāb al-Murīdīn*]. On the other hand, anti-interpretivism also had a decisive influence on the Arabic Sufi manuals that began to emerge around the time when it was increasingly becoming popular among Sufis. The prominence of anti-interpretivism in the Sufi manuals mirrored a rising fashion among tenth- and eleventh-century Sufis in participation with the growing "Sunnī consensus," rather than merely an apologetic reimagination of the past.

71. Al-Daylamī, *Treatise on Mystical Love*, xxx–xxxiii. Al-Qushayrī says that Ibn Khafīf studied with the great Ḥanbalī Sufi master, and a close friend of al-Ḥallāj, Abū al-ʿAbbās Ibn ʿAṭāʾ al-Ādamī, which is historically untenable. At another point, Ibn Khafīf reports from al-Ādamī through the narration of ʿAbd al-Raḥmān Aḥmad al-Ṣūfī (fl.10th CE), which is more likely to represent the indirect connection between al-Ādamī and Ibn Khafīf. (al-Qushayrī, *Epistle*, 56, 70.)

72. E.g., al-Daylamī, *Treatise on Mystical Love*, 12–13, 129.

Anti-Interpretivism during the Formalization of Sufism

ʿAbd al-Karīm al-Qushayrī

Like other authors of Sufi manuals, al-Qushayrī, a Shāfiʿī in law and Ashʿarī in theology, narrates in his *Epistle* the undeniably anti-anthropomorphic interpretive positions of earlier Sufis on divine nature. Accordingly, these examples "prove that the beliefs of Sufi masters agree with the teachings of the People of the Truth [i.e., Ashʿarī Sunnīs], as far as the fundamentals of religion are concerned."[73] But a closer look displays a rather sharp difference between the interpretive positions of earlier Sufis and his own traditionist Ashʿarī anti-interpretivism in the *Epistle*. Immediately after reporting rich Sufi interpretations that emphasize divine otherness and dissimilarity, al-Qushayrī presents an alleged "summary" of these Sufi approaches to make his point. Surprisingly, his "summary" follows a rather traditionist Ashʿarī creed and emphasizes the *bilā kayfa* acceptance of anthropomorphic descriptions of God in the sacred sources without further interpretation. The stark contrast is striking:

> God . . . is existent [*mawjūd*], eternal, One, wise, all-powerful, all-knowing, overpowering, compassionate, willing, hearing, glorious, exalted, speaking, seeing, proud, strong, all-living, everlasting, and everlasting refuge. He knows by His knowledge; He is powerful by His power; He wills by His will; He sees by His sight; He speaks by His speech; He lives by His life; He is everlasting by His everlastingness. *He has two hands, which are His attributes and with which He creates what He wishes and gives it a specific form. He has a face.* The attributes of His essence are unique to Him. One must not say that they are He or that they are not He. They are [His] eternal attributes and [His] everlasting properties. He is unique in His essence. He is not similar to any originated thing, nor is any created being similar to Him. . . . About Him one ought not ask "where," "in what way," or "how." . . . *He will be seen [on the Judgment Day], but not by positioning Himself in front of the viewers, while He will see others without applying [His] eyesight.* He fashions [creatures] without

73. Al-Qushayrī, *Epistle on Sufism*, 14. Al-Khatīb al-Baghdādī's (d.1071) biography of al-Qushayrī portrays him as an Ashʿarī without mentioning Sufism. See Melchert, "Origins and Early Sufism," 19.

> touching them directly or handling. . . . *These are the passages that present in brief the principles of the Sufi masters.*[74]

These were certainly *not* "the principles of the Sufi masters" that al-Qushayrī had been transmitting in the previous passages! The *Epistle*'s official Sufism, and its Ashʿarī *bilā kayfa* acceptance of corporeal depictions of God, were dramatically different from the intensively interpretive anti-anthropomorphism of the earlier Sufis. As in the case of his report on al-Tustarī on the vision of God, here again al-Qushayrī projected on Sufism a clearly scripturalist, anti-interpretivist Ashʿarism.

Al-Qushayrī's semi-official creedal description of the "consensus of Sufis" on the divine nature entailed an even more significant problem of representation. The Ashʿarized, anti-interpretive Sufi theology in the *Epistle* actually differed from al-Qushayrī's own interpretive position. A look at his *Subtle Allusions* [*Laṭāʾif al-Ishārāt*] suggests that the creedal opening of al-Qushayrī's monumental *Epistle* is primarily a showcase or introduction for outsiders and Sufi novices. His exegetical work on the Qurʾan, the *Subtle Allusions* displays for us the rather double-layered hermeneutics of al-Qushayrī:

> God has classified the discourse for them. From its apparent sense, there is the clarity of its revelation [*tanzīl*] and from its obscure sense [*ghāmiḍ*], there is the problem of its interpretation. The first kind is for the purpose of unfolding the law and guiding the people of the outwardly manifest. The second kind is for the purpose of protecting secrets from the scrutiny of outsiders.[75]

The *Epistle* gives us merely the first, apparent sense, in the anti-interpretive style of traditionism of his time, with its manifold practical and political implications. Both of the layers, thus including al-Qushayrī's own deeper and interpretive hermeneutics, were uncovered in his *Subtle Allusions*. Here, we find two layers in his approach to God's "throne": The first one is

---

74. Al-Qushayrī, *Epistle on Sufism*, 14–16. For the Arabic original, see al-Qushayrī, *al-Risāla al-Qushayriyya fī ʿIlm al-Taṣawwuf*, 38–39.

75. Al-Qushayrī, *Laṭāʾif al-Ishārāt*, Q.3:7. For English translations, see Sands, *Sufi Commentaries on the Qurʾan in Classical Islam*, 15; al-Qushayrī, *Subtle Allusions*, Q.3:7, 207. At the outset of the *Epistle*, al-Qushayrī declares that the work addresses "to all the Sufi community" [*jamāʿat al-ṣūfiyya*]. (al-Qushayrī, *Epistle*, 1.)

a non-cognitive, non-interpretive repetition of the Qur'anic phrase—a *bilā kayfa* apophatic move harmonious with the *Epistle*. The second is rather a violation of this amodality via interpretation. Accordingly, the "throne" of God on earth is the hearts of the people of unity [*qulūb ahl al-tawḥīd*].[76] These all-welcoming hearts are the throne of the all-merciful and the locus of divine unveilings [*maḥall naẓar al-Ḥaqq*]. Hence he interprets not only the "throne" but also "vision" metaphysically in line with earlier Sufis. The hermeneutical tradition and practice that al-Qushayrī inherits is that of the sustained, anti-anthropomorphism of the early Sufi masters. Yet, on the surface, "Sufism" officially follows anti-interpretivist apophaticism as a conservative Sunnī institution in the eleventh century.

Abū Ṭālib al-Makkī

Another key author of Sufi manuals in the late formative period is al-Makkī, who adopted a hermeneutical position close to the one that al-Qushayrī defended in the *Epistle*. His sizable *Sustenance of the Hearts* [*Qūt al-Qulūb*] defended a *bilā kayfa* apophaticism by considering the sacred scripture as the eternal, divine discourse that cannot be understood or interpreted when it talks about the divine nature. Due to its unknowability, al-Makkī declares that he agrees with the traditionists "on the submission to the reports on the divine attributes and keeping silent on their interpretation." This resistance to discursive understanding of the divine nature is accompanied by a strong negation of modalities from such descriptions:

> God is manifested via His attributes, or via anything else that He pleases, without any limitation, without any number—He is manifested with an attribute however He pleases. He is not restricted by any attribute. Nor is He confined by them in any form. Without manifesting His jealousy, how can it be rather manifested? With which description can it be manifest? *With negating howness [nafy al-kayfiyya] and similitude [mithliyya] that removes categories and substantiation [from Him]. . . . Whoever inquires this via reasoning, and interprets them with his own opinion [ra'y], enters into the comparability*

76. Al-Qushayrī, *Laṭā'if al-Ishārāt*, Q.20:5.

> *[tashbīh] of the divine, or departs to His negation and annulment [nafy wa ibṭāl].*[77]

With its strong emphasis on negativity, the monumental *Sustenance of the Hearts* has clear parallels with the *bilā kayfa* apophaticism of the Ḥanafism of Central Asia. Al-Makkī holds the ultimate inaccessibility of the nature of the divine essence, as well as its relationship with divine attributes. Hence he affirms, though amodally, the divine discourse and cancels the constructed ones. Any interpretive inquiry makes the immodest assumption that it can access the meaning of the divine discourse with its created, limited terms and categories. Al-Makkī's position is consistent concerning various issues related to anthropomorphism, such as the "vision" of God in the afterlife, Her "establishment" on the "throne," or Her "speech" with Moses. He admits [*taslīm*] and affirms [*ithbāt*] these reports on the divine attributes without interpretation [either *tafsīr* or *taʾwīl*], with a bunch of negations of comparability and howness [*nafy al-tashbīh wa-l-takyīf*] that indicate the self-cancellation of theological discourse in favor of the unknowable transcendent discourse. "*It is not interpreted. . . . We don't compare; we don't describe; we don't assimilate; we don't make known; we don't condition*" [*lā yuʾawwal. . . . lā nushabbih wa naṣif, lā numaththil wa nuʿarrif, wa lā nukayyif*].[78]

Al-Makkī fiercely criticizes not only anthropomorphism but also negative theologies of divine attributes from the perspective of *bilā kayfa* apophaticism. By his time, a variety of schools from diverse backgrounds, such as early Ibāḍīs, a few Muʿtazilīs, Jahmīs, prominent Peripatetic philosophers, and some Imāmī theologians had adopted a negativist position by arguing that the divine attributes should be understood not as affirmations but as the negations of their deprivation. "God is omnipotent," for example, meant from this perspective that She is not incapable. The *bilā kayfa* non-cognitivist critique of such negative reading of the divine attributes points to the ultimate symmetry in language when it concerns the divine nature: negations are not in a more advantaged position than

---

77. Abū Ṭālib al-Makkī, *Qūt al-Qulūb*, 1:414.

78. Ibid., 3:1270–1271.

Al-Makkī also does not share the general Sufi and wider pietist distaste with religious dispensations [*rukhaṣ*]. In this sense, his *Sustenance* approaches to Ḥanafī creeds, such as the early *Waṣiyya* attributed to Abū Ḥanīfa. (See ibid., 2:608; Abū Ḥanīfa in Wensinck, *The Muslim Creed*, 129, 185–187.)

positive discourses on God. In other words, negative discourses, as much as positive discourses, assume the accessibility of their subject. Adopting a negative interpretation is ultimately a construction, hence it is inescapably anthropomorphic. In order to emphasize the amodal affirmation of the inaccessible meaning of the divine attributes, *bilā kayfa* theologians developed a seemingly repetitive approach. This approach was already present in Abū Ṭālib al-Makkī's *Sustenance*:

> The prerequisite [*farḍ*] of the divine unity is the heartfelt belief [*iʿtiqād al-qalb*] that God is one not as a number; the first without the second; existent without any doubt; *present not absent; all-knowing not ignorant; all-powerful not incapable; all-living not lifeless; self-subsistent not ignorant; mild not crude; all-hearing all-seeing; sovereign no end to His sovereignty; ancient not in term of time; last without limitation;* . . . Last in His firstness; first in His lastness; His names and attributes are His uncreated lights, not separated from Him; He is the front of everything; and the beyond of everything; with all; closer to everything than their very selves, yet He is not a location for anything, nor is anything a location of Him; *He is established on His throne as he pleases, without howness, without comparison* [*kayfa shāʾ bilā takyīf wa lā tashbīh*].[79]

Redundant verbalism as it might appear, the phrases "present not absent," "all-knowing not ignorant," "all-powerful not incapable," "all-living not lifeless" directly criticize the negative theology of divine attributes in favor of unknowability. The attribute "all-knowing" amodally affirmed here is not the opposite of "ignorance." "All-knowing" is not "not-ignorant." It is rather the non-cognitive, unknown, transcendent discursive term that does not have an opposite. The transcendent discourse on the divine essence cannot be understood by any terms except itself: these apparently redundant but rather amodal statements constituted a popular way to transmit this apophatic theology.

79. Ibid., 3:1171–1172.

Muḥammad al-Kalābādhī

The section on divine unity in al-Makkī's *Sustenance* occupies around two full pages and contains around a hundred Arabic negative particles. Radical as it might sound, the creeds of other Sufis were quite consistent with al-Makkī's love of negations that follows a *bilā kayfa* non-cognitivism. Al-Kalābādhī's *Doctrine of the Ṣūfīs* neatly fits into the philosophically oriented Ḥanafī context of Transoxania under the Sāmānid rule. Indeed, the author of the *Greatest Abode,* al-Samarqandī was not only a judge but also a pietist in the Central Asian group of Sages [Ḥukamāʾ] that Hujvīrī described. The *Greatest Abode* played an important role not only by defining a post-Karrāmī Ḥanafism, with its *bilā kayfa* apophaticism, but also by normalizing Sufi themes and wonder-workings and putting its principles or discourses on stable theological ground. The *Doctrine of the Ṣūfīs* is penned within this stronghold of non-cognitive amodalism. It opens with a negativist description of God strongly critical of anthropomorphism. As the source of creation, God is necessarily dissimilar to anything human faculties can imagine, perceive, or contain. Our descriptions of God do not reach Her: the attributes that we give God are not Hers but our own attributes. Quoting the great Sufi master al-Ḥallāj without explicitly naming him, al-Kalābādhī introduces a long series of negations demonstrating that no worldly category applies to Her.[80] The pages-long negations devoted to the explication of the divine essence and attributes suggests that in al-Kalābādhī's view Sufis, while they had disagreements on many other topics, had a unanimous consensus on a strong negative theology of the divine essence emphasizing divine unknowability.

In typical *bilā kayfa* format, al-Kalābādhī affirms "all attributes with which He described Himself"—that is, the amodal affirmation of the transcendent discourse on the divine attributes. The conventional Qurʾanic attributes are affirmed non-discursively, while al-Kalābādhī ensures through a long list of negations that God remains utterly unknowable, "not compassed by thoughts, nor covered by veils, nor attained by eyes." Neither God nor the way in which attributes apply to Her is knowable. Al-Kalābādhī introduces here a philosophical argument on language that has a fundamental place in Sufism. Comparing the transcendent "mentioning"—that

80. Al-Kalābādhī, *Kitāb al-Taʿarruf,* 33–35. For an English translation, see al-Kalābādhī, *Doctrine of the Ṣūfīs,* 15–16.

is, the Qurʾan—with our created discourses, he argues that our descriptions "return" back to us—they have nothing to do with the unknowable relationship between the divine essence and attributes:

> Our description of Him with these attributes in no way is an attribute to Him. On the contrary, *our description is our own attribute* [*waṣfunā ṣifatunā*], a narration of an attribute that subsists with Him. Whoever makes their own description an attribute of God, without affirming His attribute in reality, he is a liar against Him in reality, for he mentions Him without His [Real] description. It cannot be like the Mentioning, insofar as He will be mentioned by other than Him. For *mentioning is an attribute of the mentioner, not an attribute of the mentioned.* The mentioned one becomes so by the mentioning of the mentioner. But the described one does not become so by the description of the describer. . . . God has unsullied Himself from their descriptions.[81]

God can be described only via Her own transcendent discourse; our descriptions of Her are our own attributes instead of belonging to God. Al-Kalābādhī traced the apophatic insight that "human discourse on God returns to itself" back to the reports from Baghdadian Sufis like al-Shiblī, which widely circulated among the most popular Sufi manuals.[82] Hence the idea would have repercussions among well-known Sufis including Abū Ḥāmid al-Ghazālī, ʿAyn al-Qużāt Hamadānī, ʿAṭṭār, and Ibn al-ʿArabī. Al-Kalābādhī also provided an elaborate, sophisticated discussion on the *bilā kayfa* negative theological implications of the gap between the transcendent discourse and our linguistic constructions. His non-cognitive approach to the transcendent discourse did not lack a critique of the negative reading of the divine attributes. In the same way as Abū Ṭālib al-Makkī, al-Kalābādhī underlined that a divine attribute marks the *bilā kayfa*

81. Al-Kalābādhī, *Kitāb al-Taʿarruf,* 36v37; al-Kalābādhī, *Doctrine of the Ṣūfīs,* 17.

82. Al-Qushayrī, *al-Risāla,* 496; al-Qushayrī, *Epistle,* 310; al-Ṭabarī, *Salwat al-ʿĀrifīn,* 18 (Arabic text); al-Sīrjānī, *Sufism, Black and White,* 52 (Arabic text).

A parallel version of this reversive approach to theological language flourished among the Muʿtazilites as well. Abū ʿAlī al-Jubbāʾī argued that an attribute has no extralinguistic reality. Accordingly, attribute was identical with the act of description or attribution. Thiele, "Abū Hāshim al-Jubbāʾī's (d. 321/933) Theory of 'States,'" 367.

affirmation of the unknowable, transcendent discourse, not just the negation of an imperfection:

> The meaning of the divine attributes is the negation of their opposites, *and* the affirmation that they exist in themselves, and subsist through Him. Neither is the meaning of knowledge only the negation of ignorance, nor is the meaning of power simply the negation of incapacity, but also the affirmation of knowledge and power. If one could become knowing by negating ignorance, or powerful by negating incapacity, then the meaning of negating ignorance and incapacity would be being knowing and powerful. And so with all attributes.[83]

Al-Kalābādhī argued that all divine attributes mean a negation at the level of human understanding but also an affirmation at the non-discursive, transcendent level of revelation. "God is all-knowing" means "God is not ignorant" at our speculative level, and the perfection of divine knowledge remains unknown even if it is affirmed by Qurʾanic transcendent discourse. In other words, we know and logically prove that God cannot be ignorant or impotent, but we cannot grasp the way in which She possesses these qualities.[84]

Abū Ḥāmid al-Ghazālī

The description of Sufism in line with *bilā kayfa* non-cognitivism since the tenth-century manuals of al-Kalābādhī and al-Makkī was followed by al-Qushayrī in the next century. Another giant of Sufism followed al-Qushayrī in the next generation. Like the other Sufi manuals, the monumental *Revivification of Religious Sciences* [*Iḥyāʾ al-ʿUlūm al-Dīn*] by Abū Ḥāmid al-Ghazālī is one of the most celebrated texts ever written in the history of Islam. Penned in the eleven-year period following Abū Ḥāmid al-Ghazālī's retirement in 1095, the *Revivification* is a post-Sufism work of al-Ghazālī. The main model of the *Revivification* was al-Makkī's *Sustenance*, and the *Revivification* is widely presented as a Sufi work. Yet it is also a deeply Ashʿarī work in many ways. It affirms, for example, Ashʿarī

83. Al-Kalābādhī, *Kitāb al-Taʿarruf*, 36; al-Kalābādhī, *Doctrine of the Ṣūfīs*, 17.

84. Cf. Mayer, "Theology and Sufism," 269–270.

occasionalism. The part titled "The Rules of Beliefs" ["Qawāʾid al-ʿAqāʾid"] presents a strongly early Ashʿarī depiction of the divine nature with *bilā kayfa* anti-interpretivism and divine knowability. Yet al-Ghazālī does not introduce this part as a distinctly Ashʿarī or Sufi creed but rather as a more ecumenical set of core beliefs that should be taught to a wide audience, including children.[85]

In typical Ashʿarī format, Abū Ḥāmid's creed begins with Qurʾanic verses, mixed with a list of negations from God, including partner, opposite, similitude, beginning, or an end. Then he embarks on a section on "incomparability" [*tanzīh*], which brings a new wave of negations. This emphasis on divine transcendence is followed by the anti-interpretive acceptance of the Qurʾanic passages related to anthropomorphism. Al-Ghazālī denies the accessibility of the transcendent discourse to interpretation:

> *He is sitting on the throne as it appears in His discourse, and with the meaning that He intended by "sitting" [istiwāʾ].* He transcends touching and being placed in space, and from incarnation [*ḥulūl*]. . . . He is nearer to a human being than his jugular vein [Q.5:16]. Over everything He is a witness, since His nearness does not resemble the nearness of bodies, just as His essence does not resemble the essence of bodies. . . . *In His ipseity, God's existence is known [maʿlūm] to intellects. His ipseity will be seen by the eyes in the afterlife as a blessing from Him* and a grace to the upright [*abrār*]. *He completes His favor with sight of His noble countenance.*[86]

Although the anti-interpretivism we find here is non-cognitivist, it also makes peace with transcendent anthropomorphism, especially in terms of God's visibility in the afterlife in physical terms. Among others, al-Sarrāj's famous *Book of Flashes* [*Kitāb al-Lumaʿ*], a major source of al-Ghazālī's *Revivification*, had already categorized the vision of God via physical eyes in the afterlife as an anthropomorphic error. In fact, the *Book of Flashes* not only resisted such a claim, but it also situated Sufism in its opposition. Al-Sarrāj wrote that he saw an admonishing letter penned by al-Kharrāz to the people of Damascus, who were said to make such embarrassing claims. In the same place, al-Sarrāj also cites an example of al-Tustarī's interpretivist

85. Marmura, "Al-Ghazālī," 149–150; Abū Ḥāmid al-Ghazālī, *Iḥyāʾ al-ʿUlūm al-Dīn*, 1:93.
86. Abū Ḥāmid al-Ghazālī, *Iḥyāʾ*, 1:89.

theology and argues that those who claim to see God on a throne are actually deceived by Satan.[87] Hence the *Revivification* diverges from the Sufi hermeneutical tradition exposed by al-Sarrāj, according to which vision belongs to hearts. In the following pages of the creed, al-Ghazālī affirms that the attributes of vision, hearing, and speech apply to God, even if they should not be understood in physical or human terms. Except a vague hint in terms of divine nearness [*qurb*] to physical bodies, al-Ghazālī does not engage in any interpretation but accepts the transcendent discourse amodally. We know what these attributes are *not*—a long list of negations follow these descriptions—but not what they are. The dissimilarity of the divine nature is amodally followed in canceling all interpretive inquiries, however anti-anthropomorphic they would be.

Al-Ghazālī's *bilā kayfa* position regarding the divine nature is not limited to the *Revivification*. His last work on speculative theology that we know to be authentic, *Restraining the Lay Public from Approaching Speculative Theology*, is in perfect harmony with the approach summarized in the *Revivification*. According to this post-Sufism work of Abū Ḥāmid, the way of the pious ancestors [*madhhab al-ṣalaf*], which is the true path in his view, is to follow one of seven strategies concerning the ambiguous, apparently anthropomorphic, or controversial verses and prophetic reports:

1. *Exoneration* [*taqdīs*]—that is, to absolve [*tanzīh*] Him from such bodily descriptions.
2. *Affirmation* [*taṣdīq*]—that is, to believe in the sacred discourse, and in its truth with the meaning intended by God.
3. *Confession of one's inability* [*al-iʿtirāf bi al-ʿajz*]—that is, acknowledging that the intended meaning is beyond the scope of one's knowledge, that the meaning is not of one's business or discursive limits [*ḥarf*].
4. *Silence* [*sukūt*]—that is, not to elaborate on the transcendent meaning, as it is beyond human knowledge.
5. *Abstinence* [*imsāk*]—that is, refraining from any discursive activity, such as playing words, translation, adding or subtracting words.
6. *Restraint* [*kaff*]—that is, reining back one's heart and mind from search [*baḥth*] or reflection [*tafakkur*] on the transcendent intention or meaning.

87. Al-Sarrāj, *Kitāb al-Lumaʿ*, 428–429.

7. *Yielding to its expert* [*taslīm li-ahlihi*]—that is, not assuming that its meaning is hidden from the prophets and the saints.[88]

Most, if not all, of these hermeneutical principles indicate the importance of adopting anti-anthropomorphic, but also anti-interpretive, *bilā kayfa* positions for al-Ghazālī. *Restraining the Lay Public* is replete with examples that exemplify this position. Accordingly, interpretation can give only what the real meaning *is not*. *"If a person is aware of the negation of this [physical, hence] unthinkable reference in relation to the divinity, then nothing more is required of him."*[89] It is sufficient to know what these verses do *not* mean. The theological position that al-Ghazālī associates with Sufism toward the end of his life is distinctly and broadly "Sunnī" with its emphasis on the pious ancestors and its non-cognitivism on the divine nature. This anti-interpretive Sunnī-Sufi position is expressed in the other key work of post-Sufi al-Ghazālī: the *Decisive Criterion*. Here al-Ghazālī underlines the essentiality of interpretation for the verses and sacred reports, the meaning of which would be absurd if taken literally. Yet, when it comes to God's "throne" and "footstool," He insists that these are real things that are not subject to interpretation. He begins with dividing existence into five levels: ontological [*dhātī*], sensory [*ḥissī*], conceptual [*khayālī*], noetic [*ʿaqlī*], and analogous [*shabahī*]. Divine throne and footstool belong to the first category of things that have an objective, "absolute and real existence" [*al-wujūd al-muṭlaq al-ḥaqīqī*]: they must be "understood according to the apparent meaning of these terms, devoid of any figurative interpretation. For these corporeal entities exist in their own right, whether they are apprehended by the senses or the imagination or not."[90] We do not know or understand them; thus speculative, cognitive human approaches and modalities should not apply to them.

Al-Ghazālī's intensified interest in Sufism toward the end of his life curiously coincided with his adoption of more anti-interpretivist approaches to the divine nature, when Ashʿarism had been moving toward interpretivism at least for a century. Prominent Ashʿarī teachers like ʿAbd al-Qāhir al-Baghdādī, al-Bayhaqī, Abū Isḥāq al-Shīrāzī, and al-Juwaynī all

88. Abū Ḥāmid al-Ghazālī, *Iljām al-ʿAwāmm ʿan ʿIlm al-Kalām*; for an English translation, see Abū Ḥāmid al-Ghazālī, *A Return to Purity in Creed*, 23–24.

89. See Shu'ayb, "Al-Ghazzālī's Final Word on Kalām," 151–172.

90. Abū Ḥāmid al-Ghazālī, *Fayṣal al-Tafriqa*, 33; Abū Ḥāmid al-Ghazālī, *On the Boundaries*, 96–97; Sands, *Sufi Commentaries*, 57.

had refused the anti-interpretive theological approaches toward anthropomorphism. Post-Sufi al-Ghazālī, like al-Qushayrī, turned this interpretivist tide. If the late al-Ghazālī *revived* something, it was first and foremost the anti-interpretivist Ashʿarī theological hermeneutics under the rubric of a Sunnī, "*uṣūl*-ized" Sufism.

These eminent examples give an idea about the theology that we find in the Sufi manuals that emerged in the tenth century. Influential authors of Sufi manuals such as al-Makkī, al-Kalābādhī, al-Kharkūshī, al-Qushayrī, ʿAbd Allāh al-Anṣārī (d.1089), Abū Ḥāmid al-Ghazālī, al-Sarrāj, and Abū Khalaf al-Ṭabarī ascribed *bilā kayfa* non-cognitivism to the normative, increasingly formalized Sufism. Yet not all writers of Sufi manuals followed this prominent anti-interpretive theological fashion. The very first Persian Sufi compendium by the Ḥanafī Sufi author of Ghazna, Hujvīrī, was the most important and suggestive exception in insistently following the interpretivism of earlier Sufis.

Interpretivism in Persian Sufism

Unlike other Sufi manuals of the formalization period, Hujvīrī's *Unveiling of the Hidden* [*Kashf al-Maḥjūb*] insisted on interpretive approaches to anthropomorphism. Among a long list of negations, Hujvīrī affirmed the vision of God [*dīdārash*] in paradise. Yet he immediately added that one should avoid comparison [*tashbīh*], or thinking about such vision as "confrontation or facing" [*muqābala va muvājaha*]. In this non-physical visionary sense, God's saints [*avliyā'*] can witness [*mushāhadat*] Her in this world. In other sections of the *Unveiling*, Hujvīrī interprets the prophetic vision of God in his night journey as happening not via his physical eyes but in the "eye of his innermost heart" [*chashm-e sirr*]—in line with al-Kharkūshī's *Refining the Secrets* [*Tahdhīb al-Asrār*], and quoting Sahl al-Tustarī.[91]

Hujvīrī also directly criticizes the anthropomorphic anti-interpretivism. In one of his discussions on the Sufi auditions [*samāʿ*], he argues that audition will only increase the perversity of those whose hearts are not ready for it:

> Another group interpreted "then He established Himself on the throne" [Q.7:54] as an affirmation of spatiality and modality for

91. Hujvīrī, *Kitāb Kashf al-Maḥjūb*, 359 (For English translations, see Hujvīrī, *A Persian Treatise on Sufism*, 279–280; Hujvīrī, *Kashf al-Maḥjūb*, 376.) Hujvīrī, *Kashf al-Maḥjūb*, 430–431.

> Him. Others showed "and thy lord comes, and the angels rank on rank" [Q.89:22] as a proof for His "coming"! As their hearts were a locus of error, hearing the discourse of their sublime lord didn't give them any profit. The unifiers [*muvaḥḥidān*], however, when they look at the poet of a poem, they regard the creator of his nature, and the designator of his thoughts. They draw the proof for the agent from the action.[92]

Here Hujvīrī not only criticizes the anthropomorphist approaches but also indicates that the vision of God in this world is a metaphysical, non-corporeal way of moving from creation to the creator. His approach to creation as a sign of the creator was a popular philosophical proof that circulated not only among Ghaznavid philosophers and Muʿtazilīs but also Ḥanafī scholars for more than a century. Hujvīrī also reads the "throne" of God in metaphorical terms as the "inward direction of prayer" [*qibla-ye bāṭin*]; the mysteries of divine contemplation [*sirr al-mushāhadat*] emerge from it.[93] In other words, the throne, like in earlier Sufism, indicates a high cosmological level that can be visited by visionary wayfaring and purification of one's own soul.

Hujvīrī is definitely not the only Farsi-writing Sufi of his time to enthusiastically adopt interpretive, discursive positions toward the anthropomorphic depictions of the divine essence. The less-known work of the Sufi master and theologian Aḥmad al-Ghazālī, devoted to systematical theology, is of great importance here. Aḥmad is famous for his great poetical work on love theology, *Inspirations from the World of Pure Spirits*. The *Inspirations* is a rhapsodic series of letters to the radically other, yet excessive, overwhelming, all-consuming Beloved—a perfect paradoxical combination of divine incomparability and immanence. Aḥmad's students also compiled the sessions [*majālis*] he conducted when he was in Baghdad. These discourses became a lesser-known Arabic book on divine unity titled *Excursus Regarding the Expression of Unity*. A powerful text that witnesses Aḥmad al-Ghazālī's oratory skills as an eloquent Sufi preacher, the *Excursus* is in stark contrast with the anti-interpretive position espoused by the Sufis who surrounded him.

92. Hujvīrī, *Kashf al-Maḥjūb*, 508–509.

93. Ibid., 397.

The *Revivification* of his brother Abū Ḥāmid, the *Sufi Etiquette for Novices* of his pupil Abū al-Najīb al-Suhrawardī, and the *Epistle* of al-Qushayrī, who was the master of Ali al-Fārmadhī—the joint teacher of the Ghazālī brothers—all adopted anti-interpretivist theologies. Aḥmad al-Ghazālī's divergence is palpable. Very much like the Sufis of Baghdad, Aḥmad al-Ghazālī's *Excursus* understands from "divine unity" [*tawḥīd*] the entire path, aims, and states of spiritual progress, and the related practices, instead of a set of doctrinal ideas. In all of his extant discourses, Aḥmad clearly adopts an intensively interpretive position toward the sacred sources. His readings unveil the deeper meanings of the sacred sources that relate to the Sufi path. He does not consider beatific vision possible, as God cannot be an object. God is infinitely veiled from vision and, already, excessively present—only God actually exists. Aḥmad al-Ghazālī's discourses consistently violate the anti-interpretive position. A few of these discourses explicitly address God's double fingers, throne, face, vision, or blowing into the soul; literalism in all of them is sharply criticized by Aḥmad on strongly anti-anthropomorphic interpretive grounds. In one of his discourses, he interprets the "double fingers" of God as the binary states through which the soul passes in its progress. In another discourse, he proposes another interpretation. Accordingly, the expression might be an allusion [*ishāra*] to the quick transformation of the soul from one state into another, or anything else but its literal sense. He is open to other interpretations as well, because the literal reading of the verse would be anthropomorphism. He introduces a rather long list of negations that target similar problems: God's throne, vision, and nearness in particular.[94]

Such interpretive anti-anthropomorphism, as opposed to *bilā kayfa* positions, was very prominent in Persian Sufism of the eleventh and twelfth centuries. Sanāʾī (d.1131), another Ghaznavid Sufi and poet, was even more direct in his critique of anti-interpretivism and anthropomorphism. His influential *mathnawī*, the *Walled Garden of Truth* [*Ḥadīqat al-Ḥaqīqat*] contained an extensive discussion of the anthropomorphic depictions of God. Sanāʾī expounds his interpretive position within the context of his emphasis on divine otherness, negativity, unknowability, and the inapplicability of modalities. Here Sanāʾī goes on to interpret "hand" as Her capacity, "face" Her subsistence, "coming" Her wisdom, "descent"

94. Aḥmad al-Ghazālī, *al-Tajrīd fī Kalimat al-Tawḥīd*, ch.43, 104–107.
For his metaphorical reading of "seeing" and "hearing" God, see ibid., 109–111.

Her gift, "two feet" Her majesty of chastisement and danger, "two fingers" the pervasiveness of Her judgment and power. Associating the divine throne with the heart of the mystic [*ʿārif*], he criticizes those who attribute "speech," "throne," and such corporeal qualities: none of them actually apply to God.[95]

The cosmological, visionary interpretation of the throne verse, and the role of the heart as the genuine seat of God, supported by popular prophetic traditions, were the most common and interrelated interpretative approaches to the anthropomorphic depictions of the divine nature. Ibn Abī al-Khayr, Aḥmad-i Jām, and the former's hagiographer, Ibn Munavvar, were following such interpretive positions.[96] An interesting anecdote on the prominence of interpretivism as opposed to *bilā kayfa* apophaticism or anthropomorphism comes from Ibn Abī al-Khayr of Mihna. Accordingly, the Persian interpretive position on the throne verse was so obvious and simple that the shaykh refused to bother himself explaining it. The shaykh takes such a trivial question as an offense:

> When the shaykh was on his way, there was somebody from the populace of Harat, who grasped the reins of his mount and had entered his service [*khidmat*]. He asked the shaykh a question on what he would say on the verse "the all-merciful, established on the throne" [Q.20:5]. Our shaykh said: *"In Mihna even the crones know that the lord was there when the throne wasn't!"*[97]

On the eve of the emergence of the distinct methods, lineages, and networks associated with charismatic masters, Persian Sufism did not experience the invasion of *bilā kayfa* apophatic fashion that we find in Arabic compendia of Sufism. Instead, it was the visionary interpretive approaches of the earlier Sufis that flourished in approaching the divine essence. With

95. Sanāʾī in Renard, *Islamic Theological Themes*, 271–276.

96. Ibn al-Munavvar, *Asrār al-Tawḥīd fī Maqāmāt al-Shaykh Abī Saʿīd*, 36–37; Aḥmad-i Jām, *The Colossal Elephant and His Spiritual Feats*, 271, 296.

ʿAbd al-Raḥmān ʿĀbādī (fl.ea.12th CE) and Aḥmad-i Jām, the two competing Sufi masters of Nishapur reportedly entered a Qurʾanic exegesis contest. Aḥmad-i Jām wrote an exegesis of Q.55, the chapter of *All-Merciful* [*Al-Raḥmān*]. The leitmotif "O which of your lord's bounties will you and you deny?" is repeated thirty-one times in the chapter, and Aḥmad-i Jām proudly interprets all of them differently. (Aḥmad-i i Jām, *The Colossal Elephant and His Spiritual Feats*, 1.21, 140–141.)

97. Ibn al-Munavvar, *Asrār al-Tawḥīd fī Maqāmāt al-Shaykh Abī Saʿīd*, 297–298.

properly regulated study and practice, one could, and should, interpret the transcendent discourse on God's ipseity. As ʿAyn al-Qużāt put it, one could interpret, if not apprehend, God's creation of man in Her/her "likeness," Her "establishment" on the "throne," and Her "descent," once having inhaled the scent of "who has known her self."[98]

Sufis of the ninth and tenth centuries were strongly anti-anthropomorphist, with little sympathy for anti-interpretive approaches to the corporeal descriptions of God, even if with a *bilā kayfa* apophatic lens. Their eagerness to interpret such reports, if we consider the power of transcendent anthropomorphism of traditionism during this period, indicates their receptiveness to speculative—rationalist or imaginative—theologies on the divine nature. Both Baghdadian and Basran Sufis from early on had a strong interest in a theologically conscious, anti-anthropomorphist exegesis that underlined divine otherness in the strongest terms. Authors of Sufi manuals like al-Sarrāj, al-Kalābādhī, al-Kharkūshī, al-Sīrjānī, Abū Khalaf al-Ṭabarī, al-Qushayrī, or Hujvīrī devoted pages to Sufi approaches to the divine nature. Even if many of these writers themselves were inclined to *bilā kayfa* apophaticism of their time, none of them could actually find reliable evidence for the earlier Sufis adopting that approach to the divine nature. While al-Qushayrī's "summary" claimed that Sufis affirmed divine face, hands, vision, or throne *bilā kayfa*, even he could not present tangible proof for such a position. None of these vast manuals actually provided evidence of earlier Sufis affirming the divine face or hands *prima facie*. Yet, as al-Qushayrī vividly showed, the Ashʿarite authors were particularly interested in placing earlier Sufis in their *bilā kayfa* apophatic line. Such an endeavor also appears in the *Comfort of the Mystics* [*Salwat al-ʿĀrifīn*]. Its compiler, Abū Khalaf al-Ṭabarī, was another scholar of Shāfiʿī law and Ashʿarite theology who lived in Nishapur, the provincial capital and cultural center of Khurasan. The section on divine unity in the *Comfort of the Mystics*, very much like other Sufi manuals, contains pages of negations, emphasizing divine transcendence and unknowability with examples from a plethora of Sufis. In his presentation, however, Dhū al-Nūn al-Miṣrī accepted a verse on God's "throne," Q.20:5, without interpretation and as it is, in the *bilā kayfa* apophatic line. Such representation of Dhū al-Nūn was in sharp contrast to his general theological approach to the divine essence as well as the rather widespread reports about his

98. ʿAyn al-Qużāt Hamadānī in Papan-Matin, *Beyond Death*, 218.

anti-anthropomorphic interpretation of this verse. Less than ten percent of the entire *Comfort of the Mystics* actually embodied Abū Khalaf al-Ṭabarī's own declarations, which tried to situate the chapters into a theological framework of the Ashʿarī School.[99] The ascription of *bilā kayfa* apophaticism was integral to this Ashʿarization of earlier Sufis by Abū Khalaf and al-Qushayrī.

Elusive as it was, a tension did exist between the *bilā kayfa* apophaticism of the Arabic Sufi manuals that were describing (and partially constructing) the normative Sufi theological approaches and the prominence of rather anti-anthropomorphic interpretivism among the late tenth- and eleventh-century Sufis. Which position would prevail among Sufis in the later couple of centuries? The answer was a complex one, as both approaches would play important authenticating roles.

Ḥanbalī Sufism and the Qādiriyya

Sunnism of the tenth century still had strong transcendent anthropomorphist strands that accepted the literal reading of physical depictions of God in the scripture or the prophetic reports. Such inclinations were more powerful among traditionists in the anti-*kalām* camp. A rescript of Caliph al-Rāḍī (r.934–940) issued in 935 against the Baghdadian Ḥanbalīs under the leadership of al-Barbahārī strongly denounced them for their anthropomorphist traditions, such as the Prophet's vision of God as white-skinned and dark-haired, or as an adolescent whose hair was shorn, among other embarrassments:

> *You claim that your ugly and disgusting faces are in the image of the Lord of the worlds and that your vile appearance is in His image; you talk of His feet and fingers and legs and gilded shoes and curly hair, and going up to heaven and coming down to the world—may God be raised above what wrongdoers and unbelievers say about Him.*[100]

As a Ḥanbalī champion of anti-interpretivism, al-Barbahārī is said to have been a direct disciple of Sahl al-Tustarī. Still, unlike al-Tustarī, he was

---

99. Abū Khalaf al-Ṭabarī, *Salwat al-ʿĀrifīn*, 20; al-Qushayrī, *Epistle on Sufism*, 12; Böwering and Orfali in Abū Khalaf al-Ṭabarī, *Salwat al-ʿĀrifīn*, 1–28.

100. Williams, "Aspects of the Creed," 454 (emphasis mine).

affirming all anthropomorphic depictions of God without qualification, and he claimed that asking "how" or "why" concerning the divine attributes means to doubt God Herself.[101] The leading Sunnī *ḥadīth* scholar of the next generation in the second half of the century was al-Dāraquṭnī, who, as al-Dhahabī reports, hated *kalām* and fiercely defended transcendent anthropomorphism with a *bilā kayfa* discourse. In his *Book of Divine Attributes* [*Kitāb al-Ṣifāt*], al-Dāraquṭnī affirms virtually all anthropomorphic depictions of God we know: man's creation in God's image [*ṣūra*]; Her having fingers, laughing, sitting on a throne and having a footstool; the similarity [*tashbīh*] of Her face to human faces; Her literal descent [*nuzūl*] to the lowest heavens during the night; or Her height, which is accordingly about sixty arm-lengths. Al-Dāraquṭnī insists that these descriptions have no interpretation [*tafsīr*], which means that they should be accepted literally, as they appear, *bilā kayfa*:

> These prophetic reports are reliable [*saḥīḥ*]. . . . They are real [*ḥaqq*] in our view, without any doubt. But if it is asked: What is the situation about His footstool? How does He laugh? We say: There is no interpretation for these. We have not heard a single interpretation about these.[102]

Ibn Baṭṭa's position seems to be in line with al-Barbahārī and al-Dāraquṭnī. "God closes and opens His hand, He takes and gives, He is on his throne."[103] Abū Yaʿlā (d.1066) was another prominent Ḥanbalī to write a pro-transcendent anthropomorphism book of traditions with the same title, the *Book of Divine Attributes*. As an influential jurist of Baghdad, Abū Yaʿlā was instrumental in the dissemination of Ḥanbalism. Still, the strengthening anti-anthropomorphist *bilā kayfa* trend within Ḥanbalism would be later hardly pleased with his memory. Mentioning Abū Yaʿlā's death, the historian Ibn al-Athīr (d.1233) added a tellingly bold note: "[Abū Yaʿlā's book] gives evidence of unadulterated anthropomorphism, and God is indeed far above all that. [Abū Muḥammad Rizq Allāh ibn ʿAbd al-Wahhāb] Ibn Tamīmī the Ḥanbalī used to say, 'Abū Yaʿlā al-Farrāʾ has

---

101. Abū al-Ḥasan al-Daylamī, *A Treatise on Mystical Love*, xxiii–xxxiv; Melchert, "Origins and Early Sufism," 20–22; Melchert, "The Ḥanābila and the Early Sufis."

102. Al-Dāraquṭnī, *Kitāb al-Ṣifāt*, 115; also see ibid., 73–121; Brown "al-Dāraquṭnī."

103. Ibn Baṭṭa in al-Daylamī, *A Treatise on Mystical Love*, xxxiii.

covered the Ḥanbalites in shit that no water can clean off.' "[104] The prominent anti-anthropomorphist Ḥanbalī scholar, Ibn al-Jawzī also narrated the same saying. Yet the anthropomorphist trend remained alive well into the twelfth century, as recorded in Abū Ḥāmid al-Ghazālī's *Decisive Criterion* and in various works of Ibn al-Jawzī. Especially the latter, the most well-known insider critic of Ḥanbalism, shows that transcendent anthropomorphism was popular during his times:

> Abū ʿAbd Allāh ibn Ḥāmid [d.1013], his disciple, Qāḍī Abū Yaʿlā, and Ibn al-Zāghūnī [d.1132] who composed books by which they have disgraced the [Ḥanbalī] school. They held the attributes of God to be subject to human understanding and perception. They heard that God, glorified and exalted be He, created Adam in his image, upon him be blessing and peace. On that basis, they acknowledged for Him an image and a physical form, a face attributable to His essence, two eyes, a mouth, uvulas, molar teeth, and lights for His face which represent His majestic splendor, two hands, fingers, a palm, a little [pinky] finger, a thumb, a chest, a thigh, two shins, and two feet.[105]

Hence the transcendental anthropomorphist trend in Ḥanbalism would survive, and keep appearing in various theological contexts. Even Ibn Taymiyya, who is accepted today by most Salafīs as the champion of anti-interpretive amodalism, found himself charged multiple times with anthropomorphism. The famous authority on law, *ḥadīth*, and historian, Ibn Ḥajar al-ʿAsqalānī (d.1449) narrates from al-Ṭūfī that anthropomorphic inclinations of Ibn Taymiyya stirred conflict in Damascus in 705/1306. The traveler Ibn Baṭṭūṭa's (d.1377) description of this incident is more colorful, although the claim for his own eyewitness testimony (and the authenticity of this event in general) should be taken with a grain of salt:

> Among the chief Ḥanbalī jurists in Damascus was Taqī al-Dīn Ibn Taymiyya who, although he enjoyed great prestige and could discourse on the scholarly disciplines, had a screw loose [*fī ʿaqlihi*

104. Ibn al-Athīr, *Annals of the Saljūq Turks: Selections from al-Kāmil fī'l-Ta'rikh*, 159. See Ibn al-Jawzī, *Attributes of God*, 46n13.

105. Ibn al-Jawzī, *Attributes of God*, 42.

> *shay'an*]. . . . While I was in Damascus, I was in attendance on a Friday, when he was preaching to the people and exhorting them from the pulpit [*minbar*] of the cathedral mosque. In the course of his speech he said, "*God comes down to the sky of this world just as I come down now,*" and he descended one step of the pulpit. A Mālikī jurist known as Ibn al-Zahrā' remonstrated with him and denounced what he had said, whereupon the congregation rose against this jurist, striking him with their hands and shoes.[106]

Sufism played an ambivalent role between anthropomorphism and anti-anthropomorphic *bilā kayfa* within this unsettled Ḥanbalī context. Abū Nuʿaym al-Iṣfahānī (d.1038), one of the earliest and celebrated sources on Sufism, was a descendant, and perhaps grandson, of Yūsuf al-Bannā' (d.bef.899), who was a member of the Ḥanbalī pietist school in Isfahan. This school promoted transcendent anthropomorphism more than amodality, at least until the eleventh century. Abū al-Shaykh al-Iṣfahānī (d.979) compiled a large collection of anthropomorphic prophetic traditions, titled the *Book of Majesty* [*Kitāb al-ʿAẓāma*]. While it might be just a well-worn pretext, Abū Nuʿaym al-Iṣfahānī himself was expelled from the city by Muḥammad ibn Isḥāq (d.1005) of the powerful Banū Manda family on the grounds of his anthropomorphism. Ibn Taymiyya depicts Abū Nuʿaym as closer to amodality than anthropomorphism, but this is the former's general tendency toward earlier pietist traditionists. Abū Nuʿaym's own work testifies rather to his anti-interpretive, literalist acceptance of the physical depictions of God. Accordingly,

> God is *above* the heavens, and is seated on His throne; it is not that He simply "rules," as the Jahmiyya would interpret His mode of sitting [*istiwā'*], on the basis that God is everywhere. . . . The throne of God is a real entity: it is not simply intended to symbolize divine knowledge, as the Jahmiyya would have it. On the Day of Judgment, His throne is really placed before His creatures as a judgment

106. Ibn Baṭṭūṭa, *Tuḥfat al-Nuẓẓār*, 1:316–317; Little, "Did Ibn Taymiyya Have a Screw Loose?" 95–97.

Recent studies have questioned the authenticity of this event, while they also acknowledge that Ibn Taymiyya was involved in heated controversies related to anthropomorphism, such as pointing with the finger upward to indicate God's spatiality, and raising hands during supplications. See Holtzman, *Anthropomorphism in Islam*, 330–333.

seat from which to deliver the verdicts and decrees regarding His subjects.[107]

A fellow townsman of Abū Nuʿaym, Abū Manṣūr Maʿmar (d.1027) was another early associate with Ḥanbalī pietism of Isfahan. His work lists not only well-known early ascetics and jurists but also key scholars of anthropomorphic traditionism among the early generations of Muslims, whom he deeply revered. The work also acknowledges anthropomorphic depictions of God in the sacred scripture, denying to comment further on the issue. The defining document of Ḥanbalism at the turn of the century was the creed of the ʿAbbāsid Caliph al-Qādir (r.991–1031), affirmed by his son and successor, al-Qāʾim (r.1031–1075). Expressed in some verses, which originally circulated in Farsi, the Ḥanbalī creed was forcefully anthropomorphic:

Our God can be seen; is established on his throne
His speech is eternal; his prophet Arab,

Anyone who says anything other than this is an Ashʿarī
Our path [*madhhab*] is the Ḥanbalī *madhhab*.[108]

It is this anti-interpretivist swing between anthropomorphism and amodality against the backdrop of which Ḥanbalī Sufism would reach its apogee with ʿAbd Allāh Anṣārī in Khurasan and ʿAbd al-Qādir al-Jīlānī in Baghdad. Ḥanbalism was probably the most powerful school in Baghdad in the eleventh century. The Saljūqī vizier Niẓām al-Mulk (d.1092) in his letter to Abū Isḥāq al-Shīrāzī, the leading Ashʿarī in Baghdad, testified to the dominance of the Ḥanbalī school in the ʿAbbāsid capital and its political significance.[109] But Khurasan was home to Ḥanbalīs as well. Indeed, one of the great Ḥanbalī leaders of Baghdad, al-Sharīf Abū Jaʿfar (fl.l.11th

107. Gharagozlou, Anṣārī, and Negahban, "Abū Nuʿaym al-Iṣfahānī." Also see Blankinship, "The Early Creed," 52.

108. Peacock, *Early Seljuq History*, 116. Also see ibid., 99–104; Annabel Keeler, "Mystical Theology and the Traditionalist Hermeneutics of Maybudī's Kashf al-Asrār," 28; Meier, *Essays on Islamic Piety and Mysticism*, 145–146, 154.

109. "The policy of the Sulṭān and fairness require that we do not incline towards one *madhhab* more than another. . . . We do not have the power to overcome Baghdad and its surroundings and to alter forcibly [its people's] established customs, for the majority here belong to the school [*madhhab*] of the Imām Ibn Ḥanbal." (Niẓām al-Mulk in Peacock, *Early Seljuq History*, 104–105.)

CE), claimed that the Qādirī-Qāʾimī creed "was borne by Khurasanians and pilgrims to the ends of the earth." The anti-interpretivist creed reflected that of al-Anṣārī as well, while his student Maybudī was more clearly adopting *bilā kayfa* amodalism. Al-Anṣārī strongly defended divine unknowability in all of his extant works. He was also a strong critic of dialectical theology, and even wrote a polemical attack against the Ashʿarīs. Here he fiercely and categorically opposed the interpretations of God's face, eye, ear, throne, and footstool. He opposes the theologians' claim that "God has no place," which may suggest that al-Anṣārī's own understanding of God's establishment is either transcendent anthropomorphist or unknowable. Al-Anṣārī seems to follow the latter, apophatic position, insofar as he left the interpretation to God Herself when affirmed God's physical appearance to the Prophet:

> [Q.7:180] What God showed of Himself, that He is, and such is His attribute. God is the explication of Himself, and Muṣṭafā [i.e., the Prophet] has face-to-face vision of Him.[110]

Hence Anṣārī is a reluctant exegete with reference to the divine nature, while he is a very active interpreter in other contexts. His canceling of further interpretation is on the verge of literal acceptance. It is his foremost pupil, Maybudī, who pulls al-Anṣārī's image toward a clear *bilā kayfa* apophaticism.[111] For example, immediately after quoting al-Anṣārī's

---

110. Maybudī, *Unveiling of the Mysteries*, Q.7:180, 282.

> [Q.20:5] The all-merciful sat on the throne. The sitting of the lord on the throne is in the Qurʾan, and I have faith in it. I do not seek interpretation, for interpretation in such topics is rebellion. I accept the outward meaning and surrender to the inner meaning. This is the belief of the Sunnīs, whose path is to accept with the spirit what is not perceived. . . . Nonetheless, I know for sure that He is not one who takes up place out of need, for He shows place by argument. The throne does not elevate God, for God elevates and preserves the throne. He made the throne for seekers of God, not recognizers of God. The God-seeker is one thing, the God-recognizer something else. He says to the God-seekers, "The all-merciful sat on the throne." He says to the God recognizers, "And He is with you" [Q.57:4] on the throne by essence, in knowledge everywhere, through companionship with the spirit, and through nearness with the soul. (Maybudī, *Unveiling of the Mysteries*, 402.)

111. Maybudī played a parallel role in transforming al-Anṣārī into a mainstay of the Sufi school of thought known as the "Religion of Love" [*mazhab-i ʿishq*] in classical Persian poetry. Al-Anṣārī never used the term "passionate love" [*ʿishq*], and preferred the Qurʾanic "compassionate love" [*maḥabba*] in describing God's relationship with creation. Maybudī replaced *maḥabba* with *ʿishq* all throughout the *Kashf al-Asrār*, which was instrumental in firmly situating al-Anṣārī into the *mazhab-i ʿishq*. See Lewisohn, "Sufism's Religion of Love," 165–166.

unqualified claim that the Prophet met God face-to-face, Maybudī added the following passage that moved his shaykh toward amodality more clearly:

> It is not appropriate for someone to affirm attributes for God on his own, nor to declare Him incomparable on his own. Keep your ears fixed on the Book and the *Sunna*! Whatever they say, you say that it is that. God said there are attributes, there are names, so you should also say that. Since He did not say that there are not, you should not say that there are not. He did not say "how" He is. If He had said "how" He is, we would say that. God said, "I am." He did not speak of howness. *You should speak of being, but you should not speak of howness.*[112]

Al-Anṣārī, with his ups and downs, was a polemical traditionist, whose overt attacks against theologians caused headaches for the rulers. As early as in 1038, when he appeared before the Ghaznavid Sulṭān Masʿūd (r.1030–1040), the charge against him was the same as the one against Abū Nuʿaym al-Iṣfahānī: anthropomorphism. Life got initially easier for al-Anṣārī with the Saljūqī conquest, but the charge of anthropomorphism against him did persist, even if the Sulṭān Alp Arslan (r.1063–1072) protected him from his detractors. His Shāfiʿī (yet not Ashʿarī) student Maybudī, on the other hand, developed a two-layered hermeneutical system, which juxtaposed "a traditionalist commentary containing a literalist interpretation of the text, and a Sufi commentary which often interprets the text allegorically. . . . Maybudī's double-layered theological outlook accentuating the absolute omnipotence and ineffability of God."[113] Following al-Anṣārī, Maybudī emphasized divine unknowability, and he insisted that the anthropomorphic expressions in the Qur'an, such as God's descent, establishment on the throne, or two hands, should be accepted as they are, without attempting to interpret them. Yet Maybudī supplied this literal acceptance of anthropomorphism with another reading, which he defined as comprising "the allegories of mystics, allusions of Sufis, and subtle associations of preachers" [*rumūz-i ʿārifān, ishārāt-i ṣūfiyyān, laṭāʾif-i*

112. Maybudī, *Unveiling of the Mysteries*, Q.7:180, 282 (emphasis mine).

113. Shihadeh, *Sufism and Theology*, 4; de Laugier de Beaureceuil, "Abdāllah Anṣārī"; Peacock, *Early Seljuq History*, 116.

muzakkirān].[114] From this perspective, the "throne" of God was the heart of Her lovers. This is the same two-layered hermeneutical system of al-Qushayrī's *Subtle Allusions*. In contexts other than anthropomorphism, Maybudī is a fascinatingly creative exegete. The phrase "In the name of God, the all-merciful, the ever-merciful" [*bismillāh al-raḥmān al-raḥīm*] gets a new, different meaning in each of its appearances. Maybudī also interprets the enigmatic disjointed letters, which Ḥanafīs considered ultimately unknowable and inscrutable. He undertakes these allegorical interpretations, as in the case of the disjointed letters in Q.2:1, in support of Ḥanbalī doctrines, such as the uncreatedness of the letters and sounds of the transcendent discourse. Concerning the depictions of God in human terms, he is a much more reticent exegete, like al-Anṣārī. He insists that the Prophet did see God's face, which defies discursive explanation—hence to be accepted *prima facie*. God's "hand" in Q.5:64, similarly, is another point where we observe his double-layered *bilā kayfa* apophatic approach:

> A hand of attribute [*yad-i ṣifāt*], a hand of essence [*yad-i ẕāt*], the outward meaning of which [should be] accepted, the inner meaning surrendered [to God], and the reality unapprehended [*ḥaqīqat dar nayāfta*], [so that one] desists from the way of [asking] how [*rāh-i chigūnagī*], the exertion [of reason] [*taṣarruf*] and metaphorical interpretation [*ta'wīl*].[115]

The great Ḥanbalī ascetic and orator ʿAbd al-Qādir al-Jīlānī shares the ambivalence of al-Anṣārī in terms of *bilā kayfa* apophaticism. Al-Jīlānī's anti-interpretivism was clear early in his life. Upon his arrival at Baghdad as a young aspirant, he chose to join a Ḥanbalī circle to get legal training, instead of coming to the Niẓāmiyya madrasa of the Saljūqīs, which was, tellingly, headed by Aḥmad al-Ghazālī at that time. The discourses of al-Jīlānī known as the *Sublime Revelation* [al-*Fatḥ al-Rabbānī*] oscillate between the literal acceptance of anthropomorphic depictions of God and the *bilā kayfa* critique of such anthropomorphism. Delivered in 1150–1151 in Baghdad, al-Jīlānī's *Sublime Revelation* emphasizes the uncreated nature

---

114. See Keeler, "Mystical Theology and the Traditionalist Hermeneutics of Maybudī's Kashf al-Asrār," 15–16.

115. Maybudī in Keeler, "Mystical Theology and the Traditionalist Hermeneutics of Maybudī's Kashf al-Asrār," 17. Also see Maybudī, *Unveiling of the Mysteries*, 12; al-Māturīdī, *Kitāb al-Tawḥīd*, 138; Coppens, *Seeing God in This World and the Otherworld*, 76–77.

of the Qur'an and the importance of the meticulous observance of the letter of the sacred law. His depiction of divine unity, on the other hand, is connected to the progress of the wayfarer on the Sufi path. Hence, instead of a list of dogmatic doctrines on divine nature, we rather find an organic, multilayered response that ties its realization to the diverse levels of wayfaring. Yet a few theological convictions consistently appear in these discourses. One of them is the vision of (and nearness to) God and Her face in the afterlife. Al-Jīlānī explains that the decisive difference between creation and the creator does not allow the vision of Her face in this world. Yet Her nearness, Her vision, and Her face will be seen: death will remove the veil from the physical eyes [*baṣar*] of the believers, and in the afterlife God will say: "This My face is for you, and My nearness is for you." Such descriptions, which are found in various discourses of al-Jīlānī, are very close to Maybudī's approach to the vision of God in the afterlife. More characteristically, al-Jīlānī rebukes his audience not to interpret [*ta'wīl*] the anthropomorphic depiction of God as sitting on the throne, but to accept *prima facie*:

> The Real qualifies Himself with attributes [*ṣifāt*] He permits to Himself; but would you interpret them, and refuse them as they are? What was good enough for your predecessors, the Companions and the Successors, is not good enough for you! *Our lord is upon the throne, as He said, without comparison [tashbīh], ineffectualism [taʿṭīl], or embodiment [tajsīm].*[116]

Organized around al-Jīlānī's name by his sons and followers, the emerging Qādirī circle had strong associations with Ḥanbalism. As a theological dimension of this connection, both groups promulgated the same anti-interpretive approach to the divine nature during the thirteenth century, when al-Jīlānī's followers firmly established themselves in Iraq and expanded to Syria, Yemen, and Egypt. Al-Jīlānī invested Ibn Qudāma with a cloak [*khirqa*] in Baghdad around fifty days before his death. Afterward, Ibn Qudāma studied under the celebrated Ḥanbalī scholar Ibn al-Jawzī. Ibn Qudāma, along with Ibn Taymiyya, would emerge among the famous

116. ʿAbd al-Qādir al-Jīlānī, *al-Fatḥ al-Rabbānī*, 95; 248–261 (for an English translation, see ʿAbd al-Qādir al-Jīlānī, *The Sublime Revelation (al-Fatḥ al-Rabbānī)*, 141, 426–449.) Cf. Maybudī, *Unveiling of the Mysteries*, Q.75:22–23, 661.

Ḥanbalīs in the Qādirī initiatic [*lubs al-khirqa*] lineage that came down to Ibn al-Qayyim al-Jawziyya's well-known disciple, Ibn Rajab (d.1392). The emergence of this Ḥanbalī-Qādirī lineage was initially surprising, for two main reasons. First, if we believe Avḥad al-Dīn Kirmānī's Persian hagiography, Ibn al-Jawzī was actually a devout disciple of Avḥad's own Sufi master, Rukn al-Dīn al-Sujāsī (d.1209). Al-Sujāsī was a pupil of Quṭb al-Dīn Abharī (d.1181) and his successor as the head of the Daraja Sufi lodge [*ribāṭ*] in Baghdad. If true, his discipleship would make Ibn al-Jawzī closer to Abhariyya. Second, and more significantly, in the last decades of the twelfth century, Baghdad witnessed a fierce conflict between al-Jīlānī and Ibn al-Jawzī. The intensity of the conflict between the two powerful Ḥanbalīs went so far that Ibn al-Jawzī penned a refutation of al-Jīlānī. Ibn al-Jawzī seems to have taken an active part in the condemnation of al-Jīlānī for harboring in his madrasa books of philosophy suspected of heresy. Eventually, the madrasa was taken away from al-Jīlānī and given to Ibn al-Jawzī.[117] The conflict survived after al-Jīlānī's death. In the last years of his life, Ibn al-Jawzī would seriously suffer under the virulent opposition of al-Jīlānī's rapidly expanding community of followers. All of this despite (or due to) the fact that they shared the Ḥanbalī anti-interpretive position on the anthropomorphism of the divine nature.

Prolific scholar that he was, Ibn al-Jawzī defended *bilā kayfa* apophaticism in a variety of his works. In line with his vision of the Ḥanbalī tradition, one should accept God's "throne," "footstool," "fingers," "vision," and so on "as they are revealed, without explanation [*tafsīr*] or interpretation [*ta'wīl*]." His non-interpretivism was strongly couched in amodalism and unknowability, instead of anthropomorphism. He argued that one should accept the transcendent discourse without reducing it into metaphor [*ḍarb*] or allegory [*mathal*], and defer the interpretation of the unknowable discourse [*irjāʿ mā ghāba*] to God Herself. While he could neatly fit into the *bilā kayfa* apophatic position, Ibn al-Jawzī makes a surprising yet clear interpretive move in terms of divine actions. Accordingly, there are three hermeneutical approaches to the sacred reports that have an anthropomorphic bent:

> The first position is to let them pass as they came without explanation or interpretation *unless it is necessary as in the case of His*

117. Laoust, "Ibn al-Djawzī"; Makdisi, "The Ḥanbalī School and Sufism," 115–126; Avḥad al-Dīn Kirmānī, *Manāqeb-e Owḥad al-Dīn Ḥāmed Ibn-e Abi al-Fakhr-e Kermānī*, 13–16.

> *saying, "Exalted be He: And your lord comes"* [Q.89:22], *which means, "When His command comes." This is the understanding of the pious ancestors*. The second method is figurative interpretation, which is a dangerous position, and the third way is speaking about them according to human understanding and perception. This method is pervasive amongst the ignorant transmitters.[118]

Ibn al-Jawzī is actually suggesting an actively interpretive response to the ascription of the anthropomorphic action of "coming" to God. Accordingly, "rational sciences" close the door of anti-interpretivism in terms of "coming." Interpretivism is necessary only in terms of God's "coming." Otherwise, he is explicitly critical toward such rationalist interpretive inquiries, as in the case of the "establishment" on a "throne."[119]

In general, the non-anthropomorphic, *bilā kayfa* anti-interpretive position on the divine nature was shared by al-Jīlānī and Ibn al-Jawzī. Hence from Ibn Qudāma—their immediate pupil—onward, Ḥanbalism aligned with the rising order of the Qādiriyya. As Ibn Qudāma's *Illuminating Creed* [*Lumʿat al-iʿtiqād*] and *Prohibition of the Study of the Books of the Partisans of Theology* [*Taḥrīm al-Naẓar fī Kutub Ahl al-Kalām*]—and later, Ibn Taymiyya's vast corpus—indicate, at least since its association with the idiosyncratic methods associated with al-Jīlānī, Ḥanbalī Sufism had diverted from transcendent anthropomorphism and more closely aligned with *bilā kayfa* apophaticism.

The Emergence of the Rifāʿiyya

Aḥmad al-Rifāʿī had very close ties with the other two eponyms, al-Jīlānī and ʿUmar al-Suhrawardī. Aḥmad was the nephew and the foremost pupil of Manṣūr al-Baṭāʾihī (d.1145), who left him the leadership [*mashyakha*] of his convent [*zāwiya*] in southern Iraq. Al-Baṭāʾihī was also the master of the stern ascetic, Ḥammād "the Syrup Merchant" al-Dabbās (d.1131), who in turn taught Sufi discipline to al-Jīlānī and Abū al-Najīb al-Suhrawardī. Abū al-Najīb studied with al-Dabbās until the latter died, and then he established his own Sufi lodge and Shāfiʿite madrasa. ʿUmar al-Suhrawardī, on the other hand, called al-Dabbās "the master of our master" in the *Gifts*

118. Ibn al-Jawzī, *Attributes of God*, 94–95 (my emphasis; with my minor modifications). Ibn al-Jawzī, *Virtues of the Imām Aḥmad ibn Ḥanbal*, 286–287.

119. Ibn al-Jawzī, *Attributes of God*, 44.

of Gnosis.[120] Al-Jīlānī studied with al-Dabbās for a few years and reportedly did not get along well with his fellow students.

The circles and followers of the three masters had also overlaps and rivalry. In his early hagiography of al-Jīlānī, the *Garden of Mysteries* [*Bahjat al-Asrār*], Nūr al-Dīn al-Shaṭṭanawfī (d.1314) depicted al-Rifāʿī as a disciple of al-Jīlānī. Accordingly, when ʿAbd al-Qādir was in Baghdad in 1180, he declared that his foot was on the neck of every saint; al-Rifāʿī, who was in far-off Umm ʿUbayda, heard this and testified loudly that he was one of his disciples. On the other hand, the biographer of Aḥmad al-Rifāʿī, ʿAbd al-Raḥmān al-Wāsiṭī (d.1343), fiercely challenges this spiritual hierarchy, accusing al-Shaṭṭanawfī of being an "indicted liar" [*kadhdhāb al-muttahim*]. While their rivalry was real, the orders were only fluid in the thirteenth century. The Wāsiṭī Sufi Aḥmad al-Fārūthī (d.1295), for example, was primarily associated with the Rifāʿiyya through his father, Ibrāhīm, and his grandfather ʿUmar, who was a direct disciple of Aḥmad al-Rifāʿī. Yet as he mentions in his *Guidance of Muslims* [*Irshād al-Muslimīn*], al-Fārūthī also associated with ʿUmar al-Suhrawardī, heard *ḥadīth* from him, and later, studied his *Gifts of Gnosis*—one of the most important Sufi manuals ever written. He received a ratification [*ijāza*] to transmit the *Gifts of Gnosis* and the Suhrawardiyya cloak [*khirqa*], both from ʿUmar al-Suhrawardī himself, without actually cutting his stronger ties with the Rifāʿiyya.[121]

In theological terms, al-Rifāʿī is very close to al-Suhrawardī and al-Jīlānī in his *bilā kayfa* apophaticism. He underlines the decisive role of the transcendent discourse itself concerning the divine nature. His brief responses to the questions on God's ipseity, attributes, names, and actions are all Qurʾanic verses that emphasize divine incomparability. The ultimate meaning of the transcendent discourse is itself unknowable, and delegated to God. In this delegation, al-Rifāʿī explicitly criticizes anthropomorphist, literal understandings of the transcendent discourse on the divine nature: "The path of the God-fearing among the pious ancestors is to absolve God from that which literalism indicates. *Delegation of its intended meaning to the exalted, transcendent Real: therein resides the soundness in religion.*"[122]

120. ʿUmar al-Suhrawardī, *ʿAwārif al-Maʿārif*, ch.44, 247.

121. Margoliouth, "al-Rifāʿī"; Trimingham, *Sufi Orders in Islam*, 41. "*Innī ṣaḥabtu al-shaykh al-ʿārif Shihāb al-dīn ʿUmar al-Suhrawardī ṣuḥbat al-tabarruk wa samaʿtu minhu.*" (Aḥmad al-Fārūthī, *Irshād al-Muslimīn*, 133.)

122. Aḥmad al-Rifāʿī, *Kitāb al-Burhān al-Muʿayyad*, 19.

Citing “our imām” al-Shāfiʿī (d.820), al-Rifāʿī claims that the seeker of gnosis is an anthropomorphist if she stops in her own reasoning, an ineffectualist if she stops in pure negation [*al-ʿadam al-ṣirf*], and a genuine monotheist if she stops in admitting her own incapacity to apprehend Her. He continues uniting all eponyms of the Sunnī and Shīʿī schools of law under the banner of *bilā kayfa* apophaticism against anthropomorphism:

> They have purified your beliefs [*ʿaqāʾid*] from interpreting the meaning of establishment applied to God as “sitting,” like that of bodies on bodies. It would require His incarnation [*ḥulūl*], and He is beyond that. Lest you attribute upness and downness to Him. And [His] “place,” “hand,” “seeing via organs,” His “descent,” and “coming” and “going” . . . Everything that came to us through the Book and *Sunna*, the literal appearance of which is like this. . . . One has to believe in all of them with their literal appearance, remove the knowledge of their intention to Him and His Prophet, and absolve the exalted creator from the modalities and the attributes of creation. This is the way for the entire community on everything with which He describes Himself in His book, on its interpretation, its recitation, and silence about it. None but God and His Prophet should interpret it. You should take such ambiguous parts in conformity with the meaning of the clear part, because it is the fundamentals of the Book. The ambiguous parts cannot contradict the fundamentals. A man asked Imām Mālik ibn Anas about “the all-merciful is established on the throne” [Q.20:5]. He said: “His establishment is not unknown. Yet it's ‘howness’ cannot be comprehended. Faith in it is obligatory, and inquiry about it is innovation.” . . . Our imām, al-Shāfiʿī said:
>
> I have faith in it without anthropomorphism.
> I confirm it without imagery [*tamthīl*].
>
> I denounce myself from apprehending it.
> I abstain wholeheartedly from delving into its pool.
>
> Imām Abū Ḥanīfa said: “whoever says ‘I don't know whether God is in the heaven or on earth’ commits blasphemy, because this statement fancies that the Real has a space. Whoever fancies that the Real has a space is an anthropomorphist.”

> Imām Aḥmad ibn Ḥanbal was asked about God's "sitting." He said: "sitting is as it is reported, not as how human beings consider."
>
> And his majesty Imām, the son of Imām, Jaʿfar al-Ṣādiq said: "whoever assumes that God is in, from, or on something associates Him with another God."[123]

Al-Rifāʿī's non-cognitive anti-interpretivism can be traced later to one of the greatest Sufis in Yemenī history, Ibn ʿAlwān (d.1266). The biographer of Aḥmad al-Rifāʿī, ʿAbd al-Raḥmān al-Wāsiṭī placed Ibn ʿAlwān in the lineage of Aḥmad al-Badawī (d.1276) and ʿIzz al-Dīn Aḥmad al-Ṣayyād (d.1271)—the latter being a successor and grandson of Aḥmad al-Rifāʿī.[124] Ibn ʿAlwān's *Greatest Unity* [*al-Tawḥīd al-Aʿẓam*] has been one of the most influential sources of Sufi literature in Yemen until the present day. The work begins with a statement of his theological creed that is both intellectual and mystical. The divine oneness is associated with negativity and unknowability. Human discourse has no way to access the divine essence, and intellect has no understanding of the transcendent discourse when it addresses God. Hence the final interpretation is left to God Herself on the issues of the divine nature, divine attributes, the knowledge of the throne, footstool, and afterlife in general. Ibn ʿAlwān's approach to the vision of God is similarly anti-interpretive. She will be seen *in the way She intended*, and *in the way She says*—it is beyond human understanding. What is known is that such an encounter will be unlike what we can imagine: talking to Her will be without a tongue, and seeing Her will be without eyes—non-corporeal.[125]

The practices and teachings organized around the figure of al-Rifāʿī rapidly expanded in southern Iraq, and spread to Egypt, Syria, Yemen and Anatolia in the thirteenth century. In al-Rifāʿī's hands, the *bilā kayfa* position became the shared heritage of all eponyms of legal schools, both Sunnī and Shīʿī. While al-Rifāʿī's harmonization is more on legal grounds, in favor of a broad depiction of the pious ancestors, ʿUmar al-Suhrawardī appealed to *bilā kayfa* in unifying Ḥanbalism and Ashʿarism. The latter

---

123. Aḥmad al-Rifāʿī, *Kitāb al-Burhān al-Muʿayyad*, 19–20.

124. Ibn ʿAlwān's connections with these names may be weak, since he had never left Yemen. See Aziz, "Aḥmad b. ʿAlwān."

125. Aziz, *Religion and Mysticism in Early Islam*, 60, 74, 83–84, 120–123.

was admittedly a more difficult task to undertake without state sponsorship which al-Rifāʿī lacked.

Suhrawardiyya and the State-Sponsored "Sunnī Bilā Kayfa" *Project*

Abū al-Najīb al-Suhrawardī was a prominent traditionist and a great Sufi master who established various Sufi lodges [*ribāṭ*]. He is known to have traveled to Isfahan a couple times, where he became a disciple of Aḥmad al-Ghazālī. Along with Aḥmad al-Ghazālī, Abū al-Najīb was also familiar with another influential Sufi master of southern Persia, Ibn Khafīf al-Shīrāzī. In his anti-interpretivist theology, Abū al-Najīb was closer to Ibn Khafīf than Aḥmad al-Ghazālī, as attested in his citations to Ibn Khafīf's creeds. Abū al-Najīb's *Sufi Etiquette for Novices* was of fundamental importance as it vividly witnesses the transmission of *bilā kayfa* apophaticism into the formation of specific authoritative Sufi methods. The *Sufi Etiquette*, in line with al-Qushayrī's and al-Kalābādhī's Sufi manuals, began with a creedal declaration that situates Sufism within the path of pious ancestors. The creed is strongly in line with the *bilā kayfa* apophaticism of its time. Abū al-Najīb begins by introducing a long list of negations, underlining not only the otherness of God, but also that of Her transcendent discourse—the only legitimate speech about Her:

> [The pious ancestors] agreed [*ijmāʿ*] that God the transcendent is One, has no partner, no opposite, no match, no similar; *He is described by that which He describes Himself, and He is named by that which* He *names Himself.* He is not a body, insofar as bodies are compositions [*muʾallaf*], and compositions need a composer. Nor is He a substance, insofar as substances can be enclosed. Yet the Lord cannot be enclosed, but He is the creator of all enclosers and enclosings. He is not an accident, because accidents don't persist temporally, but the Lord, glorified He is, persists necessarily. There is no combination, no division, no thingness for Him. Invocation does not sway on Him. Thought does not reach Him, and words don't draw near to Him. Indications don't designate Him, thoughts don't encompass Him, [and visions don't comprehend Him]. Everything is limited for Him. One cannot say "His existence," but "His being," because not all beings are existent, while every existent is. He is

> dissimilar to whatever imagination fancies or understanding apprehends. If you ask "when": His existence antecedes temporality. If you ask "how": the description of His essence is veiled. If you ask "where": His being precedes space. His making is the cause of everything, and there is no cause of His making. There is no howness to His ipseity, and no commissioning to His actions. He is veiled from the intellects, as He is also veiled from eyes. His essence is not like essences; His attributes are not like attributes. *The meaning of "knowledge" in His description is not the negation of ignorance [nafy al-jahl] from Him. Nor is the meaning of His "power" the negation of inability [nafy al-ʿajz] from Him.*[126]

The last sentences are of particular significance, as they follow Abū Ṭālib al-Makkī and al-Kalābādhī's emphasis on the irreducibility of the transcendent Qurʾanic speech to the human understanding. Accordingly, these divine attributes have a meaning not accessible to human understanding. Abū al-Najīb follows the apophatic affirmation of all anthropomorphic depictions of God, negating anthropomorphism itself, together with all human modes of thought:

> They agreed on affirming [*ithbāt*] whatever is mentioned in His Book, and confirming the reports of the Prophet (peace be upon him) about His face, hand, soul, hearing, and vision, without similitude [*tamthīl*] or ineffectualism [*taʿṭīl*]. . . . Their doctrine on the "sitting" [on the throne] is what Mālik ibn Anas said when asked about it: "God's 'sitting' on the throne is known [*maʿlūm*], but its modality is unknown. The belief in His 'establishment' is obligatory, and the inquiry about it is an innovation." Their doctrine regarding [the prophetic report on] the "descent" [of God] is also like this.
>
> They agreed that the Qurʾan is the word of God, and it is uncreated. . . . They agreed on the *permissibility of the vision of God in the paradise via eyes*. God has negated the apprehension via eyes

---

126. Abū al-Najīb al-Suhrawardī, *Ādāb al-Murīdīn*, 1–2. On the influence of Ibn Khafīf al-Shīrāzī's *Minor Creed* [*al-ʿAqīdat al-Ṣughrā*] on Abū al-Najīb's creed in the *Ādāb al-Murīdīn*, see Sobiero, "Ibn Khafīf's Kitāb al-Iqtiṣād and Abū al-Najīb al-Suhrawardī's Ādāb al-Murīdīn."

> [*al-idrāk bi-l-abṣār*], as it necessitates howness and comprehension, which is not the case for vision.[127]

Abū al-Najīb's *bilā kayfa* affirmation of the vision of God, and negation of Her apprehension, insofar as it entails howness and comprehension, is similar with Abū Ḥāmid al-Ghazālī's work. But more elusively and importantly, it almost verbatim follows al-Māturīdī's Ḥanafī creed as well as Juwaynī's Ashʿarite masterpiece the *Guidance*. Abū al-Najīb al-Suhrawardī's influential book on proper Sufi conduct, beliefs, and ethics adopts a *bilā kayfa* apophaticism that is equally Ashʿarite and Māturīdite and yet depicts itself as neither of those. Rather, it is the theological dimension of an emerging performative identity, the primary concern of which is not theology, but proper conduct [*adab*] in the lineage of the pious ancestors—Sufism.

ʿUmar al-Suhrawardī's more famous and voluminous *Gifts of Gnosis*, like his *Guidance of the Aspirants*, is exclusively directed toward proper Sufi conduct, religious practices, and their deeper meanings in relevance to the spiritual quest. His discursive theology is found in the *Signposts of Right Guidance*, a creedal work that probably circulated in al-Suhrawardī's convents together with the *Gifts of Gnosis*. Composed in Mecca, the *Signposts of Right Guidance* is a strong statement of *bilā kayfa* apophaticism in line with al-Qushayrī and Abū al-Najīb. Like in all of ʿUmar's works, the *Signposts of Right Guidance* has a strong emphasis on divine unknowability, and otherness. The uncreated, transcendent word of God enjoys full authority as the only legitimate discourse on the divine nature. The *Signposts of Right Guidance* follows Ashʿarite theology by adopting the seven essential names of God that included "all-seeing" and "all-hearing." All justifications for any affirmative discourse on God comes from the sacred reports via a *bilā kayfa* attitude. All attributes of God, both the essential ones and the attributes of actions, are inscrutable and are to be accepted amodally. They are known only through revelation; they fall far beyond the capacity of the intellect and its rational judgments to even begin to conceive their nature and significance.[128] ʿUmar al-Suhrawardī underlines this apophatic position by

127. Abū al-Najīb al-Suhrawardī, *Ādāb al-Murīdīn*, 1–3. For an English summary, see Abū al-Najīb al-Suhrawardī, *A Sufi Rule for Novices*, 28. The same argument appears later in ʿUmar al-Suhrawardī's Sufi creed, *Aʿlām al-Hudā*. See ʿUmar al-Suhrawardī, *Rasāʾil Aʿlām al-Hudā*, 77.

128. "He has the beautiful names, and the lofty attributes; we don't name Him except with what He names Himself." (ʿUmar al-Suhrawardī, *Rasāʾil Aʿlām al-Hudā*, 57.) "He hears . . .

devoting a chapter to the anthropomorphist aspect that appears in the sacred reports [*fī-l-āyāt wa-l-akhbār al-wārida fī-l-ṣifāt*]. He writes:

> The Real . . . has reported that He is "sitting" [on His throne]. . . and the Prophet has reported His "descent," among things like this, such as His "hand," "foot," "astonishment," and "hesitance." All of the revelations like these are proofs of divine unity; similitude or ineffectualism have no effect here. . . . All of the sacred reports on His attributes are divine manifestations, unveilings, subtle secrets; some understand them, and some remain ignorant about them. Don't distance yourself from Him through similitude, for He is near to you. Don't approach Him via ineffectualism, for this is vile for you. The "sitting" is certain, and it is beyond howness; this is the case for all divine attributes. He is Manifest as He unveils Himself to His believers through these sacred reports; and He is Hidden as intellects fall short from the apprehension of their profundity and their howness [*kunhuhā wa kayfiyyatuhā*]. *Nothing of what He hid is uncovered.*[129]

Hence the reports themselves, with their unknowable modalities and inaccessible meanings, should be accepted as negations of human understanding and of anthropomorphism. While this *bilā kayfa* position is strongly supported both by Ashʿarite and Māturīdite theologies, al-Suhrawardī's chosen groups of conversation are strategic, highlighting the audience in the rise of the Suhrawardiyya. Al-Suhrawardī appeals to the *bilā kayfa* apophaticism as a way to reconcile Ashʿarites and Ḥanbalites:

> O my Ḥanbalī brother! Your Ashʿarī brother didn't go to the path of interpretation [*taʾwīl*] except . . . [avoiding] similitude and resemblance. If he just affirmed His "sitting" [on the throne], he wouldn't interpret it. Hence the need [for interpretation] appeared only because of his fear of similitude. And O my Ashʿarī brother! Your Ḥanbalī brother headed to exaggeration and firmness from the fear

---

without interpretation [*taʿbīr*] by means of language, and without exegesis." (ʿUmar al-Suhrawardī, *Rasāʾil Aʿlām al-Hudā*, 60.) Ohlander, *Sufism in an Age of Transition*, 265.

129. ʿUmar al-Suhrawardī, *Rasāʾil Aʿlām al-Hudā*, 69–70.

> of negation and ineffectualism . . . So, one should make peace with the other . . . and not insist on interpretation, as the mere recognition of "sitting" will not harm.[130]

In these fascinating sections, the *Signposts of Right Guidance* depicts Ḥanbalīs and Ashʿarīs as Sunnī brothers who scrupulously avoid the fallacies of anthropomorphism, ineffectualism, and similitude. Their strategies are different, but a *bilā kayfa* position toward such controversial depictions of God, in line with Mālik ibn Anas, whom al-Suhrawardī cites, is the way of the pious ancestors that actually unites them. Al-Suhrawardī's state-sponsored efforts to unify Ḥanbalism and Ashʿarism was a desideratum at least since the time of Niẓām al-Mulk and al-Ghazālī, who witnessed the hatred between the two prominent groups that divided Sunnism. Hence his unification under the *bilā kayfa* apophaticism of an institutionalized, order-based Sufism was spiritually and politically rewarding. This broad reconciliation project of organized Sunnism was strongly supported, and to some extent administered, by the energetic ʿAbbāsid Caliph al-Nāṣir (r.1158–1225). Indeed, with its *bilā kayfa* apophaticism,

> [The *Signposts of Right Guidance*] can be situated in the ethos of al-Nāṣir's ideological program, the *daʿwa hādiya*, a program of propaganda which called for a certain rapprochement between various sectarian communities and dogmatic trends and the (re)centralization of identity and allegiance in a broader *jamāʿī-Sunnī* community under the all-embracing shadow of the caliph himself. This program was propagated early on by, among many others, Shāfiʿī *ʿulamāʾ* and Sufi masters.[131]

The earlier caliphs had a strong support for Ḥanbalī scholars of Baghdad such as the celebrated Ibn al-Jawzī. The latter seized this opportunity to undermine other groups, including Sufi pietists like Abū Ḥafṣ's uncle, Abū al-Najīb al-Suhrawardī. Al-Nāṣir, however, diverted from the pro-Ḥanbalī policies of the previous caliphs, and he aimed at broadening his authority by attaching the men's confederation [*futuwwa*] organizations to himself

130. Ibid., 70. For an alternative translation, see ʿUmar al-Suhrawardī in Ohlander, *Sufism in an Age of Transition*, 267.

131. Ohlander, *Sufism in an Age of Transition*, 258. Cf. Abū Ḥāmid al-Ghāzalī in Jackson, *On the Boundaries of Theological Tolerance in Islam*, 93.

and bringing the *ʿulamāʾ* under his influence. ʿUmar al-Suhrawardī's parallel Sufi project incorporated the Ḥanbalīs, and non-cognitive apophatic theology was a common theological ground. Establishing his own rules of conduct, litanies, and wider theology, al-Suhrawardī was in negotiation with already well-established masters, particularly ʿAbd al-Qādir al-Jīlānī, whose legacy was appropriated mostly by Shāfiʿī Sufis and spread outside Iraq. Al-Suhrawardī's alliance with Ḥanbalism, supported by a systematic defense of Ashʿarism against it, provided him with a vast Sunnī ground to develop his method with its insistence on the normative authority of the pious ancestors and their non-cognitive apophaticism.[132]

Kubrawī Interpretivism

Najm al-Dīn Kubrā was born in Khiwa, the small Shāfiʿite enclave in an otherwise Ḥanafī and Muʿtazilī dominated area of Khuwarazm. Through his masters Bābā Faraj (d.1172), Ismāʿīl Qaṣrī (d.1193) and ʿAmmār al-Bidlīsī, Kubrā's spiritual as well as theological lineage runs back to Abū al-Najīb al-Suhrawardī. Yet, the formal Sunnī-Sufi *bilā kayfa* apophaticism of the master Abū al-Najīb had already changed by the time of his immediate students. The official, creedal non-cognitivism of Abū al-Najīb's normative *Sufi Etiquette for Novices* already ceded its place to non-anthropomorphic, mystical interpretivism in ʿAmmār al-Bidlīsī's writings. In both his *Delight of the People* [*Bahjat al-Ṭāʾifa*] and the *Fasting of the Heart* [*Ṣawm al-Qalb*], al-Bidlīsī typically forbade the vision of God via human organs except for the prophets. Our "vision" of God happens as clairvoyance, and our "conversation" with Her happens through inner voice rather than actual talking. God's "throne," following earlier Sufis of Baghdad, is actually a reference to the heart.[133] Al-Bidlīsī consistently insisted on the same non-anthropomorphic, interpretive approach in his writings: the heart is the real throne of divine

---

132. See Mayer, "Theology and Sufism," 272; Ohlander, *Sufism in an Age of Transition*, 32–33.

133. The attribute of the heart in the station of witnessing [*maqām al-mushāhada*] corresponds to the throne of manifestations. For, manifestation is in terms of their hearts for the friends of God, and in terms of their eyes for the prophets. In the station of conversation [*maqām al-muḥaddathiyya*], the attribute of the heart corresponds to the Preserved Tablet [*lawḥ al-mahfūẓ*]. For, conversation with God is in the heart, and with the heart. As a proof of its being the throne of manifestations, it is said, "My heart saw my Lord." And as a proof of its being the throne of manifestations, it is said: "My heart spoke to me about my Lord." (Al-Bidlīsī, "Bahjat al-Ṭāʾifa," 137–138.)

For God's countenance, see ibid., 116; al-Bidlīsī, "Ṣawm al-Qalb," Q.30:38, 44. Also see al-Bidlīsī, "Bahjat al-Ṭāʾifa," 72–73, 79, 112; al-Bidlīsī, "Ṣawm al-Qalb," 14, 39, 26–27.

manifestations. The official, creedal non-interpretive position of Abū al-Najīb, who was one of his teachers, and ʿUmar al-Suhrawardī is left behind in favor of the less formally defined, though sustained, interpretive Sufi heritage in al-Bidlīsī's works. The corpus of his Persian student, Najm al-Dīn Kubrā, follows this hermeneutics.

The voluminous Qurʾanic exegesis that has various titles, one of which is the *Expositions* [*Taʾwīlāt*] is a collective, "Kubrawī" project in two ways. First, the master Najm al-Dīn Kubrā initiated it, and was able to write up to Q.51:17-18 before he passed away. It was ʿAlāʾ al-Dawla Simnānī, an energetic Sufi in Kubrā's lineage, who completed the work. Second, a number of manuscripts credit Kubrā's prominent pupil Najm al-Dīn Dāya Rāzī with the work, but we do not clearly know the extent of his involvement as an author or editor in the exegesis of the first fifty-one chapters. At least in its theological approach to the divine essence, the *Expositions* is harmonious with Dāya Rāzī's influential Sufi manual the *Path of God's Bondsmen* [*Mirṣād al-ʿIbād*]. The *Expositions* ingeniously uses Q.2:255, the verse mentioning the "footstool," as an occasion to discuss Q.20:5, the verse on God's "throne" and the more general hermeneutical principle of its author in approaching such anthropomorphic depictions of God. First, Kubrā underlines that these terms of the transcendent discourse indicate the highest levels of perfection—hence one cannot ignore the literal dimension of the Qurʾan and simply interpret them:

> [Q.2:255] "*His footstool comprises the heavens and earth.*" This (verse) informs us of the beauty [*jamāl*] of His secrets via His creation—that is, it means the darkening [*sīd*] of His perfection [*kamāl*] in order to encompass the heavens, earth, and fire. This is, as His name is supreme, like His creation of circles in a desert in relation to His throne. Look at the perfection of the beauty of His throne! As for the meaning of His "footstool," you should know that religion and faith necessitate not interpreting anything of the essences [*al-aʿyān*] according to their meanings without their forms.[134]

Kubrā here does not invalidate interpretive or discursive inquiries. He rather argues that the non-anthropomorphic interpretations of such

134. Najm al-Dīn Kubrā and Simnānī, *al-Taʾwīlāt al-Najmiyya*, 1:330. Also see Elias, *Throne Carrier of God*, 204–205; Sands, *Sufi Commentaries on the Qurʾan in Classical Islam*, 77.

verses add another, a deeper layer. Hence, one should not assume that the interpretation violates the literal form, or the surface of these verses. Rather than himself adopting *bilā kayfa*, anti-interpretive, non-cognitive positions, Kubrā is actually addressing the concerns of those who adopt it. He stresses that non-anthropomorphic, deeper interpretations do not violate the sacred form; rather, they affirm and celebrate it:

> The Prophet, his companions, and the scholars among the pious ancestors interpreted them only through the realization apportioned to them by God, via unveiling of truths, hidden meanings, secrets, scriptural indications, and realization of interpretation. If a special meaning, indication, and realization is unveiled, as much as it can be, without annulling the forms of essences (as in the cases of paradise and hell, the weighing, the narrow path, the houris, palaces, the flowing rivers and other things in the paradise), it may seem to annul its form, but it rather confirms the essence as it was revealed, and understands their truths and meanings. God has not created anything in this world of forms that can rival something in the world of meanings; and He has not created anything in the world of meanings (which is the afterlife) that does not have a reality in the world of truth (which is the hidden of the hidden).[135]

Kubrā highlights that these verses have two layers of truth, one literal and non-interpretive, the other anti-anthropomorphic and interpretive. From this deeper interpretive approach, God's "throne" and "footstool," unsurprisingly, indicate the center of the micro-cosmos, in line with al-Qushayrī, Maybudī, his own master al-Bidlīsī, and later, Najm al-Dīn Dāya Rāzī, ʿIzz al-Dīn Kāshānī, and other prominent Sufis:

> God has not created anything in this or the next world that does not have an allegory or an example in the human world. So, know this, and understand that the allegory of the "throne" in the human world is the heart: it is the place of sitting of the spirit in vicegerency for God. And the allegory of the "footstool" is the innermost of the human. . . . "*The all-merciful, established on the throne.*" [Q.20:5] . . . The wonder of all wonders is the capacity of the throne

135. Najm al-Dīn Kubrā and Simnānī, *al-Taʾwīlāt al-Najmiyya*, 1:330.

for the establishment of the all-mercifulness. So it is said that it is like His creation of circles between the heavens and the earth, in correspondence with the capacity of the heart of the faithful.[136]

Kubrā's double-layered interpretive approach to anthropomorphic depictions of God was well-received among his pupils from early on. The exchange of letters between two Persian Kubrawīs, Majd al-Dīn Baghdādī and Sharaf al-Dīn Balkhī, displays the prominence of interpretive approaches, particularly with relevance to Sufi wayfaring. The exchange of letters has a clear emphasis on divine transcendence and unknowability. No wayfarer, no matter how long they pursue their spiritual travel, can actually attain the gnosis of the path to the real [*ṭarīq al-ḥaqq*]; it exclusively belongs to the lord Herself [*istiḥqāq-e rubūbiyyat ast*]. Once the wayfarer negates and erases [*nafy va maḥv*] all of their attributes, the sultan of truth [*sulṭān-e ḥaqīqat*] permeates the already emptied heart of the wayfarer; "*He establishes Himself on the throne of the heart*" [*istivā-ye ū bar ʿarsh-e dal*].[137]

The Sufi poet of Nishapur, Farīd al-Dīn ʿAṭṭār, adopts an interpretive approach to the divine throne that is strikingly similar to that of Kubrā. His mystical allegorical feast, the *Conference of the Birds*, follows a double-layered hermeneutics and theology. In the opening of the work, where ʿAṭṭār describes the apophatic nature of God, he introduces Her "throne" and "footstool" as realms where no interpretation operates. Insofar as they transcend the levels of human apprehension, one should not even ask their meaning—discourse is canceled in the very beginning due to human limits and the divine transcendence:

> Reason, soul, religion, heart. . . We have lost all,
> Still we are yet to understand a minimum of His perfection!
>
> Shut your lips: don't ask of the "throne," or of the "footstool,"
> Even just for a letter—don't ask!
>
> Your reason will burn from a minimum of it, thus:
> Both of your lips should be seamlessly detached from asking of it.
>
> Nobody genuinely knows the profundity of a minimum of it,

136. Ibid., 1:331.

137. Meier, *Essays on Islamic Piety and Mysticism*, 278.

How long will you talk, how long will you ask? Just stop![138]

Yet, as we proceed, ʿAṭṭār explains the cosmological role of the throne and footstool. Accordingly, God first creates the prophetic light, or the Muḥammadan Reality. Then it is followed by the levels of heavenly realms, such as the "throne," "footstool," "tablet" [*lavḥ*], and "pen." The throne and the footstool are actually created from the mirror image of the prophetic reality [*ʿaks-e ẕātash*]. This hierarchical depiction of cosmology corresponds to the levels of wayfaring. Eventually, like all cosmological levels, the divine throne is contained in the heart of the wayfarer. Finding God in Her proper house—that is, the heart—also means finding Her throne. The heart is the mirror of the divine beloved, and everything it contains is a manifestation, or shadow, of the divine.[139]

Kubrā's prominent pupil Dāya Rāzī's *Path of God's Bondsmen* is also fundamentally interpretive. Human creation in the form [*ṣūrat*] of God, a bone of contention around anthropomorphism during the Inquisition, is interpreted here in light of a wider cosmology of manifestation, hence, non-anthropomorphically. In the same vein, the "double fingers" indicate God's *jalāl* and *jamāl*: divine majesty and beauty. His interpretations of "throne" and "footstool" are similarly cosmological, corresponding to the higher levels of creation—that is, immutable spiritual verities. "Throne" is the all-encompassing center of the cosmos, and the equivalent of the universal soul [*nafs-e kulliyya*]. The phrases emphasizing the all-encompassing role of the heart, are verbatim from the *Expositions*: "The relationship of the heart to the body is like that of God's throne to the world." It is here where the excessive, life-bequeathing, existence-giving grace first emerges, and permeates creation. In this deeper metaphorical sense, the heart is not only Her throne but also Her never-perishing face.[140]

With prominent Sufis like Saʿd al-Dīn Ḥammūya (or Ḥamuwayh), Shams al-Dīn Kīshī (d.1295), and ʿAlāʾ al-Dawla Simnānī, early Sufis in the Kubrawī network perpetuate the divergence from *bilā kayfa* apophaticism. Their interpretive positions were rich. In his Arabic commentary on a biblical theme and prophetic report, Kīshī developed a highly philosophical

138. ʿAṭṭār, *Manṭiq al-Ṭayr*, verses 154–158.

139. Ibid., verses 283–284, 295–296, 1124–1129.

140. Dāya Rāzī, *Path of God's Bondsmen*, 27, 70, 76, 80, 84, 85, 106, 111–112, 201–202, 219.

interpretation of the anthropomorphic depictions of God.[141] Simnānī extends the two-layered interpretive schema of Maybudī, Kubrā, and others to four on the basis of a noncanonical prophetic tradition. Each level of meaning appeals to a different source of interpretation and corresponds to a different level of existence: the human realm [*nāsūt*], the kingdom [*malakūt*], the omnipotence [*jabarūt*], and the divinity [*lāhūt*]. This cosmology, of course, is related to the four levels of the human soul as well. It is not the first, "literal," traditionist level of reading, but the last, highest rank of "witnessing," in the highest realm of divinity, where interpretation and discourse are canceled. Having interpretively ascended to this level, the seeker attains an apophatic apotheosis where her presence, agency, body, intellect, and discourse are perfected in their very negation. In other words, theological discourse cancels itself at the very end of wayfaring, in correspondence with a Sufi cosmology and under the regulation of Sufi discipline.[142] Simnānī more directly appeals to the divine "throne" and "hands" when he sets the hermeneutical principles of his continuation of the *Explications*, sometimes called the *Wellhead of Life* [*ʿAyn al-Ḥayāt*]. Accordingly, "throne" and "footstool" are cosmological as well as spiritual levels that the seeker attains in their transformative, interpretive wayfaring. The two "hands" of God with which She created human beings are Her grace and disfavor [*yadayy al-luṭf wa-l-qahr*]. His approach to the vision of the "face" of God in this world, similarly, is non-physical and related to the purification of one's own mirror of the heart, to Her identity [*huwiyya*], or to the endlessness of the manifestations of Her majesty and beauty.[143]

Simnānī's four levels of existence—the human realm, the kingdom, the omnipotence, and the divinity—were actually developed earlier by another Khurasanian Sufi master and a disciple of Kubrā, Saʿd al-Dīn Ḥammūya. Ḥammūya wrote a Persian hermeneutical feast, titled the *Lamp of Sufism* [*al-Miṣbāḥ fī al-Taṣavvuf*]. The work was devoted to the mystical and allegorical interpretations [*taʾwīl*] of Qurʾanic concepts, phrases, or even letters in a wider mystical, philosophical lens. Here Ḥammūya devoted a section

141. Shams al-Dīn Kīshī, *Majmūʿa-yi āsār*, 299–300.

142. Elias, *Throne Carrier of God*, 107–109; Sands, *Sufi Commentaries on the Qurʾan in Classical Islam*, 11–12, 62; Elias, *Sufi Thought and Practice in the Teachings of ʿAlāʾ ad-Dawla as-Simnānī*, 211.

143. Elias, *Throne Carrier of God*, 81, 106; Elias, *Sufi Thought and Practice in the Teachings of ʿAlāʾ ad-Dawla as-Simnānī*, 172; Najm al-Dīn Kubrā and Simnānī, *al-Taʾwīlāt al-Najmiyya*, 6:3, 6:68.

titled "the Interpretation of the 'Throne' [*ta'vīl-e 'arsh*]," where the interpretation was connected to cosmology as well as the levels of the wayfarer.[144] Ḥammūya's pupil [*tilmīẕ*] in the Sufi hospice [*khānaqāh*] in Khurasan, ʿAzīz Nasafī's depiction of the divine throne and footstool is typical: They correspond to the two highest levels of the nine heavenly bodies. They have a cosmic, physical reality, but they also correspond to the highest spiritual stations that the most elite wayfarers and prophets can achieve. He also appeals to the homology of creation and human nature as macro- and micro-cosmos. Yet, instead of the heart, it is now the intellect acclaimed in relation to the throne: "Intelligence is God's deputy in the microcosm, and the human spirit is the throne of God's deputy, the animal spirit is the footstool of God's deputy."[145] ʿAzīz Nasafī's move from the heart to intellect is the same as that of Shams al-Dīn Kīshī, who was the Kubrawī Sufi master of the astronomer and philosopher Quṭb al-Dīn Shīrāzī.

Simnānī's ideas became influential in Iran, Central Asia, and India, largely through the endeavors of his prolific nephew Sayyid ʿAlī Hamadānī (d.1385), who had been instructed by two of Simnānī's main disciples, Maḥmūd Mazdaqānī (d.1365) and ʿAlī Dūstī (d.1336). The prominent Persian astronomer and Qurʾan commentator Niẓām al-Dīn al-Nīsābūrī (d.1329) also follows Simnānī in interpreting the beatific vision in this world. To counter the Qurʾanic verse, "eyes do not apprehend Him" [Q.103:6], he appeals to the argument that the negation of the apprehension via eyes [*al-idrāk bi-l-abṣār*] is different than the vision of God. As we saw, this argument was present in the major works of al-Māturīdī, al-Juwaynī, Abū al-Najīb al-Suhrawardī, and ʿUmar al-Suhrawardī. Yet al-Nīsābūrī benefited much more extensively from the Kubrawī *Expositions* than is appreciated in contemporary scholarship. Not only in his interpretations of specific verses, or the cosmology that parallels human micro-cosmos and the spiritual path, but also in his very hermeneutical principles, al-Nīsābūrī follows Najm al-Dīn Kubrā. Indeed, the above quoted passages of Kubrā on not interpreting the transcendent discourse appear verbatim in al-Nīsābūrī's commentary as well. Like Kubrā, he even appeals to the key term "unentified essences" [*al-aʿyān*] in distinguishing the inviolable interior meaning from its exterior. Al-Nīsābūrī's indebtedness to the Kubrawī interpretive theology is striking, considering his faith

144. Saʿd al-Dīn Ḥammūya, *al-Miṣbāḥ fī al-Taṣavvuf*, 122–123.

145. ʿAzīz Nasafī, *Persian Metaphysics and Mysticism*, 77–79, 134, 136, 141, 158, 180, 181.

in scientific epistemology in general, and in astronomical observations in particular.[146] The Kubrawī non-anthropomorphic interpretive tradition on the divine nature became influential beyond Sufism, particularly in Central Asia and Persia by the end of the century.

Bilā Kayfa *Mysticism in Andalusia: The Background*

Imām Mālik's by-the-book approach, both in its *bilā kayfa* apophatic and transcendent anthropomorphist readings, was dominant in the West until the mid-twelfth century. The first generation of Mālikī jurists did write refutations to Khārijī, Ismāʿīlī, and Muʿtazilī doctrines from the ninth century onward, but they carefully abstained from, or simply disliked, theological speculation and had a strong tradition of asceticism. Ashʿarism initially took root in cultural metropolises like Qayrawan with prominent scholars such as Ibn Abī Zayd, Abū al-Ṭayyib al-Asfāqisī (fl.10th-11th CE), Abū al-Ḥasan al-Qābisī (d.1013), al-Qalānisī, and al-Bāqillānī. This was predominantly an anti-interpretive environment, with a rivalrous mix of early Ashʿarism and Mālikism, both of which harbored not only transcendent anthropomorphism but also *bilā kayfa* apophaticism on the divine nature.

The popularization of Ashʿarism in Andalusia began to take place only in the late eleventh century, during the Almoravid period. This was a key development because Ashʿarites had begun to adopt more discursive and interpretive approaches to the divine essence at the beginning of the century. Instead of the anti-interpretive Ashʿarites, such as al-Bāqillānī or al-Qalānisī, it was the prominent Ashʿarites with a strong appeal to reasoning in theology who became influential. Among Andalusian Ashʿarites, Abū al-Ḥajjāj al-Kalbī al-Ḍarīr's (d.1126) *Instruction and Guidance Concerning the Science of Creed* [*al-Tanbīh wa-l-Irshād fī ʿIlm al-Iʿtiqād*], al-Salālijī's (d.1178)

146. Elias, "Sufism," 595–613; Sands, *Sufi Commentaries on the Qur'an in Classical Islam*, 11; al-Māturīdī, *Kitāb al-Tawḥīd*, 145; al-Juwaynī, *Kitāb al-Irshād*, 181–183; Abū al-Najīb al-Suhrawardī, *Ādāb al-Murīdīn*, 1–3; ʿUmar al-Suhrawardī, *Rasāʾil Aʿlām al-Hudā*, 77; Morrison, *The Intellectual Development of Niẓām al-Dīn al-Nisābūrī*, 158–171, 256.

> Know that the requirement of religion is that the Muslim should not interpret [*yuʾawwilu*] anything in the Qurʾan or the *ḥadīth* according to meanings which would invalidate the essentials which the Prophet and the pious first generations commented on, like the garden, the fire, the path, the balance, the palaces, the rivers, the trees, etc. Instead, he must affirm these essentials just as they have been set forth. (Niẓām al-Dīn al-Nisābūrī in Sands, *Sufi Commentaries on the Qurʾan in Classical Islam*, 42.)

Demonstrations [*Burhāniyya*], and Muḥammad Ibn Tūmart's (d.1130) *Guides* [*al-Murshidāt*] were all inspired in one form or another by Imām al-Ḥaramayn al-Juwaynī's seminal *Book of Guidance* [*Kitāb al-Irshād*]. The *Book of Guidance*, with its interpretive theology, dominated Andalusia, while the Mālikī, anti-interpretive al-Bāqillānī had more influence in North Africa. Still, Juwaynī's *Book of Guidance* elicited an astonishing number of commentaries in the following three centuries in the Maghrib. He would be so influential in Andalusia that Ibn Rushd's *Exposition of the Methods of Proof* would mention an interpretive theological path [*ṭarīqa*] of al-Juwaynī along with the path of the Ashʿarites in general.[147]

Yet interpretive theologies on the divine nature did not emerge only with rationalist versions of Ashʿarism in Andalusia. Members of the juridico-theological trend of mysticism in Madrid already resorted to allegorical interpretation [*ta'wīl*] to respond to the corporeal depictions of God. For example, Abū ʿUmar al-Ṭalamankī (d.1037), an ascetic mystic, polemicist theologian, traditionist, and Shāfiʿī lawyer, argued that the verse "He is *with* you wherever you are" had to be interpreted as "God is with you *by His knowledge*."[148] There were other interpretive mystics: al-Ṭalamankī himself was deeply critical toward another indigenous mystical movement associated with Ibn Masarra that described interpretation as the cornerstone of their teachings.[149] This was a distinctly Andalusian ascetic mystical tradition that was rather irreducible to "Sufism." The applicability of "Sufism" to this Masarran interpretivism has been questioned, while recent studies propose the alternative "Contemplators" [Muʿtabirūn]—literally, "those who cross over"—as a more representative and authentic self-designation of this mystical tradition.[150] The term "crossing over," from the time of Ibn Masarra onward, indicates a general ontological disposition in Andalusian mysticism to go beyond the visible phenomena via constant interpretation. As traversing the visible via interpretation, the Contemplators undertook an attitude toward scripture and the natural world that can be called "hermeneutical" in its etymological sense. Only with the twelfth century, the

147. Ibn Rushd, *al-Kashf ʿan Manāhij al-Adilla*, 111–116.

148. See Casewit, *The Forgotten Mystic*, 77 (my emphasis).

149. Ibn Masarra interpreted the "throne" as the prime matter from which the universe is created. See Abrahamov, *Ibn al-ʿArabī and the Sufis*, 101.

150. See Casewit, *The Mystics of al-Andalus*; Böwering and Casewit in Ibn Barrajān, *A Qur'an Commentary*, 7–15.

indigenous movement of the Contemplators, under diverse influences, began acquiring distinctly Sufi institutional forms, especially with the generation of mystics of the failed *murīdūn* revolt: Ibn Barrajān, Ibn al-ʿArīf, and Ibn Qasī (d.1151). The twelfth century was a watershed in Andalusia for the incorporation of mysticism, law, traditionism, asceticism, and various (including Ismāʿīlī) theological traditions within the rising framework of Sufism.

In line with this interpretive heritage, the noted Andalusian traditionist scholar of Almeria and a late convert to mysticism, Ibn al-ʿArīf, had an approach to the depictions of the divine essence and divine attributes that was strongly interpretive. Discussions on anthropomorphism, or related themes like "throne," "fingers," or "footstool," do not directly appear in Ibn al-ʿArīf's *Splendors of Sessions* [*Maḥāsin al-Majālis*], *Key to Happiness* [*Miftāḥ al-Saʿāda*], or *Letters*. The integration of mysticism with a larger traditionist, but also interpretive, discursive Sunnism can be observed in the *Splendors of Sessions*. Here Ibn al-ʿArīf begins by introducing creation [*mā siwāʾ*]—that is, everything other than God—as Her veil, suggesting that God's vision in this world is not possible. The elect gnostic can "see" [*rāʾā*] and "witness" [*mushāhada*] Her in this world. Yet this vision happens non-physically, through the "eye of the heart" [*ʿayn al-qalb*], and, more importantly, within the performative context of paradoxes instead of a *bilā kayfa* unknowability. The vision of God [*naẓar ilā Allāh*] is also possible in the afterlife, as one of the wonders [*karāmāt*] that God bequeaths to the gnostics. This encounter [*liqāʾ*] of God will be an amodal [*bilā kayfa*] one.[151] Transcendent anthropomorphism emerges neither in this world nor in the next one; it is a venue that Ibn al-ʿArīf never intended.

In the omission of controversial topics in terms of anthropomorphic depictions of God, Ibn al-ʿArīf was not an isolated case of his time. The founding figure of the Almohadī movement, Muḥammad Ibn Tūmart, deliberately avoided entering into debates on anthropomorphism in his creedal works the *Guides*, and the *Most Precious One Can Ask For* [*Aʿazz Mā Yuṭlab*]. The absence of the terms "throne," "footstool," "fingers," "hands," and so forth is striking in these theological works. Like rationalist Ashʿarites, Ibn Tūmart saw reason as our main source on the nature of God, even if he appealed to prophetic traditions much more often in his writings. He argued that knowledge of God [*ʿilm billāh*, or *maʿrifat al-maʿbūd*]

151. Ibn al-ʿArīf, *Maḥāsin al-Majālis*, 76–103.

is incumbent on everybody, because this is a purely logical necessity that anybody, Muslim or non-Muslim, can attain. We can know God through natural rational means, and through Her actions. Ibn Tūmart criticized the Mālikī traditionist emphasis on following earlier authorities [*taqlīd*] and underlined the key role of reasoning in theological matters.[152] His depictions of God, from this perspective, were—not surprisingly—negative ones: we find pages of negations of Her nature in the *Most Precious One* as well as in the *Guides*. The transcendent discourse on the names of God is venerated without asking how, but this is a strongly negativist rationalist context, wherein no human category applies to God; anthropomorphism and comparability are utterly negated. In his discussions on the vision of God, Ibn Tūmart underlines that it does not entail Her apprehension [*idrāk*], which is impossible. He situates the beatific vision in a context of rationalist negation of modalities:

> He is seen without comparison [*lā tashbīh*], without qualification [*lā takyīf*]; eyes do not apprehend Him in the sense of exhausting [*nihāya*], encompassing [*iḥāṭa*], connection [*ittiṣāl*], separation [*infiṣāl*], insofar as His description with the definitions of creation. . . . Visions do not apprehend Him, but He apprehends the visions.[153]

In his clear negativism, Ibn Tūmart was strongly resisting against transcendent anthropomorphism. His negativist approach to the divine nature that removes all human categories, and his conception of the beatific vision, are rooted in rationalist Ashʿarism, influenced by Ibn Sīnā's ontology. This discursive removal of the applicability of human terms from the divine nature is supported by abundant references to prophetic traditions. In the *Guides*, he cites a prophetic report in support of *bilā kayfa* apophaticism on the divine nature and rejecting anthropomorphism. Here Ibn Tūmart adopts a non-interpretive position, yet in general he depicts the rules of interpretation of ambiguities in the Qurʾan and the prophetic reports as one of the five main principles of religious scholarship [*fiqh al-sunna*]. His exegesis gestures toward Q.2:255 in full, but drops the part

152. Muḥammad Ibn Tūmart, *Aʿazz mā Yuṭlab*, 210–214; Muḥammad Ibn Tūmart, *Sharḥ Murshida*, 9–10; Cornell, "Understanding Is the Mother of Ability," 96.

153. Muḥammad Ibn Tūmart, *Aʿazz mā Yuṭlab*, 220–221; Muḥammad Ibn Tūmart, *Sharḥ Murshida*, 15–16. Cf. al-Māturīdī, *Kitāb al-Tawḥīd*, 151.

on the footstool, carefully avoiding direct references to topics related to anthropomorphism.[154] While his interpretive, rationalist tendencies are obvious, Ibn Tūmart deliberately avoided entering into debates that would certainly bring him into conflict with the popular non-interpretive positions toward these verses.

Ibn al-ʿArīf's venerated master, Ibn Barrajān also interpretively eliminated the literal applicability of divine names, such as "the Firm" [al-Matīn], as they have corporeal implications.[155] His two Qurʾan commentaries provide us with highly personal interpretations on select verses, evidently in the interpretive lineage of the Contemplators. This line, in contrast to the philosophical and Sufi lines of indicative [*ishārī*] interpretation, adopted a contemplative [*iʿtibārī*]—literally, "hermeneutical"—approach wherein cosmology is directly implicated in the interpretive encounter. The discovery of the inner meanings of the Qurʾan went hand in hand with an ever-ascending apprehension of the natural order. The divine throne, within this context, was the all-encompassing cosmological level that mediates the divine word. This interpretive, visionary reality, however, did not indicate a physical one. Instead, each level of heaven has its own "footstool" and "throne."[156] A similarly hierarchical spiritual anthropology corresponded to different levels of understanding the scripture, and ascending through contemplation. At the highest level attainable by non-prophets, such as saints, one's lowly attributes [*ṣifāt dunyā*] are transformed into lofty divine attributes [*ṣifāt ʿulyā*], where one hears the direct word of God [*mukhāṭaba wa-l-taklīm*], and receives direct communication [*muḥādatha*] and discourse [*taklīm*] with Her. Yet, as in the case of Her vision happening via insight [*baṣīra*], none of these terms had a corporeal meaning for Ibn Barrajān. With his interpretive approach, Ibn Barrajān distanced himself from anthropomorphism and *bilā kayfa* apophaticism, approaching the position of later Ashʿarites in interpretively removing

154. Muḥammad Ibn Tūmart, *Aʿazz mā Yuṭlab*, 224; Muḥammad Ibn Tūmart, *Sharḥ Murshida*, 20; Griffel, "Ibn Tūmart's Rational Proof for God's Existence and Unity," 806; Cornell, "Understanding Is the Mother of Ability," 94.

155. See Ibn al-ʿArīf and ʿAtīq ibn ʿĪsā, *Miftāḥ al-Saʿāda*, 108–109; Ibn Barrajān, *A Qurʾan Commentary*, 18–19, 160.

156. Ibn Barrajān, *A Qurʾan Commentary*, 148–149 (Arabic text). As the prominent Khalwatī scholar of the seventeenth century would put it in Ottoman Turkish, "Every existent in creation is each a throne and a footstool, seven-layered earth, and seven-layered heaven" [*her ne kadar mevcudat var ise her birisi başka başka birer arş ve kürs ve yedi kat yer ve yedi kat göktür*]. (Niyāzī Mıṣrī, *Risāle-yi Tevḥīd*, MS 06 Mil Yz A 853/3, f.13a.)

corporeal implications. He explicitly criticized the *bilā kayfa* approach of the earlier Ashʿarism and appealed to interpretivist Ashʿarism in support of his constant hermeneutical quest for the hidden meaning.[157]

Sufism and Bilā Kayfa *in the Thirteenth-Century Muslim West*

The first openly and consciously "Sufi" movement of the West emerged only with the circle of Abū Madyan and his directing-master [*shaykh al-tarbiya*], Abū Yaʾza (d.1177). Mysticism in Andalusia on the eve of the rise of Sufism adopted interpretive approaches toward the divine nature, instead of *bilā kayfa* apophaticism. The Contemplators such as Ibn al-ʿArīf and Ibn Barrajān in Ibn Masarra's line, or other ascetics like al-Ṭalamankī, increasingly chose philosophical, rationalist Ashʿarite, or mystical hermeneutical responses instead of the prominent non-interpretive creeds of Mālikī scholars such as Ibn Abī Zayd or al-Bāqillānī. These mystics, on the other hand, integrated *ḥadīth, uṣūl al-fiqh,* and mysticism with a systematic focus on the teachings and practices of the *Sunna* and the pious predecessors, opening religious dogmatics in the Iberian Peninsula to a more universal, Sunnī ecumenism.[158] Formal Sufism in the West emerged with a similar claim for Sunnism, projecting itself back onto the earlier mystical tradition. Yet unlike earlier mysticism, it depicted itself initially as non-interpretive, closely following *bilā kayfa* apophaticism on the divine essence. Hence the rise of institutional Sufism in both the East and the West was dramatically similar: both communities were inheritors of interpretive, discursive mysticisms yet initially associated themselves with anti-interpretive, non-cognitive theologies.

When al-Ghazālī's *Revivification* was put to the torch in 1109 and 1143, Ashʿarism, and some direct disciples of al-Ghazālī, were already settled in Andalusia. Yet al-Ghazālī's influence on Ibn Barrajān and Ibn al-ʿArīf were rather negligible. The *bilā kayfa* apophaticism that al-Ghazālī widely preached in his corpus did not find a footing in the writings of these later mystics. It began to make its mark with the rise of Sufism, once the *Revivification* controversy was settled, and the earliest Sufi hagiographies of

157. Casewit, *The Mystics of al-Andalus*, 145–146; Casewit, *The Forgotten Mystic*, 4, 209, 247–248.

158. Casewit, *The Mystics of al-Andalus*, 43.

the West began emerging. The Mālikī legist and mystic ʿAlī ibn Ḥirzihim (d.1162) had a Sufi convent [*zāwiya*] in Fez, where the *Revivification* was among the required readings.[159] Later, Abū Madyan himself made the work the obligatory source for his own disciples. He also quoted the *Epistle* of al-Qushayrī in his discourses; al-Tamīmī (d.ca.1206), his disciple in Fez, asked him to read the *Epistle* under his supervision. As both of these monumental works strongly expounded *bilā kayfa* apophaticism as the normative Sufi teaching, it would be hardly surprising to find Abū Madyan following this path. Indeed, the short but powerful *Blessed Creed* [*al-ʿAqīda al-Mubāraka*] attributed to him is a perfect example of *bilā kayfa* apophaticism of the divine essence. It begins with negations of modalities, binaries, comparability, and knowability from God. Then it affirms the typical Ashʿarite attributes without any further explanation. God spoke to Moses amodally; Her "hand" has no arm; Her "face" has no defect; Her "hearing" and "vision" are non-physical—all are beyond human understanding, to be accepted non-cognitively. She is "established" on the "throne," neither in the sense of fixedness nor physical sitting.[160] We know that these terms of the transcendent discourse are not physical, or within the limits of human understanding, and we do not have discursive access to their meaning.

Fitting perfectly into al-Ghazālī and al-Qushayrī's *bilā kayfa* apophaticism, the *Blessed Creed* was actually penned by a much later Sufi of Fez, Abū Madyan ibn Muḥammad (d.1768). On the other hand, the meeting or the fraternal bond of Abū Madyan with two great Sufis, Aḥmad al-Rifāʿī and ʿAbd al-Qādir al-Jīlānī, began to circulate already in the thirteenth century. Both al-Rifāʿī and al-Jīlānī had a clear anti-interpretive approach similar to that of the *Blessed Creed*, and Abū Madyan began to be depicted in the same *bilā kayfa* orientation in the next century. It is difficult to ascertain that Abū Madyan actually fitted into *bilā kayfa* apophaticism, but we may propose a strong parallel, if not overlap, with al-Qushayrī, Abū Ḥāmid al-Ghazālī, al-Rifāʿī, and al-Jīlānī in his theological outlook.

Nonetheless, such an anti-interpretivism was in contrast with the Andalusian mystical strands as well as the Almohadī interpretivist

---

159. ʿAlī Ibn Ḥirzihim was the nephew of Ṣāliḥ ibn Ḥirzihim (d.af.1111) and a student of the great jurist Abū Bakr Ibn al-ʿArabī (d.1148), both of whom were pupils of Abū Ḥāmid al-Ghazālī. (Cornell in Abū Madyan, *The Way of Abū Madyan*, 19–21.) Meier, *Essays on Islamic Piety and Mysticism*, 423–427. For the *Iḥyāʾ* controversy in Andalusia, see Casewit, *The Mystics of al-Andalus*, 50–57.

160. Abū Madyan, *The Way of Abū Madyan*, 4–5, 13, 48–53; Gril, "Abū Madyan."

theology tactfully suggested in Ibn Tūmart's works. An early Sufi from Fez and contemporary of Abū Madyan, Abū al-Qāsim al-Lajāʾī (d.1202) demonstrates that al-Juwaynī's interpretivist *Book of Guidance* played a role among Western Sufis as significant as Abū Ḥāmid al-Ghazālī's post-Sufism works. Al-Lajāʾī's two books on Sufism are perfect examples that display the prominence of interpretivism in the wake of institutional Sufism in the Almohadī West. His best-known work, the *Pole of the Gnostics in Creed and Sufism* [*Quṭb al-ʿĀrifīn fī al-ʿAqāʾid wa-l-Taṣawwuf*], begins with a clearly interpretivist philosophical theology. The table of contents of the work suffices to show its powerful negative theology of the divine essence. The book is composed of three parts, and the list of early sections covered in the first part are as follows:

> The knowledge of creation, and the distinction between the eternal attributes and the created attributes
> The negation [*nafy*] of precedence and subsequence from God
> The negation of movement and stability from God
> The negation of imaginability, modality, representability, and variegation from God
> The negation of similitude between the creator and creation
> The negation of injustice and tyranny from God
> The negation of partnership from God
> The negation of spatiality from God[161]

These sections contain pages of negative statements. The terminology that al-Lajāʾī applies is philosophical, and he follows the sharp philosophical distinction between the created and eternal attributes, which renders the latter unknowable by the former. Yet al-Lajāʾī does not stop with the unknowability of the divine attributes and the essence. He rather embarks on a sweeping interpretive operation in the following sections of the part. The establishment, throne, speech, vision, smile, coming, hands, proximity, and so forth attributed to God go through a rigorous interpretive process. Her "establishment" means Her power, overcoming, and agency—the same interpretation as al-Juwaynī, and even the same

161. Al-Lajāʾī, *Quṭb al-ʿĀrifīn*, 187. All three of his extant works are on Sufism. See al-Dībājī in al-Lajāʾī, *Shams al-Qulūb*, 2–3.

examples concerning the linguistic usage of the term.[162] Her "proximity" is a metaphor for Her knowledge and supervision, while Her "smile" is an allegory [*ḍarb mathālan*] to Her blessings and generosity. "His 'hands' mean His power . . . His 'hearing' means His apprehension of all audibles; and His 'vision' means His apprehension of visibles. His 'face' means His being, which is unlike that of creation." All of these examples are identical with the interpretations of al-Juwaynī.[163]

Al-Lajāʾī's Sufi manual the *Sun of Hearts* [*Shams al-Qulūb*] follows a similar theological path. The book is oriented toward the practice of wayfaring, describing Sufi states, stations, and main concepts. Still, with its strong emphasis on negative descriptions of God, it does not hesitate to negate all of Her descriptions, along with the knowability of Her essence and even attributes. Here al-Lajāʾī also negates Her being "above" [*fawq*] or "on" [*ʿalā*] something, or being carried by a "throne." "Throne" marks the ascription of createdness and violates Her unique, unknowable, eternal singularity. He follows the sharp philosophical distinction between the created and eternal attributes, which renders the latter unknowable by the former. Hence Her "establishment" on the throne is "without reciprocity, neighboring, without touching, without indwelling, without similarity, and without modality." Her "coming" is, similarly, "without transferring, without movement, without similarity, and without modality. . . . He was pre-eternal without space, without similarity or modality." God is exalted from being above something, from being carried by a throne, from having a face, or any attribute that applies to creation.[164]

Al-Lajāʾī quoted a poem of Ibn al-ʿArīf in the *Sun of Hearts*, calling him the "venerated teacher" [*al-ustādh al-fāḍil*], and he cited al-Juwaynī in the *Pole of the Gnostics* as the "*imām*." It is the interpretive position of al-Juwaynī, instead of the anti-interpretive *bilā kayfa* position of al-Ghazālī, that makes its mark on al-Lajāʾī's works on normative Sufism. Yet it would not be wrong to attribute some prominence to *bilā kayfa* apophaticism among Sufis of the late twelfth century under the influence of al-Qushayrī and Abū Ḥāmid al-Ghazālī. Many of these early Western Sufis are reported to dislike engaging in producing theological discourses or writing books.

162. Al-Lajāʾī, *Quṭb al-ʿĀrifīn*, 51, 57–58; al-Lajāʾī, *Shams al-Qulūb*, 187v188; al-Juwaynī, *Kitāb al-Irshād*, 40.

163. Al-Lajāʾī, *Quṭb al-ʿĀrifīn*, 59–61; al-Juwaynī, *Kitāb al-Irshād*, 155.

164. Al-Lajāʾī, *Quṭb al-ʿĀrifīn*, 51–53; al-Lajāʾī, *Shams al-Qulūb*, 64, 187–189.

Ibn al-ʿArabī's Malāmatī Sufi master Abū Muḥammad al-Qaṭṭān (fl.l.12th CE) admonished those who write or compile books, arguing that the transcendent discourse—that is, "the Book of God and the traditions of His messenger—are sufficient."[165] They kept a distaste for speculation, and adhered rather to the transcendent discourse of the sacred scripture, or to the *bilā kayfa* position of al-Ghazālī and al-Qushayrī's monumental works. It was the pupil of Abū Madyan, Isḥāq al-Kūmī (d.1180), who introduced the *Epistle* of al-Qushayrī to the young aspirants Badr al-Dīn al-Ḥabashī and Ibn al-ʿArabī. Ibn al-ʿArabī beautifully narrates how the two companions followed al-Kūmī to a mosque on the top of a mountain, where al-Ḥabashī and Ibn al-ʿArabī recited the *Epistle*, and the master expounded upon it.[166] On the other hand, even if the generation of Abū Madyan, al-Qaṭṭān, and al-Kūmī adopted the *bilā kayfa* position, it did not extend to the next one in Andalusia.

Al-Ḥabashī, a freed slave of Ethiopian origin, had already acquired a copy of the *Epistle* before Ibn al-ʿArabī. Al-Ḥabashī's *Awakening to the Path of God* [*Kitāb al-Inbāh*] claims to transmit what the author heard from Ibn al-ʿArabī, "our master, our shaykh and our guide, the *imām*, the most pure man of knowledge, the Red Sulphur."[167] Hence the *Awakening* is an excellent witness to the mystical ideas of not only the Ethiopian Sufi but also the young Ibn al-ʿArabī. The *Awakening* adopts a *bilā kayfa* approach to the beatific vision, limiting it to the afterlife. It cites Q.75:22-23 and Q.83:15 in justification of the meeting and vision [*waṣl ilayhi wa rāʾhu*] in the afterlife, while the vision in this world is a non-discursive, non-corporeal, mystical one. It also interprets the "hand of God" as a metaphor for divine agency. Ibn al-ʿArabī's own hermeneutical, anti-corporeal paradoxical approach closely follows that of Ibn Barrajān. He depicts God's "throne" and "footstool" as real cosmological entities that manifest the divine mercy and veil the unknowable ipseity simultaneously. The "throne" and "footstool" are higher cosmological realities and loci of divine manifestations, which can

---

165. Muḥyī al-Dīn Ibn al-ʿArabī, *Sufis of Andalusia*, 112.

166. See ibid., 71–72.

167. Al-Ḥabashī in Gril, "Le Kitāb al-Inbāh ʿalā ṭarīq Allāh de ʿAbdallāh Badr al-Habasi," 104 (Arabic text), 123 (French translation).

be witnessed through spiritual wayfaring because of the correspondence between the macro-cosmos and the micro-cosmos.[168]

As a critic of allegorical interpretation [*ta'wīl*], yet a master of a fundamental hermeneutics of constant traversal, Ibn al-ʿArabī squarely fits in the interpretive tradition of the Contemplators. God's "hands," "fingers," and "face" turn into experiential signifiers in a hierarchical metaphysical system. He venerates the literal surface of the scripture, underlines its ultimately unknowable nature as the transcendent discourse, but also depicts a depth-hermeneutics as the best way of celebrating this transcendence. In terms of this interpretive theology, Ibn al-ʿArabī is closer to Ibn Barrajān's *Wisdom Deciphered* [*Īḍāḥ al-Ḥikma*] that he studied with ʿAbd al-ʿAzīz al-Mahdawī in the latter's center in Tunis in 1194. Al-Mahdawī himself wrote a Qur'an commentary that would be later transmitted to Ṣadr al-Dīn Qūnavī's library. In Barrajān's interpretive lineage, the *Blessed Prayer* [*al-Ṣalāh al-Mubāraka*] attributed to al-Mahdawī associates the "throne" of God with the Muḥammadan Reality where all divine names emanate.[169] Al-Mahdawī was a student of Abū Madyan, yet he connected Ibn al-ʿArabī to Ibn Barrajān's interpretive tradition instead of to the *bilā kayfa* position of al-Qushayrī and Abū Ḥāmid al-Ghazālī.

If there ever was a *bilā kayfa* apophaticism in the first self-consciously "Sufi" generation of Abū Madyan, it did not find wide resonance in the next generation. Among others, Abū Madyan was the spiritual master of Abū al-Ḥasan al-Shādhilī (d.1258), through his direct disciples Ibn Mashīsh (d.1228) and Ibn Ḥarāzim (d.1235). Strictly limiting himself to the transcendent discourse, al-Shādhilī saw any of his inclination to a discursive formation except the Qur'an and the prophetic reports as vain passions. Yet unlike the other two eponyms, ʿAbd al-Qādir al-Jīlānī and Aḥmad al-Rifāʿī, with whom Abū Madyan would be associated after his death, al-Shādhilī did not adopt a *bilā kayfa* approach to the anthropomorphic depictions of God. Instead, he situated them in a cosmology where they lose their corporeal implications but attain a rather visionary dimension. Accordingly, God created the prophetic soul and gave her Her "command" so that the prophetic intellect became manifest in Her "throne" under the light of the

---

168. Muḥyī al-Dīn Ibn al-ʿArabī in Renard, *Islamic Theological Themes*, 30; Muḥyī al-Dīn Ibn al-ʿArabī, *Sufis of Andalusia*, 34; al-Ḥabashī in Gril, "Le Kitāb al-Inbāh ʿalā ṭarīq Allāh de ʿAbdallāh Badr al-Habasi," 114–115, 108.

169. Al-Mahdawī in Elmore, "Shaykh ʿAbd al-ʿAzīz al-Mahdawī, Ibn al-ʿArabī's Mentor," 607–608. Also see ibid., 610–611.

command. Then Her "spirit" became manifest through the prophetic intellect, and through Her "spirit" Her "footstool" became manifest under the light of the throne. This complex system of emanations descends to the lower, bodily world of veils. The wayfarer should ascend in this system by purifying her soul.[170] Hence, "throne" or "footstool" signify both cosmological realities and the highest spiritual levels that the wayfarer can attain. Al-Shādhilī himself reports in various places that he transcended the "veil of throne," saw his Sufi teacher under the throne, or traveled there with the martyr grandson of the Prophet, al-Ḥusayn (d.680):

> My ancestor, al-Ḥusayn, took me and put his finger in my navel and turned me around over his head until the heavens, the earth, the throne, and the footstool became before me like the country round about.[171]

Within a non-anthropomorphist, interpretive context reminiscent of Ibn Barrajān, the "throne" is named as the highest heavenly realm in al-Shādhilī's cosmology. It had no physical implications for the nature of God. Al-Shādhilī's disciple and successor Abū al-ʿAbbās al-Mursī (d.1287) and his pupils followed this visionary interpretive perspective. Al-Mursī used to veil his eyes during his own discourses lest he be consumed by the illuminations of the divine throne that he saw. Like his master, he reportedly claimed that he knew the throne "as he knew the palm of his hand."[172] His successor, Ibn ʿAṭāʾ Allāh al-Iskandarī (d.1309) depicts God's "hand" or "throne" as non-physical metaphors for deeper metaphysical realities. "Throne," as the highest cosmological level associated with the prophetic soul, is where the excessive mercy of God emanates. He is "settled on the throne through His mercifulness, such that the throne disappeared into His mercifulness, as the universe disappeared into His throne." As this is a cosmological level that marks the prophetic intellect, Abū al-ʿAbbās al-Tanjī (fl.bef.14th CE) makes the same point on the divine excess with

---

170. Ibn al-Sabbāgh, *Mystical Teachings of al-Shādhilī*, 190–191, 148–149.

He also intensively mentioned the verses that address the divine throne or footstool in devotional contexts. See e.g. Q.2:255, Q.9:129, Q.20:5, in Ibn al-Sabbāgh, *Mystical Teachings of al-Shādhilī*, 111, 78, 66. For the "throne of honor," see ibid., 73.

171. Ibn al-Sabbāgh, *Mystical Teachings of al-Shādhilī*, 157; 78, 149.

172. Ibid., 215, 184, 158.

reference to the Prophet: "behold, heaven and earth, God's throne and God's footstool, are filled with the Apostle of God!"[173]

In brief, Shādhilism from its very emergence followed an interpretive approach to the divine nature, instead of the normative Sunnī Sufi creed promulgated in the *Revivification* of al-Ghazālī, the *Epistle* of al-Qushayrī, or other Arabic Sufi manuals. While Sufis intensively cited al-Ghazālī as the great Sufi authority, they preferred to follow interpretive theologies. Ibn ʿAṭāʾ Allāh, for example, repeatedly cites al-Ghazālī as the great "imām" in his manual on invocation, *Key to Salvation* [*Miftāḥ al-Falāḥ*], yet he carefully sorts out the *bilā kayfa* dimensions of it. It is rather the *Book of Guidance* of Ghazālī's teacher, al-Juwaynī, that makes an unmistakable imprint on his works, including his mystical aphorisms.[174] Among early Shādhilī Sufis, al-Juwaynī's theological interpretivism was much more powerful than the *bilā kayfa* apophaticism of his celebrated Sufi student.

Shādhilī interpretivism in North Africa mirrored Andalusia. The *bilā kayfa* apophatic position evidenced in the later Sufi creed attributed to Abū Madyan did not find any inheritors among Sufis of Andalusia in the thirteenth century, and even in his own times. Ibn al-ʿArabī's generation and his students adopted similarly interpretive, mostly paradoxical or philosophical approaches to the divine essence. The inapplicability of modalities to the divine nature among Andalusian Sufis operates mainly within an interpretive framework instead of *bilā kayfa*. Ibn Sabʿīn provides an excellent demonstration of the philosophical rigor in anti-anthropomorphic interpretive positions that Sufis adopted. The third issue that Ibn Sabʿīn addresses in the *Sicilian Questions* is the definition of categories [*maqūlāt*]. After introducing the four possible causalities in Aristotle's works, Ibn Sabʿīn discusses the nine "questions" [*maṭlab*], such as "what," "which," "how," "why," "how many," "where," "when," that can be asked about any object. As God does not have a cause [*ʿilla*], "none of the nine principle questions, except '*is?*' [*hal?*], can be asked about God."[175] In other words, Ibn Sabʿīn employs logic, instead of the transcendent discourse to cancel human discourse on the divine nature. He also interprets God's "eye"

---

173. Meier, *Essays on Islamic Piety and Mysticism*, 537; Ibn ʿAṭāʾ Allāh al-Iskandarī, *Tāj al-ʿArūs*, 102; Ibn ʿAṭāʾ Allāh al-Iskandarī in Jackson, *Sufism for Non-Sufis? Ibn ʿAṭāʾ Allāh al-Sakandarī's Tāj al-ʿArūs*, 146; Ibn ʿAṭāʾ Allāh al-Iskandarī, *Kitāb al-ḥikam*, 40 (Arabic text), 36 (English translation).

174. Mayer, "Theology and Sufism," 272.

175. Ibn Sabʿīn, *al-Kalām ʿalā al-Masāʾil al-Ṣiqilliyya*, 60, 85–88.

[*ʿayn*] and "hand" as Her apprehension and power respectively. In his extensive discussion of anthropomorphism, he does not even bother himself with interpreting the non-Qurʾanic attributions that have corporeal implications; he rather refuses them outright as unacceptable and inapplicable. In his interpretive, philosophical approach to the divine essence, the transcendent discourse does not have any less authority than it has in non-cognitive approaches.

Summary

In the formative period of Islamic thought, the term *bilā kayfa* marks two closely related, yet different anti-interpretive positions on the nature of the divine essence. First, it indicates the literal acceptance of transcendent anthropomorphism without adding an interpretation. Such anthropomorphism in the ancient Near Eastern tradition circulated among Sunnī traditionists well into the thirteenth century. Second, *bilā kayfa* names the non-cognitive, apophatic theological position wherein neither God nor the meaning of Her transcendent discourse is accessible. Human speculations cancel themselves in favor of the incomprehensible transcendent discourse on the unknowable ipseity. As al-Māturīdī puts it, "*The principle here is this: to say as much as it is revealed; to negate all of the meanings that are about creation; and no interpretation [tafsīr]—as nothing is revealed.*"[176]

Instead of such anti-interpretive paths, early Sufis active in Baghdad and Basra adopted primarily interpretive approaches to the anthropomorphic depictions of God in the sacred sources. Only in association with Ḥanbalism and scripturalist Ashʿarism did anti-interpretivism on the divine essence appear among Sufis. Yet it would have a sustained career among the Sufi manuals and (under the manuals' clear influence) in the founding generation of the Suhrawardiyya, Rifāʿiyya, and Qādiriyya. The Sufi manuals met an important task by presenting Sufism as a *bilā kayfa* apophatic institution in an anti-interpretive scholarly and political context. With these manuals, "Sufism" emerged as a broad, formalized piety that not only projects its conception of Sunnī mysticism and the *bilā kayfa* apophatic theology onto the previous generations but also selectively claims a large variety of local movements and groups. This canonized Sufism

176. Al-Māturīdī, *Kitāb al-Tawḥīd*, 145–146.

provided the bedrock for the emerging eponyms. The *bilā kayfa*, non-cognitive, anti-interpretive theology played an integral role in the rise of these first and foremost practice-oriented institutions of piety that were forming around the methods and teachings associated with charismatic Sufi masters. In the West, on the other hand, the interpretivism of the Andalusian mystical movements and the Almohadī rational Ashʿarism prevailed over the anti-interpretivism of the prominent Sufi manuals. It was against this interpretive background that the Shādhilī method emerged.

With a couple exceptions, Sufism in Persian language did not undergo the *bilā kayfa* interruption in the formalization, and later, institutional period that we observe in Arabic. Among the early Sufi manuals, that of Hujvīrī was an exception not only in being written in Farsi but also in criticizing the *bilā kayfa* positions on the divine nature. Persian Sufis of diverse backgrounds and loose affiliations with the rising orders followed the general rule of interpretivism. Sayyid Burhān al-Dīn, Rūmī's early master, interprets God's "fingers" as Her agency and Her "hand" as Her power. The latter interpretation is similar to early Sufi approaches that we find in al-Tustarī, or in al-Sulamī's compilation of Sufi exegesis on the Qurʾan. Naṣīr al-Dīn Qūnavī follows a rationalist Ashʿarite approach to the categorization of the divine attributes, which he supplies with the paradox of the veil. On par with Ibn al-ʿArabī, Naṣīr al-Dīn argues that the true knowledge of God's essence cannot be accessed by creation. We can only "witness that essence in respect of its manifestation within the loci of manifestation."[177] God's throne and footstool are, in line with Ibn al-ʿArabī once again, cosmic levels with visionary mystical significance, instead of corporeal relations to God. In other words, they signify the divine dominion [*mulk*]. Naṣīr al-Dīn's non-corporeal interpretation jointly responds to divine "nearness," and the "throne," pulling the reader toward paradoxical apophaticism:

> *He is nearer to the servants than the jugular vein* [Q.5:16], *and further from them than any distance that comes to mind.* His relationship of nearness to the majestic throne is the same as His relationship with the bottom of the earth. He is hidden because of extreme evidence,

177. Naṣīr al-Dīn Qūnavī in Chittick, *Faith and Practice of Islam*, 61. Sayyid Burhān al-Dīn, *Maʿārif*, 62, 122 [Q.48:10]. Burhān al-Dīn also appears skeptical on the vision of God, arguing that only God witnessed God. (Ibid., 67.)

> and evident because of extreme hiddenness. . . . Whatever may pass into the fancies, imaginations, and minds of human beings—He is not that, and He is not like that. [178]

The *Discourses* of Rūmī's enigmatic master Shams Tabrīzī is also deeply interpretive. Each of his *Discourses*, very much like Dāya Rāzī's *Path of God's Bondsmen*, begins with a Qur'anic verse, each time giving fresh interpretations. His discussions on the anthropomorphic depictions of God are critical to the *bilā kayfa* anti-interpretivism that he (correctly) associates with al-Ashʿarī. "Throne" and "footstool" mark the highest cosmological levels, but he also adds to them a personal, visionary dimension by attaching them to the heart.[179]

While Shams' rich, interpretive response to anthropomorphism is evident, theology is an integral dimension of a primarily practice-oriented institution that regulates discourse, spiritual wayfaring, and human conduct [*adab*] at large. No matter whether Sufis followed the *bilā kayfa* apophatic creeds or rather interpretive positions, discourses on the divine ipseity were firmly situated within larger visionary metaphysical systems and normative practices that regulated wayfaring, purification of the soul, and human conduct.

---

178. Naṣīr al-Dīn Qūnavī in Chittick, *Faith and Practice of Islam*, 121, 80, 73 [Q.20:5].

179. Shams Tabrīzī, *Me and Rūmī*, 157–160, 90, 92, 136-138. For the wonderful anecdote on a wise woman and her husband, who is bewildered between the interpretation-oriented and the *bilā kayfa*-minded preachers, see ibid., 60–62.

Conclusion

Associations

What we have been witnessing in recent decades can be described as an "apophatic rage."[1] It is not only that studies on apophaticism and negative theologies have been exponentially increasing in constructive theology and the study of religion. Interest has soared across the humanities, including in the arts, philosophy, gender and sexuality, and literary studies. This increasing appeal to negative theologies and apophaticism has also given rise to a variety of highly contested scholarly perspectives.

Islamic intellectual history has been an understudied field in this context. This book has aimed to fill this gap by providing contextual approaches to apophatic performances in medieval Islam. In the first chapter, I asked the broad question "What is negative theology?" in order to pin it down with reference to Islam in general, and medieval Sufism in particular. I argued that "negative theology" is a blanket term that tends to confuse various theological questions. Moreover, the term reduces the rich field of theology into a single question—theomania, and its negation. As modern religionists, we have not been able to imagine a "negative theology of religious leadership," "negative theology of theodicy," or "negative theology of eschatology," precisely because the term "negative theology" spans the entire field of theology, reducing it to the divine nature. Intellectual history provided us with conceptual correctives. I argued that the Muʿtazilites generally had a *negative theology of divine attributes* but that the majority of them were far from following a *negative theology of divine essence*. Many Sufis, on the other hand, adopted a negative theology of divine essence, yet their approach to the divine attributes was far from, and even critical

1. See Laird, "Whereof We Speak: Gregory of Nyssa, Jean-Luc Marion and the Current Apophatic Rage."

to, being purely negativist. Following medieval Muslim scholars, I differentiated the questions of the "divine essence" and "divine attributes" and demonstrated that a negativist position toward one of these questions does not ineluctably guarantee a negativist position on the other. This analysis showed that negative speech is contextual, insofar as an apophatic approach to a specific discursive field does not automatically prove apophaticism in another discursive field.

Throughout the study, we observed that negation played an important role in theological discourse in Muslim contexts. Theological debates were refined, and terminology was rich; scholars employed plenty of terms for negation: *salb, nafy, taʿṭīl,* and *tanzīh* being the most common Arabic ones. These terms could often bear unfavorable connotations, and detractors had an important role to play in defining the negativism of their rivals. Eventually, to go back to the unfriendly schema of Ibn Khalīfa al-Tamīmī, the funny labels "Knower Unknowers," "I-Don't-Knower Unknowers," or "Negationists" were not self-descriptive at all. Rather they were often used to define, and denigrate, one's intellectual opponent. Instead of addressing a historically fixed—say, "Neoplatonic"—group or identity, "negative theology" had changing meanings in diverse contexts throughout the first seven centuries of Islam. There was no "negative theology" in the first place; rather, there were diverse positions taken in terms of various theological questions that were associated with negativity. Focusing solely on the question of the divine nature, we examined the discursive formations that *we* can label as self-negating. In other words, rather than depicting "negative theology" as a *sui generis,* Neoplatonic, or mystical category, this study approached it as a self-negating apophatic strategy in the field of theology, the historical significance of which was not fixed, but negotiated.

The following four chapters introduced different negative theologies of the divine essence that circulated in the Islamicate world, with a focus on Sufis. Here I introduced the emergence and historical development of four prominent negative theologies of the divine essence: Ismāʿīlī, philosophical, paradoxical, and amodal apophaticism. These broad traditions marked families of negative language performances that share not only historical networks and linguistic strategies but also various assumptions on epistemology, language, and cosmology. In other words, I have argued that apophatic speech affirms various cosmological or epistemological assumptions in order to operate. Ismāʿīlī apophaticism, for example, required the acceptance of its unique cosmology that deepened divine hiddenness. Similarly, paradoxical apophaticism demanded the careful matching of the binaries in given theological discourses, and their subversion through a dialectical logic. The specific paradoxes that were chosen, and their performative dimensions and sociopolitical implications, were determined by the specific theological context in each unique case. The performative aspects of paradoxical apophaticism, such as the "healing with paradoxes" as in the case of Kubrawī Sufis, were set and regulated by theological, mystical, and social institutions.

Prominent intellectuals such as Jacques Derrida, Jean-Luc Marion, Henry Corbin, and many contemporary religionists today often overlook this inherent context-dependence of apophatic performances and take it for granted that apophasis enjoys an "infinite critical capacity." Just to give one example, William Franke has repeatedly argued that a self-negating speech formation on infinity must itself be infinite:

> Like divinity, negation is infinite. . . . Thus, negative theology points to certain limits of all disciplinary discourses, their inability to circumscribe their domains and give an adequate account of themselves. . . . *Theology, as the discourse of the unlimited, or as discourse without limits, turns out to be radically negative.* . . . There is no negative theology as such; there can only be a negative theology of negative theology: a discourse that cancels itself out by its very nature and necessity and that exists only in and as this act of self-annihilation or self-erasure.[2]

In theoretical terms, this study has suggested the opposite: the discourse of the unlimited is still *a* discourse *with* limits. Apophasis, like any speech-act, must affirm the logical, terminological, or performative norms of the specific discursive formation that it negates. As Michel Foucault put it eloquently, "A proposition must fulfil some onerous and complex conditions before it can be admitted within a discipline; *before it can be pronounced true or false it must be 'within the true.'*"[3] The inherent affirmativity in any given speech performance challenges the hasty association of apophasis with broad themes like critical thinking and morality. Amodal apophaticism, with its conservative and sometimes anti-intellectual versions, further undermines such ethicalizing roles that contemporary scholars widely attribute to negative speech.

2. Franke and Woods, "Negative Theology," 1444–1445 (my emphasis).

3. Foucault, "The Discourse on Language," 323 (my emphasis).

The common equivalence of apophaticism and mysticism has proven equally problematic in the current study. This equivalence has a strong Christian background; eventually, the founding text of Christian apophaticism penned by Pseudo-Dionysius (fl.5th–6th CE) is titled *Mystical Theology*. Hence many scholars of religion today associate "negative theology" with mysticism without acknowledging the possibility of apophatic performances without mysticism. The Russian philosopher Nikolai Berdyaev (d.1948), for example, argued that the superiority of "apophatic theology" lies in its inherent mysticism: "Apophatic-negative theology is more mystical than kataphatic-positive theology, which always includes within itself *a strong dose of rationalism*." More recent studies, such as *Apophatic Bodies*, analyze "mystical and apophatic traditions," where "*apophatic mystics*—Jewish, Christian, Muslim—speak and unspeak volumes."[4] The current study put a question mark to such widespread yet, I would argue, historically unwarranted associations in the study of Muslim and Jewish negative theologies. But we should challenge the equation of "negative theology" to mysticism in the study of Christianity as well. Even the explicit followers of Pseudo-Dionysius do not fit into Nikolai Berdyaev's description of mystical apophaticism. The prominent Roman Catholic theologian Denys the Carthusian (d.1471), for example, commended the via negativa of philosophers like Aristotle, al-Fārābī, Ibn Sīnā, and al-Ghazālī, and he saw apophaticism as an integral component of not only theological but also philosophical contemplation.[5] Philosophical, Ismāʿīlī, and amodal forms of negative theology of the divine essence suggest that theology in Abrahamic contexts did not require that it be mystical, irrational, or suprarational in order to negate itself. Instead, with its popular claim for an experiential or visionary knowledge of the ultimate object of theological speculation, mysticism could rather undermine apophaticism on divine nature.

4. Berdyaev, "A Consideration Concerning Theodicy"; Boesel and Keller, *Apophatic Bodies: Negative Theology, Incarnation and Relationality*, 1; Ward, "In the Daylight Forever? Language and Silence," 164; Sells, *Mystical Languages of Unsaying*, 5–11; 220–221n14; Clayton, "The Infinite Found in Human Form," 288.

5. In other words, his definition of the mystical contemplation was broad enough to include rationalist forms of theology as well. See Turner, *The Darkness of God*, 212–213. Richard King's studies provide a good introduction to the strong association of mysticism with apophaticism in Christianity from Pseudo-Dionysius and Meister Eckhart to influential religionists like William James (d.1910). See, e.g., King, "Mysticism and Spirituality," 324–327.

If "apophasis," "negative theology," "via negativa," or "negation" do not necessarily connote mysticism, critical thinking, or morality, how did we come up with strong associations of apophaticism with these key modern values? A critical history of these concepts can help us develop more self-conscious and decolonized perspectives toward the apophatic heritage across intellectual and religious traditions around the world. This much-needed genealogy should be the subject of another study.

Multiplicity

The plurality of medieval apophatic positions on a single question in the vast field of theology has wider theoretical implications. First, it reminds us that a given discursive formation yields itself to negation in neither a single nor infinite ways. Such plurality is neglected in the singular use of the phrase "negative theology." Once we overlook the diversity of the ways in which theological discourse can be negated from within, "negative theology" inescapably reduces to a single path. This path, for many contemporary scholars of apophaticism, including Jean-Luc Marion, Michael Sells, and Denys Turner, is that of "yes and no"—the paradox. For example, Jacques Derrida argues that "negative theology" always represents a "paradoxical hyperbole" in different religious and cultural traditions.[6] While Marion defends "negative theology" against Derrida's critique, he too presumes that paradox is the only way of "negative theology." Accordingly, as the "third way," "negative theology" goes beyond the affirmation of the object of the discourse through paradox:

> The third way is played out beyond the oppositions between affirmation and negation, synthesis and separation, in short, between the true and the false. Strictly speaking, if thesis and negation have it in common to speak the truth (and spurn the false), the way that transcends them should also transcend the true and the false. The third way would transgress nothing less than the two truth values, between which the entire logic of metaphysics is carried out. Therefore, if the third way is no longer about saying the true or the

6. See Derrida, *On the Name*, 63–67, 78; cf. Marion, *In Excess: Studies of Saturated Phenomena*, 133.

> false, if it is precisely a matter of its not saying them, one can no longer claim that it means to affirm a predicate of a subject.[7]

While such equation of "negative theology" with paradox is common in the literature, it tends to ignore the historical as well as potential diversity of negative theologies. Other than turning in their graves, how would philosophers like Moses Maimonides or Ibn Sīnā respond to such claims to violate the principle of non-contradiction? Their philosophical path of negative theology of divine essence was clearly not that of Marion or Derrida. This study has suggested that "yes and no" was a prominent, yet not the sole, way of negating discourse on God. We observed that Muslims could follow these paths in different levels of intensity, often dependent on the sociopolitical atmosphere. Sufis shared some of these apophatic paths with non-Sufis, non-Muslims, and even anti-Sufis. Depending on the context, a given scholar could adopt more than one of these apophatic paths. We are familiar with such shifts between multiple apophatic positions since at least Plotinus.[8] In other words, the available apophatic paths were not mutually exclusive, and it was possible to swing between them, or beyond them.

Marion's reference to *the third way that transgresses the two truth values* lays bare another common theme in the current literature on "negative theology" that is difficult to corroborate historically. Even the followers of the path of paradox, as we have seen, were keen to follow logical principles rather than ignore or transgress them. The apophatic path of paradox did follow a rigorous logical structure: the key binaries of a given discourse had to be carefully chosen, and brought together in the right context and moment to create the intended logical and performative attack on propositional discourse. What paradoxographers did was to indicate the limits of propositional logic thorough a dialectical system that rigorously appeals to logic rather than lacking or abandoning it. They were far from questioning the principle of non-contradiction. In other words, the claim to violate the principle of non-contradiction, which we find widely in the study of Jewish, Muslim, and Christian apophaticism today,[9] is difficult to

7. Marion, *In Excess: Studies of Saturated Phenomena*, 137–138.

8. Sells, *Mystical Languages of Unsaying*, 16–22; Kars, "Two Modes of Unsaying in the Early Thirteenth Century Islamic Lands," 276.

9. See, e.g., E. R. Wolfson, "Revisioning the Body Apophatically," 189; Schumann, *Logic in Religious Discourse*, 15–16; Clayton, "The Infinite Found in Human Form," 302.

ascribe not only to the precolonial logicians and philosophers but even to the paradoxographers.

Second, this plurality challenges the efforts to construct single, unified negative theological traditions within religious systems. We often find in the literature claims for an "ancient tradition of apophasis"—that is, a distinct, singular, Western negative theological tradition raised by Jewish and Christian scholars on the Greek bedrock, particularly within the matrix of the commentary tradition on Plato's *Parmenides*. On this shared "Neoplatonic" basis, the argument goes, Christianity, Judaism, and Islam each developed a unique and distinct negative theological tradition of their own. Accordingly,

> Each tradition has manifested its own systematic outline of negative theology through the medieval, modern, and postmodern eras. Thus, while the several traditions often share a desire to limit the reach of human discourse vis-a-vis God, they each have developed their own idiosyncratic patterns of negation that should not be conflated indiscriminately.[10]

Such a construction of singular and distinct "negative theological traditions" not only overlooks the diversity, and sometimes conflicts, among various theological positions within religious traditions. More elusively, it also misses the historical fact that the negative theological positions among scholars and mystics from different religious backgrounds had strong overlaps. For example, Maimonides, who was the head of the Jewish community in Egypt, and the Muslim scholar al-Baṭalyawsī followed the same philosophical negative theological strategies in approaching both the divine ipseity and divine attributes. Yet, Nethanel al-Fayyūmī, the head of the Jews in Yemen, followed a negative theology of the divine essence that was arguably much closer to that of the Ismāʿīlīs than to Maimonides. These two prominent Jewish scholars were active around the same time, wrote in the same language, and flourished under Muslim rule, while their paths of apophaticism were different from each other, reflecting their sociopolitical context and intellectual orientations. Why insist on putting Maimonides, al-Fayyūmī, and Azriel into one box, and Ibn Sīnā, Abū Yaʿqūb al-Sijistānī, and Ibn Masarra in another? The trans-religious theological networks we

10. Franke and Woods, "Negative Theology," 1443.

explored in the book have highlighted the intellectual porosities not only between Sufism, mysticism, theology, and philosophy but also between religious traditions.

In brief, there is no exclusively Muslim, or for that matter, Jewish or Christian, "negative theological tradition," for three reasons. First, "negative theology" does not address a *sui generis* category or an enduring, well-defined group of intellectuals; it is rather a conceptual construct with debated meanings and significance in changing historical settings. Today it is often used as a blanket term that confuses various theological questions and negativities, and it widely serves to our contemporary agendas to selectively ethicalize specific groups in history to make them fit into modernity. Second, there were numerous negative theological positions regarding but a single question in a rich field of intellectual activity. These positions could and did transcend disciplinary boundaries as they were adopted by scholars with diverse orientations and backgrounds. Finally, negative theological positions that Muslims adopted were shared with, informed by, or impacted upon non-Muslims. "Intellectual history characteristically disregards any national, religious, cultural and economic borders, and intellectual symbiosis was often the norm rather than the exception in medieval and pre-modern time."[11] Negative theologies of divine essence were an integral component of this shared intellectual heritage.

11. Schmidtke, "Theological Rationalism in the Medieval World of Islam," 25.

Bibliography

ʿAbd al-Jabbār, Ibn Aḥmad al-Asadābādī. 1996. *Sharḥ al-Uṣūl al-Khamsa*. 3rd ed. With notes by Aḥmad ibn al-Ḥusayn ibn Abī Hāshim and an introduction by ʿAbd al-Karīm ʿUthmān. Cairo: Maktabat Wahbah.

Abdel-Kader, Ali Hassan. 1962. *The Life, Personality and Writings of al-Junayd*. London: Luzac, printed for the Trustees of the E. J. W. Gibb Memorial.

al-Abharī, Athīr al-Dīn. 2008. *Hidayetü'l-Hikme'nin Tenkitli Neşri*. Edited by Abdullāh Yormaz. *Marmara Üniversitesi İlâhiyat Fakültesi Dergisi* 34, no. 1: 145–202. Critical edition of the Arabic text.

al-Abharī, Athīr al-Dīn. 2009. *A Guide to Philosophy*. Translated by Syed Ali Tawfik al-ʿAttas. Selangor, Malaysia: Pelanduk.

Abrahamov, Binyamin. 1995. "The 'Bi-lā Kayfa' Doctrine and Its Foundations in Islamic Theology." *Arabica*, T. 42, fasc. 3: 365–379.

Abrahamov, Binyamin. 1998. *Islamic Theology: Traditionalism and Rationalism*. Edinburgh: Edinburgh University Press.

Abrahamov, Binyamin. 2002. "Fakhr al-Dīn al-Rāzī on the Knowability of God's Essence and Attributes." *Arabica*, T. 49, fasc. 2: 204–230.

Abrahamov, Binyamin. 2014. *Ibn al-ʿArabī and the Sufis*. Oxford: Anqa.

Abū Ḥanīfa and Muḥammad ibn Maḥmūd Akmal al-Dīn al-Bābartī. 2009. *Sharḥ Waṣiyyat al-Imām Abī Ḥanīfa*. Edited and with notes by Muḥammad Ṣubḥī ʿĀydī and Ḥamza Muḥammad Wasīm Bakrī. Amman, Jordan: Dār al-Fatḥ lil-Dirāsāt wa-al-Nashr.

Abū Madyan, Shuʿayb ibn al-Ḥusayn al-Anṣārī. 1996. *The Way of Abū Madyan: Doctrinal and Poetic Works of Abū Madyan Shuʿayb ibn al-Ḥusayn al-Anṣārī*. Edited, translated, and with an introduction and notes by Vincent Cornell. Cambridge: Islamic Texts Society.

Abū Tammām. 1998. *An Ismaili Heresiography: The "Bāb al-Shayṭān" from Abū Tammām's Kitāb al-Shajara*. Edited, translated, and with an introduction by Wilferd Madelung and P. Walker. Leiden and Boston: Brill.

Adamson, Peter. 2000. "The Arabic Plotinus: A Study of the *Theology of Aristotle* and Related Texts." PhD diss., University of Notre Dame.

Adamson, Peter. 2003. "Al-Kindī and the Muʿtazila: Divine Attributes, Creation and Freedom." *Arabic Sciences and Philosophy* 13, no. 1: 45–77.

Adamson, Peter. 2004. "Non-Discursive Thought in Avicenna's Commentary on the *Theology of Aristotle*." In *Interpreting Avicenna: Science and Philosophy in Medieval Islam*, 87–111. Edited by Jon McGinnis with David Reisman. Leiden and Boston: Brill.

Adamson, Peter. 2005. "On Knowledge of Particulars." *Proceedings of the Aristotelian Society* 105, no. 3: 257–278.

Adamson, Peter. 2007. *Al-Kindī*. Oxford: Oxford University Press.

Adamson, Peter, ed. 2013. *Interpreting Avicenna: Critical Essays*. Cambridge: Cambridge University Press.

Addas, C. 1994. "The Paradox of the Duty of Perfection in the Doctrine of Ibn al-ʿArabī." Translated by C. Twinch. *Journal of the Muhyiddin Ibn ʿArabi Society* 15:37–49.

Aflākī, Shams al-Dīn Aḥmad. 2001. *Ariflerin Menkıbeleri*. 2 vols. Translated by Tahsin Yazıcı. Istanbul: Milli Eğitim Bakanlığı.

al-Aharī, ʿAbd al-Qādir ibn Ḥamzah ibn Yāqūt. (1358) 1979. *Al-Aqṭāb al-Quṭbiyya, aw, al-Bulgha fī al-Ḥikma*. Intishārāt-i Anjuman-i Falsafa-yi Īrān, no. 45, Tehran: Anjuman-i Falsafa-yi Īrān.

Aḥmad-i Jām. 2004. *The Colossal Elephant and His Spiritual Feats: Shaykh Aḥmad-E Jām; The Life and Legend of a Popular Sufi Saint of 12th-Century Iran*. Translated and with annotation by Heshmat Moayyad and Franklin Lewis. Costa Mesa, CA: Mazda.

Ajhar, ʻAbd al-Ḥakīm. 2000. "The Metaphysics of the Idea of God in Ibn Taymiyyah's Thought." PhD diss., McGill University.

Akasoy, Anna Ayşe. 2008. "Ibn Sabʿīn's *Sicilian Questions*: The Text, Its Sources, and Their Historical Context." *al-Qantara* 29:115–146.

Alfino, Mark Richard. 1988. "Plotinus and the Possibility of Non-Propositional Thought." *Ancient Philosophy* 8, no. 2: 273–284.

ʿAlī ibn Abī Ṭālib, ʿAlī al-Qāḍī al-Quḍāʿī and al-Jāḥiẓ. 2013. *A Treasury of Virtues: Sayings, Sermons, and Teachings of ʿAlī al-Qāḍī al-Quḍāʿī; With the One Hundred Proverbs Attributed to al-Jāḥiẓ*. Edited and translated by T. Qutbuddin. New York: New York University Press.

ʿAlī ibn al-Ḥusayn, Zayn al-ʿĀbidīn. 1988. *The Psalms of Islam* [*al-Saḥīfat al-Kāmilat al-Sajjādiyya*]. Translated and with an introduction and annotations by William C. Chittick. With a foreword by S. H. M. Jafri. London: Muhammadi Trust of Great Britain and Northern Ireland.

Alibhai, Mohamed Abualy. 1983. *Abū Yaʿqūb al-Sijistānī and Kitāb Sullam al-Najāt*. PhD diss., Harvard University.

Ali-Shah, Zulfiqar. 2012. *Anthropomorphic Depictions of God: The Concept of God in Judaic, Christian, and Islamic Traditions; Representing the Unrepresentable.* Herndon, VA: International Institute of Islamic Thought.

Almond, Ian. 2004. *Sufism and Deconstruction: A Comparative Study of Derrida and Ibn al-ʿArabī.* London: Routledge.

AlSarhan, Saud Saleh. 2011. "Early Muslim Traditionalism: A Critical Study of the Works and Political Theology of Aḥmad Ibn Ḥanbal." PhD diss., University of Exeter.

Alwishah, Ahmed, and David Sanson. 2009. "The Early Arabic Liar: The Liar Paradox in the Islamic World from the Mid-Ninth to the Mid-Thirteenth Centuries CE." *Vivarium* 47:97–127.

al-ʿĀmirī, Abū al-Ḥasan Muḥammad ibn Yūsuf. 1988. *A Muslim Philosopher on the Soul and Its Fate: Al-ʿĀmirī's Kitāb al-Amad ʿalā l-Abad.* With an introduction and notes by Everett K. Rowson. New Haven, CT: American Oriental Society.

Anonymous. 2008. "The Mother of Books (from *Umm al-kitāb*)." In *An Anthology of Philosophy in Persia.* Vol. 2, *Ismaili Thought in the Classical Age from Jābir ibn Ḥayyān to Naṣīr al-Dīn Ṭūsī,* 18–34. Translated by L. P. Peerwani. Edited by Seyyed Hossein Nasr and Mehdi Aminrazavi. London: Tauris.

Anonymous. 2012. *ʿIlm al-Taṣawwuf.* Edited by Naṣr Allāh Pūrjavādī and Muḥammad Sūrī. Tehran: Mu'assasah-'i Pizhūhishī-i Ḥikmat va Falsafah-'i Īrān; Berlin: Mu'assasah-'i Muṭālaʿāt-i Islāmī-i Dānishgāh-i Āzād-i Barlīn.

Ansari, Hassan Farhang. 2016. *Al-Mutabaqqī min Kutub Mafqūda.* Isfahan: Daftar-i Tablīghāt-i Islāmī.

Ansari, Hassan Farhang, and Sabine Schmidtke. 2010. "Muʿtazilism after ʿAbd al-Jabbār: Abū Rashīd al-Nīsābūrī's Kitāb Masāʾil al-Khilāf fī l-Uṣūl." *Studia Iranica* 39: 225–276.

Amir-Moezzi, Mohammed Ali. 1994. *The Divine Guide in Early Shiʿism: The Sources of Esotericism in Islam.* Albany: State University of New York Press.

Arberry, Arthur John. 1950. *Sufism: An Account of the Mystics of Islam.* London: George Allen & Unwin.

Aristotle. 1995. *Aristotle: Selections.* Translated and with an introduction, notes, and glosses by Terence Irwin and Gail Fine. Indianapolis, IN: Hackett.

Asad, Talal. 1993. *Genealogies of Religion: Discipline and Reasons of Power in Christianity and Islam.* Baltimore: Johns Hopkins University Press.

al-Ashʿarī, Abū al-Ḥasan ʿAlī ibn Ismāʿīl. 1950. *Maqālāt al-Islāmiyyin wa Ikhtilāf al-Muṣallīn.* Edited by Muḥammad Muḥyī al-Dīn ʿAbd al-Ḥamīd. 1st ed. Cairo: Maktabat al-Nahḍa al-Miṣriyya.

ʿAṭṭār, Farīd al-Dīn. 2000. *Muslim Saints and Mystics.* Translated by Arthur John Arberry. Ames, IA: Omphaloskepsis.

ʿAṭṭār, Farīd al-Dīn. Undated. *Manṭiq al-Ṭayr.* Tehran: Noorsoft DVD.

Austin, John Langshaw. 1962. *How to Do Things with Words.* Oxford: Clarendon Press.

Avery, K. 2014. *Shiblī: His Life and Thought in the Sufi Tradition*. Albany: State University of New York Press.

Aziz, Muḥammad Ali. 2011. *Religion and Mysticism in Early Islam: Theology and Sufism in Yemen, the Legacy of Aḥmad Ibn ʿAlwān*. London: Tauris.

Aziz, Muḥammad Ali. 2018. "Aḥmad b. ʿAlwān." In *Encyclopaedia of Islam, Three*. Edited by Kate Fleet, Gudrun Krämer, Denis Matringe, John Nawas, and Everett Rowson. Leiden: Brill.

Baffioni, Carmela. 2013. "The Role of the Divine Imperative (*Amr*) in the Ikhwān al-Ṣafāʾ and Related Works." *Ishrāq: Islamic Philosophy Yearbook*, no.4, 46–70. Moscow: Vostochnaya Literatura.

al-Baghdādī. ʿAbd al-Qāhir Ibn Ṭāhir. (1346) 1928. *Kitāb Uṣūl al-Dīn*. Istanbul: Maṭbaʿat al-Dawla.

al-Baghdādī, ʿAbd al-Qāhir Ibn Ṭāhir. Undated. *Kitāb al-Farq bayn al-Firaq: Wa Bayān al-Firqa al-Nājiya Minhum*. Cairo: Maktabat Ibn Sīnā.

al-Balyānī, Awḥad al-Dīn (misattributed to Muḥyī al-Dīn Ibn al-ʿArabī). 1976. *Whoso Knoweth Himself*. Translated by T. H. Weir BD. Cheltenham, PA: Beshara, in collaboration with the Muhyiddin Ibn ʿArabi Society.

al-Bāqillānī, Muḥammad ibn al-Ṭayyib. 1987. *Kitāb Tamhīd al-Awāʾil wa Talkhīṣ al-Dalāʾil*. Beirut: Muʾassasat al-Kutub al-Thaqāfiyya.

Baqlī, Rūzbihān ibn Abī Naṣr. 2008. *ʿArāʾis al-Bayān fī Ḥaqāʾiq al-Qurʾān*. 3 vols. With notes by Aḥmad Farīd al-Mazīdī. Beirut: Dār al-Kutub al-ʿIlmiyya.

al-Baṭalyawsī, ʿAbd Allāh ibn Muḥammad. (1408) 1988. *Al-Ḥadāʾiq fī al-Maṭālib al-ʿĀliya al-Falsafiyya al-ʿAwīṣa*. Edited by Muḥammad Riḍwān Dāya. With an introduction by ʿAbd al-Karīm al-Yāfī. Damascus: Dār al-Fikr.

al-Bayhaqī, Aḥmad ibn al-Ḥusayn. (1358) 1939. *Kitāb al-Asmāʾ wa-l-Ṣifāt*. With an introduction and notes by M. Zahid al-Kawthari. Cairo: al-Maktabat al-Azhariyya Lil-Turath.

Bennett, David. 2016. "The Muʿtazilite Movement (II: The Early Muʿtazilites)." In *The Oxford Handbook of Islamic Theology*, 142–158. Edited by Sabine Schmidtke. Oxford: Oxford University Press.

Berdyaev, Nikolai. 1927. "A Consideration Concerning Theodicy." Translated (2000) by Fr. S. Janos. *Put'*, no. 7: 50–62. http://www.berdyaev.com/berdiaev/berd_lib/1927_321.html

Bernstein, Andrew. 2012. "Religion versus Morality." *Objective Standard* 7, no. 3: 29–42.

al-Bidlīsī, ʿAmmār. 1999. "Ṣawm al-Qalb." In *Zwei Mystische Schriften des ʿAmmār al-Bidlīsī*, 5–59. Edited by Edward Badeen. Beirut and Stuttgart: Steiner.

al-Bidlīsī, ʿAmmār ibn Muḥammad. 1999. "Bahjat al-Ṭāʾifa." In *Zwei Mystische Schriften des ʿAmmār al-Bidlīsī*, 12–146. Edited by Edward Badeen. Beirut and Stuttgart: Steiner.

Black, Deborah L. 2008. "Al-Fārābī on Meno's Paradox." In *In the Age of al-Fārābī: Arabic Philosophy in the Fourth/Tenth Century*, 15–34. Edited by Peter Adamson. London: Warburg Institute.

Blankinship, Khalid. 2008 "The Early Creed." In *The Cambridge Companion to Classical Islamic Theology*, 33–54. Edited by T. Winter. Cambridge: Cambridge University Press.

Boesel, Chris., and Catherine. Keller, eds. 2010. *Apophatic Bodies: Negative Theology, Incarnation, and Relationality*. New York: Fordham University Press.

Böwering, Gerhard. 1980. *Mystical Vision of Existence in Classical Islam: The Qur'anic Hermeneutics of the Sufi Sahl At-Tustarī*. Berlin and New York: De Gruyter.

Böwering, Gerhard. 1999. "Ideas of Time in Persian Sufism." In *The Heritage of Sufism*. Vol. 1, *Classical Persian Sufism from Its Origins to Rūmī (700–1300)*, 199–233. Edited by Leonard Lewisohn. Oxford: Oneworld.

Brown, Jonathan A. C. 2012. "al-Dāraquṭnī." In *Encyclopaedia of Islam, Three*. Edited by Kate Fleet, Gudrun Krämer, Denis Matringe, John Nawas, and Everett Rowson. Leiden: Brill.

Bunzel, Cole. 2015. *From Paper State to Caliphate: The Ideology of the Islamic State*. Brookings Project on US Relations with the Islamic World, Analysis Paper, no. 19, March 2015. https://www.brookings.edu/wp-content/uploads/2016/06/The-ideology-of-the-Islamic-State.pdf.

Burrell, David. 1986. *Knowing the Unknowable God: Ibn-Sina, Maimonides, Aquinas*. Notre Dame, IN: University of Notre Dame Press.

Casewit, Yousef A. 2014. *The Forgotten Mystic: Ibn Barrajān (d. 536/1141) and the Andalusian Muʿtabirūn*. PhD diss., Yale University.

Casewit, Yousef. 2017. *The Mystics of al-Andalus: Ibn Barrajān and Islamic Thought in the Twelfth Century*. Cambridge: Cambridge University Press.

Cerić, Mustafa. 1995. *Roots of Synthetic Theology in Islam: A Study of the Theology of Abū Manṣūr al-Māturīdī*. Kuala Lumpur: International Institute of Islamic Thought and Civilization.

Chittick, William C. 1989. *The Sufi Path of Knowledge: Ibn al-ʿArabī's Metaphysics of Imagination*. Albany: State University of New York Press.

Chittick, William C. 1992. *Faith and Practice of Islam: Three Thirteenth-Century Sufi Texts*. Albany: State University of New York Press.

Chittick, William C. 2000. *Sufism: A Beginner's Guide*. Oxford: Oneworld.

Chittick, William C. 2001. *The Heart of Islamic Philosophy: The Quest for Self-Knowledge in the Teachings of Afḍal al-Dīn Kāshānī*. Oxford: Oxford University Press.

Chittick, William C. 2008. "Worship." In *The Cambridge Companion to Classical Islamic Theology*, 218–236. Edited by T. J. Winter. New York: Cambridge University Press.

Chodkiewicz, Michel. 1993. *An Ocean without Shore: Ibn al-ʿArabī, the Book, and the Law*. Albany: State University of New York Press.

Clayton, Philip. 2010. "The Infinite Found in Human Form: Intertwinings of Cosmology and Incarnation." In *Apophatic Bodies: Negative Theology, Incarnation and Relationality*, 286–303. Edited by C. Boesel and C. Keller. New York: Fordham University Press.

Coppens, Pieter. 2015. *Seeing God in This World and the Otherworld: Crossing Boundaries in Sufi Commentaries on the Qurʾān*. Utrecht: Utrecht University.

Corbin, Henry. 1977. "De la Théologie Apophatique comme Antidote du Nihilisme." Paper presented in the Iranian Centre for the Study of Civilizations Conference. https://www.amiscorbin.com/bibliographie/de-la-theologie-apophatique-comme-antidote-du-nihilisme/.

Corbin, Henry. 1976. "The Paradox of the Monotheism." Translated by Matthew Evans-Cockle. https://www.amiscorbin.com/bibliographie/the-paradoxe-of-the-monotheism/. First published as "Le paradoxe du monothéisme." *Eranos-Jahrbuch* 65 (1976): 69–133. Reprinted in *Le Paradoxe du Monothéisme*. Paris: L'Herne, 1981.

Corbin, Henry. 1994. *The Man of Light in Iranian Sufism*. Translated by Nancy Pearson. New York: Omega.

Cornell, Vincent. 1987. "Understanding Is the Mother of Ability: Responsibility and Action in the Doctrine of Ibn Tūmart." *Studia Islamica*, no. 66: 71–103.

Cornell, Vincent. 2007. "The All-Comprehensive Circle (*al-lhata*): Soul, Intellect, and the Oneness of Existence in the Doctrine of Ibn Sabʿīn." In *Sufism and Theology*, 31–48. Edited by A. Shihadeh. Edinburgh: Edinburgh University Press.

Cowell, Dustin, and Ibn Rashīq al-Qayrawānī. 1982. "On the Ancients and the Moderns." *Alif: Journal of Comparative Poetics*, no. 2: 67–75.

Daadbeh, Asghar, and Matthew Melvin-Koushki. 2008. "ʿAṭṭār Nīsābūrī." In *Encyclopaedia Islamica*. Edited by Wilferd Madelung and Farhad Daftary. Leiden: Brill.

Daftary, Farhad. 2005. *Ismailis in Medieval Muslim Societies*. London and New York: Tauris in association with the Institute of Ismaili Studies.

Daftary, Farhad. 2013. "The Iranian School of Philosophical Ismailism." *Ishrāq: Islamic Philosophy Yearbook*, no.4, 13–24. Moscow: Vostochnaya Literatura.

Daiber, Hans. 1995. *The Islamic Concept of Belief in the 4th/10th Century: Abū l-Laiṯ as-Samarqandī's Commentary on Abū Ḥanīfa (Died 150/767) al-Fiqh al-Absaṭ*. Tokyo: Institute for the Study of Languages and Cultures of Asia and Africa.

al-Dāraquṭnī, ʿAlī ibn ʿUmar. 2005. *Kitāb al-Ṣifāt*. Analyzed, edited, and commented by Muḥammad ibn Yaḥyá ibn ʿAlī ibn ʿAbd Allāh Abū ʿAbd al-Qahhār Āl Ḥuṭāmī al-Waṣābī thumma al-Hamadānī, introduced by Muqbil ibn Hādī al-Wādiʿī. Riyadh: Dār al-Ṣamīʿī.

Dan, Joseph, ed., and Ronald C. Kiener, trans. 1986. *The Early Kabbalah*. With a preface by Moshe Idel. New York: Paulist Press.

Davlatshāh. (1382) 2003. *Tazkirat al-Shuʿarāʾ*. Tehran: Asāṭīr.

Dāya Rāzī, Najm al-Dīn. 1958. *Mirṣād al-ʿIbād min al-Mabdaʾ ilā al-Maʾād*. Edited by Ḥusayn al-Ḥusaynī al-Niʿmat-Allāhī Shams al-ʿUrafā. Tehran: Maṭbaʾat Majlis.

Dāya Rāzī, Najm al-Dīn. 1982. *The Path of God's Bondsmen from Origin to Return: Merṣād al-ʿebād men al-Mabdāʾ elāʾl-Maʿād: A Sufi Compendium*. Translated and with an introduction and annotation by H. Algar. Delmar, NY: Caravan Books.

al-Daylamī, Abū al-Ḥasan ʿAlī ibn Muḥammad. 2005. *A Treatise on Mystical Love*. Translated by Joseph Norment Bell and Hassan Mahmood Abdul Latif Shafie. Edinburgh: Edinburgh University Press.

De Smet, Daniel. 2016. "Ismāʿīlī Theology." In *Handbook of Islamic Theology*, 314–323. Edited by Sabine Schmidtke. Oxford: Oxford University Press.

Derrida, Jacques. 1995. *On the Name*. Edited by Thomas Dutoit. Translated by D. Wood, J. P. Leavey, and I. McLeod. Stanford, CA: Stanford University Press.

DeWeese, Devin A. 1985. "The Kashf al-Huda of Kamal ad-din Husayn Khorezmi." PhD diss., Indiana University.

al-Dhahabī, Muḥammad ibn Aḥmad. 1999. *Kitāb al-ʿArsh*. 2 vols. Edited and introduced by Muḥammad ibn Khalīfa al-Tamīmī. Riyadh: Aḍwāʾ al-Salaf.

Dickinson, Eerik Nael. 1992. "The Development of Early Muslim Ḥadīth Criticism: The 'Taqdima' of Ibn Abī Ḥātim al-Rāzī (d.327/938)." Phd diss., Yale University.

Dickinson, Eerik Nael. 2001. *The Development of Early Sunnite Hadith Criticism: The Taqdima of Ibn Abī Ḥātim al-Rāzī (240/854–327/938)*. Leiden and Boston: Brill.

Donnolo, Shabbatai. 2010. *Shabbatai Donnolo's Sefer Hakhmoni*. Edited, translated, and with an introduction by Piergabriele. Mancuso. Leiden and Boston: Brill.

Druart, Thérèse-Anne. 2005. "Metaphysics." In *The Cambridge Companion to Arabic Philosophy*, 327–348. Edited by Peter Adamson and Richard C. Taylor. Cambridge and New York: Cambridge University Press.

Dunlop, D. M. 2012. "Ibn Badjdja." In *Encyclopaedia of Islam*. 2nd ed. Edited by Peri Bearman, Thierry Bianquis, C. Edmund Bosworth, E. J. van Donzel, and Wolfhart Heinrichs. Leiden: Brill, 2016.

Ebstein, Michael. 2014. *Mysticism and Philosophy in al-Andalus: Ibn Masarra, Ibn al-ʿArabi, and the Ismāʿīlī Tradition*. Islamic History and Civilization, vol. 103. Leiden and Boston: Brill.

El-Bizri, Nader. 2008. "God: Essence and Attributes." In *The Cambridge Companion to Classical Islamic Theology*, 121–140. Edited by Tim Winter. New York: Cambridge University Press.

Elias, Jamal J. 1991. "Sufi Thought and Practice in the Teachings of ʿAlāʾ ad-Dawla as-Simnānī." PhD diss., Yale University.

Elias, Jamal J. 1995. *The Throne Carrier of God: The Life and Thought of ʿAlāʾ ad-Dawla As-Simnānī*. Albany: State University of New York Press.

Elias, Jamal J. 1998. "Sufism." *Iranian Studies* 31, nos. 3–4 (Summer–Autumn): 595–613.

Eliyahu, Ayala. 2013. "Muslim and Jewish Philosophy in al-Andalus: Ibn al-Sīd al-Baṭalyawsī and Moses ibn Ezra." In *Judaeo-Arabic Culture in al-Andalus: Proceedings of the 13th Conference of the Society for Judaeo-Arabic Studies, Córdoba 2007*. Edited by Amīr Ashur. Córdoba, Spain: Córdoba Near Eastern Research Unit, Oriens Academic.

Elmore, Gerald. 1995. "The Fabulous Gryphon (ʿAnqāʾ Mughrib), on the Seal of the Saints and the Sun Rising in the West: An Early, Maghribine Work by Ibn al-ʿArabī." PhD diss., Yale University.

Elmore, Gerald. 2001. "Shaykh ʿAbd al-ʿAzīz al-Mahdawī, Ibn al-ʿArabī's Mentor." *Journal of the American Oriental Society* 121, no. 4 (October–December): 593–613.

El-Rouayheb, Khaled. 2010. *Relational Syllogisms and the History of Arabic Logic, 900–1900*. Leiden and Boston: Brill.

Ernst, Carl. W. 1985. *Words of Ecstasy in Sufism*. Albany: State University of New York Press.

Ernst, Carl. W. 1993. "The Man without Attributes: Ibn al-ʿArabī's Interpretation of Abū Yazīd al-Bisṭāmī." *Journal of the Muhyiddin Ibn ʿArabi Society* 13:1–18.

Fakhry, Majid. 2004. *A History of Islamic Philosophy*. 3rd ed. New York: Columbia University Press.

al-Fārābī, Abū Naṣr. 1989. *Kitāb al-Wāḥid wa-l-Waḥda*. Edited by Muhsin Mahdī. Casablanca: Les Editions Toubkal.

al-Fārābī, Abū Naṣr. 1998. *On the Perfect State: Mabādiʾ Ārāʾ Ahl al-Madīnat al-Fāḍilah*. Translated and with an introduction and commentary by Richard Walzer. Great Books of the Islamic World. Chicago: Kazi.

al-Fārūthī, Aḥmad ibn Ibrāhīm. (1307) 1889. *Irshād al-Muslimīn li-Ṭarīqat Shaykh al-Muttaqīn*. Cairo: Maṭbaʿat Muḥammad Muṣṭafā.

al-Fayyūmī, Nethanel ben. 1908. *The Bustan al-Ukul*. Bilingual edition, edited and translated by David Levine. New York: Columbia University Press.

al-Fazārī, ʿAbd Allāh ibn Yazīd. 2014. *Early Ibāḍī Theology: Six Texts by ʿAbd Allāh b. Yazīd al-Fazārī*. Edited by A. al-Salimi and Wilferd Madelung. Leiden and Boston: Brill.

Finlayson, James Gordon. 2012. "On Not Being Silent in the Darkness: Adorno's Singular Apophaticism." *Harvard Theological Review* 105, no. 1: 1–32.

Foucault, Michel. 2005. "The Discourse on Language." In *Truth: Engagements across Philosophical Traditions*, 315–333. Edited by José Medina and David Wood. Malden, MA: Blackwell.

Frank, Richard M. 2005. "'Lam Yazal' as a Formal Term in Muslim Theological Discourse." In *Philosophy, Theology, and Mysticism in Medieval Islam: Texts and Studies on the Development and History of Kalām*, vol. 1, 243–270. Edited by Dimitri Gutas. Variorum Collected Studies Series. Burlington, VT: Ashgate.

Franke, William. 2007. *On What Cannot Be Said*. 2 vols. Notre Dame, IN: University of Notre Dame Press.

Franke, William, and Chance B. Woods. 2013. "Negative Theology." In *Encyclopedia of Sciences and Religions*, 1443–1450. Edited by Anne L. C. Runehov and Lluis Oviedo. Dordrecht, Germany: Springer.

Garakani, Morteza Gharaee, and Farzin Negahban. 2008. "Bābā Afḍal." In *Encyclopaedia Islamica*. Edited by Wilferd Madelung and Farhad Daftary. Leiden: Brill.

Garrido Clemente, Pilar. 2007. "Edición Crítica de la *Risalat al-Iʿtibar* de Ibn Masarra de Córdoba." *Miscelánea de estudios árabes y hebraicos: Sección Árabe-Islam* 56:91–104.

Garro, Ibrahim. 1994. "The Paradox of the Infinite by al-Kindī." *Journal for the History of Arabic Science/Majallat Tārīkh al-ʿUlūm al-ʿArabiyya* 10, nos. 1–2: 111–118.

Geertz, Clifford. 1973. *The Interpretation of Cultures: Selected Essays.* New York: Basic Books.

Gharagozlou, Alireza Zekavati, Hassan Anṣārī, and Farzin Negahban. 2008. "Abū Nuʿaym al-Iṣfahānī." In *Encyclopaedia Islamica.* Edited by Wilferd Madelung and Farhad Daftary. Leiden and Boston: Brill.

al-Ghazālī, Abū Ḥāmid. 1957. *Iḥyāʾ ʿUlūm al-Dīn.* 4 vols. Edited and with an introduction by Aḥmad Badawī Ṭabāna. Cairo: Dār Iḥyāʾ al-Kutub al-ʿArabiyya.

al-Ghazālī, Abū Ḥāmid. 1993. *Fayṣal al-Tafriqa Bayn al-Islām wa-l-Zandaqa.* Edited by Maḥmūd Bījū. Damascus: Dār al-Beirutī.

al-Ghazālī, Abū Ḥāmid. 1999. *Al-Maqṣad al-Asnā fī Sharḥ Asmāʾ Allāh al-Ḥusnā.* Damascus: Matbaʾat al-Sabah.

al-Ghazālī, Abū Ḥāmid. 2000. *The Incoherence of the Philosophers: Tahāfut al-Falāsifa, a Parallel English-Arabic Text.* 2nd ed. Translated, annotated, and with an introduction by Michael E. Marmura. Provo, UT: Brigham Young University Press.

al-Ghazālī, Abū Ḥāmid. 2007. *Al-Ghazālī, The Ninety-Nine Beautiful Names of God: Al-Maqṣad al-Asnā fī Sharḥ Asmāʾ Allāh al-Husnā.* Translated and with notes by David Burrell and Nazih Daher. Cambridge: Islamic Texts Society.

al-Ghazālī, Abū Ḥāmid. 2008. *A Return to Purity in Creed.* Translated by ʿAbd Allāh ibn Ḥāmid ʿAlī. Philadelphia: Lamppost.

al-Ghazālī, Abū Ḥāmid. 2012. "The Niche of Lights (from Mishkāt al-anwār)." In *An Anthology of Philosophy in Persia.* Vol. 4, *From the School of Illumination to Philosophical Mysticism,* 317–335. Translated by David Buchman. Edited by Seyyed Hossein Nasr with Mehdi Aminrazavi. London: Tauris, in association with the Institute of Ismaili Studies.

al-Ghazālī, Abū Ḥāmid. Undated. *Iljām al-ʿAwāmm ʿan ʿIlm al-Kalām.* http://www.Ghazali.org/works/iljam.pdf.

al-Ghazālī, Aḥmad. 1986. *Sawāniḥ: Inspirations from the World of Pure Spirits.* Translated and with commentary and notes by Nasrollah Pourjavady. London: Kegan Paul.

al-Ghazālī, Aḥmad. 2012. *Al-Tajrīd fī Kalimat al-Tawḥīd.* Edited by Aḥmad Mujāhid. Beirut: Manshūrāt al-Jamāl.

al-Ghazālī, Aḥmad. Undated. *Kitāb Savāniḥ al-ʿUshshāq.* Tehran: Noorsoft DVD.

Gillon, Fârès. 2013. "Aperçus sur les Origines de lʾismaélisme à Travers le Kitāb al-Kašf, Attribué au Dâʿî Gaʿfar b. Manṣūr al-Yaman." *Ishrāq: Islamic Philosophy Yearbook,* no.4. Moscow: Vostochnaya Literatura, 90–111.

Goldziher, Ignaz. 1893. "Ibn Hûd, the Mohammedan Mystic, and the Jews of Damascus." *Jewish Quarterly Review* 6, no. 1 (October): 218–220.

Goldziher, Ignaz. 1917. *Mohammed and Islam.* Translated by K. C. Seelye. New Haven, CT: Yale University Press.

Griffel, Frank. 2005. "Ibn Tūmart's Rational Proof for God's Existence and Unity, and His Connection to the Niẓāmiyya Madrasa in Baghdād." In *Los Almohades: Problemas y Perspectivas*, vol. 2, 753–813. Edited by P. Cressier, M. Fierro, and L. Molina. Madrid: Consejo Superior de Investigaciones Cientificas.

Griffel, Frank, and Klaus Hachmeier. 2010–2011. "Prophets as Physicians of the Soul: A Dispute about the Relationship between Reason and Revelation Reported by al-Tawḥīdī in His Book of Delightful and Intimate Conversations (*Kitāb al-Imtāᶜ wa-l-muʾānasa*)." *Mélanges de l'Université Saint-Joseph* 63:223–257.

Gril, Denis. 1979. "Le Kitāb al-Inbāh ᶜalā Ṭarīq Allāh de ᶜAbdallāh Badr al-Habasi." *Annales Islamologiques* 15:97–164.

Gril, Denis. 2016. "Abū Madyan." In *Encyclopaedia of Islam, Three*. Edited by Kate Fleet, Gudrun Krämer, Denis Matringe, John Nawas, and Everett Rowson. Leiden and Boston: Brill.

Groff, Peter S. 2007. *Islamic Philosophy A–Z*. Edinburgh: Edinburgh University Press.

al-Ḥabashī, Badr al-Dīn. 1994. "The Kitāb al-Inbāh of ᶜAbdallah Badr al-Ḥabashī." Translated by Karen Holding. *Journal of the Muhyiddin Ibn ᶜArabi Society* 15. http://www.ibnarabisociety.org/articles/Habashi_text.html.

al-Ḥallāj, al-Ḥusayn ibn Manṣūr. 1913. *Kitāb al-Ṭawāsīn*. Translated, edited, and with notes by Louis Massignon. Paris: Librairie Paul Geuthner.

al-Ḥallāj, al-Ḥusayn ibn Manṣūr. 2002. *Al-Ḥallāj: al-Aᶜmāl al-Kāmila*. Edited by Qāsim Muḥammad ᶜAbbās. Beirut: Riyāḍ al-Rayyis lil-Kutub wa-al-Nashr.

Hamadānī, ᶜAbd Allāh ibn Muḥammad ᶜAyn al-Qużāt. 1962. *Tamhīdāt*. Introduction, commentary, and notes by ᶜAfīf ᶜUsayrān. Tehran: Chāphāna-i Dānishgāh.

Hamadānī, Yūsuf. 2007. "Seyyid Yusuf-i Hemedani'nin Tasavvufa İlişkin Bir Risalesi." *Şarkiyat Mecmuası*, no. 10: 23–39.

al-Ḥāmidī, Ibrāhīm ibn al-Ḥusayn. 1971. *Die Ismailitische Theologie des Ibrāhīm ibn al-Ḥusain al-Hāmidī*. Edited by M. Ghalib Wiesbaden: Franz Steiner.

al-Ḥāmidī, Ibrāhīm ibn Ḥusayn ibn Abī al-Saᶜūd Yaᶜqūb. 2012. *Risālat Tuḥfat al-Qulūb wa Furjat al-Makrūb, aw, Kitāb Tuḥfat al-Qulūb: fī Tartīb al-Hudā wa al-Duᶜā fī Jazīrat al-Yaman*. Ismaili texts and translations series (Institute of Ismaili Studies). Beirut: Dār al-Sāqī.

Ḥammūya, Saᶜd al-Dīn. (1362) 1983. *Al-Miṣbāḥ fī al-Taṣavvuf*. Edited by Najīb Māyil Hiravī. Tehran: Mawla.

Hamza, F., S. Rizvi, and F. Mayer. 2008. *An Anthology of Qurʾanic Commentaries*. Vol. 1, *On the Nature of the Divine*. Oxford: Oxford University Press.

Hanif, N. 2000. *Biographical Encyclopaedia of Sufis: South Asia*. New Delhi: Sarup & Sons.

Hanif, N. 2002. *Biographical Encyclopaedia of Sufis: Central Asia and Middle East*. New Delhi: Sarup & Sons.

Harlan, Mark Alan. 2013. *A Model for Theologizing in Arab Muslim Contexts*. Evangelical Missiological Society Dissertation Series. Pasadena, CA: William Carey International University Press.

Harmless, William. 2008. *Mystics.* Oxford: Oxford University Press.

Heinrichs, Wolfhart. 2008. "*Takhyil*: Make-Believe and Image Creation in Arabic Literary Theory." *Takhyil: The Imaginary in Classical Arabic Poetics*, 1–14. Edited by Geert Jan Van Gelder and M. Hammond. Cambridge: Trustees of the E. J. W. Gibb Memorial, 2008.

Hendel, Ronald S. 1997. "Aniconism and Anthropomorphism in Ancient Israel." In *The Image and the* Book, 205–228. Edited by Karel Van der Toorn. Leuven, Belgium: Peeters.

Hinds, Martin. 2006. "Miḥna." In *Encyclopaedia of Islam.* 2nd ed. Edited by Peri Bearman, Thierry Bianquis, C. Edmund Bosworth, E. J. van Donzel, and Wolfhart Heinrichs. Leiden: Brill, 2016.

Hodgson, Marshall. 2012. "Bāṭiniyya." In *Encyclopaedia of Islam.* 2nd ed. Edited by Peri Bearman, Thierry Bianquis, C. Edmund Bosworth, E. J. van Donzel, and Wolfhart Heinrichs. Leiden: Brill, 2016.

Holtzman, Livnat. 2010. "Islamic Theology." In *De Gruyter Handbook of Medieval Studies*, vol. 1, 56–68. Edited by A. Classen. Berlin: De Gruyter.

Holtzman, Livnat. 2011. "Anthropomorphism." In *Encyclopaedia of Islam, Three.* Edited by Kate Fleet, Gudrun Krämer, Denis Matringe, John Nawas, and Everett Rowson. Leiden: Brill.

Holtzman, Livnat. 2016. "Accused of Anthropomorphism: Ibn Taymiyya's Miḥan as Reflected in Ibn Qayyim al-Jawziyya's al-Kāfiya al-Shāfiya." *Muslim World* 166 (July): 561–587.

Holtzman, Livnat. 2018. *Anthropomorphism in Islam: The Challenge of Traditionalism (700–1350).* Edinburgh: Edinburgh University Press.

Hollenberg, David. 2006. "Interpretation after the End of Days: The Fāṭimid-Ismāʿīlī Taʾwīl (Interpretation of Jaʿfar ibn Manṣūr al-Yaman." PhD diss., University of Pennsylvania.

Homerin, Emil. 2015. "A Distant Fire: Ibn al-Shahrazūrī's Mystical Ode and Arabic Sufi Verse." *Journal of Sufi Studies* 4:27–58.

Horn, Laurence R. 2014. "Contradiction." In *Stanford Encyclopedia of Philosophy.* Edited by Edward N. Zalta. https://plato.stanford.edu/.

Hujvīrī, ʿAlī ibn ʿUs̱mān. 1911. *The Kashf al-Maḥjūb: The Oldest Persian Treatise on Sufiism.* Edited and translated by R. Nicholson. Leiden: Brill.

Hujvīrī, ʿAlī ibn ʿUs̱mān. 1926. *Kitāb Kashf al-Maḥjūb.* Edited by V. A. Zhukovskīī. Leningrad: Maṭbaʿah-ʾi Dār al-ʿUlūm-i Ittiḥād-i Jamāhīr-i Shūravī-i Sūsiyālīstī.

Hujvīrī, ʿAlī ibn ʿUs̱mān. 2001. *A Persian Treatise on Sufism: The Kashf al-Maḥjūb.* Lahore: Zia-ul-Quran.

Huntington, C. W. 1995. "A Way of Reading." *Journal of the International Association of Buddhist Studies* 18, no. 2: 279–308.

Ibn al-ʿArabī, Muḥyī al-Dīn. (1428) 2007. "Kitāb al-Fanāʾ fī al-Mushāhada." In *Rasāʾil Ibn al-ʿArabī*, 17–23. Beirut: Dār al-Kutub al-ʿIlmiyya.

Ibn al-ʿArabī, Muḥyī al-Dīn. (1428) 2007. "Kitāb al-Jalāla, wa Huwa Kalimat 'Allāh.'" In *Rasāʾil Ibn al-ʿArabī*, 46–54. Beirut: Dār al-Kutub al-ʿIlmiyya.

Ibn al-ʿArabī, Muḥyī al-Dīn. (1428) 2007. "Kitāb al-Aʿlām bi-Ishārāt Ahl al-Ilhām." In *Rasāʾil Ibn al-ʿArabī*, 75–82. Beirut: Dār al-Kutub al-ʿIlmiyya.

Ibn al-ʿArabī, Muḥyī al-Dīn. (1428) 2007. "Kitāb al-Yāʾ." In *Rasāʾil Ibn al-ʿArabī*, 107–114. Beirut: Dār al-Kutub al-ʿIlmiyya.

Ibn al-ʿArabī, Muḥyī al-Dīn. (1428) 2007. "Kitāb al-Azal." In *Rasāʾil Ibn al-ʿArabī*, 115–122. Beirut: Dār al-Kutub al-ʿIlmiyya.

Ibn al-ʿArabī, Muḥyī al-Dīn. (1428) 2007. "Risāla ilā al-Imām al-Rāzī." In *Rasāʾil Ibn al-ʿArabī*, 184–191. Beirut: Dār al-Kutub al-ʿIlmiyya.

Ibn al-ʿArabī, Muḥyī al-Dīn. (1428) 2007. "Kitāb al-Masāʾil." In *Rasāʾil Ibn al-ʿArabī*, 303–321. Beirut: Dār al-Kutub al-ʿIlmiyya.

Ibn al-ʿArabī, Muḥyī al-Dīn. (1428) 2007. "Kitāb al-Tajalliyāt." In *Rasāʾil Ibn al-ʿArabī*, 322–354. Beirut: Dār al-Kutub al-ʿIlmiyya.

Ibn al-ʿArabī, Muḥyī al-Dīn. (1428) 2007. "Kitāb Naqsh al-Fuṣūṣ." In *Rasāʾil Ibn al-ʿArabī*, 394–400. Beirut: Dār al-Kutub al-ʿIlmiyya.

Ibn al-ʿArabī, Muḥyī al-Dīn. 1946. *Fuṣūṣ al-Ḥikam*. Edited and introduced by Abuʾl ʿAla ʿAfifi. Beirut: Dār al-Kitāb al-ʿArabī,.

Ibn al-ʿArabī, Muḥyī al-Dīn. 1971. *Sufis of Andalusia: The Ruh al-Quds and al-Durrat al-Fakhirah of Ibn al-ʿArabī*. Translated and with an introduction and notes by R. W. J. Austin. With a foreword by Martin Lings. Berkeley and Los Angeles: University of California Press.

Ibn al-ʿArabī, Muḥyī al-Dīn. 2001. *Contemplation of the Holy Mysteries: Mashāhid al-Asrār al-Qudsiyya*. Translated by Cecilia Twinch and Pablo Beneito. Oxford: Anqa.

Ibn al-ʿArīf, Aḥmad ibn Muḥammad. 1933. *Maḥāsin al-Majālis*. Translated and with notes by M. A. Palacios. Paris: L. O. P. Geuthner.

Ibn al-ʿArīf, Aḥmad ibn Muḥammad. 2012. *Splenderus des Enseignements Soufis: Maḥāsin al-Majālis*. Beirut: Dar Albouraq.

Ibn al-ʿArīf, Aḥmad ibn Muḥammad, and ʿAtīq ibn ʿĪsā. 1993. *Miftāḥ al-Saʿāda wa Taḥqīq Ṭarīq al-Saʿāda*. Edited by ʿIṣmat ʿAbd al-Laṭīf Dandash. Beirut: Dār al-Gharb al-Islāmī.

Ibn al-Athīr, ʿIzz al-Dīn. 2002. *The Annals of the Saljūq Turks: Selections from al-Kāmil fīʾl-Taʾrikh of ʿIzz al-Dīn Ibn al-Athīr*. Translated and annotated by Donald Sidney Richards. London: Routledge.

Ibn al-Jawzī, Abū al-Faraj ʿAbd al-Raḥmān ibn ʿAlī. 2006. *The Attributes of God: Dafʿ Shubah al-Tashbīh bi-Akaff al-Tanzīh*. With an introduction by Khālid Yaḥyā Blankinship. Translated and with notes and appendices by 'Abdullāh bin Ḥamīd 'Alī. Original notes by Zāhid al-Kawtharī. Bristol, UK: Amal Press.

Ibn al-Jawzī, Abū al-Faraj ʿAbd al-Raḥmān ibn ʿAlī. 2013. *Virtues of the Imām Aḥmad ibn Ḥanbal*, vol. 1. Edited and translated by Michael Cooperson. New York: New York University Press.

Ibn al-Jawzī, Abū al-Faraj ʿAbd al-Raḥmān ibn ʿAlī. 2016. *The Life of Ibn Ḥanbal.* Translated by Michael Cooperson, G. Fowden, and T. Qutbuddin. New York: New York University Press.

Ibn al-Munavvar, Muḥammad. (1313) 1934. *Asrār al-Tawḥīd fī Maqāmāt al-Shaykh Abī Saʿīd.* Edited by Aḥmad Bāhmanyār. Tehran: Chāpkhānʾi Farīdīn va-Barādar.

Ibn al-Ṣabbāgh, Muḥammad ibn Abī al-Qāsim. 1993. *The Mystical Teachings of al-Shādhilī.* Translated by E. H. Douglas. Edited and with an introduction by I. M. Abu-Rabiʿ. Albany: State University of New York Press.

Ibn al-Wālid, ʿAlī ibn Muḥammad. (1403) 1982. *Kitāb Tāj al-ʿAqāʾid wa Maʿdin al-Fawāʾid.* Edited by ʿĀrif Tāmir. Beirut: Muʾassasat ʿIzz al-Dīn.

Ibn Bābawayh, Shaykh Ṣadūq. 1993. *Al-Iʿtiqādāt fī Dīn al-Imāmiyya.* Lebanon: al-Mufīd al-Tibaʾah wa-l-Nashr wa-l-Tawziʿ.

Ibn Bājja, Abū Bakr. 1961. *ʿIlm al-Nafs.* Karachi: Pakistan Historical Society Publication, no. 26.

Ibn Bājja, Abū Bakr. 2007. "Conjunction of the Intellect with Man." In *Classical Arabic Philosophy: An Anthology of Sources*, 269–283. Translated and with introduction, notes, and gloss by J. McGinnis and D. C. Reisman. Indianapolis, IN, and Cambridge: Hackett.

Ibn Barrajān, ʿAbd al-Salām ibn ʿAbd al-Raḥmān ibn Muḥammad. 2015. *A Qurʾan Commentary by Ibn Barrajān of Seville, d. 536/1141: Wisdom Deciphered, the Unseen Discovered.* Edited by G. Bowering and Y. Casewit. Leiden and Boston: Brill.

Ibn Baṭṭūṭa, Abū ʿAbd Allāh Muḥammad. (1417) 1997. *Tuḥfat al-Nuẓẓār fī Gharāʾib al-Amṣār wa Ajāʾib al-Asfār.* Edited and with an introduction and notes by ʿAbd al-Hādī al-Tāzī. Rabat: Maṭbūʿāt Akādīmiyya al-Mamlaka al-Maghribiyya.

Ibn Fātik, al-Mubashshir. 2013. *Mukhtār al-Ḥikam wa Maḥāsin al-Kalim.* Translated from Arabic to Turkish by O. Guman. Bilingual edition by A. Coskun. Istanbul: Türkiye Yazma Eserler Kurumu.

Ibn Ḥazm, ʿAlī Ibn Aḥmad.134) 1) 1928. *Kitāb al-Fiṣal fī al-Milal wa-l-Ahwāʾ wa-l-Niḥal.* 5 vols. Cairo: Maktabat al-Islām al-ʿĀlamiyya.

Ibn Ḥazm, ʿAlī Ibn Aḥmad. (1420) 1999. *Al-Nubadh fī Uṣūl al-Fiqh al-Ẓāhirī.* Edited by Muḥammad Ṣ. Ḥallāq. Beirut: Dār Ibn Ḥazm.

Ibn Khallikān, Abū al-ʿAbbās Aḥmad. (1398) 1978. *Kitāb Wafayāt al-Aʿyān*, vol. 4. With an introduction by Ihsan ʿAbbās. Beirut: Dar Sader.

Ibn Khallikān, Abū al-ʿAbbās Aḥmad. 1843. *Ibn Khallikān's Biographical Dictionary*, vol. 3. Translated by William MacGuckin de Slane. Paris: Duprat.

Ibn Miskawayh, Abū ʿAlī Aḥmad ibn Muḥammad. 1993. *Miskawayh: De lʾâme et de lʾintellect.* Edited and with an introduction by Y. Michot and V. Harika. Louvain, Belgium: Université Catholique de Louvain.

Ibn Rushd, Abū al-Walīd Muḥammad. 1954. *Averroes' Tahāfut al-Tahāfut.* Translated and with an introduction and notes by S. Van den Bergh. Cambridge: Cambridge University Press for Trustees of the E. J. W. Gibb Memorial.

Ibn Rushd, Abū al-Walīd Muḥammad. 1963. "The Decisive Treatise: Determining What the Connection Is Between Religion and Philosophy." Translated by G. F. Hourani. In *Medieval Political Philosophy*, 163–185. Edited by Ralph Lerner and Muhsin Mahdī. New York: Free Press of Glencoe.

Ibn Rushd, Abū al-Walīd Muḥammad. 1998. *Al-Kashf ʿan Manāhij al-Adilla fī ʿAqāʾid al-Milla.* Edited by Muḥammad ʿĀbid Jābirī. Beirut: Markaz Dirāsat al-Waḥda al-ʿArabiyya.

Ibn Sabʿīn, ʿAbd al-Ḥaqq ibn Ibrāhīm. 1941. *Al-Kalām ʿalā al-Masāʾil al-Ṣiqilliyya.* Edited and with notes by Muḥammad Sharaf al-Dīn Yāltaqāyā. Beirut: al-Maṭbaʿa al-Kāthūlīkiyya.

Ibn Sabʿīn, ʿAbd al-Ḥaqq ibn Ibrāhīm. 1978. *Budd al-ʿĀrif.* Edited and with an introduction by Jūrj Kattūrah. Beirut: Dār al-Andalus/Dār al-Kindī.

Ibn Sīnā, Abū ʿAlī. 1935. "al-Risāla al-ʿArshiyya." In *Majmūʿ Rasāʾil*, 241–258. Hyderabad, India: Dā'irat al-Maʿārif al-ʿUthmāniyya.

Ibn Sīnā, Abū ʿAlī. 1996. *Ibn Sīnā and Mysticism: Remarks and Admonitions*, vol. 4, Translated by Shams C. Inati. London and New York: Kegan Paul.

Ibn Sīnā, Abū ʿAlī. 2005. *The Metaphysics of "The Healing": A Parallel English-Arabic Text, al-Ilahīyāt min al-Shifāʾ.* Translated, annotated, and with an introduction by Michael E. Marmura. Provo, UT: Brigham Young University Press.

Ibn Sīnā, Abū ʿAlī, and Naṣīr al-Dīn Ṭūsī. 1960. *Al-Ishārāt wa-l-Tanbīhāt, maʿa Sharḥ Naṣīr al-Dīn Ṭūsī*, vol. 4. Edited by Sulaymān Dunyā. Cairo, Dār al-Maʿārif.

Ibn Sīnā, Abū ʿAlī, and Naṣīr al-Dīn Ṭūsī. 1983. *Al-Ishārāt wa-l-Tanbīhāt, maʿa Sharḥ Naṣīr al-Dīn Ṭūsī*, vol. 1. Edited by Sulaymān Dunyā. 2nd ed., Cairo, Dār al-Maʿārif.

Ibn Taymiyya, Aḥmad ibn ʿAbd al-Ḥalīm. 1991. *Darʾ Taʿāruḍ al-ʿAql wa-l-Naql.* Edited by Muḥammad Rashād Sālim. 2nd ed. Riyadh, S. Arabia: Jāmiʿat al-Imām Muḥammad ibn Saʿūd al-Islāmiyya.

Ibn Taymiyya, Aḥmad ibn ʿAbd al-Ḥalīm. 1993. *Against Greek Logicians.* Translated and with an introduction and notes by W. Hallaq. Oxford: Clarendon Press.

Ibn Ṭufayl, Muḥammad ibn ʿAbd al-Malik. 2009. *Ibn Ṭufayl's Ḥayy ibn Yaqẓān: A Philosophical Tale.* Edited, translated, and with an introduction and notes by L. Goodman. Chicago; London: University of Chicago Press.

Ibn Tūmart al-Andalusī, Jamāl al-Dīn. 1999. *Kanz al-ʿUlūm wa-l-Durr al-Manẓūm fī Ḥaqāʾiq ʿIlm al-Sharīʿa wa Daqāʾiq ʿIlm al-Ṭabīʿa.* Edited and with an introduction by Ayman ʿAbd al-Jābir Buḥayrī. Cairo: Dār al-Āfāq al-ʿArabiyya.

Ibn Tūmart, Muḥammad Ibn ʿAbd Allāh. 1993. *Sharḥ Murshida Muḥammad ibn Tūmart.* Edited by Muḥammad ibn Khalīl Sakūnī al-Ishbīlī. Beirut: Dār al-Gharb al-Islāmī.

Ibn Tūmart, Muḥammad Ibn ʿAbd Allāh. 1997. *Aʿazz mā Yuṭlab.* Edited by ʿAbd al-Ghanī Abū al-ʿAzm. Rabat, Morocco: Muʾassasat al-Ghanī lil-Nashr.

Idel, Moshe. 2005. *Ascensions on High in Jewish Mysticism: Pillars, Lines, Ladders.* New York: Central European University Press.

Ikhwān al-Ṣafā᾽. 1983. *Rasā᾽il Ikhwān al-Ṣafā᾽ wa Khullān al-Wafā᾽: al-ʿUlūm al-Nāmūsiyya al-Ilāhiyya wa-l-Sharʿiyya al-Dīniyya*, vol. 4. Analysis by B. al-Bustānī. Beirut: Dār Ṣādir.

Ikhwān al-Ṣafā᾽. 2009. *Epistles of the Brethren of Purity*. Epistle 22, *The Case of the Animals versus Man before the King of the Jinn: An Arabic Critical Edition and English Translation of Epistle 22*. Edited and translated by Lenn E. Goodman and Richard McGregor. With a foreword by Nader El-Bizri. Oxford: Oxford University Press, in association with the Institute of Ismaili Studies.

Iqbal, Muḥammad. 2013. *The Reconstruction of Religious Thought in Islam*. Edited and annotated by M. S. Sheikh. With an introduction by J. Majeed. Stanford, CA: Stanford University Press.

ʿIrāqī, Fakhr al-Dīn. 1982. *Divine Flashes*. Translated and with an introduction by William C. Chittick and P. L. Wilson. Ramsey, NJ: Paulist Press.

al-Isfarā᾽īnī, Abū al-Muẓaffar Ṭāhir. (1403) 1983. *Al-Tabṣīr fī al-Dīn wa Tamyīz al-Firqa al-Nājiya ʿan al-Firaq al-Hālikīn*. Beirut: ʿĀlam al-Kutub.

al-Iskandarī, Ibn ʿAṭā᾽ Allāh Aḥmad ibn Muḥammad. 199?. *Kitāb al-Ḥikam*. Introduced by ʿAbd al-Ḥamīd Ṣāliḥ Ḥamdān. Cairo: Maktabat Madbūlī.

al-Iskandarī, Ibn ʿAṭā᾽ Allāh Aḥmad ibn Muḥammad. 2006. *Kitāb Tāj al-ʿArūs wa Anas al-Nufūs*. Introduced and analyzed by Makatab al-Rawḍah al-sharīfah lil-Baḥth al-ʿIlmī. Cairo: al-Jazīrah lil-Nashr wa-al-Tawzīʿ.

Ivanow, Wladimir. 1936. *A Creed of the Fāṭimids: A Summary of the Taju᾽l-ʿAqa᾽id, by Sayyid-na ʿAlī b. Muḥammad b. al-Walid*. Bombay: Qayyima Press.

Jackson, Sherman. 2002. *On the Boundaries of Theological Tolerance in Islam: Abū Ḥāmid al-Ghāzalī's Fayṣal al-Tafriqa bayna al-Islām wa-l-Zandaqa*. Oxford: Oxford University Press.

Jackson, Sherman. 2012. *Sufism for Non-Sufis? Ibn ʿAṭā᾽ Allāh al-Sakandarī's Tāj al-ʿArūs*. New York: Oxford University Press.

Jaffer, Tariq. 2012. "Muʿtazilite Aspects of Faḫr al-Dīn al-Rāzī's Thought." *Arabica* 59:510–535.

Janz, Denis R. 1998. "Syllogism or Paradox: Aquinas and Luther on Theological Method." *Theological Studies* 59:3–21.

al-Jīlānī, ʿAbd al-Qādir. (1427) 2006. *Al-Fatḥ al-Rabbānī wa-l-Fayḍ al-Raḥmānī*. Beirut: Dār al-Kutub al-ʿIlmiyya.

al-Jīlānī, ʿAbd al-Qādir. 1992. *The Sublime Revelation (al-Fatḥ al-Rabbānī): A Collection of Sixty-Two Discourses*. Translated by M. Holland. Houston: Al-Baz Pub.

Jokisch, Benjamin. 2007. *Islamic Imperial Law: Harun-al-Rashīd's Codification Project*. Berlin: De Gruyter.

Jones, Tamsin. 2011. *A Genealogy of Marion's Philosophy of Religion: Apparent Darkness*. Bloomington: Indiana University Press.

al-Junayd, Abū al-Qāsim ibn Muḥammad. 2003. *Rasā᾽il al-Junayd*. Edited by A. H. Abdel-Kader. Cairo: Buraʿī wa-Jiddāy.

al-Juvaynī, ʿAlā al-Dīn ʿAṭāʾ Malik. 1958. *Jehān Gūshā: The History of the World-Conqueror*. 2 vols. Translated by J. A. Boyle. Cambridge, MA: Harvard University Press.

al-Juwaynī, ʿAbd al-Malik ibn ʿAbd Allāh Imām al-Ḥaramayn. 1950. *Kitāb al-Irshād ilā Qawāṭiʿ al-Adilla fī Uṣūl al-Iʿtiqād*. Edited and with an introduction and notes by Muḥammad Yūsuf Mūsa and ʿAlī ʿAbd al-Munʿim ʿAbd al-Ḥamīd Kabīr. Cairo: Maktabat al-Khānjī.

al-Kalābādhī, Muḥammad ibn Ibrāhīm. 1935. *The Doctrine of the Ṣūfīs: Kitāb al-Taʿarruf li-Madhhab Ahl al-Taṣawwuf.* Translated by Arthur John Arberry. Cambridge: Cambridge University Press.

al-Kalābādhī, Muḥammad ibn Ibrāhīm. 1993. *Kitāb al-Taʿarruf li-Madhhab Ahl al-Taṣawwuf.* Edited by Aḥmad Shams al-Dīn. Beirut: Dār al-Kutub al-ʿIlmiyya.

Karamustafa, A. T. 2007. *Sufism: Formative Period.* Edinburgh: Edinburgh University Press.

Karamustafa, A. T. 2014. "Antinomian Sufis." In *The Cambridge Companion to Sufism*, 101–124. Edited by Lloyd Ridgeon. Cambridge: Cambridge University Press.

Kars, Aydogan. 2013. "Two Modes of Unsaying in the Early Thirteenth Century Islamic Lands: Theorizing Apophasis through Maimonides and Ibn ʿArabī." *International Journal for Philosophy of Religion* 74, no. 3: 261–278.

Kars, Aydogan. 2017. "Sufis and Muʿtazilites: Theological Engagements of Ibn ʿArabī." *Journal of the Muhyiddin Ibn ʿArabi Society* 62:49–78.

Kars, Aydogan. 2017. "Ṭūsī Reloaded: Ismāʿīlī Paths of Sufi Wayfaring and Sufi Paths of Ismāʿīlī Apophaticism." *Iranian Studies* 50, no. 3: 369–390.

Kars, Aydogan. 2018. "What Is 'Negative Theology'? Lessons from the Encounter of Two Sufis." *Journal of the American Academy of Religion* 86, no. 1: 181–211.

Kāshānī, ʿAbd al-Razzāq. Undated. *Tafsīr Kāshānī*, part 1. Royal Aal al-Bayt Institute for Islamic Thought. Louisville, KY: Fons Vitae.

Kāshānī, ʿIzz al-Dīn Maḥmūd. (1394) 2016. *Miṣbāḥ al-Hidāya*. 12th ed. Edited and with an introduction and notes by Jalāl-ad-Dīn Humāʾī. Tehrān: Chāphāna-i Majlis. (First published in 1323/1944.)

Katz, Steven T. 1992. *Mysticism and Language*. Oxford: Oxford University Press.

Katz, Steven T., ed. 1978. *Mysticism and Philosophical Analysis*. New York: Oxford University Press.

Keeler, Annabel. 2007. "Mystical Theology and the Traditionalist Hermeneutics of Maybudī's Kashf al-Asrār." In *Sufism and Theology*, 15–30. Edited by A. Shihadeh. Edinburgh: Edinburgh University Press.

Keshavarz, Fatemeh. 1998. *Reading Mystical Lyric: The Case of Jalāl al-Dīn Rūmī*. Columbia: University of South Carolina Press.

al-Kharkūshī, ʿAbd al-Malik ibn Muḥammad. 1999. *Kitāb Tahdhīb al-Asrār*. Edited by Bassām Muḥammad Bārūd. Abu Dhabi: al-Majmaʿ al-Thaqāfī.

al-Kharrāz, Abū Saʿīd. 1937. *The Book of Truthfulness (Kitāb al-Ṣidq)*. Bilingual edition, edited and translated by Arthur John Arberry. Islamic Research Association, no. 6. Oxford: Oxford University Press.

Kiener, Ronald C. 1984. "Jewish Ismāʿīlism in Twelfth Century Yemen: R. Nethanel Ben al-Fayyūmī." *Jewish Quarterly Review* 74, no. 3: 249–266.

al-Kindī, Yaʿqūb ibn Isḥāq. 1974. *Al-Kindī's Metaphysics: A Translation of Yaʿqūb ibn Isḥāq al-Kindī's "On First Philosophy."* Translated and with an introduction by Alfred L. Ivry. Albany: State University of New York Press.

al-Kindī, Yaʿqūb ibn Isḥāq. 1978. *Rasāʾil al-Kindī al-Falsafiyya*. Edited and with an introduction by Muhammad ʿAbd al-Hadi Abu-Rida. Cairo: Dār al-Fikr.

al-Kindī, Yaʿqūb ibn Isḥāq. 1989. "al-Ḥudūd wa-l-Rusūm." In *al-Muṣṭalaḥ al-Falsafī ʿinda al-ʿArab*. Study and edition by ʿAbd al-Amīr Aʿsam, 188–203. Cairo: al-Hayʾa al-Miṣriyya al-ʿĀmma lil-Kitāb.

King, Richard. 2009. "Mysticism and Spirituality." In *The Routledge Companion to the Study of Religion*, 2nd ed., 323–338. Edited by John Hinnels. London and New York: Routledge.

al-Kirmānī, Aḥmad ibn ʿAbd Allāh Ḥamīd al-Dīn. 1983. *Rāḥat al-ʿAql*. 3rd ed. With an introduction by Muṣṭafa Ghālib. Beirut: Dār al-Andalus lil-Ṭibāʿah wa-al-Nashr wa-al-tawzīʿ.

al-Kirmānī, Aḥmad ibn ʿAbd Allāh Ḥamīd al-Dīn. 2008. "*al-Risāla al-Durriyya*." In *An Anthology of Ismaili Literature*, 89–97. Edited by Hermann Landolt, Samira Sheikh, and Kutub Kassam. London and New York: Tauris, in association with the Institute of Ismaili Studies.

Kirmānī, Ḥāmid Ibn Abī al-Fakhr Avḥad al-Dīn. 1969. *Manāqeb-e Owḥad al-Dīn Ḥāmed Ibn-e Abi al-Fakhr-e Kermānī*. Edited by Badīʿ al-Zamān Furūzānfar. Tehran: Bungāh Tarjuma wa Nashr Kitāb.

Kīshī, Shams al-Dīn Muḥammad. 2011. *Majmūʿa-yi Āsār-i Shams al-Dīn Muḥammad Kīshī*. Analysis and edition by Najaf Jawkār. Tehran: Muʾassasah-ʾi Pizhūhishī-i Ḥikmat va Falsafah-ʾi Īrān.

Kubrā, Najm al-Dīn Aḥmad Ibn ʿUmar. 1993. *Fawāʾiḥ al-Jamāl wa Fawātiḥ al-Jalāl*. Edited by Yūsuf Zaidān. Cairo: Dār Suʿād aṣ-Ṣabāḥ.

Kubrā, Najm al-Dīn Aḥmad Ibn ʿUmar, and ʿAlāʾ al-Dawla Simnānī. 2009. *Al-Taʾwīlāt al-Najmiyya fī al-Tafsīr al-Ishārī al-Ṣūfī; Wa-yalīhi tatimmatuhu ʿAyn al-Ḥayā*. Edited by Aḥmad Farīd al- Mazīdī. 6 vols. Beirut: Dār al-Kutub al-ʿIlmiyya.

Kubrā, Najm al-Dīn Aḥmad Ibn ʿUmar, and Ismāʿīl Ḥaqqi Bursawī. 1980. *Tasavvufi Hayat*. Edited by M. Kara. Istanbul: Dergah Yayınları.

al-Kutubī, Muḥammad Ibn Shakir. Undated. *Fawāt al-Wafayāt*. http://www.al-mostafa.com/ https://archive.org/details/fawat-alwafayat.

Laird, Martin. 2001 "Whereof We Speak: Gregory of Nyssa, Jean- Luc Marion, and the Current Apophatic Rage." *Heythrop Journal* 42, no. 1: 1–12.

al-Lajāʾī, ʿAbd al-Raḥmān ibn Yūsuf. 2001. *Quṭb al-ʿĀrifīn fī al-ʿAqāʾid wa-l-Taṣawwuf*. Introduced and annotated by Muḥammad Dībājī. Beirut: Dār Ṣādir.

al-Lajāʾī, ʿAbd al-Raḥmān ibn Yūsuf. 2003. *Shams al-Qulūb*. Introduced and annotated by Muḥammad Dībājī. Beirut: Dār Ṣādir.

Landolt, Hermann. 2002. "Nasafī, ʿAzīz." *Encyclopedia Iranica*. Edited by Ehsan Yarshater. New York: Encyclopaedia Iranica Foundation. http://www.iranicaonline.org/articles/nasafi

Landolt, Hermann. 2006. "ʿAttar, Sufism and Ismailism." In *ʿAṭṭār and the Persian Sufi tradition: The Art of Spiritual Flight*, 3–26. Edited by L. Lewisohn and C. Shackle. London: Tauris, in association with the Institute of Ismaili Studies.

Landolt, Hermann. 2012. "Khalwa." *Encyclopaedia of Islam*, 2nd ed. Edited by Peri Bearman, Thierry Bianquis, C. Edmund Bosworth, E. J. van Donzel, and Wolfhart Heinrichs. Leiden: Brill Online. https://referenceworks.brillonline.com/entries/encyclopaedia-of-islam-2/khalwa-SIM_4178.

Landolt, Hermann. 2013. "Khwājah Naṣīr al-Dīn Ṭūsī (597/1201–672/1274), Ismāʿīlism, and Ishrāqī Philosophy." *Ishrāq: Islamic Philosophy Yearbook*, no.4. Moscow: Vostochnaya Literatura, 360–378.

Landolt, Hermann, Samira Sheikh, and Kutub Kassam, eds. 2008. *An Anthology of Ismaili Literature*. London and New York: Tauris, in association with the Institute of Ismaili Studies.

Laoust, Henri. 2012. "Ibn al-Djawzī." In *Encyclopaedia of Islam*. 2nd ed. Edited by Peri Bearman, Thierry Bianquis, C. Edmund Bosworth, E. J. van Donzel, and Wolfhart Heinrichs. Leiden: Brill Online. http://dx.doi.org/10.1163/1573-3912_islam_SIM_3139.

de Laugier de Beaureceuil, S. 2011. "Abdāllah Anṣārī." In *Encyclopædia Iranica*. Edited by Ehsan Yarshater. New York: Encyclopaedia Iranica Foundation. http://www.iranicaonline.org/articles/abdallah-al-ansari.

Lav, Daniel. 2012. *Radical Islam and the Revival of Medieval Theology*. Cambridge: Cambridge University Press.

Lewisohn Leonard, And Christopher Shackle. 2006. *ʿAṭṭār and the Persian Sufi Tradition: The Art of Spiritual Flight*. London: Tauris, in association with the Institute Of Ismaili Studies.

Lewisohn, Leonard. 2003. "Sufism and Ismāʿīlī Doctrine in the Persian Poetry of Nizārī Qūhistānī (645–721/1247–1321)." *Iran* 41:229–251.

Lewisohn, Leonard. 2014. "Sufism's Religion of Love, from Rābiʿa to Ibn ʿArabī." In *The Cambridge Companion to Sufism*, 150–180. Edited by Lloyd Ridgeon. Cambridge: Cambridge University Press.

Lewisohn, Leonard., ed. 1999. *Heritage of Sufism*. Vol.1, *Classical Persian Sufism from Its Origins to Rūmī (700–1300)*. Oxford: Oneworld.

Little, Donald. 1975. "Did Ibn Taymiyya Have a Screw Loose?" *Studia Islamica*, no. 41: 93–111.

Madelung, Wilferd. 1988. *Religious Trends in Early Islamic Iran*. Bibliotheca Persica. Albany, NY: Persian Heritage Foundation.

Madelung, Wilferd. 2013. *Studies in Medieval Muslim Thought*. Edited by Sabine Schmidtke. Ashgate, VT: Variorum.

Maimonides, Moses. 2008. *Dalālat al-Ḥā'irīn*. 2nd Arabic ed. Edited and with an introduction and notes by Huseyin Atay. Cairo: Maktabah TḤaqqāfah al-Dīniyya,.

Makdisi, George. 1979. "The Ḥanbalī School and Sufism." *Boletin de la Asociacion Espanola de Orientalistas* 15:115–126.

al-Makkī, Abū Ṭālib. 2001. *Qūt al-Qulūb fī Muʿāmalat al-Maḥbūb wa Waṣf Ṭarīq al-Murīd ilā Maqām al-Tawḥīd*. 3 vols. Edited by Maḥmūd Ibrāhīm Raḍwānī. Cairo: Maktabat Dār al-Turāth.

Marcotte, Roxanne D. 1992. "Ibn Miskawayh's Concept of the Intellect (*ʿAql*)." PhD diss., McGill University.

Margoliouth, D. S. 2012. "al-Rifāʿī." In *Encyclopaedia of Islam*. 2nd ed. Edited by Peri Bearman, Thierry Bianquis, C. Edmund Bosworth, E. J. van Donzel, and Wolfhart Heinrichs. Leiden: Brill Online. http://dx.doi.org/10.1163/1573-3912_islam_SIM_6295.

Marion, Jean-Luc. 2002. *In Excess: Studies of Saturated Phenomena*. Perspectives in Continental Philosophy. New York: Fordham University Press.

Marmura, Michael E. 2005. "Al-Ghazālī." In *The Cambridge Companion to Arabic Philosophy*, 137–154. Edited by Peter Adamson and Richard C. Taylor. Cambridge and New York: Cambridge University Press.

Marmura, Michael E. 2010. "Avicenna on Meno's Paradox: On 'Apprehending' Unknown Things through Known Things." *Mediaeval Studie* 71:47–62.

Massignon, Louis. 1997. *Essays on the Origins on the Technical Language of Islamic Mysticism*. Translated by B. Clark. Notre Dame, IN: University of Notre Dame Press. (First published in 1922.)

al-Māturīdī, Abū Manṣūr. 2003. *Kitāb al-Tawḥīd*. Edited by B. Topaloğlu and M. Aruci. Beirut: Dar Sader.

Mayer, Toby. 2008. "Theology and Sufism." In *The Cambridge Companion to Classical Islamic Theology*, 285–287. Edited by T. Winter. Cambridge: Cambridge University Press.

Maybudī, Rashīd al-Dīn. 2015. *Unveiling of the Mysteries*. Translated by William Chittick. Royal Aal al-Bayt Institute for Islamic Thought. Louisville, KY: Fons Vitae.

Meier, Fritz. 1999. *Essays on Islamic Piety and Mysticism*. Translated by J. O'Kane. Edited by B. Radtke. Leiden and Boston: Brill.

Melchert, Christopher. 2001. "The Ḥanābila and the Early Sufis." *Arabica*, T. 48, fasc. 3: 352–367.

Melchert, Christopher. 2014. "Origins and Early Sufism." In *The Cambridge Companion to Sufism*, 3–23. Edited by Lloyd Ridgeon. Cambridge: Cambridge University Press.

Michot, Yahya. 2007. "Ibn Taymiyya's Commentary on the Creed of al-Ḥallāj." In *Sufism and Theology*, 123–136. Edited by A. Shihadeh. Edinburgh: University Press.

Mole, Marijan. 1963. "Traites Mineurs de Nagm al-Dīn Kubrā." *Annales Islamologiques* 4:1–78.

Montada, J. Puig. 2005. "Philosophy in Andalusia: Ibn Bājja and Ibn Ṭufayl." In *The Cambridge Companion to Arabic Philosophy*, 155–179. Edited by Peter Adamson and Richard C. Taylor. Cambridge and New York: Cambridge University Press.

Morris, James Winston. 1973. *Ibn Masarra: A Reconsideration of Primary Sources.* http://dlib.bc.edu/islandora/object/bc-ir:100180.

Morrison, Robert Gordon. 1998. "The Intellectual Development of Niẓām al-Dīn al-Nisābūrī (d. 1329 AD)." PhD diss, Columbia University.

Morrow, John A., ed. 2013. *Islamic Images and Ideas: Essays on Sacred Symbolism.* Jefferson, NC: McFarland.

Mourad, Suleiman A. 2010. "The Survival of the Muʿtazila Tradition of Qurʾanic Exegesis in Shīʿī and Sunnī tafāsīr." *Journal of Qurʾanic Studies*12:83–108.

al-Mufīd, Ibn Muḥammad Ibn al-Nuʿmān. (1371) 1951. *Taṣḥīḥ Iʿtiqādāt al-Imāmiyya.* Qum: al-Muʾtamar al-ʿAlami Li-Allafiyyat al-Shaykh al-Mufīd.

Muḥammad Pārsā, ibn Muḥammad. 1975. *Qudsiyya: Kalimāt-i Bahāʾ al-Dīn Naqshband.* Tehran: Ṭahūrī.

Murata, Sachiko. 1992. *The Tao of Islam: A Sourcebook on Gender Relationships in Islamic Thought.* Albany: State University of New York Press.

al-Najrānī, Taqī al-Dīn. 1999. *Al-Kāmil fī al-Istiqṣāʾ fīmā Balaghnā min Kalām al-Qudamāʾ.* Studied by Muḥammad Shāhid. Cairo: Lajnat Iḥyāʾ al-Turāth.

Narāqī, Muḥammad Mahdī ibn Abī Ḍarr. 2010. "The Delight of the Eyes (from Qurrat al-ʿuyūn)." In *An Anthology of Philosophy in Persia.* Vol. 3, *Philosophical Theology in the Middle Ages and beyond from Muʿtazilī and Ashʿarī to Shīʿī Texts*, 433–456. Edited and with an introduction by Seyyed Hossein Nasr and Mehdi Aminrazavi. Translated by J. E. Lumbard. London: Tauris.

Nasafī, ʿAzīz. 2002. *Persian Metaphysics and Mysticism.* Translated and with an introduction by Lloyd Ridgeon. London: Routledge.

al-Nasafī, Maymūn ibn Muḥammad. 2000. *Baḥr al-Kalām.* Edited by Muḥammad Ṣāliḥ Farfūr. 2nd ed. Damascus: Maktabat Dār al-Farfūr.

Nāṣir Khusrav. 1949. *Six Chapters; or, Shish Faṣl: Also Called Rawshanāʾī-nāma.* Edited and translated by Wladimir Ivanow. Leiden: Brill for the Ismaili Society. http://www.ismaili.net/Source/khusraw/nk3/nasir_kusraw3.html.

Nāṣir Khusrav. 2012. *Between Reason and Revelation: Twin Wisdoms Reconciled; An Annotated English Translation of Nāṣir-i Khusraw's Kitāb-i Jāmiʿ al-Ḥikmatayn.* Translated by Eric Ormsby. London: Tauris.

Nasr, Seyyed Hossein. 1984. "Afḍāl al-Dīn Kāshānī and the Philosophical World of Khwāja Naṣīr al-Dīn Ṭūsī." In *Islamic Theology and Philosophy: Studies in Honor of George F. Hourani*, 249–264. Edited by Michael E. Marmura. Albany: State University of New York Press.

al-Naysābūrī, Aḥmad ibn Ibrāhīm. 2010. *Degrees of Excellence: A Fāṭimid Treatise on Leadership in Islam: A New Arabic Edition and English Translation of Aḥmad b. Ibrāhīm al-Naysābūrī's Kitāb Ithbāt al-Imāma.* Edited and translated by A.

Lalani. London and New York: Tauris, in association with the Institute of Ismaili Studies.

Netton, Ian Richard. 1989. *Allah Transcendent: Studies in the Structure and Semiotics of Islamic Philosophy, Theology, and Cosmology*. London and New York: Routledge.

Netton, Ian Richard. 1998. "Al-Fārābī, Abū Naṣr." In *Routledge Encyclopedia of Philosophy*, vol. 8, 554–558. Edited by Edward Craig. London: Routledge.

Nicholas of Cusa. 1957. "On Learned Ignorance." In *Late Medieval Mysticism*, 360–366. Edited by R. C. Petry. Louisville, KY: Westminster Press.

Nicholson, Reynold A. 2005. *Studies in Islamic Mysticism*. Curson Press E-books. (First published in 1921.)

al-Niffarī, Muḥammad ibn ʿAbd al-Jabbār. 1987. *The Mawāqif and Mukhāṭabāt of Muḥammad Ibn ʿAbdi'l-Jabbār al-Niffarī, with Other Fragments*. Edited and translated by Arthur John Arberry. London: Trustees of the E. J. W. Gibb Memorial.

al-Nisābūrī, Abū al-Qāsim. 1987. *ʿUqalā' al-Majānīn*. Edited byʿUmar Asʿad. Beirut: Dār al-Nafā'is.

Niyāzī Mıṣrī. *Risāle-yi Tevḥīd*, MS 06 Mil Yz A 853/3, Ankara: Milli Kütüphane Manuscript Collection, ff.8a–17a.

Nomoto, Shin. 1999. "Early Ismāʿīlī Thought on Prophecy according to the *Kitāb al-Iṣlāḥ* by Abü Ḥātim al-Rāzī." PhD diss., McGill University.

Ogren, Brian. 2009. *Renaissance and Rebirth: Reincarnation in Early Modern Italian Kabbalah*. Leiden and Boston: Brill.

Ohlander, Erik. 2008. *Sufism in an Age of Transition: Umar al-Suhrawardī and the Rise of the Islamic Mystical Brotherhoods*. Leiden and Boston: Brill.

al-ʿOmar, Farouq ʿOmar. ʿAbd-Allāh. 1974. "The Doctrines of the Māturīdīte School with Special Reference to As-Sawād al-Aʿẓam of al-Ḥakīm al-Samarqandī." PhD diss., University of Edinburgh.

Osman, Amr. 2014. *The Ẓāhirī Madhhab (3rd/9th–10th/16th Century)*. Studies in Islamic Law and Society. Leiden and Boston: Brill.

Ovadia, Miriam. 2018. *Ibn Qayyim al-Jawziyya and the Divine Attributes*. Leiden and Boston: Brill.

Özbalıkçı, M. Reşit. 1988. "Batalyevsi." *Türkiye Diyanet Vakfi Ansiklopedisi*, Istanbul, vol. 5, 138–139.

Papan-Matin, Firoozeh. 2010. *Beyond Death: The Mystical Teachings of ʿAyn al-Quḍāt al-Hamadhānī*. Leiden and Boston: Brill.

Peacock, Andrew C. S. 2010. *Early Seljuq History: A New Interpretation*. Routledge Studies in the History of Iran and Turkey. London: Routledge.

Pellat, Ch. 2012. "Nābita." In *Encyclopaedia of Islam*. 2nd ed. Edited by Peri Bearman, Thierry Bianquis, C. Edmund Bosworth, E. J. van Donzel, and Wolfhart Heinrichs. Leiden: Brill Online. http://dx.doi.org/10.1163/1573-3912_islam_SIM_5705.

Plato. 2010. *Plato's Parmenides: Text, Translation, and Introductory Essay*. Translated and with an introductory essay by Arnold D. Hermann. With a foreword by

Douglas Hedley. Translated in collaboration with Sylvana Chrysakopoulou . Edited by Glenn W. Most. Las Vegas, NV: Parmenides.

Plotinus. 2014. *Enneads.* 6 vols. Translated by A. H. Armstrong. Cambridge, MA: Harvard University Press.

Poonawala, Ismail K. 2013. "Al-Sijistānī and His Kitāb al-Maqālid al-Malakūtiyya." *Ishrāq: Islamic Philosophy Yearbook,* no. 4, 162–185. Moscow: Vostochnaya Literatura.

Pourjavady, Nasrollah. 1992. "El-Büstî, Ebü'l-Hasen Alî b. Muhammed." In *Türkiye Diyanet Vakfi İslam Ansiklopedisi,* Istanbul, vol. 6, 495–496.

Proudfoot, Wayne. 1985. *Religious Experience.* Berkeley: University of California Press.

al-Qāsim ibn Ibrāhīm. 1990. *Al-Qāsim b. Ibrāhīm on the Proof of God's Existence: Kitāb al-Dalīl al-Kabīr.* Edited, translated, and with an introduction and notes by B. Abrahamov. Leiden and Boston: Brill.

al-Qāsim ibn Ibrāhīm. 1996. *Anthropomorphism and Interpretation of the Qur'an in the Theology of al-Qāsim Ibn Ibrāhīm: Kitāb al-Mustarshid.* Edited, translated, and with an introduction and notes by B. Abrahamov. Leiden and Boston: Brill.

al-Qayrawānī, ʿAbd Allāh ibn ʿAbd al-Raḥmān Ibn Abī Zayd. 1997. *Al-Risāla al-Fiqhiyya.* Edited by al-Hādī Ḥimmū, Muḥammad Abū al-Ajfān, and Muḥammad ibn Manṣūr Maghrāwī. 2nd ed., Beirut: Dār al-Gharb al-Islāmī.

al-Qaysarī, Dāwūd. 1997. *Al-Rasā'il li-Dāwūd al-Qaysarī.* Edited and with an introduction by Mehmet Bayraktar. Kayseri, Turkey: Kayseri Büyükşehir Belediyesi.

al-Qifṭī, ʿAlī Ibn Yūsuf. 1903. *Ibn al-Qifṭī's Ta'rīkh al-Ḥukamā'.* Edited by A. Müller. Translated by J. Lippert. Leipzig: Dieterichsche Verlagsbuchhandlung.

Qūnavī, Ṣadr al-Dīn. 193(?). *Miftāḥ Ghayb al-Jamʿ wa-l-Wujūd.* http://babel.hathitrust.org/cgi/pt?id=mdp.39015079131804.

Qūnavī, Ṣadr al-Dīn. 2003. *Al-Nuṣūṣ fī Taḥqīq al-Ṭawr al-Makhṣūṣ.* Edited and with an introduction by Ibrāhīm Ibrāhīm Muḥammad Yasin. Alexandria, Egypt: Munsha'at al-Maʿārif.

Qūnavī, Ṣadr al-Dīn. Undated. *Ṣadr al-Dīn Qūnavī: The Texts (al-Nuṣūṣ).* Translated by William Chittick. https://www.academia.edu/8101330/Sadr_al-Dīn_Qūnawī_The_Texts_al-Nusus_.

al-Qurashī, Idrīs ʿImād al-Dīn. 1991. *Kitāb Zahr al-Maʿānī.* Introduced and studied by Muṣṭafā Ghālib. Beirut: al-Mu'assasa al-Jāmiʿiyya.

al-Qushayrī, ʿAbd al-Karīm ibn Hawāzin. (1409) 1989. *Al-Risāla al-Qushayriyya fī ʿIlm al-Taṣawwuf.* Edited by ʿAbd al-Halim Maḥmūd and Maḥmūd ibn al-Sharif. Cairo: M. Dar al-Sha'b.

al-Qushayrī, ʿAbd al-Karīm ibn Hawāzin. 1969. *Sharḥ Asmā' Allāh al-Ḥusna (al-Taḥbīr fī al-Tadhkīr).* 3rd ed. With notes by Aḥmad ʿAbd al-Munʿim ʿAbd al-Salām Ḥalawānī. Cairo: Maṭbaʿat al-Amāna.

al-Qushayrī, ʿAbd al-Karīm ibn Hawāzin. 2014. *Laṭā'if al-Ishārāt.* https://www.altafsīr.com.

al-Qushayrī, ʿAbd al-Karīm ibn Hawāzin. 2007. *Al-Qushayrī's Epistle on Sufism: al-Risāla al-Qushayriyya fī ʿIlm al-Taṣawwuf.* Translated by Alexander D. Knysh. Reviewed by Muhammad S. Eissa. Reading, UK: Garnet.

al-Qushayrī, ʿAbd al-Karīm ibn Hawāzin. 2017. *Great Commentaries on the Holy Qurʾān.* Vol. 7, *Laṭāʾif al-Ishārāt/Subtle Allusions.* Translated by Kristin Zahra Sands. Edited by Royal Aal al-Bayt Institute for Islamic Thought. Louisville, KY: Fons Vitae. http://www.altafsir.com/Books/lataif.pdf.

al-Rāzī, Abū Ḥātim. 2008. "On al-Wāḥid/al-Aḥad." In *An Anthology of Qurʾanic Commentaries.* Vol. 1, *On the Nature of the Divine,* 509–512. Translated by F. Hamza, S. Rizvi, and F. Mayer. Oxford: Oxford University Press.

al-Rāzī, Abū Ḥātim. 2011. *The Proofs of Prophecy: A Parallel Arabic-English Text.* Translated, introduced, and with annotations by T. Khalidi. Islamic Translation Series. Provo, UT: Brigham Young University Press.

al-Rāzī, Fakhr al-Dīn. 1966. *Munāẓarāt Fakhr al-Dīn al-Rāzī fī Bilād Mā warāʾ al-Nahr.* Edited by Fatḥ Allāh Khulaif. Beirut: Dār al-Mashriq.

al-Rāzī, Fakhr al-Dīn. 1978. *Muḥaṣṣal Afkār al-Mutaqaddimīn wa-l-Mutaʾakhkhirīn min al-ʿulamāʾ wa-l-Mutakallimīn. Wa-bi-dhaylihi kitāb Talkhīṣ al-Muḥaṣṣal li-Naṣīr al-Dīn Ṭūsī.* Introduced by Ṭāha ʿAbd al-Raʾūf Saʿd. Cairo: Maktabat al-Kulliyyāt al-Azhariyya.

al-Rāzī, Fakhr al-Dīn. 2009. "Iʿtiqād al-Firaq al-Muslimīn wa-l-Mushrikīn" [İtikadatu Firaki'l-Müslimin Ve'l-Müşrikin]. Translated into Turkish by Faruk Sancar. *Dinbilimleri Akademik Araştırma Dergisi* 9, no. 2: 235–274.

Renard, John, ed. and trans. 2014. *Islamic Theological Themes: A Primary Source Reader.* Oakland: University of California Press.

Ridgeon, Lloyd, ed. 2014. *The Cambridge Companion to Sufism.* Cambridge: Cambridge University Press.

al-Rifāʿī, Aḥmad ibn ʿAlī. (1425) 2004. *Ḥālat Ahl al-Ḥaqīqa maʿa Allāh Taʿāla.* Analysis by Aḥmad ibn Farīd ibn Aḥmad Mazīdī. 1st ed., Beirut: Dār al-Kutub al-ʿIlmiyya.

al-Rifāʿī, Aḥmad ibn ʿAlī. 1904. *Kitāb al-Burhān al-Muʿayyad.* Cairo: Maṭbaʿat al-Ẓāhir.

Rippin, Andrew, and Jan Knappert. 1990. *Textual Sources for the Study of Islam.* University of Chicago Press.

Rosenthal, Franz. 1988. "Ibn al-ʿArabī Between 'Philosophy' and 'Mysticism': 'Sufism and Philosophy Are Neighbors and Visit Each Other' (*Fa-inna at-taṣawwuf wa-t-tafalsuf yatajāwarāni wa-yatazāwarāni*)." *Oriens* 31:1–35.

Rudolph, Ulrich. 2015. *Al-Māturīdī and the Development of Sunnī Theology in Samarqand.* Translated by Rodrigo Adem. Leiden and Boston: Brill.

Rūmī, Jalāl al-Dīn. (1348) 1969. *Kitāb-i Fīhi mā Fīhi: Az Guftār-i Mawlānā Jalāl al-Dīn Ibn Muḥammad Mashūr bi-Mawlawī.* Edited by Badīʿ al-Zamān Furūzān-far. Ṭehrān: Amīr Kabīr.

Rūmī, Jalāl al-Dīn. (1376) 1998. *Kulliyyāt-i Dīvān-i Shams.* Edited by Badīʿ al-Zamān Furūzān-far. Tehran: Muʾassasat Intisharat Amīr Kabir.

Rūmī, Jalāl al-Dīn. 2015. *Maṣnavī-ya Maʿnavī*. Edited by R. Nicholson. http://www.masnavi.net/.

Rustom, Mohammed. 2018. *Inrushes of the Spirit: The Mystical Theology of ʿAyn al-Qudat*. Albany: State University of New York Press.

Safi, Omid. 2006. *The Politics of Knowledge in Premodern Islam: Negotiating Ideology and Religious Inquiry*. Chapel Hill: University of North Carolina Press.

Salamah-Qudsi, Arin S. 2010. "'The Sealed Nectar': An Overview of a Sufi Treatise of ʿUmar al-Suhrawardī (d. 632 AH/1234 AD." *Arabica* 57:30–56.

Sands, Kristin Zahra. 2006. *Sufi Commentaries on the Qurʾan in Classical Islam*. Routledge Studies in the Quran. London: Routledge.

al-Sarrāj, Abū Naṣr (1914). *Kitāb al-Lumaʿ*. Edited, translated, and with notes by Reynold Nicholson. Leiden: Brill.

Sayyid Burhān al-Dīn, Ḥusayn Muḥaqqiq al-Tirmidhī. 1973. *Maʿārif*. Translated and with an introduction by Abdülbaki Gölpınarlı. Ankara: İş Bankası Kültür Yayınları.

Schimmel, Annemarie.1975. *Mystical Dimensions of Islam*. Chapel Hill: University of North Carolina Press.

Schimmel, Annemarie. 1976. *Pain and Grace: A Study of Two Mystical Writers of Eighteenth-Century Muslim India*. Leiden: Brill.

Schimmel, Annemarie. 1982. *As Through a Veil: Mystical Poetry in Islam*. New York: Columbia University Press.

Schimmel, Annemarie. 1993. *The Triumphal Sun: A Study of the Works of Jalāloddin Rūmī*. Albany: State University of New York Press.

Schimmel, Annemarie. 2001. *Make a Shield from Wisdom: Selected Verses from Nāṣir-i Khusraw's Dīvān*. London and New York: Tauris, in association with the Institute of Ismaili Studies.

Schmidtke, Sabine. 2008. "Theological Rationalism in the Medieval World of Islam." *Al-ʿUsur al-Wusta* 20, no. 1 (April): 17–29.

Schumann, Andrew, ed. 2010. *Logic in Religious Discourse*. Frankfurt: Ontos.

Sells, Michael A. 1994. *Mystical Languages of Unsaying*. Chicago: University of Chicago Press.

al-Shahrastānī, Muḥammad Ibn ʿAbd al-Karīm. 1992. *Al-Milal wa-l-Niḥal*. Edited and commented by Aḥmad Fahmī Muḥammad. Beirut: Dār al-Kutub al-ʿIlmiyya.

al-Shahrastānī, Muḥammad Ibn ʿAbd al-Karīm. 2001. *Struggling with the Philosopher: A Refutation of Avicenna's Metaphysics*. Edited and translated by Wilferd Madelung and T. Mayer. London: Tauris.

al-Shahrastānī, Muḥammad ibn ʿAbd al-Karīm. 2009. *Keys to the Arcana: Shahrastānī's Esoteric Commentary on the Qurʾan*. Edited by M. A. Adharshab. Translated by T. Mayer. London: Oxford University Press in association with the Institute of Ismaili Studies.

al-Shahrastānī, Muḥammad Ibn ʿAbd al-Karīm. 2014. "Shahrastānī's Doxography of Muslim Schools." In *Islamic Theological Themes: A Primary Source Reader*. Edited and translated by John Renard. Oakland: University of California Press.

al-Shahrazūrī, Shams al-Dīn Muḥammad. 2007. *Taʾrīkh al-Ḥukamāʾ Qabl Ẓuhūr al-Islām wa Baʿdahu: Nuzhat al-Arwāḥ wa Rawḍat al-Afrāḥ*. Edited by ʿAbd al-Karīm Abū Shuwayrib. Paris: Dar Byblion.

al-Shahrazūrī, Shams al-Dīn Muḥammad. 2012. "Excursion of Spirits and Garden of Delights (from *Nuzhat al-Arwāḥ wa Rawḍat al-Afrāḥ*)." In *An Anthology of Philosophy in Persia*. Vol. 4, *From the School of Illumination to Philosophical Mysticism*, 56–76. Translated by M. Fakhry. Edited by Seyyed Hossein Nasr, and Mehdi Aminrazavi. London: Tauris, in association with the Institute of Ismaili Studies.

al-Shīrāzī, Abū Isḥāq Ibrāhīm ibn ʿAlī ibn Yūsuf Fīrūzābādī. (1420) 1999. *Al-Ishāra ilā Madhhab Ahl al-Ḥaqq*. Analysis by Muḥammad al-Sayyid Jalaynad. Cairo: Wizārat al-Awqāf, al-Majlis al-Aʿla lil-Shuʾūn al-Islāmiyya, Markaz al-Sīra wa-al-Sunna.

Shīrāzī, Quṭb al-Dīn Maḥmūd ibn Masʿūd. 2005. *Sharḥ-i Ḥikmat al-ishrāq-i Suhravardī*. Edited by ʿAbd Allāh Nūrānī and Mahdī Muḥaqqiq. Tehran: Anjuman-i Ās̱ār va Mafākhir-i Farhangī.

Shehadi, Fadlou. 1964. *Ghazali's Unique Unknowable God*. Leiden: Brill.

Shihadeh, Ayman. 2006. "Three Apologetic Stances in al-Ṭūfī: Theological Cognitivism, Noncognitivism, and a Proof of Prophecy from Scriptural Contradiction." *Journal of Qurʾanic Studies* 8, no. 2: 1–23.

Shihadeh, Ayman. 2008. "The Existence of God." In *The Cambridge Companion to Classical Islamic Theology*, 197–217. Edited by T. J. Winter. New York: Cambridge University Press.

Shihadeh, Ayman, ed. 2007. *Sufism and Theology*. Edinburgh: Edinburgh University Press.

Shuʿayb, Fiazuddin. 2011. "Al-Ghazzālī's Final Word on Kalām." *Islam & Science* 9, no. 2 (Winter): 151–172.

al-Sijistānī, Isḥāq ibn Aḥmad Abū Yaʿqūb. 1965. *Kitāb al-Yanābīʿ*. With an introduction by Mustafa Ghalib. Beirut: al-Maktab al-Tijari.

al-Sijistānī, Isḥāq ibn Aḥmad Abū Yaʿqūb. 1994. *The Wellsprings of Wisdom: A Study of Abū Yaʿqūb al-Sijistānī's "Kitāb al-Yanābīʿ," including a Complete English Translation with Commentary and Notes on the Arabic Text*. Translated, edited, and with an introduction by P. Walker. Salt Lake City: University of Utah Press.

al-Sijistānī, Isḥāq ibn Aḥmad Abū Yaʿqūb. 2008. "Unveiling of the Hidden (from *Kashf al-Maḥjūb*)." Translated by Hermann Landolt. In *An Anthology of Philosophy in Persia*. Vol. 2, *Ismaili Thought in the Classical Age from Jābir ibn Ḥayyān to Naṣīr al-Dīn Ṭūsī*, 83–129. Edited by Seyyed Hossein Nasr and Mehdi Aminrazavi. London: Tauris.

al-Sijistānī, Isḥāq ibn Aḥmad Abū Yaʿqūb. 2011. *Kitāb al-Maqālīd al-Malkūtiyya*. Edited and with an introduction and notes by Ismail K. Poonawala. Tunis: Dār al-Gharb al-Islāmi.

Silvers, Laury. 2002. "Tawḥīd in Early Sufism: The Life and Work of Abū Bakr al-Wāsiṭī (d. ca. 320/928)." Phd diss., State University of New York at Stony Brook.

al-Sīrjānī, ʿAlī ibn al-Ḥasan. 2012. *Sufism, Black and White: A Critical Edition of Kitāb al-Bayād wa-l-Sawād*. Edited by Bilal Orfali and Nada Saab. Leiden and Boston: Brill.

Sirry, Munʿim. 2012. "Muqātil b. Sulaymān and Anthropomorphism." *Studia Islamica*, n.s., 3:51–82.

Sobieroj, Florian. (1998. "Ibn Khafīf's Kitāb al-Iqtiṣād and Abū al-Najīb al-Suhrawardī's Ādāb al-Murīdīn: A Comparison between Two Works on the Training of Novices." *Journal of Semitic Studies* 18, no. 2: 327–345.

Steigerwald, Diane. 1996. "The Divine Word (*Kalima*) in Shahrastānī's *Majlis*." *Studies in Religion/Sciences Religieuses* 25, no. 3 (September): 335–352.

Stelzer, Steffen. 1996. "Decisive Meetings: Ibn Rushd, Ibn al-ʿArabī, and the Matter of Knowledge." *Alif*, no. 16: 19–55.

Stetkevych, Suzanne Pinckney. 1994. *Reorientations: Arabic and Persian Poetry*. Bloomington: Indiana University Press.

Street, Tony. 2005. "Logic." In *The Cambridge Companion to Arabic Philosophy*, 247–265. Edited by Peter Adamson and Richard C. Taylor. Cambridge and New York: Cambridge University Press.

Street, Tony. 2015. "Arabic and Islamic Philosophy of Language and Logic." In *The Stanford Encyclopedia of Philosophy*. Edited by Edward N. Zalta. https://plato.stanford.edu/archives/spr2015/entries/arabic-islamic-language/.

Stronach, David, Michael Roaf, Ruth Stronach, and S. Bökönyi. 1978. "Excavations at Tepe Nush-i Jan." *Iran* 16:1–28.

Stroumsa, Sarah. 2014. "The Muʿtazila in al-Andalus: The Footprints of a Phantom." *Intellectual History of the Islamicate World* 2, nos. 1–2: 80–100.

Stroumsa, Sarah, and Sara Sviri. 2009. "The Beginnings of Mystical Philosophy in al-Andalus: Ibn Masarrah and His *Epistle on Contemplation*." *Jerusalem Studies in Arabic and Islam* 36:201–253.

al-Suhrawardī, ʿAbd al-Qāhir ibn ʿAbd Allāh Abū al-Najīb. 1975. *A Sufi Rule for Novices: Kitāb Ādāb al-Murīdīn of Abū al-Najīb al-Suhrawardī*. Abridged, translated, and with an introduction by Menahem Milson. Cambridge, MA: Harvard University Press.

al-Suhrawardī, ʿAbd al-Qāhir ibn ʿAbd Allāh Abū al-Najīb. 1977. *Kitāb Ādāb al-Murīdīn*. Edited by Menahem Milson. Al-Quds: Maʿhad al-Dirāsāt al-Asyawiyya wa-al-Afrīqiyya, al-Jāmiʿah al-ʿIbriyya fī Urushalīm.

al-Suhrawardī, Shihāb al-Dīn Yaḥyā. (1373) 1994. *Majmūʿa-yi Muṣannafāt-i Shaykh-i Ishrāq*. Vol. 2, *Kitāb Ḥikmat al-Ishrāq, Risālah fī Iʿtiqād al-Ḥukamāʾ wa Qiṣṣat al-Ghurbah al-Ghurbiyya*. Edited and with an introduction by H. Corbin. Tehran: Pizhūhishgāh-i ʿUlūm-i Insānī va Mutālaʿāt-i Farhangī.

al-Suhrawardī, Shihāb al-Dīn Yaḥyā. 1935. *Three Treatises on Mysticism*. Edited and translated by O. Spies and S. K. Khatak. Stuttgart: W. Kohlhammer.

al-Suhrawardī, Shihāb al-Dīn Yaḥyā. 2002. *Maqāmāt al-Ṣūfiyya*. Edited and with an introduction and notes by Émile Ide Maalouf. 2nd ed. Beirut: Dār al-Mashriq.

al-Suhrawardī, ʿUmar ibn Muḥammad. 1939. *Kitāb ʿAwārif al-Maʿārif*. Cairo: al-Maktaba al-ʿAlāmiyya.

al-Suhrawardī, ʿUmar ibn Muḥammad. 1996. *Rasāʾil Aʿlām al-Hudā wa ʿAqīdat Arbāb al-Tuqā*. Edited by ʿAbd al-ʿAzīz ʿIzz al-Dīn Sayrawānī. Damascus: Dār al-Anwār.

al-Suhrawardī, ʿUmar ibn Muḥammad. Undated. *Irshād al-Murīdīn*. Şehit Ali Paşa Library, Istanbul, MS 1397, ff. 1b–47b.

al-Sulamī, Abū ʿAbd Allāh. 2014. *Ḥaqāʾiq al-Tafsīr*. https://www.altafsir.com/Tafasir.asp?tMadhNo=3&tTafsirNo=30&tSoraNo=2&tAyahNo=115&tDisplay=yes&UserProfile=0&LanguageId=1

al-Suyūṭī, ʿAbd al-Raḥmān ibn Abī Bakr. 1934. *Taʾyīd al-Ḥaqīqa al-ʿAliyya wa Tashyīd al-Ṭarīqa al-Shādhiliyya*. Edited by ʿAbd Allāh b Muḥammad al- Ġumārī. Cairo: al-Maṭbaʿa al-Islāmiyya.

Sviri, Sara. 1987. "Between Fear and Hope: On the Coincidence of Opposites in Islamic Mysticism." *Jerusalem Studies in Arabic and Islam* 9:316–349.

al-Ṭabarī, Abū Khalaf Muḥammad ibn ʿAbd al-Mālik. 2013a. *Salwat al-ʿĀrifīn wa Uns al-Mushtāqīn: The Comfort of the Mystics: A Manual and Anthology of Early Sufism*. Edited by G. Bowering and B. Orfali. Leiden and Boston: Brill.

al-Ṭabarī, Abū Khalaf Muḥammad ibn ʿAbd al-Mālik. 2013b. *Khalwat al-ʿĀkifīn: Muntajib min Salwat al-ʿĀrifīn li-Abī Khalaf al-Ṭabarī*. Edited by Bilal Orfali and Gerhard Bowering. Beirut: Dār al-Mashriq.

Tabrīzī, Shams. 2004. *Me and Rūmī: The Autobiography of Shams Tabrīzī*. Edited and translated by William C. Chittick. Louisville, KY: Fons Vitae.

al-Tamīmī, Muḥammad ibn Khalīfa. 1996. *Muʿtaqad Ahl al-Sunna wa-l-Jamāʿa fī Tawḥīd al-Asmāʾ wa-l-Ṣifāt*. Kuwait: Dār īlāf al-Dawliyya.

al-Tamīmī, Muḥammad ibn Khalīfa. 1999. *Muʿtaqad Ahl al-Sunna wa-l-Jamāʿa fī Asmāʾ Allāh al-Ḥusnā*. Riyadh: Aḍwāʾ al-Salaf.

al-Tawḥīdī, ʿAlī ibn Muḥammad Abū Ḥayyān. 1992. *Al-Muqābasāt*. With commentary by Ḥasan Sandūbī. 2nd ed. Kuwait: Dār Suʿād al-Ṣabāḥ.

al-Tawḥīdī, ʿAlī ibn Muḥammad Abū Ḥayyān. 2013. "Essayistic Prose: Al-Tawḥīdī on the Superiority of the Arabs." Translated by Geert Jan van Gelder. In *Classical Arabic Literature: A Library of Arabic Literature Anthology*, 195–207. New York: New York University Press.

Thiele, Jan. 2016. "Abū Hāshim al-Jubbāʾī's (d. 321/933) Theory of 'States' (*Aḥwāl*) and Its Adaption by Ashʿarite Theologians." In *The Oxford Handbook of Islamic Theology*, 364–382. Edited by Sabine Schmidtke. Oxford: Oxford University Press.

al-Tilimsānī, ʿAfīf al-Dīn Sulaymān Ibn ʿAlī, and ʿAbd Allāh al-Anṣārī. 1989. *Sharḥ Manāzil al-Sā'irīn*. Edited by ʿAbd-al-Ḥafīẓ Manṣūr. Tunis: Dār at-Turkī li al-nashr.

al-Tilimsānī, ʿAfīf al-Dīn Sulaymān Ibn ʿAlī, and Muḥammad Ibn-ʿAbd al-Jabbār al-Niffarī. 1997. *Sharḥ Mawāqif al-Niffarī*. First ed., Cairo: Markaz al-Maḥrūsah.

Todd, Richard. 2014. *The Sufi Doctrine of Man: Ṣadr al-Dīn Qūnavī's Metaphysical Anthropology*. Leiden and Boston: Brill.

Trimingham, J. Spencer. 1971. *The Sufi Orders in Islam*. Oxford: Clarendon Press.

Turner, Denys. 1995. *The Darkness of God: Negativity in Christian Mysticism.* Cambridge: Cambridge University Press.

Ṭūsī, Naṣīr al-Dīn. (1369) 1990. *Avṣāf al-Ashrāf.* With an introduction by Mahdī Shams al-Dīn. Tehran: Sāzmān-i Chāp va Intishārāt, Vizārat-i Farhang va Irshād-i Islāmī.

Ṭūsī, Naṣīr al-Dīn. 1998. *Contemplation and Action: The Spiritual Autobiography of a Muslim Scholar.* Edited, translated, and with an introduction by S. J. Badakhchani. London: Tauris, in association with the Institute of Ismaili Studies.

Ṭūsī, Naṣīr al-Dīn. 2005. *Paradise of Submission: A Medieval Treatise on Ismāʿīlī Thought.* Edited and translated by S. J. Badakhchani. With an introduction by Hermann Landolt and philosophical commentary by Christian Jambert. London; New York: Tauris.

Ṭūsī, Naṣīr al-Dīn. 2010. "Āghāz va Anjām." In *Shīʿī Interpretations of Islam: Three Treatises on Islamic Theology and Eschatology,* 45–88. Translated by J. Badakhchani. London: Tauris.

Ṭūsī, Naṣīr al-Dīn. 2010. "Tavallā va Tabarrā." In *Shīʿī Interpretations of Islam: Three Treatises on Islamic Theology and Eschatology,* 23–32. Translated by J. Badakhchani. London: Tauris.

Ṭūsī, Naṣīr al-Dīn, and Ṣadr al-Dīn Ibn Isḥāq Qūnavī. 1995. *Al-Murāsalāt bayna Ṣadr al-Dīn Qūnavī wa Naṣīr al-Dīn Ṭūsī.* Edited by G. Schubert. Stuttgart, Germany: Yuṭlabu min Dār al-Nashr Frānts Shtāynar.

al-Tustarī, Sahl ibn ʿAbd Allāh. 2011. *Commentaries on the Holy Qurʾān.* Vol. 4, *Tafsīr al-Tustarī.* Translated by Annabel Keeler and Ali Keeler. Edited by Royal Aal al-Bayt Institute for Islamic Thought. Louisville, KY: Fons Vitae.

Valabregue-Perry, Sandra. 2012. "The Concept of Infinity (*Eyn-sof*) and the Rise of Theosophical Kabbalah." *Jewish Quarterly Review* 102, no. 3 (Summer): 405–430.

Van Ess, Josef. 1997. *Theologie und Gesellschaft im 2. und 3. Jahrhundert Hidschra.* 6 vols. Berlin and New York: De Gruyter.

Van Ess, Josef. 2006. *The Flowering of Muslim Theology.* Translated by Jane Marie Todd. Cambridge, MA: Harvard University Press.

Van Gelder, Geert Jan. 2003. "Beautifying the Ugly and Uglifying the Beautiful: The Paradox in Classical Arabic Literature." *Journal of Semitic Studies* 48, no. 2 (Autumn): 321–351.

Vasiltsov, Konstantin S. 2004. "Afḍal al-Dīn Kāshānī and His Treaties 'The Book of Everlasting.'" *Manuscripta Orientalia* 10, no. 4: 6–19.

Vaṭvāṭ, Rashīd al-Dīn. (1308) 1929. *Ḥadāʾiq al-Siḥr fī Daqāʾiq al-Shiʿr.* Edited by ʿAbbās Iqbāl. Tehran: Kitābkhāna-yi Kāvah.

Virani, Shafique. 2007. *The Ismailis in the Middle Ages: A History of Survival, a Search for Salvation.* Oxford: Oxford University Press.

Walbridge, John. 1992. *The Science of Mystic Lights: Quṭb al-Dīn Shīrāzī and the Illuminationist Tradition in Islamic Philosophy.* Harvard Middle Eastern Monographs. Cambridge, MA: Harvard University Press.

Waley, Muhammad Isa. 1999. "Contemplative Disciplines in Early Persian Sufism." In *the Heritage of Sufism*. Vol.1, *Classical Persian Sufism from Its Origins to Rūmī (700–1300)*, 497–548. Edited by Leonard Lewisohn. Oxford: Oneworld.

Walker, Paul Ernest. 1974. "An Ismaili Answer to the Problem of Worshipping the Unknowable, Neoplatonic God." *American Journal of Arabic Studies* 2:7–21.

Walker, Paul Ernest. 1993. *Early Philosophical Shiism: The Ismaili Neoplatonism of Abū Yaʿqūb al-Sijistānī*. Cambridge Studies in Islamic Civilization. Cambridge: Cambridge University Press.

Walker, Paul Ernest. 1996. *Abū Yaʿqūb al-Sijistānī: Intellectual Missionary*. London and New York: Tauris, in association with the Institute of Ismaili Studies.

Walker, Paul Ernest. 1999. *Ḥamīd al-Dīn al-Kirmānī: Ismaili Thought in the Age of al-Ḥākim*. New York: Tauris, in association with the Institute of Ismaili Studies.

Walker, Paul Ernest. 2005. "The Ismāʿīlīs." In *The Cambridge Companion to Arabic Philosophy*, 72–91. Edited by Peter Adamson and Richard C. Taylor. Cambridge and New York: Cambridge University Press.

Walker, Paul Ernest. 2009. *Orations of the Fāṭimid Caliphs Festival Sermons of the Ismaili Imāms: An Edition of the Arabic Texts and English Translation of Fāṭimid Khuṭba*. London and New York: Tauris, in association with the Institute of Ismaili Studies.

Ward, Graham. 2002. "In the Daylight Forever? Language and Silence." In *Silence and the Word: Negative Theology and Incarnation*, 159–184. Edited by Oliver Davies and Denys Turner. Cambridge and New York: Cambridge University Press.

Watt, William Montgomery. 1994. *Islamic Creeds: A Selection*. Edinburgh: Edinburgh University Press.

Weismann, Itzchak. 2014. "Sufism in the Age of Globalization." In *The Cambridge Companion to Sufism*, 257–281. Edited by Lloyd Ridgeon. Cambridge: Cambridge University Press.

Wensinck, Arent Jan. 2008. *The Muslim Creed: Its Genesis and Historical Development*. London: Routledge. (First published in 1932.)

Williams, Wesley. 2002. "Aspects of the Creed of Imām Aḥmad Ibn Ḥanbal: A Study of Anthropomorphism in Early Islamic Discourse." *International Journal of Middle East Studies* 34, no. 3 (August): 441–463.

Williams, Wesley. 2009. "A Body Unlike Bodies: Transcendent Anthropomorphism in Ancient Semitic Tradition and Early Islam." *Journal of the American Oriental Society* 129, no. 1 (January–March): 19–44.

Winter, Tim J., ed. 2008. *Cambridge Companion to Classical Islamic Theology*. New York: Cambridge University Press.

Wisnovsky, Robert. 2000. "Notes on Avicenna's Concept of Thingness." *Arabic Sciences and Philosophy* 10:181–221.

Wisnovsky, Robert. 2003. *Avicenna's Metaphysics in Context*. Ithaca, NY: Cornell University Press.

Wisnovsky, Robert. 2004. "One Aspect of the Avicennian Turn in Sunnī Theology." *Arabic Sciences and Philosophy* 14:65–100.

Wisnovsky, Robert. 2005. "Avicenna and the Avicennian Tradition." In *The Cambridge Companion to Arabic Philosophy*, 92–136. Edited by Peter Adamson and R. C. Taylor. Cambridge and New York: Cambridge University Press.

Wisnovsky, Robert. 2012. "Essence and Existence in the Eleventh- and Twelfth-Century Islamic East (Masriq): A Sketch." In *The Arabic, Hebrew, and Latin Reception of Avicenna's Metaphysics*, 27–50. Edited by Dag Nikolaus Hasse and Amos Bertolacci. Boston: De Gruyter.

Wisnovsky, Robert. 2014. "Towards a Genealogy of Avicennism." *Oriens* 42:323–363.

Wolfson, Elliot. R. 2008. "Via Negativa in Maimonides and Its Impact on Thirteenth-Century Kabbalah." In *Maimonidean Studies*, vol. 5, 393–442. Edited by Arthur Hyman and Alfred L. Ivry. Ktav. New York: Michael Scharf Publication Trust of the Yeshiva University Press.

Wolfson, Elliot. R. 2010. "Revisioning the Body Apophatically: Incarnation and the Acosmic Naturalism of Habad Hasidism." In *Apophatic Bodies: Negative Theology, Incarnation, and Relationality*, 147–199. Edited by C. Boesel and C. Keller. New York: Fordham University Press.

Wolfson, Harry. A. 1976. *The Philosophy of the Kalām*. Cambridge, MA: Harvard University Press.

Yaman, Hikmet. 2011. *Prophetic Niche in the Virtuous City: The Concept of Ḥikmah in Early Islamic Thought*. Islamic Philosophy, Theology, and Science Series. Leiden and Boston: Brill.

Zaman, M. Qasim. 1988. "The Relevance of Religion and the Response to It: A Study of Religious Perceptions in Early Islam." *Journal of the Royal Asiatic Society of Great Britain and Ireland*, no. 2: 265–287.

Zargar, Cyrus Ali. 2013. "The Ten Principles: Theoretical Implications of Volitional Death in Najm al-Dīn Kubrā's *al-Uṣūl al-ʿAshara* (a Study and Translation)." *Muslim World* 103 (January): 107–130.

Ziai, Hossein. 2005. "Recent Trends in Arabic and Persian Philosophy." In *The Cambridge Companion to Arabic Philosophy*, 405–425. Edited by Peter Adamson and Richard C. Taylor. Cambridge and New York: Cambridge University Press.

Ziyadah, Maʿan. 1968. "Ibn Bājja's Book: Tadbīr al-Mutawaḥḥid." PhD diss., McGill University.

Index